Table of Contents

Table of Contents

Tables, Figures, and Exhibits

Tables

i

Figures

Exhibits

Foreword

This book addresses the central question of education—what to teach—in a refreshingly candid manner, raising issues that will make some readers uneasy or even angry. With their extensive knowledge of curriculum and several years experience analyzing, classifying, and clarifying standards prepared by state and national organizations, the authors are superbly qualified to raise these issues. Their work on standards has brought them face to face with the unavoidable fact that there is far more that is worth teaching than students have time to learn.

In theory, deciding the content of schooling shouldn't be difficult. Everyone agrees on the importance of reading and writing, on the need for mathematics, history, science, and so on. But beyond these generalizations, the apparent consensus begins to disintegrate. What particular mathematics, how much history, and what aspects of science? What about other possibilities: music theory, sewing, swimming, Latin, child care, Japanese, interviewing for a job, the major rivers of each continent, advertising, the history of pottery making, and so on and so on?

All the topics and skills I have listed, along with thousands of others, have their justifications, their advocates, and their enemies. Wherever there is formal schooling, there is necessarily consideration of what schools should teach. And in a democracy, with people of differing backgrounds, values, and motives—and especially in times of change—the curriculum debate becomes a free-for-all.

Into this conflict, like the good guys in a Hollywood western encountering a barroom brawl, stride the authors of *Essential Knowledge*. Asserting that schools must not avoid making tough choices, they examine three contrasting sources of judgment. One way to proceed is to accept the insights of an influential individual—E. D. Hirsch, Jr.— who with a few colleagues compiled the list of terms that became the Core Knowledge curriculum. Another is to draw upon the pooled wisdom of the numerous subject-matter experts who participated in the development of national standards in the various subject fields. Bob Marzano and his coauthors believe this second source is clearly preferable to the first, but by calculating the time needed to teach the standards, they prove that schools cannot just adopt them all; the list is far too long. So, to establish priorities among the specialists' recommendations, educators might ask members of the public which are essential. In connection with this third approach, the authors present some fascinating data on what people actually say.

Some readers will like some of this, but few will applaud everything. Supporters of E. D. Hirsch and the Core Knowledge program will not appreciate the critique of "cultural literacy" and its comparison with national standards. Supporters of the national standards will not be pleased to hear that all of the standards cannot possibly be taught because there are too many of them. And many academics may be outraged by the suggestion that ordinary people, especially people with limited education themselves, should help decide the content of schooling.

The authors acknowledge that they are raising troublesome issues, which are not easily resolved, and they strive to be fair. Although they criticize the specifics of Hirsch's lists, they agree with him about the mushiness of typical public school curriculums and accept his concept of an extensive and intensive curriculum. Although they show that, as a whole, the body of educator-devised standards is overwhelming, they strongly support the use of some form of standards. And though they report survey data, they concede that it would be foolish to rely solely on public opinion about what to teach. Their basic message, though, is inescapable: Decisions must be made, and the views of various constituencies must be weighted intelligently in making them.

Essential Knowledge presents no definitive list of what students should learn, or even a recipe for deriving such a list. Instead, it offers possibilities, valuable information, and practical advice, which in the long run will prove even more useful.

Ron Brandt
Education Writer and Consultant

Preface

What should be taught to America's students is by no means a novel question. Yet, just about everyone who has anything to do with education—from parents and community members, to educators, consultants and researchers, even the President, the Congress, and the state governors—has been more intensely engaged in answering this question in recent years than ever before. National education summits have been held, year 2000 goals established, and numerous articles published in education journals and the popular press. Suddenly, it seems, a topic once reserved for faculty meetings and in-service workshops has jumped into the mainstream of American public conversation.

One of the best-known voices in the public forum is E. D. Hirsch, Jr. From the publication in the late 1980s of his initial work, *Cultural Literacy*, to the more recent release of *The Dictionary of Cultural Literacy* and the series *What Every Kindergartner* (first grader, etc., through sixth grade) *Needs to Know*, Hirsch has established himself as an individual whom thousands of Americans regard as a leader in the movement to identify the body of knowledge that should be passed on to students. Today, his movement—the Core Knowledge movement—has taken on a life of its own, counting hundreds of schools as implementers of its approach. Indeed, thousands of schools are reportedly following him down the "core knowledge" path.

But how valid is the list of core knowledge that Hirsch and his colleagues advocate? As we argue in these pages, the process used to develop many of Hirsch's lists resulted in the inclusion or exclusion of items that—although perhaps reflecting knowledge that is familiar to some "literate" Americans—do not necessarily reflect expert opinion about the ideas that are significant to each of the subject-matter disciplines. We quite clearly state our position that the criterion of "significance of content" rather than "familiarity to literate people" should be the measure against which knowledge is selected, or rejected, as essential for students to learn across the K–12 years.

Although we find fault with the process Hirsch used to create his lists, we give him due credit for other worthwhile and useful ideas. In particular, we agree wholeheartedly with the importance of identifying a body of essential knowledge; everyone who plays a role in education—in particular, teachers, administrators, students, and parents—benefits when it is clear what knowledge students are to learn. In addition, we find Hirsch's conception of the intensive and extensive curriculums particularly useful in developing curricular solutions to the intersecting problems of time and an abundance of content.

An overview of this book and the essential ideas we advance in each of the chapters should help the reader. This book begins (i.e., **Chapter 1**) with an analysis of the arguments presented by Hirsch and other "literacy reformers," as we call them, including the evidence that these writers use to assert that American students are failing and that American education continues to be in crisis. In particular, we focus on Hirsch's plea for the reinstatement in public education of the knowledge base that is the foundation of American culture—as Hirsch refers to it, the foundation for our cultural literacy. Chapter 1 also briefly reviews the arguments and evidence presented by those who counter these assertions, maintaining that American education has not been accurately portrayed by the literacy reformers. This section includes excerpts from the commentaries of David Berliner, Bruce Biddle, and Gerald Bracey, among others.

A detailed approach to the issue of essential knowledge begins in **Chapter 2**, where we analyze in depth Hirsch's lists of the terms and phrases necessary for all American students to learn and the processes by which those lists were constructed.

Chapter 3 begins the development of our argument for a research-based approach to the identification of the knowledge students should possess prior to high school graduation. It is our contention that any effort to identify this core knowledge—the essential knowledge—that students should possess should be based on the preliminary work undertaken by thousands of subject-matter specialists in a variety of content areas. Chapter 3 reviews the standards movement, which encompassed the comprehensive work of this corps of specialists, and the nationally recognized documents that resulted from their efforts. This chapter also considers three basic problems with these documents: (1) differing approaches to standards development, (2) multiple perspectives on standards, and therefore, multiple documents within a subject area, and (3) an abundance of content within and across content areas—in fact, *too much* content given the instructional time available, on average, as schooling currently is structured. The national documents have provided conceptual leadership to thousands of educators, yet, as a group, they are difficult to use at the local level because of these problems.

Chapter 4 describes the McREL standards database, the result of a major research effort undertaken to address the first two problems with the national documents. This chapter describes the content that can be found in the database and makes the point that in addition to teaching traditional subject-matter knowledge, the K–12 years should include education in thinking and reasoning skills and other important life skills, a recommendation supported by the national documents.

Chapter 5 addresses the third problem identified relative to the nationally recognized standards documents: an abundance of content. In the face of the sheer volume of the documents, the question arises, Is there enough time in the school day to teach all of the content identified by professionals in their respective areas of expertise? The answer, in short, is "no." Thus, educators are presented with two obvious solutions to the time problem: increase the amount of instructional time or decrease the number of standards addressed K–12. Chapter 5 focuses primarily on the first option and presents a process that educators might use to assess—and ultimately enhance—the efficiency with which they use time.

Regardless of whether schools and districts use time more efficiently, in all likelihood, we argue, they will still face the problem of "too much" content. In **Chapter 6**, we consider in more detail the option of decreasing the content taught in depth across the K–12 years (or, conversely, identifying the content that *will* be taught in depth). Several approaches might be taken to this task; Chapter 6 highlights one: Surveying community groups about their preferences and then using those preferences to inform the decision-making process. Chapter 6 reviews the results of just such a survey undertaken by the Mid-continent Regional Educational Laboratory (McREL) with the assistance of the Gallup Organization. Some findings from this poll of U.S. adults may disturb some readers, largely because of the particular standards, and types of standards, that survey respondents considered unnecessary for students to learn prior to venturing beyond their high school classrooms.

Although Chapter 6 offers one solution to dealing with the problem of more content than time, it does not address what to do—if anything—with all of the content that cannot be taught in depth in the 13 years of schooling from kindergarten through grade 12. **Chapter 7** addresses this problem, applying, in part, Hirsch's conception of the two-part curriculum: the extensive curriculum—content that students should have at least a general understanding of—and the intensive curriculum—content that should be taught in depth. Specifically, in Chapter 7 we present a five-step vocabulary process as a practical solution for teaching the key terms and phrases found in those standards that are not part of the intensive curriculum, whether they deal with mathematics, history, civics, physical education, life skills, or the arts.

Chapter 8 steps back from the discussion and takes a broad look at the issues that a school or district should address given the amount of content they are being urged to teach and the time available in most schools to teach this content. Regardless of whether schools choose to lengthen the school day, lengthen the school year, or use time more efficiently, they will not have enough time to teach in depth all of the content identified as essential for students to learn.

A number of questions are at the heart of the debate over what American students should know: What is the essential knowledge that all students should learn? Who should decide? How should this body of knowledge be developed? How much time will it take to teach all of this knowledge? How should it be taught? Although no definitive answers are available for these issues, a clear direction is apparent if one uses the research and theory—rather than the opinions of "literate" Americans, no matter how well educated—as a foundation from which to start.

Those involved in the debate over what students should know may well view the issues we tackle here quite differently. Yet despite our differences, we believe that we share a common effort: to ensure that our children's education rests on a solid foundation. To those who must struggle daily with the issues we have raised here—teachers, administrators, parents, and community members—we dedicate this book and hope that our work will prove to be of some benefit.

Denver, Colorado   Robert J. Marzano
January, 1999   John S. Kendall
                                                              Barbara B. Gaddy

The Authors

Robert J. Marzano is a senior fellow with the Mid-continent Regional Educational Laboratory (McREL) in Aurora, Colorado. He earned his B.A. degree (1968) in English from Iona College, his M.Ed. degree (1971) in reading and language arts from Seattle University, and his Ph.D. degree (1974) in curriculum and instruction from the University of Washington, Seattle. Prior to joining the McREL staff, he was an associate professor at the University of Colorado.

Marzano has developed numerous programs and practices, used in K–12 classrooms, that translate research and theory in cognition into instructional methods. During his 30 years in education, he has authored more than ten books and one hundred articles and chapters in books on such topics as reading and writing instruction, thinking skills, performance assessment, curriculum design, and school reform.

John S. Kendall is a senior director with the Mid-continent Regional Educational Laboratory (McREL) in Aurora, Colorado. He earned his B.A. degree in English language and literature (1978) and his M.A. degree in classics (1983) from the University of Colorado at Boulder. He is the lead author of *Content Knowledge: A Compendium of Standards and Benchmarks for K–12 Education* (Kendall & Marzano, 1996; 2nd edition, Kendall & Marzano, 1997) and coauthor of *A Comprehensive Guide to Designing Standards-Based Districts, Schools, and Classrooms* (Marzano & Kendall, 1996) and a number of articles and book chapters related to standards and student assessment.

Kendall directs a technical assistance unit that provides standards-related services to schools, districts, and states, as well as national and international organizations. He has consulted for state departments of education and other educational institutions in the United States and abroad.

Barbara B. Gaddy is a senior associate with the Mid-continent Regional Educational Laboratory (McREL) in Aurora, Colorado. She earned her B.S. degree (1975) in marketing management from Miami University (Oxford, Ohio) and her M.A. degree (1992) in mass communications and journalism from the University of Denver. Gaddy has over 20 years of experience in communications and marketing. As a writer and editor, she works with other members of McREL's senior staff on programs related to standards-based reform and other approaches to enhancing student learning.

Gaddy is the lead author of *School Wars: Resolving Our Conflicts Over Religion and Values* (Gaddy, Hall, & Marzano, 1996), which was selected by *Choice*, a journal of the American Library Association, as one of the outstanding academic titles for 1997. She is also the editor of *A Comprehensive Guide to Designing Standards-Based Districts, Schools, and Classrooms* (Marzano & Kendall, 1996), the *Dimensions of Learning Teacher's Manual* (2nd ed.) (Marzano et al., 1997), and the *Dimensions of Learning Trainer's Manual* (2nd ed.) (Marzano et al., 1997).

Chapter 1

Crisis in American Education?

The Reformers

With the 1987 publication of his book *Cultural Literacy: What Every American Needs to Know*, E. D. Hirsch, Jr., initiated a national discussion about the literacy levels of American students. Hirsch coined a term for his conception of literacy, *cultural literacy*, which he defined in the preface to his book:

> To be culturally literate is to possess the basic information needed to thrive in the modern world. The breadth of that information is great, extending over the major domains of human activity from sports to science. It is by no means confined to "culture" narrowly understood as an acquaintance with the arts. Nor is it confined to one social class. (p. xiii)

Asserting that the literacy levels of Americans had severely declined, Hirsch charged that the educational system clearly was to blame. Since schools have failed to transmit the basic, shared information that people need to function effectively in society, Hirsch asserted, they have failed to fulfill their role of enculturating students. According to Hirsch (1987), the chief culprit is a liberal philosophy embraced by educators in the early part of the 20th century:

> The decline of American literacy and the fragmentation of the American school curriculum have been chiefly caused by the ever growing dominance of romantic formalism in educational theory during the past half century. We have too readily blamed shortcomings in American education on social changes (the disorientation of the American family or the impact of television) or incompetent teachers or structural flaws in our school systems. But the chief blame should fall on faulty theories promulgated in our schools of education and accepted by educational policymakers. (p. 110)

Hirsch (1987) defined romantic formalism—or educational formalism as he also called it—as "the theory that any suitable content will inculcate reading, writing, and thinking skills" (p. 21). Where did such an approach and its "faulty theories" originate? According to Hirsch, they can be traced back to the influence of Jean Jacques Rousseau whose ideas, in turn, greatly influenced John Dewey. Rousseau's view of education as a process in which children should be left free of adult ideas in order to naturally develop their intellectual and social skills was, Hirsch asserted, only half of the picture. Dewey's later embracement of Rousseau's content-neutral approach failed to recognize the great importance of shared information to the effective functioning of a society, a mistake that led to a deemphasis on factual knowledge. "Rousseau, Dewey, and their present-day disciples," Hirsch charged, "have not shown an adequate appreciation of the need for transmission of specific cultural information" (p. xvi).

As a remedy for the declining literacy of American students, Hirsch offered, as an appendix to *Cultural Literacy*, a list of 4,552 items. The list, which Hirsch and his colleagues said they hoped would serve as a curricular foundation for American education, was advanced as one that reflected the current, literate, American culture. The list contained dates (e.g., 1492), names of important people living and dead (e.g., Jimmy Carter and Enrico Fermi), places (e.g., Moscow), events (e.g., the Cuban missile crisis), literary works (e.g., *The Iliad*), and the like.

Allan Bloom's *The Closing of the American Mind* (1987), published, coincidentally, one month before Hirsch's *Cultural Literacy*, critiqued American education and the wider intellectual crisis of the 20th century. Somewhere along the line, Bloom argued, openness to anyone and anything became a precept in American culture and particularly in American higher education. This philosophy of openness—and its partner, relativism—have led to a degradation of the intellectual life for university students. Universities no longer challenge students to inquire into the essential questions of life, nor do they give them the appropriate tools to do so. "Relativism," Bloom remarked, "has extinguished the real motive of education, the search for a good life" (p. 34). Characterizing typical American university students, Bloom noted:

> Some intend to be scientists, some humorists or professionals or businessmen; some are poor, some rich. They are unified only in their relativism and in their allegiance to equality. And the two are related in a moral intention. The relativity of truth is not a theoretical insight, but a moral postulate, the condition of a free society, or so they see it. They have all been equipped with this framework early on, and it is the modern replacement for the inalienable natural rights that used to be the traditional American grounds for a free society. (p. 25)

The result of the indoctrination of openness is students who, although professing otherwise, are closed to Western culture and who, at the same time, have little real knowledge of non-Western cultures.

Other books published in the general time frame of the late 1980s to early 1990s advanced arguments that were similar in many regards to Hirsch's work in particular. Diane Ravitch and Chester Finn's *What Do Our 17-Year-Olds Know?* (1987), which we discuss in detail in the following section, reviewed the findings of the first national assessment of the knowledge of 17-year-olds relative to history and literature. Finn's *We Must Take Charge: Our Schools and Our Future* (1991) spoke to the serious flaws in American education and the critical importance of parents, community leaders, and other concerned people becoming involved in addressing the problems head-on. Finally, William Bennett's *The De-Valuing of America: The Fight for Our Culture and Our Children* (1992) spoke to the culture wars occurring in all spheres of American life—in particular, in American education—over which values and whose values would prevail.

To say that these works represented a concerted effort to communicate a common message would probably be an overstatement. Nevertheless, the books were somehow linked in the minds of their authors, as evidenced by their explicit and implicit references to one another. For example, Bennett (1992) was highly complimentary of Bloom's *The Closing of the American Mind*, calling it an "extraordinary book" (p. 177). Bennett also signaled his approval of Hirsch's position by adding an endorsement to *Cultural Literacy*'s (1987) dust jacket, noting that "this important book could, and should, change what goes on in our nation's classrooms." Ravitch and Finn's *What Do Our 17-Year-Olds Know?* made explicit references to Hirsch's *Cultural Literacy* and Bloom's *The Closing of the American Mind*. In addition, Hirsch was identified as a consultant to the design of a major study reported in Ravitch and Finn's book (1987). Finally, Finn's *We Must Take Charge* (1991), made reference to both Bloom and Hirsch, citing each as instrumental in starting a long-awaited critical analysis of public education in America. In addition, Finn noted that he, Bennett, and Bloom were like-minded reformers, citing as evidence the fact that the trio are commonly attacked in the pages of *Chronicles*, a publication of the Rockford Institute, for their support of ideas that some conservatives find offensive. Further, implying a kind of camaraderie, Finn said that the attacks that he and Ravitch had experienced relative to *What Do Our 17-Year-Olds Know?* were "a mere drizzle" compared to the "downpour" that had fallen on Hirsch (p. 210).

We think it important to clarify here that we do not wish to characterize these authors as having only one voice about American education, like a chorus reciting its lines in unison. These authors vary in their views and essential message, some more so than others. Hirsch, Bennett, Ravitch, and Finn share a perspective about cultural literacy and the importance of identifying and transmitting the shared knowledge of the literate American. We find the essential themes of their works to be especially linked.

We do, however, wish to distinguish Bloom's work from the rest—to some extent. Bloom's work is a comprehensive analysis of the evolution of modern thought, the state of the American university, and the mind set of university students. Bloom was convinced that the Great Books should make up a central part of the curriculum, yet he did not advocate the identification of a specific list of information that should be imparted to students. Rather, he advocated the teaching of the classics as a vehicle for students' engaging in essential life questions.

Readers often have linked Bloom's book with Hirsch's *Cultural Literacy*, although they are quite different, perhaps because they were published so close together in time, because both criticize public education, or because both point to intellectual and philosophical influences as the root of the problem. In his 1996 book, *The Schools We Need and Why We Don't Have Them*, Hirsch attempted to distance himself from Bloom's thesis, asserting that the books, in fact, were "not only different, but fundamentally opposed" (p. 12). Nonetheless, given the concerns that Bloom and Hirsch shared about the current state and intellectual underpinnings of American education—and the proximity in date of the publication of these primary works—it is no wonder that these books have been thought of as a series of like-minded exposés on the weaknesses of American education. Thus, we reference Bloom's work here perhaps for the same reasons that the public often associates it with *Cultural Literacy*.

We wish to note that the books reviewed in this section represent perhaps only a partial list of similarly minded texts, published since the mid-1980s, criticizing American education. Indeed, Lawrence Levine, whose book *The Opening of the American Mind* (1996) set out to refute many of the charges leveled at universities, their changing curricula, and their students, begins his book by listing a number of titles that, he asserts, convey comparable themes. In addition to Bloom's *The Closing of the American Mind* and Bennett's *The De-Valuing of America*, Levine lists the following works:

- *Profscam: Professors and the Demise of Higher Education* (1988),
  by Charles J. Sykes

- *The War Against the Intellect: Episodes in the Decline of Discourse* (1989),
  by Peter Shaw

- *Tenured Radicals: How Politics Has Corrupted Our Higher Education* (1990),
  by Roger Kimball

- *Killing the Spirit: Higher Education in America* (1990), by Page Smith

- *The Hollow Men: Politics and Corruption in Higher Education* (1990), by Charles J. Sykes

- *Illiberal Education: The Politics of Race and Sex on Campus* (1991), by Dinesh D'Souza

- *Impostors in the Temple: American Intellectuals Are Destroying Our Universities and Cheating Our Students of Their Future* (1992), by Martin Anderson

- *Dictatorship of Virtue: Multiculturalism and the Battle for America's Future* (1994), by Richard Bernstein

The words and phrases in these titles—as well as of others works reviewed in this section—convey a common message that American education is in crisis and that a battle is afoot for the hearts and minds of American students. Taken together, these publications are indicative of a perception about American education that reached an apex in the 1980s and that continues to be widely held as we near the end of the 20th century.

- *The Closing of the American Mind: How Higher Education Has Failed Democracy and Impoverished the Souls of Today's Students* (1987), by Allan Bloom

- *Cultural Literacy: What Every American Needs to Know* (1987), by E. D. Hirsch, Jr.

- *What Do Our 17-Year-Olds Know?* (1987), by Diane Ravitch and Chester E. Finn, Jr.

- *We Must Take Charge: Our Schools and Our Future* (1991) by Chester E. Finn, Jr.

- *The De-Valuing of America: The Fight for Our Culture and Our Children* (1992), by William J. Bennett

The Logic of the Reformers

Hereinafter, for ease of discussion, we refer loosely to Hirsch, Bennett, Ravitch, and Finn as "the reformers" or "the literacy reformers," realizing that a categorization such as this does not acknowledge the differences between these authors and their works. However, we believe that, as a group, these authors convey a common message and represent a specific position about American education.

Central to the arguments advanced by Hirsch, Bennett, Ravitch, and Finn is the assertion that American education has drifted away from a historical emphasis on relatively specific information, the possession of which enables one to participate effectively in American culture. Hirsch has defended the need for a shared body of knowledge in virtually every one of his works. For example, in *The Dictionary of*

Cultural Literacy: What Every American Needs to Know (1993), Hirsch and his coauthors Joseph Kett and James Trefil noted:

> Although it is true that no two humans know exactly the same things, they often have a great deal of knowledge in common. To a large extent this common knowledge or collective memory allows people to communicate, to work together, and to live together. It forms the basis for communities, and if it is shared by enough people, it is a distinguishing characteristic of a national culture. The form and content of this common knowledge constitute one of the elements that makes each national culture unique. (p. ix)

A number of these reformers have cited compelling examples of the lack of basic knowledge of American students. Hirsch (1987), for example, cited an incident relayed by his son, John, a Latin teacher. Apparently, one student, surprised to hear that Latin is a dead language, challenged, "What do they speak in Latin America?"

Research findings also have been used by reformers to add weight to the argument that American education continues to be in a serious crisis. One of the most commonly cited studies in support of the assertion that the basic knowledge of American students has declined is reported in Ravitch and Finn's *What Do Our 17-Year-Olds Know?* (1987). This book details the results of a 1986 National Assessment of Educational Progress (NAEP) study involving a representative sample of 7,182, 17-year-old students. There is no doubt that the study was well designed from a sampling perspective.[1] The assessment given to students consisted of 262 items that dealt with "knowledge questions," 141 in history and 121 in literature. Tables 1.1 and 1.2, respectively, show sample history and literature facts that were assessed and the percentage of students who knew these facts.

---

[1] As reported by Ravitch and Finn, the sample was composed of an equal number of boys and girls and proportional numbers of white, African American, Hispanic, Asian, and Native American students. Specifically, 76.5 percent of the students were white, 12.9 percent were African American, 5.9 percent Hispanic, 2 percent Asian, and 1.1 percent Native American. In addition, the sample was representative of the population densities of the various regions in the United States: 28.8 percent of the sample was drawn from the central region, 26.2 percent from the west, 24 percent from the northeast, and 21 percent from the southeast. The sample also was representative of the wider U.S. population in terms of level of parent education and percent of students attending public versus private schools. See *What Do Our 17-Year-Olds Know?*, pages 44–45, for more details.

Table 1.1

History Facts Assessed
NAEP 1986 National Assessment: 17-Year-Olds

Fact	Percent Correct
The Underground Railroad was a secret network to help slaves escape	87.5
Woodrow Wilson appealed for American entry into League of Nations	60.2
Missouri Compromise admitted Maine as free, Missouri as slave state	43.0
"Reconstruction" refers to readmission of Confederate states	21.4

Note: Information from *What Do Our 17-Year-Olds Know?*, by D. Ravitch and C. E. Finn, Jr., 1987, New York: Harper & Row.

Table 1.2

Literature Facts Assessed
NAEP 1986 National Assessment: 17-Year-Olds

Fact	Percent Correct
In Greek mythology, ruler of gods is Zeus	86.7
Dickens' novel *Tale of Two Cities* occurs during French Revolution	59.0
Walt Whitman wrote *Leaves of Grass*, which includes line, "I celebrate myself, and sing myself"	40.2
Henrik Ibsen wrote *Hedda Gabler, A Doll's House, An Enemy of the People*	20.3

Note: Information from *What Do Our 17-Year-Olds Know?*, by D. Ravitch and C. E. Finn, Jr., 1987, New York: Harper & Row.

Student responses were analyzed in detail and results reported by specific subtopics. For example, Tables 1.3 and 1.4, respectively, show the results for specific history and literature topics.

Overall, American 17-year-olds correctly answered 54.5 percent and 51.8 percent, respectively, of the questions for history and literature. Ravitch and Finn (1987) described these findings in the following way:

> Observers looking for the bright side might suggest that the proverbial glass is half full rather than half empty. Another way of characterizing these results, however, is in the terms traditionally used by teachers: a score of less than 60 percent is failing. (p. 1)

Table 1.3

History Topics Average Scores
NAEP 1986 National Assessment: 17-Year-Olds

Topic	Percent Correct
Chronology: When it happened	51.0
Maps and geography	71.3
Important people	61.6
The Constitution	54.4
Women in history	52.6
Civil rights	58.2
Demography and migration	51.0
Science and technology	71.3
Labor and industry	61.1
International affairs	58.3
Pre-national and colonial eras	49.0
Revolution–War of 1812	58.9
Territorial expansion–Civil War	54.4
Reconstruction–WWI	49.5
WWI–WWII	60.2
Post-WWII–present	54.7

Note: Information from *What Do Our 17-Year-Olds Know?*, by D. Ravitch and C. E. Finn, Jr., 1987, New York: Harper & Row.

The report card interpretation was the one chosen by Ravitch and Finn (1987). They concluded that "if there were such a thing as a national report card for those studying American history and literature, then we would have to say that this nationally representative sample of eleventh grade students earns failing marks in both subjects" (p. 1). Ravitch and Finn used these findings to build a case that U.S. schools need to identify the critical knowledge that all students must be exposed to and for which they should be held accountable. These findings, along with Ravitch and Finn's interpretation of them, received a great deal of attention.

Table 1.4

Literature Topics Average Scores
NAEP 1986 National Assessment: 17-Year-Olds

Topic	Percent Correct
Title-author relationships	39.5
Author information	51.0
Literature of the Bible	66.8
Classical mythology and literature	56.4
Epics, myths, and legends	60.7
Shakespeare	68.4
Well-known passages and quotations	60.5
Novels and novelists	44.9
Short stories	46.2
Plays and playwrights	43.6
Poetry and poets	48.6
Historical documents & nonfiction	54.9
Literature by or involving women or Blacks	48.6

Note: Information from *What Do Our 17-Year-Olds Know?*, by D. Ravitch and C. E. Finn, Jr., 1987, New York: Harper & Row.

Convinced that the knowledge and skill of American students had declined, the literacy reformers looked for reasons for this decline. As a group, they identified a common culprit, which they referred to by different names.

As noted earlier, Hirsch blamed the "faulty" content-neutral theories adopted by educators in the early part of the century. He argued that the impact of these theories could be clearly seen by comparing two documents: *Report of the Committee of Ten on Secondary School Studies*, published in 1893 (National Education Association), and *Cardinal Principles of Secondary Education* (Kingsley, 1918), written by the Commission on the Reorganization of Secondary Education and published in 1918 by the Bureau of Education at the U.S. Department of the Interior. According to Hirsch (1987), the contrasts between these two documents, whose publication Hirsch characterized as two "decisive moments" in American education, "bring into clear relief the change in educational theory that occurred in the first quarter of this century" (p. 116). As described by Hirsch (1987), the subject-matter orientation of the 1893 *Report of the Committee of Ten* gave way to the "social adjustment" focus of the 1918 *Cardinal Principles of Secondary Education*, which held high the idea that, instead of teaching specific subject matter, schools should have as their aim "producing good, productive, and happy citizens" (p. 118). Such a focus, said Hirsch, was the result of the convergence of a number of cultural factors and new psychological theories, but clearly could be traced, in part, to the influence of the ideas of Rousseau, Dewey, and others.

Hirsch discussed these documents further in his 1996 book, *The Schools We Need and Why We Don't Have Them*. He maintained that *Cardinal Principles*'s emphasis on health, ethical character, and other elements of personal development—over traditional subject matter—could be viewed as a response to the increasingly diverse population that resulted from the mass immigration of the time. Nonetheless, Hirsch argued, the document reflected the "anti-intellectual, progressive attitudes" (p. 48) that from then on predominated in the education community. Since then, Hirsch further opined, a "hostility to academic subject matter has been the continued focus of educational 'reform' . . . [and] by the 1930s, the anti-subject-matter principles of progressive education had become the established tenets taught to elementary teachers throughout the nation" (p. 49).

As Hirsch pointed to the faulty theories embodied in educational formalism's content-neutral focus, Bennett (1992) blamed the "educational elite," whom he defined as "people who . . . are often *not* at home with the traditional beliefs of most Americans; [who] tend to be skeptical and mistrustful of American society" (p. 27). In fact, Bennett explained, the elite seek nothing less than the "wholesale rejection of American ideals. Marked by alienation, suspicion, and doubt, the liberal elite call into question what is commonly thought of as 'the American dream'" (p. 27). Such liberal ideas, Bennett claimed, are embodied in quasi-political organizations such as the National Educational Association (NEA): "The record then is clear and beyond dispute: The NEA is an organization embodying the philosophy of modern-day liberalism. When power is seized by, or ceded to an organization of this political and philosophical temperament, it has consequences" (p. 49). Bennett further argued that organizations such as the NEA and the American Federation of Teachers (AFT) constitute "the education establishment" and have "monopoly control of American education" (p. 65).

In keeping with the allegations of Bennett and Hirsch, Ravitch and Finn (1987) referred to a "theory of learning" as the force behind the deemphasis of content in American schools:

> There is a tendency in the education profession to believe that *what* children learn is unimportant compared to *how* they learn. . . . This

assumption closes resembles a nineteenth-century pedagogical theory which held that the mind is composed of a series of "faculties," each of which must be exercised, like a muscle; so long as the muscle is exercised, the content is irrelevant. . . . This theory of learning was supposedly discredited in the early twentieth century by educational psychologists, but it has reemerged in a new guise in recent years as a rationalization for teaching skills without regard to content. In his book *Cultural Literacy*, E.D. Hirsch, Jr., calls this approach "educational formalism" and demonstrates how it is used—with dire results—to substitute skills for cultural content in the curriculum (pp. 17–18).

Finn expanded on this theme in his 1991 book, *We Must Take Charge*, in which he identified schools of education, and the professors that populate them, as the instigators of the liberal education policies rampant in our schools:

Faculties of education are the brain and central nervous system of the school establishment. They are where ideas originate and get legitimated. They are also where beliefs are held—and transmitted to teachers and principals—that fly in the face of common sense, popular preference, and the express will of democratically elected policymakers. They are where the most absurd notions are promulgated, usually with an introductory phrase such as "research shows" or "we have learned."

Universities play an oppositional role in many realms of our national life, and in general this is healthy. It is why we respect the principle of academic freedom. I am not questioning the right of the professoriate to spout nonsense, even to enjoy a guaranteed income courtesy of the taxpayer while doing so. But we do not have to organize our other public policies to heed that counsel. And if we have reason to believe that teachers and principals are getting their heads stuffed full of it as they pass through colleges of education, we are within our rights to deter them from following that path into our children's schools. (p. 222)

From the discussion above, it appears that Hirsch, Bennett, Ravitch, and Finn believe that there exists an education establishment permeated by a liberal philosophy, which this establishment intends to transmit to American youth through the schools. As mentioned earlier, we refer to Hirsch, Bennett, Ravitch, and Finn as the "literacy reformers," inasmuch as they champion a return to an emphasis on a body of knowledge that is shared by the vast majority of members of American society as one possible solution to the many problems that plague public education.

A Different Perspective

Thousands of Americans have jumped on the Hirsch cultural literacy cart, so to speak, if sales of his books and numbers of schools implementing his core curriculum are an indication of success. As of 1998, Hirsch's Core Knowledge Foundation, which aids schools in the implementation of his curriculum, listed over 600 schools in 44 states and the District of Columbia that have or are in the process of implementing the *Core Knowledge Sequence*, the key Core Knowledge document. (See Chapter 2, where the *Sequence* is discussed in more depth.) Table 1.5 reports the number of schools in various states that have signaled their commitment to begin the process of implementing the Core Knowledge approach.

However, in spite of—or perhaps because of—this intense interest in cultural literacy, a number of prominent researchers have analyzed the assertions of the reformers and taken strong issue with some of their findings and conclusions. In fact, it might be more accurate to say that there are some who believe that the current, continuing spate of criticisms of public education are not based on sound evidence. For example, in their book *The Manufactured Crisis* (1995), David Berliner and Bruce Biddle assert:

> For more than a dozen years [the] groundless and damaging message [that American education is deficient] has been proclaimed by major leaders of our government and industry and has been repeated endlessly by a compliant press. Good-hearted Americans have come to believe that the public schools of their nation are in a crisis state because they have so often been given this false message by supposedly credible sources. (p. 3)

Berliner and Biddle's contentions, made in 1995, were not new. Indeed, in 1991, Peter Dow noted the lack of evidence supporting the criticisms of public education in his book *Schoolhouse Politics: Lessons from the Sputnik Era*. Dow asserted that with the 1983 publication of *A Nation at Risk* (NCEE), American education was issued the most comprehensive and drastic challenges of its 150-year history. However, these challenges were based on very little evidence. Gerald Bracey also has spoken out strongly about the criticisms of U.S. education. In his book *Setting the Record Straight* (1997), Bracey explained that those who criticize public education "continue to utter statements that are simply untrue" (p. 2). Citing ongoing commentary and alarmist statements by political and business leaders about the state of American education, Bracey declared, "Ideologues, it should be noted, are not generally interested in facts that refute their position" (p. 2). Finally, a comprehensive study of education conducted by the Sandia National Laboratories in New Mexico found that many of the criticisms of public education were not consistent with available data. However, as the Sandia researchers explain (Carson, Huelskamp, & Woodall, 1993), as they prepared to publish their results they found resistance to their findings and conclusions:

Table 1.5

Number of Schools Implementing the Core Knowledge Approach

State	Number of Implementing Schools	State	Number of Implementing Schools
Alabama	1	Montana	0
Alaska	5	Nebraska	4
Arizona	12	Nevada	1
Arkansas	19	New Hampshire	1
California	15	New Jersey	0
Colorado	35	New Mexico	0
Connecticut	4	New York	10
Delaware	0	North Carolina	21*
District of Columbia	2	North Dakota	0
Florida	128*	Ohio	10
Georgia	44*	Oklahoma	19
Hawaii	1	Oregon	4
Idaho	1	Pennsylvania	19*
Illinois	6	Rhode Island	4
Indiana	8	South Carolina	5
Iowa	1	South Dakota	0
Kansas	6	Tennessee	35
Kentucky	6	Texas	84*
Louisiana	8	Utah	2
Maine	1	Vermont	1
Maryland	57	Virginia	11
Massachusetts	5	Washington	8
Michigan	14	West Virginia	1
Minnesota	6	Wisconsin	6
Mississippi	15	Wyoming	1
Missouri	2		

Note: Figures compiled from list of schools found at the Core Knowledge website. See, specifically, http://www.coreknowledge.org/CKproto2/schools/schllst.htm. (Address current as of January 5, 1999. List of schools said to be current as of November 19, 1998.)

*During the time that we were tracking the above numbers, significant increases were observed in the number of schools reportedly committed to implementing the Core Knowledge principles in a number of states. In March 1998, ten months prior to the date the figures reported in this table were collected, these numbers were 60 for Florida, 22 for Georgia, 7 for North Carolina, 6 for Pennsylvania, and 55 for Texas. (However, the number of schools purporting to have "committed" to the core knowledge approach may fluctuate somewhat; on August 11, three months prior to the list of schools from which the above figures were compiled, the number of schools in Tennessee was 47 [compared to 35 as listed above]. Nonetheless, the vast majority of the states saw increases in the number of Core Knowledge schools.)

When Admiral Watkins, the Department of Energy (DOE) Secretary, declared education to be "a matter of mission" for the DOE laboratories, we undertook a study to elucidate key issues in education and thereby help focus our laboratories' attention on the most pressing challenges. . . .

As our work unfolded, we began to solicit feedback from various peer groups in New Mexico and throughout the nation. After a limited release of the draft in the summer of 1991, we found ourselves to be a target for various groups—both those who found our observations in conflict with their particular views, as well as those who grasped our findings as "proof" to support their own theses. Although it was not our original intention to enter into the national debate on education, we feel professionally obliged to respond to the over 500 requests we have received for the report to date. We are fully aware of the potential for controversy in any study of educational issues. Nonetheless, we present this "outsider" report as a work still in progress. Our aim remains the same—to present relevant information in a form that will foster data-based decision-making that will be as free as possible of preconceived notions or agendas. (p. 259)

Here we consider in some depth two of the many counterarguments addressed by Berliner, Biddle, Bracey, and the Sandia researchers: that American students' knowledge has not declined and that disaggregated SAT scores have remained steady or perhaps increased.

Students' General Knowledge

The allegation that American students today do not know as much as students from past generations is certainly a theme in the writings of the literacy reformers. As mentioned previously, this allegation was quite evident in Ravitch and Finn's *What Do Our 17-Year-Olds Know?* Indeed, the fact that American 17-year-olds averaged 54.5 percent correct on the history items and 51.8 percent correct on the literature items appeared to be an airtight case in support of the failure of American education.

However, researchers who have analyzed Ravitch and Finn's data have reached quite different conclusions. For example, Dale Whittington argued that Ravitch and Finn's test results were difficult, if not impossible, to interpret inasmuch as the test had never been given to any reference group. Without a reference group of similar students from past generations or even adults of today, there is no way of knowing whether the scores of 54.5 and 51.8 represented a gain or a loss in general knowledge. Although Ravitch and Finn acknowledged this lack of data with which to compare the test results, nonetheless they assumed that students should know all the items on the test. As Whittington (1991) reported:

> In other words, the study provided no indication whether 17-year-olds in the mid-1980s knew any more or less than anyone else living in the United States today. Nor can the test's results tell us how much 17-year-olds of the mid 80s knew compared to 17-year-olds of the past. The study's validity rested solely on the author's judgment that (a) all the questions in their test represented basic information about history, geography, and literature; (b) all students should have been instructed in the content covered by this test and have it permanently ingrained in their memory; (c) a test of factual knowledge, while not ideal, could adequately determine what America's 17-year-olds have and have not learned about history and literature; and (d) in order to "pass" the test, students needed to answer 60 percent of its questions correctly. (p. 763)

To more accurately interpret the findings of Ravitch and Finn, Whittington sought out history and social studies tests administered from 1915 to the present and equated them as accurately as possible with the Ravitch and Finn test. As reported by Berliner (1992), Whittington found that students in the Ravitch and Finn study were less knowledgeable than students from the past on about one-third of the items and scored better than past generations on about one-third of the items. Berliner (1992) concluded, "When compared to historical records, the data in Ravitch and Finn's study do not support their charge that today's seventeen-year-olds know less than they ever did" (p. 19).

In another attempt to determine the knowledge level of students today as opposed to students in the past, Berliner (1992) examined the research on standardized tests. He concluded that to accurately compare scores from the past with scores today, one must consider the norming procedures of standardized tests. Renorming of standardized tests takes place about every seven years; over one generation, a standardized test might be renormed about three times. Renorming means that the test makers recalculate percentile scores, making it harder to obtain a given percentile rank. Analyzing such commonly used standardized tests as the California Test of Basic Skills, the Iowa Test of Basic Skills, and the Metropolitan Achievement Test, Berliner (1992) presented evidence that student performance on standardized tests actually has *increased*:

> That means that today's youth is scoring about one standard deviation higher than their parents did when they took the test. We can estimate that around eighty-five percent of today's public school students score

higher on standardized tests of achievement than their average parent did. But the high-jump bar keeps getting higher, and it takes a higher jump today than it did around 1965 to hit the fiftieth percentile. (p. 17)

The conclusions of Berliner and Whittington are supported by C. C. Carson, R. M. Huelskemp, and T. D. Woodall (1992), authors of the report commonly referred to as the "Sandia Report." This report provides evidence of an increase in student achievement. To illustrate, consider Figure 1.1.

Figure 1.1 depicts the mathematics achievement of American students from 1977 to 1986, by ethnicity. Although it is true that the performance of white students has improved only slightly, the performance of Hispanic and African-American students has increased appreciably. The Sandia researchers interpreted these findings in light of falling drop-out rates over the last twenty years: "When viewed in conjunction with the declining drop-out rates, this chart indicates that a large percentage of minority youth are staying in school and achieving higher scores than their predecessors" (p. 271).

The same achievement patterns are observable in reading proficiency. As evidence, Sandia researchers offered the graph shown in Figure 1.2, which shows the average reading proficiency for 17-year-olds by community type, rather than by ethnic group. Again, the Sandia researchers interpreted these results quite positively:

> Students in each community type have shown steady-to-improving performance over the past 20 years. As with the previous chart [i.e., Figure 1.1], large differences in performance are seen among different groups.
>
> This chart [shows] that there have not been recent declines in performance on skills tests. If anything, today's students are performing better than previous students. (p. 271)

Overall, the Sandia researchers concluded that the achievement of U.S. students had increased steadily over the past few decades. However, the Sandia trend data stop in 1986. In a later report, Bracey (1997) offered more current data showing improvement in reading and mathematics proficiency up to 1992 (see Figures 1.3 and 1.4, respectively).

Bracey's conclusions (1997) were almost identical to those of the Sandia researchers: The performance of American 9-, 13-, and 17-year-olds has been increasing consistently over the last 20 years.

In summary, after analyzing the available data, a number of researchers have reached a conclusion that is antithetical to that reached by the reformers: The knowledge level of American students has not decreased. If anything, it has increased.

Figure 1.1

Percentage of Students with Basic Mathematics Proficiency: 17-Year-Olds

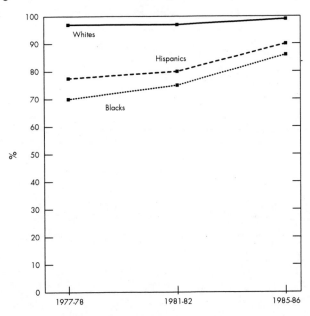

Note: From "Perspectives on Education in America: An Annotated Briefing," by C. C. Carson, R. M. Huelskamp, and T. D. Woodall, 1993, *The Journal of Educational Research, 86*(5), p. 271. (Source: National Center for Educational Statistics)

Figure 1.2

Reading Proficiency — Community Type: 17-Year-Olds

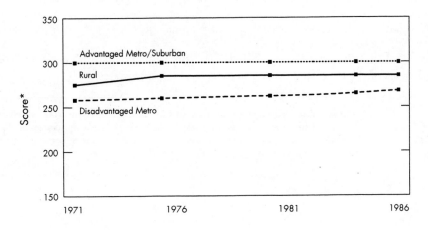

*150 = Basic, 250 = Intermediate, and 350 = Advanced

Note: From "Perspectives on Education in America: An Annotated Briefing," by C. C. Carson, R. M. Huelskamp, and T. D. Woodall, 1993, *The Journal of Educational Research, 86*(5), p. 271. (Source: National Center for Educational Statistics)

Figure 1.3

Trends in Average Reading Proficiency for the United States
as Measured by NAEP (1971–1992)

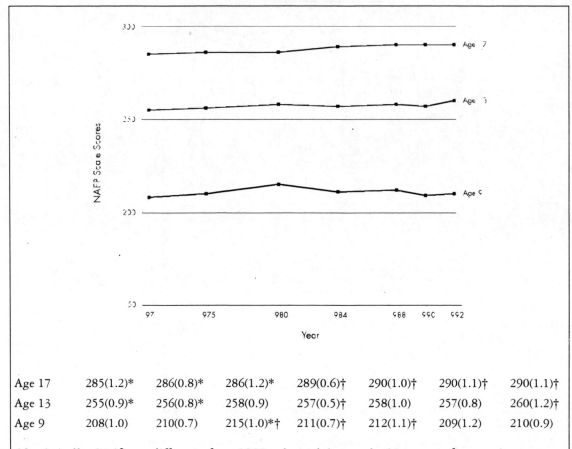

Age 17	285(1.2)*	286(0.8)*	286(1.2)*	289(0.6)†	290(1.0)†	290(1.1)†	290(1.1)†
Age 13	255(0.9)*	256(0.8)*	258(0.9)	257(0.5)†	258(1.0)	257(0.8)	260(1.2)†
Age 9	208(1.0)	210(0.7)	215(1.0)*†	211(0.7)†	212(1.1)†	209(1.2)	210(0.9)

*Statistically significant difference from 1992, where alpha equals .05 per set of comparisons.

†Statistically significant difference from 1969-1970, where alpha equals .05 per set of comparisons. The standard errors of the estimated proficiencies appear in parentheses.

Note: From *NAEP 1992 Trends in Academic Progress*, by Office of Educational Research and Improvement, 1992, Washington, DC: Author. Reprinted in *Setting the Record Straight: Responses to Misconceptions about Public Education in the United States* (p. 39), by G. W. Bracey, 1997, Alexandria, VA: Association for Supervision and Curriculum Development.

Figure 1.4

Trends in Average Mathematics Proficiency for the United States
as Measured by NAEP (1973–1992)

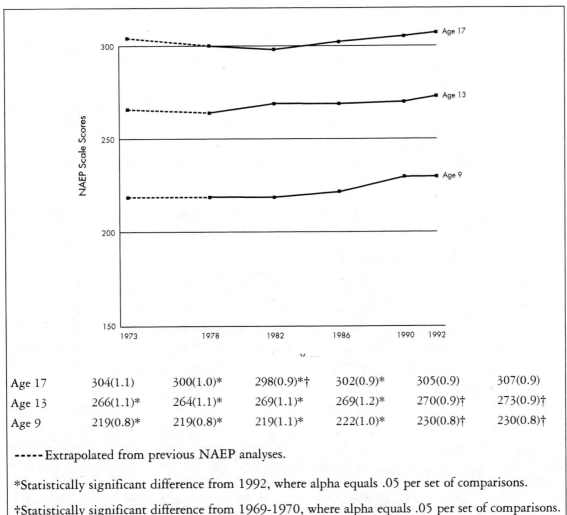

Age 17	304(1.1)	300(1.0)*	298(0.9)*†	302(0.9)*	305(0.9)	307(0.9)
Age 13	266(1.1)*	264(1.1)*	269(1.1)*	269(1.2)*	270(0.9)†	273(0.9)†
Age 9	219(0.8)*	219(0.8)*	219(1.1)*	222(1.0)*	230(0.8)†	230(0.8)†

- - - - Extrapolated from previous NAEP analyses.

*Statistically significant difference from 1992, where alpha equals .05 per set of comparisons.

†Statistically significant difference from 1969-1970, where alpha equals .05 per set of comparisons.
The standard errors of the estimated proficiencies appear in parentheses.

Note: From *NAEP 1992 Trends in Academic Progress*, by Office of Educational Research and Improvement, 1992,
Washington, DC: Author. Reprinted in *Setting the Record Straight: Responses to Misconceptions about Public Education
in the United States* (p. 39), by G. W. Bracey, 1997, Alexandria, VA: Association for Supervision and Curriculum
Development.

SAT Scores

The literacy reformers also have used the well-publicized decline in scores on the Scholastic Aptitude Test (SAT) over the last few decades as a primary piece of evidence in their criticism of American education. For example, in their book *What Do Our 17-Year-Olds Know?* Ravitch and Finn (1987) explained:

> The most widely publicized score decline was that of the Scholastic Aptitude Test, which more than a million students take annually as part of the college entry process. The revelation in 1975 that the national average had fallen precipitously over a ten-year period stirred a public furor. . . . it aroused public concern about the quality of education; it alerted the media to education issues as no other single indicator had done. (p. 7)

Hirsch (1987), too, characterized the "dramatic" decline in SAT scores as "solid evidence that literacy has been declining in this country just when our need for effective literacy has been sharply rising" (p. 5).

Again, a very different perspective has been offered by researchers. For example, Berliner (1992) noted that a decline in any test score must be interpreted in the context of the range of possible scores. That is, a decline of 10 points means one thing if there are 100 points possible; it means something quite different if there are 500 points possible. Relative to the decline in SAT scores, Berliner explained that the figures actually represent only a 3.3 percent decline in raw score total, or about five fewer items answered correctly over twenty-five years. He further maintained, "The explanation for this loss is simple and should fill educators with great pride, not shame. Why? Because much greater numbers of students in the bottom sixty percent of their class have been taking the test since the 1960s" (p. 12).

Berliner based much of his argument about SAT scores on the Sandia report. Indeed, it was the Sandia researchers who first offered a positive interpretation of the alleged decline in SAT scores. To illustrate, Figure 1.5 depicts SAT achievement as presented in the Sandia report.

Figure 1.5

Average SAT Scores
1967–1990

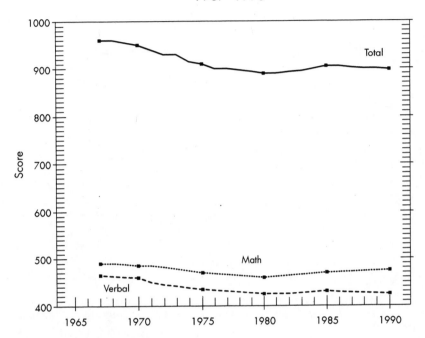

Note: From "Perspectives on Education in America: An Annotated Briefing," by C. C. Carson, R. M. Huelskamp, and T. D. Woodall, 1993, *The Journal of Educational Research*, 86(5), p. 267. (Source: National Center for Educational Statistics)

Figure 1.5 shows a decline in average SAT scores of about five percent over the interval from 1967 to 1990. Yet, the Sandia researchers noted that this decline does not translate into falling scores for comparable groups of students. As evidence, the Sandia researchers offered Figure 1.6.

Figure 1.6 indicates that following the decline in SAT scores in the 1970s for some groups, "every minority subpopulation taking the SAT has shown general improvement in its average score during the 1980s while White scores have remained relatively stable" (p. 268). Further analysis by the Sandia researchers indicated that the types of students taking the SAT tests in the late 1980s differed markedly from those who took the examination 20 years earlier. This difference is illustrated in Figure 1.7.

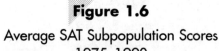

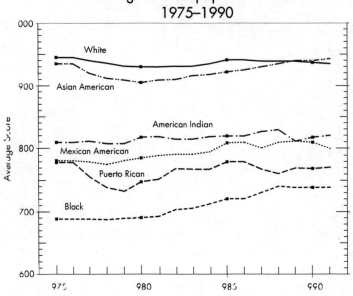

Note: From "Perspectives on Education in America: An Annotated Briefing," by C. C. Carson, R. M. Huelskamp, and T. D. Woodall, 1993, *The Journal of Educational Research, 86*(5), p. 268. (Source: National Center for Educational Statistics)

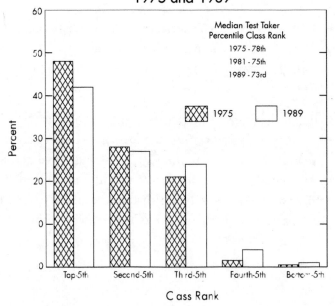

Note: From "Perspectives on Education in America: An Annotated Briefing," by C. C. Carson, R. M. Huelskamp, and T. D. Woodall, 1993, *The Journal of Educational Research, 86*(5), p. 269. (Source: The College Board)

The Sandia researchers found that more students with lower class ranks took the test in 1989 than in 1975. Specifically, as Figure 1.7 shows, fewer students in the top 20 percent of their class took the test in 1989 than did 15 years earlier, students in the next 20% made up virtually the same proportion of test takers as in the past; and that students in the lower 60% of their class made up a significantly higher percentage of test takers in 1989 than they did in 1975. One result of this shift is shown in the box in the upper right-hand corner of Figure 1.7. Specifically, the median class rank of SAT test takers in 1975 was the 78th percentile (or top 22 percent of the class), whereas in 1989, the median class rank was the 73rd percentile. The drop in SAT scores is due to this decline (i.e., to the fact that more of our youth take the entrance exams).

The Sandia researchers also explained that the drop from 78th to 73rd percentile is not trivial. The 78th percentile rank would be achieved if over 40 percent of a class took the exam. To lower the median rank to the 73rd percentile, the portion of the class between the 58th and 46th percentiles would have to be added to the group taking the test. As the Sandia researchers (Carson, Huelskamp, & Woodall, 1993) explained, "It would be a surprise if this change did not significantly lower the test results" (p. 268).

In *The Manufactured Crisis* (1995), Berliner and Biddle offered a more updated illustration of the change in the type of students taking the SAT (see Figure 1.8). Commenting on these findings, Berliner and Biddle explained:

> More students from the lower achievement ranks have recently opted to take the SAT. This would not matter if students from each achievement rank were equal in their abilities, but this is obviously not the case. Students who earn top high school grades also are much more likely to earn high SAT scores than students who earn mediocre high school grades. This means that even if the ability of schools to educate students remains constant across the nation, aggregate national SAT scores will fall when more students from the lower achievement ranks choose to take the test. (p. 18)

Berliner and Biddle concluded that aggregating SAT scores (or any scores for that matter) does not accurately reflect student achievement. They suggested that a more valid way of looking at the data is to break them down by different groups. They offered the information shown in Figure 1.9 as a more accurate accounting of student performance on the SAT examination.

Figure 1.8

Percentage of Students Taking SAT by Class Rank

1976 and 1993

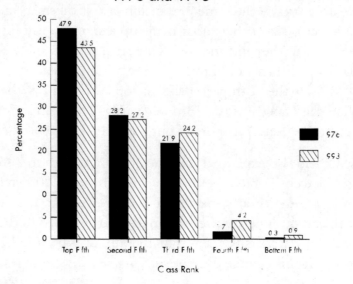

Note: From *College Bound Seniors,* by The College Entrance Examination Board, various dates, New York: Author. Found in *The Manufactured Crisis: Myths, Fraud, and the Attack on America's Public Schools* (p. 19), by D. C. Berliner and B. J. Biddle, 1995, Reading, MA: Addison-Wesley. Reprinted with permission.

Figure 1.9

Average SAT Subpopulation Scores

1976 and 1993

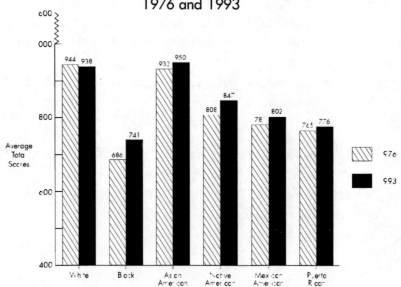

Note: From *College Bound Seniors* (p. 10), by The College Entrance Examination Board, 1993, New York: Author. Found in *The Manufactured Crisis: Myths, Fraud, and the Attack on America's Public Schools* (p. 22), by D. C. Berliner and B. J. Biddle, 1995, Reading, MA: Addison-Wesley. Reprinted with permission.

When one looks at this "disaggregated" SAT data, noted Berliner and Biddle (1995), the following trends are evident: (a) Scores for white students have shown a very slight decrease, and (b) students from minority homes are now earning higher average scores. The overall conclusion of Berliner and Biddle relative to SAT scores was that "disaggregated SAT scores suggest that student achievement in the nation has either been steady or has been climbing over the past eighteen years" (p. 23).

In short, the alleged decline in the knowledge and basic skills of American students—as well as the decline in SAT scores—are not matters of fact. Indeed, one could build a case that the literacy reformers have not provided an accurate accounting of the status of American education at least relative to the issue of student knowledge and achievement on the SAT. We strongly advise educators, parents, and other community members to gather more data on these issues—at a minimum—before drawing final conclusions.

Our Position and Recommendations

One of the purposes of this book is to highlight the findings of researchers who have challenged the data upon which many of the arguments of the reformers have been based. Again, we were motivated to present these arguments because of the large numbers of people who seem to accept as fact the declining state of public education. Our essential message relative to this topic is that educators and others should carefully review the findings and conclusions of the many ongoing research undertakings before drawing conclusions.

Since the publication of the reports reviewed in this chapter, the results of a large international study, the Third International Mathematics and Science Study (TIMSS) have been released. We discuss this study further in Chapter 3; however, at this point we wish to note that, in a general sense, the TIMSS results were relatively positive for 4th-grade students, but negative for 8th- and 12th-grade students.[2] Since the results of this study were not available until recently, the reformers did not comment on them in the books reviewed in this chapter. However, no doubt critics of public education, in particular, will seize upon the idea that U.S. students are failing when compared to students in other countries. At least one reformer, Chester Finn, commented on the

---

[2]The Third International Mathematics and Science Study (TIMSS), undertaken in 1995, assessed the knowledge of a half-million students in nearly 50 countries at three levels of schooling. Results from this study are reported in two primary sets of documents: (1) *Pursuing Excellence: A Study of U.S. Fourth-Grade Mathematics and Science Achievement*; *Pursuing Excellence: A Study of Eighth-Grade Mathematics and Science Achievement*; and *Pursuing Excellence: A Study of U.S. Twelfth-Grade Mathematics and Science Achievement*, 1997, 1996, and 1998, respectively, by the U.S. Department of Education, National Center for Education Statistics; and (2) *A Splintered Vision: An Investigation of U.S. Science and Mathematics Education*, 1997, by W. H. Schmidt, C. C. McKnight, and S. A. Raizen, at the U.S. National Research Center for the Third International Mathematics and Science Study, Michigan State University. For additional information, see http://nces.ed.gov/timss/ or http://ustimss.msu.edu/.

poor results in a March, 1998 *Wall Street Journal* article, declaring that U.S. 12th-graders "occupy the international cellar." However, other researchers, notably Berliner and Biddle (see, e.g., 1998), caution that the 12th-grade data need further analysis and debate before conclusions should be drawn.

To clarify our position, we comment here on three issues raised by the literacy reformers: the general decline in the quality of American education, the negative effect on the American education system of the liberal philosophy of the education establishment, and the need for an identifiable core of essential knowledge around which schooling should be organized.

Relative to the reformers' assertion that the quality of American education has declined, it is no doubt accurate to say—although not particularly profound—that American education is doing well in some respects and quite poorly in others. That said, we leave the debate about the current status of American education up to others, with the suggestion that readers seek multiple opinions from education researchers and professionals and consider the most current data before drawing conclusions.

Relative to the issue of the negative effect of the liberal philosophy of the education establishment, we take strong issue with the reformers' perspective that there is a liberal philosophy at work in the so-called education establishment. From our perspective, there is no education establishment, at least as described by the reformers. If one accepts their reasoning on this point, then one must accept the assertion that a large number of organizations, including the NEA, the AFT, the U.S. Department of Education, graduate and undergraduate teacher preparation programs, and research organizations funded by the U.S. Department of Education all ascribe to a common philosophy and are involved in a concerted effort to control public education. As members of a research organization funded in part by the U.S. Department of Education, we know firsthand that the organizations considered to be the "establishment" by the literacy reformers are as diverse as the individuals within them. Thus, we consider such characterizations to be inaccurate at best and a well-designed "straw man" argument at worst.

The Importance of Identifying Essential Knowledge

Finally, we agree with the position that a listing of essential knowledge should be identified and used to restructure public education. Schools and districts benefit greatly when they are organized around an agreed-upon list of information and skills that all students should master as a part of their K–12 schooling. We find three compelling reasons, in particular, for the identification and implementation of a core of essential knowledge in American education: (a) the lack of a well-articulated curriculum, (b) the lack of an emphasis on academics, and (c) the lack of an emphasis on education outputs. We discuss each of these issues in the following sections.

The Need for a Well-articulated Curriculum in Public Education

Noneducators—and many educators—commonly assume that public schools have a well-articulated curriculum. This assumption is bolstered by the fact that most school districts can produce "curriculum guides" that specify in detail the topics that will be covered in every subject area and, often, at every grade level. One might reasonably surmise, then, that the curriculum in public schools is made up of a set of carefully selected topics that form a well-articulated hierarchy of knowledge from grade level to grade level. Yet, when one probes into the curricular structure of schools, one commonly finds that the perception of a well-articulated course of study from grade to grade is just that—perception. Hirsch addressed this point in *The Schools We Need and Why We Don't Have Them* (1996):

> We know, of course, that there exists no national curriculum, but we assume, quite reasonably, that agreement has been reached locally regarding what should be taught to children at each grade level—if not within the whole district, then certainly within an individual school. . . But. . .the idea that there exists a coherent plan for teaching content within the local district, or even within the individual school, is a gravely misleading myth. (p. 26)

Hirsch (1996) further explained that the myth of a coherent curriculum is not a darkly held secret. Rather, the notion that there is a local curriculum is simply accepted by most educators as a matter of faith. To illustrate, Hirsch related the following anecdote:

> Recently, a district superintendent told me that for twenty years he had mistakenly assumed each of his schools was determining what would be taught to children at each grade level, but was shocked to find that assumption entirely false; he discovered that no principal in his district could tell him what minimal content each child in a grade was expected to learn. (pp. 26–27)

Research supports Hirsch's position relative to curriculum. For example, studies (Doyle, 1992; Stodolsky, 1989; Yoon, Burstein, & Gold, n.d.) indicate that even when highly structured textbooks are used as the basis for a curriculum, teachers commonly make independent and idiosyncratic decisions regarding what should be emphasized, what should be added, and what should be deleted. This practice commonly creates huge holes in the continuum of content to which students are exposed. To illustrate, in their book *The Learning Gap*, Stevenson and Stigler (1992) made the following observations:

> Daunted by the length of most textbooks and knowing that the children's future teachers will be likely to return to the material, American teachers often omit some topics. Different topics are omitted by different teachers thereby making it impossible for the children's later teachers to know what has been covered at earlier grades—they cannot be sure what their students know and do not know. (p. 140)

The lack of uniformity in American curriculum also is evident in the research on how teachers use time. To illustrate, in a study of the content that teachers emphasize within reading and the language arts, Berliner (1979, 1984) found that one fifth-grade teacher allocated 68 minutes a day of instruction in reading and language arts; another teacher allotted 137 minutes a day. At the second-grade level, one teacher set aside 47 minutes a day for reading and language arts; another teacher set aside 118 minutes a day—or 2 1/2 times more per day—to teach reading and language arts. Fisher and his colleagues (Fisher et al., 1980) reported the following anecdotes on variation in the curriculum:

> In one second-grade class the average student received 9 minutes of instruction over the whole school year in the arithmetic associated with the use of money. This figure can be contrasted with classes where the average second grader was allocated 315 minutes per school year in the curriculum content area of money. As another example, in the fifth grade some classes received less than 1,000 minutes of instruction in reading comprehension for the school year (about 10 minutes per day). This figure can be contrasted with classes where the average student was allocated almost 5,000 minutes of instruction related to comprehension during the school year (about 50 minutes per day).

> The differences in time allocations at the level of "reading" and "mathematics" and at the level of specific subcontent areas are substantial. These differences in how teachers allocate time are related to differences in student learning. Other things being equal, the more time allocated to a content area, the higher the academic achievement. (p. 16)

In short, the assertion by Hirsch and the other literacy reformers that American schools have failed to clearly identify the content that should be addressed at each grade level appears to be quite accurate.

The Need for an Emphasis on Academic Subjects

In addition to the negative effects of the idiosyncratic selection of content from school to school and teacher to teacher, there appears to be a notable deemphasis on time spent on academic subjects. For example, Borg (1980) documented the increase in the amount of time allocated for noninstructional activities from the late 1800s to 1980, which had the effect of decreasing the amount of time available for instruction. Borg's findings are reported in Table 1.6.

Table 1.6

Time Allocations in Minutes Per Day for Noninstructional Activities
Across the Decades (Grades 2 and 5)

Study: Noninstructional Time	1862–72 data, 6 cities (Mann)	1904 survey, 6 cities (Payne)	1914 survey, 50 cities (Holmes)	1926 survey, 444 cities (Mann	1980 (BTES)
Grade 2: Break Time[1]	23	23	38	22	76
Grade 2: Management Time[2]	16	7	12	11	45
TOTAL	39	30	50	33	121
Grade 5: Break Time[1]	24	21	34	19	80
Grade 5: Management Time[2]	18	7	10	10	46
TOTAL	42	28	44	29	126

[1]Break. Includes recess and unstructured physical education (also includes lunch period in BTES study).
[2]Management time: Includes wait and transition time. Includes opening exercises in the earlier studies.

Note: From "Time and School Learning," by W. R. Borg, 1980, *in Time to Learn* (p. 44), C. Demham and A. Lieberman (éds.), Washington, DC: National Institute of Education. Table modified for clarity.

As Table 1.6 shows, between 1926 and 1980 there was a marked increase in the amount of time allocated for breaks and other noninstructional activities. (Even allowing for a highly unlikely 60-minute lunch period, the BTES study reveals that the amount of time allocated for noninstructional activities nearly doubled between 1926 and 1980.)

A more recent study also found that U.S. schools do not characteristically allocate their time to core learning. Specifically, the National Education Commission on Time and Learning (1994) reported that when compared to eight other countries in terms of the amount of time allocated for instruction, the United States ranks in the top half. This finding, however, provides false comfort because, as the Commission's report noted, the use of instructional time in American schools is "markedly different." Calling its results "startling," the Commission noted that "students can receive a high school diploma—often sufficient in itself for university entrance—if they devote only 41 percent of their school time to core academic work" (p. 23).

Some blame the decrease in attention to core academic subjects on the erosion of the Carnegie unit. The history of the Carnegie unit dates back to 1906 when the president of the Carnegie Foundation for the Advancement of Teaching, Henry S. Prichett, defined a "unit" as "a course of five periods weekly throughout an academic year" (in Tyack & Tobin, 1994, p. 460). By convention, these periods had come to be thought of as 55 minutes long. The impetus for this categorization came from an attempt by a blue-ribbon panel of Carnegie Foundation trustees to establish criteria for distinguishing between colleges and universities. The Carnegie committee decreed that to truly be considered a university, an institution must have at least six full-time professors, require a course of study of four full years in the liberal arts and sciences, and require of entering students no less than four years of academic or high school preparation. Tyack and Tobin (1994) explained that the Carnegie committee also set what became well-established standards for the content and duration of specific courses:

> It was not enough simply to prescribe four years of secondary instruction.
> . . . It was also necessary to develop a standard measurement of time and
> credit for each subject—the Carnegie unit—and to demand that a college
> require at least fourteen of these units. The Foundation did not stop there;
> it also went on for eight pages specifying in great detail the content of
> units in subjects like English, mathematics, Latin, Greek, foreign
> languages, history, and science. Thus, they standardized not only time and
> credits, but gave pride of place to traditional academic subjects. (p. 461)

The Carnegie unit was adopted almost immediately by high schools and quickly became one of the criteria for high school accreditation by regional associations such as the North Central Association of Colleges and Secondary Schools. State laws also built the Carnegie unit system of credits into requirements for secondary schools. Initially, then, the Carnegie unit represented an implicit curriculum. It required high schools to cover specified content over a specified period of time. For decades, this system worked fairly well. However, the implicit curriculum of the Carnegie unit eventually succumbed to the perceived need to offer a wide variety of courses.

According to Ravitch (1983), by the 1930s educators were concerned that for every 1,000 children who entered the fifth grade, only 455 graduated from high school. To remedy the problem, high schools began to offer a wide array of courses to cater to the various academic and vocational interests of students. From the 1940s until the mid-1970s, the emphasis on expanding the type of courses offered in high school generated a geometric expansion of the number of courses that constituted the high school curriculum. By the mid-1970s, the U.S. Office of Education reported that more than 2,100 different courses were being offered in American high schools (see Ravitch, 1995).

Although generally it has been assumed that optimizing student choice in terms of the content they study increases their motivation to learn that content, this assumption recently has been challenged. Specifically, a 1997 survey of 1,300 randomly selected high school students, entitled *Getting By: What American Teenagers Really Think About Their Schools* (Johnson, Farkas, et al., 1997), found that American high school students value increased structure in the curriculum:

> Teenagers yearn for closer monitoring and watchfulness from teachers. These teens—in very significant numbers—want required after-school classes for youngsters who are failing. They want teachers to enforce the rules and check the homework. In focus group after focus group, teenagers voiced admiration and affection for the teacher who never lets up, who never lets go, who respects them enough to ask them to do more. (p. 35)

The Need for an Emphasis on Education Outputs

Another argument for identifying essential knowledge is the current emphasis in education on *inputs*—what schools put into the process of schooling—as opposed to *outputs*—what students get out of schools. Finn (1990) described this shift in perspective in terms of an emerging paradigm for education:

> Under the *old* conception (dare I say paradigm?), education was thought of as process and system, effort and intention, investment and hope. To improve education meant to try harder, to engage in more activity, to magnify one's plans, to give people more services, and to become more efficient in delivering them.
>
> Under the *new* definition, now struggling to be born, education is the result achieved, the learning that takes root when the process has been effective. *Only* if the process succeeds and learning occurs will we say that *education* happened. Absent evidence of such a result, there is no education—however, many attempts have been made, resources deployed, or energies expended. (p. 586)

The "input" paradigm was the norm until the mid-1960s when Congress commissioned the U.S. Office of Education to study the quality of education opportunity. Researcher James Coleman was the chief author of the resulting report, the celebrated "Coleman Report," released in 1966. Finn (1990) explained the report's conclusion that the cherished "input" variables might not have all that much to do with education equality when equality is conceived of in terms of what students actually learn as opposed to the time, money, and energy expended. In later years, Coleman (1972) summarized the importance of his study in the following way:

> The major virtue of the study as conceived and executed lay in the fact that it did not accept the [traditional] definition, and by refusing to do so, has had its major impact in shifting policy attention from its traditional focus on comparison of inputs (the traditional measures of school quality used by school administrators: per-pupil expenditures, class size, teacher salaries, age of building and equipment, and so on) to a focus on output, and the effectiveness of inputs for bringing about changes in output. (pp. 149–150)

Finn noted that President Richard Nixon was perhaps the first public official with significant power to recognize the need for an emphasis on learning: "As we get more education for the dollar," Nixon stated in 1970, "we will ask Congress to supply many more dollars for education" (in Finn, 1990, p. 588).

Finn (1990) explained that although many school reform efforts are still grounded in the old paradigm, some are beginning to embrace the output view of accountability. Among these new efforts, Finn cited the national goals established at the education summit in 1989:

> Perhaps even more portentous was the 1989 "education summit" held in Charlottesville, Virginia, at which the nation's governors and President Bush actually agreed to develop a set of national "goals" for education— goals that, as they were hammered out and made public in early 1990, have far more to do with outcomes than with service delivery. They also pledged to issue annual "report cards" on progress toward those goals. President Bush seemed to epitomize the basic philosophy of the summit—and to echo Nixon's words of almost two decades before— when he said, "We'll judge our efforts not by our intentions, but by our results." (p. 591)

The identification of essential knowledge is central to an emphasis on output variables. Obviously, the most rudimentary output variable on which schools should be judged is student mastery of essential content.

Conclusion

In this chapter, we have considered the primary assertions advanced by reformers as well as arguments made by a number of researchers who have analyzed their work. As we have seen, these researchers offer a perspective on American education that varies greatly from that of the literacy reformers. Although we disagree with the assertion that the education establishment has a negative, monopolistic grip on public education, we agree on one very important point: American education would benefit greatly from the identification of the essential information and skills to which all students should be exposed. The remainder of this book examines the question of what should be included on such a list and how schools should address such a list.

Chapter 2

The E. D. Hirsch Solution

Readers conversant with the topic of essential knowledge are well aware that an attempt already has been made to identify a list of the knowledge students should be exposed to, and ideally master, prior to high school graduation. As discussed in Chapter 1, in 1987 E. D. Hirsch, Jr., published *Cultural Literacy: What Every American Needs to Know*. The title itself conveyed the strong message that Hirsch's work included a definitive list of the essential knowledge that American students should be taught in order to be considered culturally literate. The implication was that the list should form the basis for the curriculum in K–12 education. Since the publication of *Cultural Literacy*, a number of supplemental works have been developed by Hirsch and his colleagues, all of which attempt to further identify and clarify the specific knowledge that reflects the current, literate, adult culture and that should, therefore, be transmitted to students.

Given the apparent level of success of Hirsch's approach as evidenced by the number of schools adopting it (see Chapter 1, page 13, for a state-by-state summary), one might conclude that the issue of essential knowledge has been addressed adequately. In other words, to determine what students should know and be able to do, perhaps one need only consult Hirsch's list. A careful analysis of Hirsch's work, however, reveals methodological flaws in the process used to identify the terms and phrases that constitute "core knowledge." These flaws are so serious, we contend, that they render Hirsch's list invalid as a comprehensive accounting of essential knowledge.

Hirsch's Body of Work

Hirsch's *Cultural Literacy* (1987) unabashedly proclaimed to contain the definitive list of information and skill that every American should know to be considered culturally literate. The book was reprinted in 1988 by a different publisher and with an altered list of terms and phrases. Hirsch's next work, *The Dictionary of Cultural Literacy* (coauthored with his colleagues Kett and Trefil), also was published in 1988. The book was a departure from the 1987 and 1988 lists in its inclusion of a definition for each entry term or phrase. The *Dictionary* was updated and republished in 1993.

Hirsch's *Dictionary* was followed by a product entitled the *Core Knowledge Sequence: Content Guidelines for Grades K–8* (Core Knowledge Foundation), the latest edition of which was published in 1998. This work is perhaps best described as an outline of specific content that should be taught in various subject-matter areas. After the first edition of the *Sequence* was published in 1990 and over the years that the *Sequence* was updated (1991–1998), a series of works was developed that identify what students should know at various grade levels. This highly popular series uses the titles *What Your Kindergartner Needs to Know*, *What Your First Grader Needs to Know*, and so on up through the sixth grade. Finally, in 1996, Hirsch published the book *The Schools We Need and Why We Don't Have Them*, a commentary on why Hirsch's approach had not been more widely accepted across the country.

In all, Hirsch's body of work regarding cultural literacy is an impressive one in terms of the number of publications. However, the actual listings of core knowledge provided by Hirsch in these various works are inconsistent and flawed. To illustrate, we consider each set of works separately.

Cultural Literacy

Hirsch's first accounting of essential knowledge, published in 1987 as an appendix to *Cultural Literacy*, contained six dates and 4,546 terms. Hirsch referred to this "provisional" list as "a changing entity," giving a number of reasons for such a characterization, most notably that "core knowledge changes" (p. 146). Nevertheless, as indicated by the title of the book in which it was published, the list was offered as the foundation knowledge for American culture.

In a chapter addressing the process of *explicitly* identifying the knowledge that is *implicitly* used by anyone who addresses the general public, Hirsch and his coauthors gave the following rationale for the items found on the list:

> When we address a general audience we must assume that we are addressing a "common reader," that is, a literate person who shares with us a common body of knowledge and associations. Since we so frequently have to posit a common reader in writing or public speaking, it should be possible to reach a large measure of agreement about what that common reader knows. Such agreement about literate culture should, in theory, enable a random group of literate Americans to compile a list of its core contents. (p. 135)

This simple theory is at the base of Hirsch's approach, and we submit it harbors two serious flaws. First, it presumes that the "stuff" of education is reducible to and can be defined by an imagined "common," yet "literate," reader. The theory presumes that what literate individuals know, or say they know, is an adequate summary of their education—adequate enough, in fact, to serve as the foundation for a K–12 curriculum. Thus, once children have learned to generate the same responses as literate adults, they, too, by definition, must be literate. Further, knowing a list of remembered words and phrases does not mean that one is literate anymore than parroting the index to a book means that one understands its contents.

The second flaw in the theory is that it presumes that the images, events, facts, and generalizations that an individual or group of individuals can recall on any one day, or number of days, can ultimately define the core knowledge important in a culture. As we stated earlier, we agree that there is a body of knowledge that should be transmitted to youth and that the transmission of cultural knowledge is a central purpose of education. Determining this knowledge should not be left to happenstance, either in the choice of individuals who determine what should be known or, worse, to the vagaries of human memory. This second flaw in the theory may help to explain how the lists that Hirsch's group has produced vary quite unpredictably.

One critical question, then, about Hirsch's 1987 list (as well as his subsequent lists) is, Who determined its contents? Hirsch (1987) explained the preliminary process used to identify what every student should know in the following way:

> In 1983, I persuaded two of my colleagues at the University of Virginia, Joseph Kett, chairman of the department of history, and James Trefil, professor of physics, to help me compile such a list. (p. 135)

The initial 1987 list, then, was the product of the combined input of Hirsch and two colleagues. One might argue that relying on three professors—regardless of how well informed they might be—runs the risk of a highly biased product reflecting the inevitable myopia any small set of individuals will have, given the natural limitations of knowledge and experience. As a validity check, Hirsch and his colleagues had the list reviewed. In the introductory pages to the 1987 appendix, Hirsch reported that "more than one hundred consultants reported agreement on over 90 percent of the items listed" (p. 146). Unfortunately, Hirsch did not describe who these one hundred-plus reviewers were, nor what it meant that they reached agreement on 90 percent of the items. Did it mean that 90 percent of the reviewers had perfect agreement on all items or did it mean that 100 percent of the reviewers agreed on 90 percent of the items? Given the apparent subjective methodology Hirsch used to construct his 1987 list, one might ask whether there is a certain amount of bias in the product.

The problem of selection bias in Hirsch's list was first noted in 1988 by a team of researchers from the prestigious UCLA Center for Research on Evaluation, Standards, and Student Testing (CRESST). After a detailed analysis of Hirsch's 1987 and 1988 lists, House, Emmer, and Lawrence (1988) concluded that Hirsch's listing of what every American should know was "politically conservative in what it includes and excludes" (p. 25). With regard to the 1987 list, House, Emmer, and Lawrence noted that it contained "a great many proper names of Anglo American origin, many English literary terms, a surprising number of foreign phrases, many clichés, and only a few historical dates" (p. 13). The CRESST researchers also identified what appeared to be systematic omissions in Hirsch's accounting of what every American should know:

> The list is short on athletics, health, entertainment, social science, and military terms. It systematically omits terms associated with the sixties such as the Age of Aquarius, the Beats, the Chicago Seven, counterculture, Bob Dylan, Alan Ginsburg, Howl, Jack Kerouac, One Dimensional Man, Students for a Democratic Society, We Shall Overcome, and Woodstock. It omits certain political terms such as Amnesty International, ERA, Greenpeace, Haymarket Square massacre, IWW (International Workers of the World), the Internationale, Jack London, nothing to lose but your chains, nuclear winter, and John Reed. It omits certain writers such as Henry Miller, Ezra Pound, Sam Shepherd, and John Steinbeck. It omits ethnic terms such as Black Elk Speaks, the blues, Harlem Renaissance, soul (music, food), and omits certain music terms such as the blues, Billie Holiday, punk, reggae, rock and roll, while including Fred Astaire, Ginger Rogers, and the Beatles. It omits social science terms such as Margaret Mead, Thorstein Veblen, weltanschauung. It omits health terms such as AIDS, carcinogenic, Lamaze, and stress. (p. 13)

In the final analysis, the CRESST researchers concluded, Hirsch's 1987 accounting of what every American should know simply does not meet the standards of an unbiased, expert accounting:

> Of course, any list will omit some terms that should be included: it is the systematic exclusion and inclusion of certain terms that biases the list. One cannot help but think that unacknowledged criteria of propriety, acceptability, and politics were operating, perhaps only implicitly, when the original list was constructed. After all, this is supposed to be a list of what educated Americans do know, not what they should know (or should forget). But of course the list is transformed

in reality into a prescription of what should be taught. Hirsch's subtitle after all is "What Every American Needs to Know," not what they do know. (p. 13)

In 1988, one year after the initial list was published, an updated, paperback version was released by a new publisher. The cover of the 1988 book in which the list appeared as an appendix advertised an "updated and expanded" appendix. In the preface to this second version Hirsch explained:

> The only revisions in this edition . . . are changes in the appendix, "What Literate Americans Know." We have studied about three thousand suggestions sent to us by more than two hundred readers. These have yielded a net increase of 343 items. The additions come from history, technology, literature, politics, science, and geography. The deletions are few, totaling only about twenty-five, e.g., "Edict of Nantes" and "Occam's razor," and other items that were questioned by several readers independently. Although exactitude is impossible in forming such a compilation, the many comments on the list have enabled us to make it a more reliable index to American literate culture than it was before. (p. xi)

One would expect that adding the suggestions of 200 readers would significantly reduce some of the selection bias inherent in Hirsch's original list. However, the CRESST researchers also found significant problems with the 1988 list. The CRESST researchers opined that although some omissions perhaps were simply oversights, others appeared to reflect a political bias. In addition, the CRESST researchers (House, Emmer, & Lawrence, 1988) challenged Hirsch's claim that only 25 deletions were made from the 1987 list to produce the 1988 list:

> Hirsch seems a bit confused on the deletions, his numeracy perhaps not as good as his cultural literacy. In fact, more than 300 items were deleted from the original list, including such terms as Spiro Agnew, art deco, civil liberties, Ralph Ellison, El Salvador, Jerry Falwell, Milton Friedman, ghetto, Barry Goldwater, Guatemala, Gulf of Tonkin, Lee Iacocca, Jeffersonian democracy, Edward Kennedy, Henry Kissinger, George McGovern, Ferdinand Marcos, Linus Pauling, Nelson Rockefeller, penis, phallus, Shylock, scrotum, sperm, Gloria Steinem, testes, vagina, Thornton Wilder, William Butler Yeats, and Wounded Knee massacre. Apparently, Hirsch has forgotten that a number of controversial political figures and terms were removed from the list as well as terms referring to human reproduction. (p. 13)

While preparing to write this book, we conducted a comparison of the 1987 and 1988 lists that Hirsch and his colleagues advanced as the "contents of cultural literacy" (p. 134) and found that Hirsch had expanded the 4,552 items on the 1987 list to 4,982 items on the 1988 list—an increase of 430 items, not 343 as reported by Hirsch. There were also some strong inconsistencies in the logic (or lack thereof) of Hirsch's deletions and additions. For example, Exhibits 2.1 and 2.2 list the deletions from the 1987 list and additions to the 1988 list, respectively, for entries beginning with the letter *a*. (Entries are listed alphabetically in both the 1987 and 1988 versions of the list.)

An analysis of the deletions and additions listed in Exhibits 2.1 and 2.2 raises some immediate questions. First, there are 22 deletions from the 1987 work in the *a* entries alone, providing support for the CRESST researchers finding that 300 items were deleted from the overall list as opposed to the 25 deletions claimed by Hirsch. More interesting is the idiosyncratic nature of the additions and deletions. For example, why were *Adriatic Sea*, *Alberta*, *Atlantic Ocean*, and *Austria* deleted from the 1987 list, while *Aberdeen*, *Alamo*, *Arabia*, *Arctic*, *Argentina*, and the *Azores* were added? By what logic was *active voice* deleted from the 1987 list, yet *passive voice* was not? Why was *astronomy* deleted from the 1987 list and *atom smasher* added?

Exhibit 2.1

Deletions from 1987 *Cultural Literacy* List
"a" Entries Only
(Entries found on the 1987 list but not on the 1988 list)

Abraham and Isaac	aquifer
active voice	art deco
Adriatic Sea	art nouveau
Agnew, Spiro	assembly line
agreement (grammar)	assessment (tax)
Aladdin and the Wonderful Lamp (title)	astronomy
Alberta	Atlantic Ocean
Allies (World War II)	atmosphere (earth's)
Andes Mountains	Austria
Antarctic Ocean	autonomy
apostle	axis (mathematics)

Exhibit 2.2

Additions to 1987 *Cultural Literacy* List

"a" Entries Only

(Entries found on the 1988 list but not on the 1987 list)

Aaron, Hank	ampersand (&)
Abandon all hope, all ye who enter here.	An apple a day keeps the doctor away.
Aberdeen	An army travels on its stomach.
abstract art	Andromeda
acculturation	And thereby hangs a tale.
ad absurdum	anecdote
adagio	anemia
Addis Ababa	Angelou, Maya
Adeste Fideles (song)	anon
ad infinitum	Antigone (myth)
adiós	antiparticle
Age cannot wither her, nor custom stale/ Her infinite variety.	Apostles, the Twelve
	Appomattox Court House
agreement	appraisal
Ahab, Captain	Arabia
AIDS	Arabian Nights
Aladdin's lamp	Archduke Francis Ferdinand
Alamo	archetype
Alas, poor Yorick. . .	Arctic, the
al fresco	Argentina
All animals are equal, but some animals are more equal than others.	Armenian massacres
	armistice
Allen, Woody	art for art's sake
allergy	artificial intelligence
all the news that's fit to print	Art is long, life is short.
all things to all men	As flies to wanton boys are we to the gods.
All work and no play makes Jack a dull boy.	assessment
alpha radiation	A thing of beauty is a joy forever.
Alzheimer's disease	atmosphere
a.m.	atoll
Amazing Grace (song)	atom smasher
Amazon (myth)	AT&T
America	Attila the Hun
American Gothic (image)	Auckland
American Revolution	Auld Lang Syne (Song)
Amish	A word to the wise is sufficient.
amok, run	Azores

In summary, a careful analysis of Hirsch's 1987 and 1988 *Cultural Literacy* lists leads one to the conclusion that he and his colleagues used a process that did not adequately guard against—and perhaps even promoted—selection bias. Furthermore, somewhat of an intellectual arrogance can be detected in Hirsch's stance. For example, Hirsch (1987) noted, "In the United States, only two-thirds of our citizens are literate, and even among those, the average is too low and should be raised" (p. 2). Since Hirsch offered his list as the basis of what every American should know, by inference one might conclude that if you do not know the majority of what is on his list, you are, by definition, illiterate.

Given the inherent bias in the Hirsch 1987 and 1988 lists and the lack of scientific rigor with which they were constructed, their acceptance in the education and noneducation communities is somewhat disconcerting. As mentioned in Chapter 1, a glowing endorsement from then-Secretary of Education William Bennett appeared on the back jacket of the 1987 edition of *Cultural Literacy*. On that same book jacket, an endorsement by the late Albert Shanker, then-President of the American Federation of Teachers (AFT), included an equally glowing statement of support: "I can think of no other book of recent years more important for the formulation of curriculum policy than this one."[3] It is our position that given the importance of identifying a listing of essential knowledge, candidate lists should receive a great deal more scrutiny before they are endorsed.

The Dictionary

The problem of selection bias and lack of scientific rigor also is evident in *The Dictionary of Cultural Literacy* (1988), by Hirsch and his University of Virginia colleagues Kett and Trefil. The *Dictionary* is organized into 23 sections. According to Hirsch, Kett, and Trefil, these sections reflect the divisions that students traditionally encounter by the end of twelfth grade. Some subject areas also reflect other ways of further grouping content, most notably "American History" and "World History," each of which is broken by time into two sections (e.g., "American History to 1865" and "American History since 1865"). In addition, Hirsch and his colleagues added sections on proverbs and on idioms, arguing for their addition "because cultural literacy embraces more subject matter than is usually treated in an academic setting" (p. xvii). Entries within each section are listed alphabetically. The sections of the 1988 *Dictionary* are listed in Exhibit 2.3.

---

[3]In spite of these endorsements, according to CRESST researchers House, Emmer, and Lawrence (1988), with the exception of *The American Scholar* (the Phi Beta Kappan journal that published articles by Hirsch and his coauthors), reviews in other scholarly journals "were overwhelmingly negative" (p. 3). For information on the types of criticisms leveled against Hirsch's early works in particular, see House, Emmer, & Lawrence, 1988, pp. 3–4.

Exhibit 2.3

Sections Found in the 1988 Version of *The Dictionary of Cultural Literacy*

1. The Bible	13. World Politics
2. Mythology and Folklore	14. American Politics
3. Proverbs	15. World Geography
4. Idioms	16. American Geography
5. World Literature, Philosophy, and Religion	17. Anthropology, Psychology, and Sociology
6. Literature in English	18. Business and Economics
7. Conventions of Written English	19. Physical Sciences and Mathematics
8. Fine Arts	20. Earth Sciences
9. World History to 1550	21. Life Sciences
10. World History since 1550	22. Medicine and Health
11. American History to 1865	23. Technology
12. American History since 1865	

As noted earlier, the 1988 *Dictionary* attempted to add detail to the list of cultural literacy items set forth by providing a brief description of the important information for each item. For example, Exhibit 2.4 shows the description offered in the *Dictionary* for the Lewis and Clark expedition.

Exhibit 2.4

Example Entry, 1988 *Dictionary*

Lewis and Clark expedition A journey made by Meriwether Lewis and William Clark, during the presidency of Thomas JEFFERSON, to explore the American Northwest, newly purchased from FRANCE, and some territories beyond. The expedition started from ST. LOUIS, MISSOURI, and moved up the MISSOURI RIVER and down the COLUMBIA RIVER to the PACIFIC OCEAN. The information that Lewis and Clark gathered was of great help in the settlement of the West. (*See also* LOUISIANA PURCHASE.)

Note: From *The Dictionary of Cultural Literacy: What Every American Needs to Know* (p. 247), by E. D. Hirsch, Jr., J. Kett, and J. Trefil, 1988, Boston: Houghton Mifflin. The words printed in small caps are cross-references to other entry words in the dictionary.

In the introduction to the *Dictionary*, Hirsch and his coauthors explained that although the *Dictionary* was published after *Cultural Literacy*, the idea for it arose first. *Cultural Literacy* was first envisioned "merely as a technical explanation" of the ideas that led to the *Dictionary* (Hirsch, Kett, & Trefil, 1988, p. xi.). Apparently, the positive response to *Cultural Literacy* gave Hirsch the impetus to expand the *Dictionary*.

Since the introductory section of the 1988 version of the *Dictionary* makes specific reference to the 1987 edition of *Cultural Literacy*, one might expect that the entries in the *Dictionary* would adhere to the 4,552 items in the appendix to the 1987 work. Curiously, though, the *Dictionary* includes some 6,812 items—an increase of 2,260 items from the list found in the appendix of the 1987 edition of *Cultural Literacy* and an increase of 1,830 items from the list found in the 1988 edition of *Cultural Literacy*. Nowhere in the 1988 *Dictionary* did Hirsch and his coauthors explain why the items were added. However, they did provide a description (see Exhibit 2.5) in the introduction to the *Dictionary* of the three-step process used to select items that should be included in the body of knowledge that literate Americans share.

Exhibit 2.5

Process Used for Selecting Items
The Dictionary of Cultural Literacy

First, we proposed that many things are either above or below the level of cultural literacy. Some information is so specialized that it is known only by experts and is therefore above the level of common knowledge. At the same time, some information, such as the names of colors and animals, is too basic and generally known to be included in this kind of dictionary. By definition, cultural literacy falls between the specialized and the generalized.

Our second test was to determine how widely known an item is in our culture. Only those items that are likely to be known by a broad majority of literate Americans ought to appear in this dictionary. Therefore, in selecting entries, we drew upon a wide range of national periodicals. We reasoned that if a major daily newspaper refers to an event, person, or thing without defining it, we can assume that the majority of the readers of that periodical will know what that item is. If this is true, that event, person, or thing is probably part of our common knowledge, and therefore part of cultural literacy.

Third, we proposed that cultural literacy is not knowledge of current events, although it can help us understand those events as they occur. To become part of cultural literacy, an item must have lasting significance. Either it has found a place in our collective memory or it has the promise of finding such a place. This is one of the things that contributes to the stability of cultural literacy in America. Some of the material in this dictionary has remained unchanged in our national consciousness since our nation's beginnings.

Note: Excerpt from *The Dictionary of Cultural Literacy* (pp. ix–x), by E. D. Hirsch, Jr., J. F. Kett, & J. Trefil, 1988, Boston: Houghton Mifflin. Copyright © 1988 by Houghton Mifflin Company. All rights reserved. Reprinted with permission.

Again, it is unclear whether the process described in Exhibit 2.5 was used to create the original list in the 1987 version of *Cultural Literacy*, the list in the 1988 version of *Cultural Literacy*, or the list found in the 1988 *Dictionary*. Such information would be useful inasmuch as there are significant differences among the three lists.

As noted earlier in this chapter, in preparing this publication we compared the *a* items found on the 1987 and 1988 *Cultural Literacy* lists (see Exhibits 2.1 and 2.2). Similarly, we compared the *a* items on the 1987 *Cultural Literacy* list with the *a* entries in the 1988 *Dictionary*. The results of this comparison are presented in Exhibits 2.6 and 2.7.

Exhibit 2.6

Deletions from 1987 *Cultural Literacy* List
"a" Entries Only
(Entries found in 1987 *Cultural Literacy* but not in 1988 *Dictionary*)

abominable snowman	animal/vegetable/mineral
abstract expressionism	Antarctic Ocean
aficionado	anticlericalism
aggression	Antony's speech at Caesar's funeral
á la carte	apostle
Aladdin and the Wonderful Lamp (title)	aquifer
alfresco	art deco
alkaline	art nouveau
Amazonian	asymmetry
ambiguity	As you make your bed so must you lie in it.
anarchy	Atlantic Charter
Anglican church (Church of England, Episcopal church)	autonomy
	azimuth

Exhibit 2.7

Additions to 1988 *Dictionary*
"a" Entries Only
(Entries found in 1988 *Dictionary* but not in 1987 *Cultural Literacy*)

Aaron, Henry (Hank)	Alzheimer's disease
Abandon hope, all ye who enter here.	AI
abdomen	*Aida*
abdominal cavity	AIDS
Aberdeen	alcoholism
aborigines	alderman
abscess	Ali Baba
abstract art	alkali
absurd, theater of the	All animals are equal, but some animals are
Academy, French	more equal than others.
Academy, Plato's	All for one and one for all.
Academy Awards	*All Quiet on the Western Front*
Acapulco	All the news that's fit to print
acceleration	all things to all men
according to Hoyle	all thumbs
acculturation	All work and no play makes Jack a dull boy.
ace in the hole	Allen, Woody
Achilles tendon	allergy
acorns mighty oaks do grow, From little.	*aloha*
active site	alpha radiation
acute angle	"Amazing Grace" (song)
acute disease	Amazons
ad absurdum	ambrosia
ad nauseam	"America"
adagio	*American Crisis, The*
Addis Ababa	*American Gothic*
Aden	Amish
adenoids	amniocentesis
"Adeste Fidelis"	amniotic fluid
adhesion	amplitude
adios	amplitude modulation (AM)
adipose tissue	anal stage
adsorption	analgesic
Advent	analog computer
aerobic exercise	anarchism
aerobics	anatomy
Age cannot wither her, nor custom stale/	And thereby hangs a tale.
Her infinite variety.	Anderson, Marian
Ahab, Captain	

Exhibit 2.7 (continued)

Additions to 1988 *Dictionary*
"a" Entries Only
(Entries found in 1988 *Dictionary* but not in 1987 *Cultural Literacy*)

Andromeda galaxy

anemia

anesthesia

anesthetic

Angelou, Maya

angels

angina pectoris

Anglican Communion

Animal Farm

Anna Karenina

Annunciation

anon.

anorexia nervosa

Antarctic

antiballistic missiles (ABMs)

Antichrist

anticoagulants

antidepressants

antihistamines

antiparticle

antiseptics

Antony, Mark

anus

Apocrypha

Appalachia

appendectomy

appendicitis

apple a day keeps the doctor away, An.

apple of discord

apple of one's eye

appraisal

Arabia

Arabian Nights

Arabian Peninsula

Ararat

archaeology

archetype

Arctic

Ares Argentina

Argonauts

Argus

Armenia

Armenian massacres

army marches on its stomach, An.

Around the World in Eighty Days

arson

art for art's sake

arthropods

artificial intelligence (AI)

As flies to wanton boys, are we to the gods;/
    They kill us for their sport.

As You Like It

asexuality

Ash Wednesday

Assemblies of God

asteroid

asthma

astronaut

astrophysics

Aswan Dam

at loggerheads

at sixes and sevens

atherosclerosis

athlete's foot

Atlantis

atoll

atom smasher

atomic clock

Atomic Energy Commission (AEC)

atrophy

Attila the Hun

Attucks, Crispus

Auckland

"Auld Lang Syne"

avatar

average

Since the structure of the *Dictionary* differs so much from the straightforward list of terms found in *Cultural Literacy*, it is important to explain the process we used to compare the 1987 *Cultural Literacy* list with the 1988 *Dictionary*. In compiling the lists reported in Exhibits 2.6 and 2.7, we compared the items on the 1987 *Cultural Literacy* list with the 1988 *Dictionary*'s entry words, which are printed in bold typeface throughout the *Dictionary*. We reasoned that since the entry words were the terms Hirsch and his colleagues chose to highlight, using these in our comparison would yield the fairest, most objective comparison. We did not, for example, expand our comparison to the many "cultural associations"[4] that Hirsch and his coauthors included below many entry words, reasoning that this additional information represented *related* knowledge, not the *core* knowledge that the authors seemed to be attempting to identify.

The differences noted in Exhibits 2.6 and 2.7 raise some interesting questions. For example, why were *abominable snowman*, *art deco*, and *asymmetry* deleted from the list, yet *Advent*, *allergy*, and *artificial intelligence* were added?

The *Dictionary of Cultural Literacy* was updated in a second edition, published five years later in 1993 (Hirsch, Kett, & Trefil). This edition of the *Dictionary* maintained the sections found in the 1988 edition. However, according to the preface to the text, in addition to updating and fine-tuning, some significant changes again were made to the list of core knowledge, based on the suggestions of "hundreds of readers," whom Hirsch and his coauthors acknowledged en masse as "coeditors and coparticipants" (p. vii). In spite of the changes made to the list, in the preface to the second edition of the *Dictionary*, Hirsch and his coauthors commented on the "remarkable stability" (and implied validity) of the items included on the list:

> Over ninety percent of what one needs to know has remained stable in all subjects except the obvious ones of recent history, science, and technology. And even in those subjects, the core of needed knowledge has remained very stable. The core contents of a first-rate school curriculum are not arbitrary elements, and in most areas of learning they do not change either rapidly or radically over time. These findings have enormous implications for schooling and school reform. (p. viii)

---

[4]Many cultural associations are included throughout the *Dictionary*. The *Dictionary*'s authors explain that "most definitions make the cultural sense of an entry self-evident, but such is not always the case" (pp. xvii–xviii); cultural associations are required at times to provide additional information. For example, a reference to the term apostle is included as a cultural association under the entry "Apostles, the Twelve" (see Hirsch, Kett, & Trefil, 1988, p. 3). For a further explanation of the authors' use of cultural associations, see Hirsch, Kett, & Trefil, 1988, pp. xvii–xviii. (The same explanation also can be found in the 1993 edition of the *Dictionary* on the same pages cited above.)

In keeping with the pattern established in previous works, there are substantive differences between the first and second editions of the *Dictionary*, although the numbers of changes are much smaller than those found in the other comparisons we have discussed thus far. The introduction to the 1993 *Dictionary* includes a description of a three-step process for deciding what knowledge to include that is identical to that included in the introduction to the 1988 edition. In addition, Hirsch and his coauthors explain in the preface that most of the changes in the 1993 *Dictionary* can be attributed to dramatic changes in world history since the first edition, advances in science and technology, and "the growing consensus over multiculturalism" (p. vii). Apparently, other changes are the result of "updating and fine-tuning" (p. vii).

Although the second edition reflects a net increase of only 56 entry words when compared to the 1988 edition (6,868 versus 6,812 entries), there are 249 additions and 193 deletions. In fairness to Hirsch and his coauthors, some percentage of these additions and deletions are more accurately described as items that were moved from one section of the *Dictionary* to another. For example, *Democrat* was listed in the 1988 *Dictionary* in two sections, "American History to 1865" and "American History since 1865." In 1993, this entry was deleted from both of these sections and moved to a section entitled "American Politics." In addition, a percentage of the deletions are items that were listed in two sections of the 1988 *Dictionary* but deleted from one of those sections in the 1993 *Dictionary*. For example, *That way madness lies* was listed in both "Idioms" and "Literature in English" in the 1988 *Dictionary* but was listed in only the "Literature in English" section in the 1993 *Dictionary*. Nonetheless, a number of additions and deletions were made that can be characterized as substantive. Exhibits 2.8 and 2.9 list the substantive deletions and additions for the *a* entries for the various sections of the *Dictionary* when comparing the 1988 edition to the 1993 edition.

Exhibit 2.8

Deletions from 1988 *Dictionary*
"a" Entries Only
(Entries found in 1988 *Dictionary* but not in 1993 *Dictionary*)

alias	apropos
all things to all men	arson

Exhibit 2.9

Additions to 1993 *Dictionary*

"a" Entries Only

(Entries found in 1993 *Dictionary* but not in 1988 *Dictionary*)

ACLU	arthroscope
added value tax	artificial reality
aerodynamics	astigmatism
algorithm	astronomical unit
Alvarez hypothesis	Australopithecus
A.M.E. Church	Azerbaijan
American Civil Liberties Union (ACLU)	AZT
American Dream	
angioplasty	

Again, a number of questions might be asked as to why certain items were deleted and others added. For example, since the deletion of *all things to all men* cannot be attributed to dramatic changes in world history or to advances in science and technology, was this entry deleted because of "the growing consensus over multiculturalism"? Or, if we apply the three-part test that Hirsch described (see this chapter, p. 44, or see Hirsch, Kett, & Trefil, 1993, pp. ix–x), was it deleted because

1. the phrase is only known by experts or, conversely, known by everyone, literate and illiterate alike?

2. the phrase is not widely known by most literate Americans?, or

3. because the phrase does not have "lasting significance"?

The Core Knowledge Sequence

The *Core Knowledge Sequence*, first published in 1990, was the next step in the evolution of Hirsch's accounting of what every American student should know. Of immediate interest relative to this publication is the change in name from "cultural literacy" to "core knowledge." In his 1996 book, *The Schools We Need and Why We Don't Have Them*, Hirsch commented on his reform movement in general and this name change in particular:

> Its nerve center has been a foundation I started in 1986 and first called the Cultural Literacy Foundation. But teachers pointed out that the term "Cultural" raised too many extraneous questions, whereas the term "Core Knowledge" better described the chief aim of the reform, which

was to introduce solid knowledge in a coherent way into the elementary curriculum. On their advice, I changed the name to the Core Knowledge Foundation, and the education press now calls our school reform movement the Core Knowledge Movement. (p. 13)

The apparent purpose of the *Sequence* is to serve as the basis for about half of a school's curriculum. To date, there have been seven editions of the *Sequence*, with publication dates beginning in 1990 and ending in 1998. The document is produced, marketed, and distributed through the Core Knowledge Foundation, primarily via their website. In contrast to his previous works, Hirsch provided a fairly detailed description of the process used for determining the content in the *Sequence*. This description is reproduced in Exhibit 2.10.

The Core Knowledge Series

Another product in Hirsch's impressive collection is the *Core Knowledge Series*. This product is accessible to the general public in a series of seven books that bear similar titles. Designed as resource tools for parents and teachers, the books—entitled, appropriately, as follows—specify what students should know at specific grade levels:

1. *What Your Kindergartner Needs to Know* (1996)[5]

2. *What Your First Grader Needs to Know* (1991; revised edition, 1997)

3. *What Your Second Grader Needs to Know* (1991; revised edition, 1998)

4. *What Your Third Grader Needs to Know* (1992)

5. *What Your Fourth Grader Needs to Know* (1992)

6. *What Your Fifth Grader Needs to Know* (1993)

7. *What Your Sixth Grader Needs to Know* (1993)

According to Hirsch, the content in the above books is based on the *Core Knowledge Sequence*. In fact, the consensus-building process described in the introduction to the *Sequence* (and reprinted in Exhibit 2.10) is again described in the introduction to most of the above books.

---

[5]The Kindergarten book was reprinted in 1997. However, it does not appear to be a new edition, nor is it touted as such.

Exhibit 2.10

Core Knowledge Sequence: Content Guidelines for Grades K–8
Process of Research and Consensus Building

The Core Knowledge Sequence is the result of a long process of research and consensus-building undertaken by the Core Knowledge Foundation, an independent, nonpartisan, nonprofit organization dedicated to excellence and fairness in early education.

Here is how we achieved the consensus behind the Core Knowledge Sequence. First, we analyzed the many reports issued by state departments of education and by professional organizations—such as the National Council of Teachers of Mathematics and the American Association for the Advancement of Science—which recommend general outcomes for elementary and secondary education. We also tabulated the knowledge and skills specified in the successful educational systems of several other countries, including France, Japan, Sweden, and West Germany.

In addition, we formed an advisory board on multiculturalism that proposed a core knowledge of diverse cultural traditions that American children should all share as part of their school-based common culture. We sent the resulting materials to three independent groups of teachers, scholars, and scientists around the country, asking them to create a master list of the core knowledge children should have by the end of grade six. About 150 teachers (including college professors, scientists, and administrators) were involved in this initial step.

These items were amalgamated into a draft master plan, and further groups of teachers and specialists were asked to agree on a grade-by-grade sequence of the items. That draft sequence was then sent to some one hundred educators and specialists who participated in a national conference that was called to hammer out a working agreement on core knowledge for the first six grades.

This important meeting took place in March 1990. The conferees were elementary school teachers, curriculum specialists, scientists, science writers, officers of national organizations, representatives of ethnic groups, district superintendents, and school principals from across the country. A total of twenty-four working groups decided on revisions to the draft sequence. The resulting provisional sequence was further fine-tuned during a year of implementation at a pioneering school, Three Oaks Elementary in Lee County, Florida. Also, the Visual Arts and Music sections of the Sequence were further developed based on the research of the Core Knowledge Foundation, with the assistance of advisors and teachers.

Since the content of the *Series* is said to be based on the content of the *Sequence* and since virtually the same description of the consensus-building process is printed in both the *Sequence* and the books in the *Series*, one would expect the contents of the *Series* and the *Sequence* to be virtually identical. However, when a representative of the Core Knowledge Foundation was asked to describe the similarities and differences between the seven-book series and the *Sequence*, the representative noted that the "seven-book series is based on the *Sequence*, but there are some significant differences" (Core Knowledge Foundation, 1997). A comparison of the two resources makes these differences explicit. For example, Table 2.1 offers a partial comparison of the mathematics content in the *Core Knowledge Sequence* and the *Core Knowledge Series* (i.e., *What Your Kindergartner* [First Grader, Second Grader, etc.] *Needs to Know*).

Table 2.1 illustrates that the differences between the content in the *Sequence* and the *Series* are not trivial. For example, where the *Series* covers bar graphs at third grade, the *Sequence* covers this topic at first grade; where the *Series* addresses probability at fourth grade, the *Sequence* addresses it at fifth grade. Further, an examination of the order of presentation of topics in the *Series* (which is based on the *Sequence*) raises some questions. To illustrate, consider Table 2.2, which, based on our analysis, reports some of the apparent anomalies (or at least curiosities) in the sequence of content for eight topics in mathematics as presented in the *Series*.

One might ask what the research or theory is behind requiring first graders to master addition and subtraction facts up to 12 and requiring second graders to master addition and subtraction facts up to 18. Similarly, what is the basis for the expectation that first graders learn the ordinal numbers up through 10th and second graders up through 31st? Further, what was the research that guided the decision to add (or delete) various skills to the 1998 second-grade edition, for example the skill of multiplying by 10? Were these arbitrary decisions? Or were they based on research about learning? Lacking any explanation to the contrary, one might reasonably assume that these decisions were made in the March 1990 meeting by experts who determined that first graders are capable of learning addition and subtraction facts up to 12, but not including 13 (for example). Indeed, one would hope for this level of professional review if all schools across the country are to follow Hirsch's recommendations, as is his apparent dream (see Hirsch, 1996).

Table 2.1

Partial Comparison of Mathematics Content
in *Core Knowledge Sequence* and *Core Knowledge Series* books

Concept/Skill	Grade in which Concept/Skill is Introduced	
	Sequence	*Series*
Time: A.M. vs. P.M.	2nd	1st
Roman Numerals	3rd	2nd (1991 edition; not referenced in 1998 edition)
Using dollar ($) sign	1st	2nd
Congruent shapes	Kindergarten	2nd
Measuring temperature*	2nd	N/A*
Perimeter	2nd	3rd (1991 2nd-grade edition—no; 1998 2nd-grade edition—yes)
Parallel and perpendicular lines	2nd	4th (1991 2nd-grade edition—no; 1998 2nd-grade edition—yes)
Creating and interpreting bar graphs	1st	3rd (1991 1st-grade edition—no; 1997 1st-grade edition mentioned, but not covered)
Reading and writing decimals	3rd	4th
Probability	5th	4th
Prime numbers	5th	N/A
Composite numbers	6th	N/A
Comparing fractions with unlike denominators	4th	5th
Reciprocal relationships	5th	6th
Symbols ≤, ≥	N/A	6th
Understanding multiplication and division as opposite operations	3rd	5th
Adding and subtracting fractions with like denominators	5th	4th

*Measuring temperature is not covered in the mathematics section at any grade level, but it does appear in the science section in the Grade 1 book.

Note: The books with the most recent publication dates available were used for this comparison: *Kindergartner* book (1996), *First Grader* book (1991 and 1997); *Second Grader* book (1991 and 1998); *Third Grader* book (1992); *Fourth Grader* book (1992); *Fifth Grader* book (1993); *Sixth Grader* book (1993). Any differences between the original and revised editions for first grade and second grade are noted above.

Table 2.2

Mathematics Topics
Core Knowledge Series: What Your Kindergartner [etc.] Needs to Know

Topic	Grade Level and Content Covered
Addition/Subtraction Facts	*First grade*—addition/subtraction facts to 12 *Second grade*—complete memorizing addition/subtraction facts to 18
Multiplication Tables	*Second grade*—multiplication tables for 2, 3, 4, and 5 (Latest second-grade edition [1998] also addresses multiplying by 10.) *Third grade*—memorize the multiplication table up to 9 x 9
Ordinal Numbers	*First grade*—1st through 10th *Second*—through 31st *Third*—through 100th
Roman Numerals	*Second grade*—through 12 (Latest second-grade edition [1998] does not address roman numerals.) *Fourth grade*—10–100 plus 500 and 1000
Time	*Kindergarten*—telling time to the hour *First grade*—telling time to the nearest whole and half hours; understanding days and months on a calendar *Second grade*—telling time to the nearest 5 minutes; understanding quarter hours *Third grade*—telling time to the nearest minute; finding dates a week before/after one another *Fourth grade*—changing units of time (days/hours/minutes/seconds); adding/subtracting amounts of time *Fifth grade*—multiplying/dividing amounts of time
Money	*Kindergarten*—understanding value of pennies, nickels, dimes, quarters *First grade*—understanding value of pennies, nickels, dimes, quarters (Latest first-grade edition [1997] assumes students learned this in kindergarten.) Second grade — understanding value of half dollars and dollar bills *Third grade*—understanding value of 5, 10, and 20 dollar bills
Fractions	*First grade*—$1/2$, $1/3$, $1/4$ *Second grade*—$1/5$, $1/6$, $1/10$ (Latest second-grade edition [1998] also addresses $1/8$.)
Place Value	*First grade*—ones and tens *Second grade*—whole numbers through hundreds *Third grade*—whole numbers through hundred thousands *Fourth grade*—thousandths through millions *Fifth grade*—ten-thousandths through billions *Sixth grade*—hundred-thousandths through trillions

Note: The books with the most recent publication dates available were used for this comparison: *Kindergartner* book (1996), *First Grader* book (1991 and 1997); *Second Grader* book (1991 and 1998); *Third Grader* book (1992); *Fourth Grader* book (1992); *Fifth Grader* book (1993); *Sixth Grader* book (1993). Any differences between the original and revised editions for first grade and second grade are noted above.

A Fundamental Distinction

A primary issue concerning Hirsch's list (or anyone's list, for that matter) of what every American should know is, Does it contain the right information? Stated as a specific question about Hirsch's list (or lists), one might ask, Should all students know the answers to the following questions?

> Who wrote *Macbeth*?
>
> What is a limerick?
>
> What does *nouveau riche* mean?
>
> What is a non sequitur?
>
> What is a carnivore?
>
> What does *regression* mean?
>
> Who was Spiro Agnew?

Is the information necessary to answer these questions inherently more important than that needed to answer the following, taken from Zahler and Zahler's *Test Your Countercultural Literacy* (1989) of what they humorously refer to as "countercultural literacy":

> Who was Caesar Chavez?
>
> What is the *I Ching* used for?
>
> How did Janis Joplin die?
>
> What does *macrobiotic* mean?
>
> Which countries were in SEATO?
>
> Who was Timothy Leary?

Is the term *carnivore* from Hirsch's list inherently more important than the term *macrobiotic* from the Zahler and Zahler list? Is it inherently more important to know about Spiro Agnew's life (Hirsch) than it is to know about Caesar Chavez's (Zahler & Zahler)? Ultimately, the importance of one piece of information versus another—particularly information at the level of specificity of that above—is a matter of judgment. That Caesar Chavez's life had less of an impact on American culture than Spiro Agnew's is a matter of perspective.

One might conclude, then, that a key step in the identification of essential knowledge is to consult those whose perspectives represent an unbiased, expert understanding of the field from which the information is taken. For example, those with an expert understanding of American history could be called upon to make the determination whether Spiro Agnew, Caesar Chavez, or both should be included on a list of what every American should know. Yet it is precisely this approach with which Hirsch disagreed. Writing in *Cultural Literacy* (1987, 1988) of himself and his colleagues Kett and Trefil, Hirsch said:

> Our expertise was useful in generating candidate items for the list, but it was not decisive in judging whether the items were the possession of the common reader. In fact, experts may be quite unreliable judges of items within their own domains, because their daily experiences within special fields may distort their estimates of what is and is not familiar. (p. 135)

The problem with Hirsch's argument is that it values what is familiar over what is significant. Whether experts can respond concerning what is familiar to most Americans is an interesting question. However, experts should know what ideas in their discipline are fundamental and significant. It is our position that it is this criterion of "significance of content" rather than "familiarity to literate people" that should be the criterion by which cultural knowledge is selected for transmission to students. Thus, it is essential to consult those who have a thorough grounding in their discipline and who can see the future of their areas with enough clarity and understanding that they are equipped to make reasonable judgments about the information and skills that are basic to understanding. It is this fundamental distinction between the significant and the familiar that we wish to highlight. In our estimation, the literacy landscape should first be sketched by subject-matter specialists. Thus, students should learn what subject-matter experts know to be valuable in their respective domains rather than what literate people say they know.

Conclusion

When Hirsch and his colleagues published the 1988 and 1993 editions of the Dictionary, they reported that they had received "hundreds of letters" (p. xi) from educators and the public and that their works had been positively reviewed in many places. We have no doubt that Hirsch found—and continues to find—agreement for the perspective that cultural literacy has declined.

However, Hirsch's process for identifying what American students must know and be able to do has been flawed from the outset, starting with his list in the appendix of the 1987 version of *Cultural Literacy* and ending with his *Core Knowledge Series*. Hirsch has used what appears to be an unscientific and, in some cases, unsystematic approach to identifying essential knowledge. As well intended as Hirsch's efforts might have been, the process that he and his colleagues used ran the great risk of generating a listing of knowledge that is disjointed and biased, and emphasizes knowledge identified first by Hirsch and his colleagues and then by a largely unidentified group of readers and reviewers in lieu of key knowledge as defined by experts in the various subject domains. In this chapter we have attempted to highlight a few of the inconsistencies that have resulted from the flawed approach taken by Hirsch and his colleagues.

It is our position that the first step in identifying the essential knowledge that students should know and be able to do as a result of K–12 education is to ask professionals in the diverse content areas what knowledge should be taught in their respective areas of expertise. It was the identification of precisely this body of information that was the focus of a comprehensive effort on the part of virtually thousands of subject-matter experts and subject-matter teachers over the past decade. The efforts of these professionals are commonly referred to as "the standards movement."

Chapter 3

The Standards Movement

Most educators and many noneducators are well aware of the movement to identify subject-matter standards for what American students should know and be able to do in challenging subject areas. In fact, this movement is one of the strongest reform efforts ever to impact U.S. education. Glaser and Linn (1993) note:

> In the recounting of our nation's drive toward educational reform, the last decade of this century will undoubtedly be identified as the time when a concentrated press for national education standards emerged. The press for standards was evidenced by the efforts of federal and state legislators, presidential and gubernatorial candidates, teacher and subject-matter specialists, councils, governmental agencies, and private foundations. (p. xiii)

An outline of the more salient events in the movement to establish standards in a variety of subject areas is presented in Exhibit 3.1.

Exhibit 3.1

The Standards Movement

1983	*A Nation at Risk* is published, calling for reform of the U.S. education system.
1983	Bill Honig, elected state superintendent of California public schools, begins a decade-long revision of the state public school system, developing content standards and curriculum frameworks.
1987	The National Council of Teachers of Mathematics (NCTM) writing teams begin to review curriculum documents and draft standards for curriculum and evaluation.
1989	Charlottesville, VA: The nation's fifty governors and President Bush adopt National Education Goals for the year 2000. One goal names five school subjects— English, mathematics, science, history, and geography—for which challenging national achievement standards should be established.
1989	NCTM publishes *Curriculum and Evaluation Standards for School Mathematics*.

Exhibit 3.1 (continued)

The Standards Movement

1989	Project 2061 of the American Association for the Advancement of Science (AAAS) publishes *Science for all Americans*, describing what "understandings and habits of mind are essential for all citizens in a scientifically literate society."
1990	In his State of the Union address, President Bush announces the National Education Goals for the year 2000; shortly thereafter, he and Congress establish a National Education Goals Panel (NEGP).
1990	The Secretary's Commission on Achieving Necessary Skills (SCANS) is appointed by the Secretary of Labor to determine the skills young people need to succeed in the world of work.
1990	The New Standards Project, a joint project of the National Center on Education and the Economy and the Learning Research and Development Center, is formed to create a system of standards for student performance in a number of areas.
1990, fall	The Mid-continent Regional Educational Laboratory (McREL) begins the systematic collection, review, and analysis of noteworthy national and state curriculum documents in all subject areas.
1991	SCANS produces *What Work Requires of Schools*, which describes the knowledge and skills necessary for success in the workplace.
1991, June	Secretary of Education Lamar Alexander asks Congress to establish the National Council on Education Standards and Testing (NCEST). The purpose of NCEST is to provide a vehicle for reaching bipartisan consensus on national standards and testing.
1992, Jan	NCEST releases its report, *Raising Standards for American Education*, to Congress, proposing an oversight board, the National Education Standards and Assessment Council (NESAC), to certify content and performance standards as well as "criteria" for assessments.
1992, Jan	The National Council for the Social Studies names a task force to develop curriculum standards.
1992, spring	The National History Standards Project receives funding from the National Endowment for the Humanities and the U.S. Department of Education.
1992, spring	The National Association for Sport and Physical Education begins work on *Outcomes for Quality Physical Education Programs*, which will form the basis of standards in Physical Education.
1992, June	The Consortium of National Arts Education receives funding from the U.S. Department of Education, the National Endowment for the Arts, and the National Endowment for the Humanities to write standards in the arts.

Exhibit 3.1 (continued)

The Standards Movement

1992, July	The Center for Civic Education receives funds from the U.S. Department of Education and the Pew Charitable Trusts for standards development in civics and government.
1992, July	The Geography Standards Education Project creates the first draft of geography standards.
1992, Oct	The Committee for National Health Education Standards is funded by the American Cancer Society.
1992, Nov	The Bush administration awards funds to create English standards to a consortium of three organizations: the National Council of Teachers of English, the International Reading Association, and the Center for the Study of Reading at the University of Illinois.
1993, Jan	The National Standards in Foreign Language Project becomes the seventh and final group to receive federal funds for standards development.
1993, April	McREL publishes its first technical report on standards, *The Systematic Identification and Articulation of Content Standards and Benchmarks: An Illustration Using Mathematics*.
1993	AAAS's Project 2061 publishes *Benchmarks for Science Literacy*.
1993, Nov	NEGP's Technical Planning Group issues *Promises to Keep: Creating High Standards for American Students*, referred to as the "Malcolm Report." The report calls for the development of a National Education Standards and Improvement Council (NESIC), which would give voluntary national standards a stamp of approval.
1993, Nov	The National Research Council, with major funding from the U.S. Department of Education and the National Science Foundation, establishes the National Committee on Science Education Standards and Assessment (NCSESA) to oversee standards development in content, teaching, and assessment.
1994, Jan	McREL publishes *The Systematic Identification and Articulation of Content Standards and Benchmarks: Update, January 1994*, which provides a synthesis of standards for science, mathematics, history, geography, communication and information processing, and life skills.
1994, Feb	The Standards Project for English Language Arts, a collaborative effort of the Center for the Study of Reading, the International Reading Association, and the National Council of Teachers of English, publishes the draft *Incomplete Work of the Task Forces of the Standards Project for English Language Arts*.

Exhibit 3.1 (continued)

The Standards Movement

1994, March	President Clinton signs into law Goals 2000: Educate America Act. This legislation creates the National Education Standards and Improvement Council (NESIC) to certify national and state content and performance standards, opportunity-to-learn standards, and state assessments; adds two new goals to the national education goals; brings to nine the number of areas for which students should demonstrate "competency over challenging subject matters." The subject areas now covered include foreign languages, the arts, economics, and civics and government.
1994, March	The U.S. Department of Education notifies the Standards Project for the English Language Arts that it will not continue funding for the project, citing a lack of progress.
1994, March	The Consortium of National Arts Education Associations, funded by the U.S. Department of Education, the National Endowment for the Arts, and the National Endowment for the Humanities, publishes the arts standards (dance, music, theatre, and the visual arts).
1994, fall	The National Council on Social Studies publishes *Curriculum Standards for the Social Studies: Expectations for Excellence.*
1994, Oct	Lynne Cheney, past chair of the National Endowment for the Humanities (NEH), criticizes the U.S. history standards in the *Wall Street Journal* two weeks before their release. (NEH, with the U.S. Department of Education, funded development of the U.S. history standards.)
1994, Oct	U.S. history standards are released; world history and K–4 history are released shortly thereafter.
1994, Oct	The Geography Education Standards Project publishes *Geography for Life: National Geography Standards.*
1994, Nov	The Center for Civic Education, funded by the U.S. Department of Education and the Pew Charitable Trusts, publishes standards for civics and government education.
1995, Jan	Gary Nash, National History Standards Project codirector, agrees to revise the history standards. The U.S. Senate denounces the history standards in a 99-1 vote.
1995, April	The U.S. Department of Education withdraws assurance of a $500,000 grant to the National Council on Economic Education for the development of standards in economics.
1995, May	The Joint Committee on National Health Education Standards releases *National Health Education Standards: Achieving Health Literacy.*

Exhibit 3.1 (continued)

The Standards Movement

1995, summer	The National Association for Sport and Physical Education publishes *Moving into the Future: National Standards for Physical Education*.
1995, Oct	The National Council on Economic Education, using funds from private sources, convenes a drafting committee to develop standards.
1995, Nov	The New Standards Project releases a three-volume "consultation draft" entitled *Performance Standards* for English language arts, mathematics, science, and "applied learning."
1995, Dec	McREL publishes *Content Knowledge: A Compendium of Standards and Benchmarks for K–12 Education*, a synthesis of standards in all subject areas, including behavioral studies and life skills.
1995	The National Business Education Association publishes *National Standards for Business Education: What America's Students Should Know and Be Able to Do in Business*.
1996, Jan	The National Standards in Foreign Language Education Project publishes *Foreign Language Learning: Preparing for the 21st Century*.
1996, Jan	The National Research Council publishes *National Science Education Standards*.
1996, March	The National Education Summit is held. Forty state governors and more than 45 business leaders convene. They support efforts to set clear academic standards in the core subject areas at the state and local levels. Business leaders pledge to consider the existence of state standards when locating facilities.
1996, March	The National Council of Teachers of English and the International Reading Association publish *Standards for the English Language Arts*.
1996, April	Revised history standards are published. A review in the *Wall Street Journal* by Diane Ravitch and Arthur Schlesinger, professor emeritus at City University of New York, endorses the standards. Lynn Cheney renews her criticism of the history standards, determining that the revision does not go far enough.
1996	The International Technology Education Association, supported by a grant from the National Science Foundation and the National Aeronautics and Space Administration, releases a guiding document for the development of standards in technology.
1997, Feb	In his State of the Union Address, President Clinton calls for every state to adopt high national standards and declares that "by 1999, every state should test every 4th grader in reading and every 8th grader in math to make sure these standards are met."
1997	National Council on Economic Education releases *Voluntary National Content Standards in Economics* in paper copy and on CD-ROM.

Many point to the publication of the report *A Nation at Risk* (National Commission on Excellence in Education [NCEE], 1983), commissioned during the Reagan administration, as the beginning of the modern standards movement. Who will soon forget the dramatic words often quoted from this widely publicized report: "The educational foundations of our society are presently being eroded by a rising tide of mediocrity that threatens our very future as a nation and a people. . . . We have, in effect, been committing an act of unthinking, unilateral educational disarmament" (NCEE, 1983, p. 5). Shepard (1993) notes that with the publication of the report, the rhetoric of education reform changed dramatically. Proponents of reform began to make a close link between the financial security and economic competitiveness of the nation and our education system.

Emergence of the Standards Documents

Growing concerns about the educational preparation of the nation's youth prompted President Bush and the nation's governors to call an education summit in Charlottesville, Virginia, in September, 1989. At the summit, President Bush and the nation's governors, including then-governor Bill Clinton, agreed on six broad goals for education to be reached by the year 2000.[6] These goals and the rationale for them were published under the title *The National Education Goals Report: Building a Nation of Learners* (National Education Goals Panel [NEGP], 1991). Two of those goals (3 and 4) related specifically to academic achievement:

> **Goal 3:** By the year 2000, American students will leave grades four, eight, and twelve having demonstrated competency in challenging subject matter including English, mathematics, science, history, and geography; and every school in America will ensure that all students learn to use their minds well, so they may be prepared for responsible citizenship, further learning, and productive employment in our modern economy.

> **Goal 4:** By the year 2000, U.S. students will be first in the world in science and mathematics achievement. (p. 4)

One tacit purpose of the education summit was to motivate educators to set challenging standards within all major subject areas. The National Council of Teachers of Mathematics (NCTM) had already taken the lead in this endeavor with the publication of *Curriculum and Evaluation Standards for School Mathematics* in 1989. Other groups quickly mobilized to establish content standards in their respective areas and, within a relatively short period of time, standards documents were generated for

---

[6]The initial set of goals was expanded to eight goals in 1994.

all major academic areas. The documents listed in Table 3.1 are the result of efforts of groups that either were funded by the U.S. Department of Education or identify themselves as representing the national consensus in their subject areas. Thus, collectively, these documents could be said to articulate the "official"—or nationally recognized—version of standards for K–12 subject areas. (For a more detailed discussion of the development of standards in various subject areas, see Kendall & Marzano, 1997.)

Table 3.1

Nationally Recognized Standards Documents

Content Area	Document(s)
Mathematics	National Council of Teachers of Mathematics. (1989). *Curriculum and Evaluation Standards for School Mathematics.* Reston, VA: Author.
Science	National Research Council. (1996). *National Science Education Standards.* Washington, DC: National Academy Press.
History	National Center for History in the Schools. (1994). *National Standards for History for Grades K–4: Expanding Children's World in Time and Space.* Los Angeles: Author. National Center for History in the Schools. (1994). *National Standards for United States History: Exploring the American Experience.* Los Angeles: Author. National Center for History in the Schools. (1994). *National Standards for World History: Exploring Paths to the Present.* Los Angeles: Author. National Center for History in the Schools. (1996). *National Standards for History: Basic Edition.* Los Angeles: Author.
Social Studies	National Council for the Social Studies. (1994). *Expectations of Excellence: Curriculum Standards for Social Studies.* Washington, DC: Author.
Language Arts	National Council of Teachers of English and the International Reading Association. (1996). *Standards for the English Language Arts.* Urbana, IL: National Council of Teachers of English.
The Arts	Consortium of National Arts Education Associations. (1994). *National Standards for Arts Education: What Every Young American Should Know and Be Able to Do in the Arts.* Reston, VA: Music Educators National Conference.
Civics	Center for Civic Education. (1994). *National Standards for Civics and Government.* Calabasas, CA: Author.
Economics	National Council on Economic Education. (1997). *Voluntary National Content Standards in Economics.* New York: Author.
Foreign Language	National Standards in Foreign Language Education Project. (1996). *Standards for Foreign Language Learning: Preparing for the 21st Century.* Lawrence, KS: Allen Press.
Geography	Geography Education Standards Project. (1994). *Geography for Life: National Geography Standards.* Washington, DC: National Geographic Research and Exploration.
Health	Joint Committee on National Health Education Standards. (1995). *National Health Education Standards: Achieving Health Literacy.* Reston, VA: Association for the Advancement of Health Education.
Physical Education	National Association for Sport and Physical Education. (1995). *Moving into the Future, National Standards for Physical Education: A Guide to Content and Assessment.* St. Louis: Mosby.

Each of the documents listed in Table 3.1 spells out in some detail what students in grades K–12 should know and be able to do in the respective subject areas. To illustrate, consider the subject of geography.

Geography for Life: National Geography Standards, the national geography standards document published in 1994 by the Geography Education Standards Project, lists 18 standards that are organized into six broad categories: (1) the world in spatial terms, (2) places and regions, (3) physical systems, (4) human systems, (5) environment and society, and (6) uses of geography. To illustrate the level of detail offered in the document, consider the three standards within the category "the world in spatial terms" at the fourth-grade level:

> **Standard 1:** How to use maps and other geographic representations, tools, and technologies to acquire, process, and report information from a spatial perspective
>
> **Standard 2:** How to use mental maps to organize information about people, places, and environments in a spatial context
>
> **Standard 3:** How to analyze the spatial organization of people, places, and environments on Earth's surface

For each of these standards, specific information and skills are identified. For example, for standard 1 above, the geography standards document identifies specific content and activities that students should master by the end of the fourth grade (see Exhibit 3.2).

As illustrated in Exhibit 3.2, the geography standards document identifies in specific detail what students should know and be able to do in the field of geography. Similarly, the mathematics standards document identifies what students should know and be able to do in mathematics, the science standards document identifies what students should know and be able to do in science, and so on.

A fair question here is, What makes the content identified in these documents more valid than that identified as a result of Hirsch's efforts? The answer is that the information and skills articulated in these standards documents were identified by teams of subject-matter experts using rigorous processes. To illustrate, consider the mathematics standards document *Curriculum and Evaluation Standards for School Mathematics* (1989), published by the National Council of Teachers of Mathematics (NCTM). Exhibit 3.3 lists the 60 organizations identified in the document as endorsers, supporters, or allies, respectively.

Exhibit 3.2

National Geography Standards: Geography Standard 1
Content and Activities by the End of Fourth Grade

The World in Spatial Terms

HOW TO USE MAPS AND OTHER GEOGRAPHIC REPRESENTATIONS, TOOLS, AND TECHNOLOGIES
TO ACQUIRE, PROCESS, AND REPORT INFORMATION FROM A SPATIAL PERSPECTIVE

By the end of the fourth grade, the student knows and understands:

1. **The characteristics and purposes of geographic representations—such as maps, globes, graphs, diagrams, aerial and other photographs, and satellite-produced images**
2. **The characteristics and purposes of tools and technologies—such as reference works and computer-based geographic information systems**
3. **How to display spatial information on maps and other geographic representations**
4. **How to use appropriate geographic tools and technologies**

Therefore, the student is able to:

A. **Identify and describe the characteristics and purposes of geographic representations, tools, and technologies, as exemplified by being able to**
   - Examine a variety of maps to identify and describe their basic elements (e.g., title, legend, cardinal and intermediate directions, scale, grid, principal parallels, meridians)
   - Interpret aerial photographs or satellite-produced images to locate and identify physical and human features (e.g., mountain ranges, rivers, vegetation regions, cities, dams, reservoirs)
   - Design a map that displays information selected by the student, using symbols explained in a key

B. **Show spatial information on geographic representations, as exemplified by being able to**
   - Read a narrative and then create a sketch map to illustrate the narrative (e.g., make a map showing the movement of a family of ducks as described in *Make Way for Ducklings*; or after reading the *Little House* series by Laura Ingalls Wilder make a map of where the Ingalls family lived)
   - Report regional data in both a two-dimensional format (e.g., by using proportional symbols drawn on a map) and a three-dimensional format (e.g., stacking a proportionate number of counters on each region)
   - Construct diagrams or charts to display spatial information (e.g., construct a bar graph that compares the populations of the five largest cities in a U.S. state)

C. **Use geographic representations, tools, and technologies to answer geographic questions, as exemplified by being able to**
   - Use a map grid (e.g., latitude and longitude or alphanumeric system) to answer the question—What is this location?—as applied to places chosen by the teacher and student
   - Use thematic maps to answer questions about human distributions (e.g., What explains the distribution of the human population on Earth?)
   - Use different types of map scales (linear, fractional, and word scale) to measure the distance between two places in response to the question—How far is location A from location B?

Note: From *Geography for Life: National Geography Standards* (pp. 106–107), Geography Education Standards Project, 1994, Washington, DC: National Geographic Research and Exploration. Copyright © 1994 by the National Geographic Society. Reprinted with permission.

Exhibit 3.3

Curriculum and Evaluation Standards for School Mathematics
Endorsers, Supporters, and Allies

ENDORSERS

The following mathematical science organizations join with the National Council of Teachers of Mathematics in promoting the vision of school mathematics described in the *Curriculum and Evaluation Standards for School Mathematics*:

American Mathematical Association of Two-Year Colleges
American Mathematical Society
American Statistical Association
Association for Women in Mathematics
Association of State Supervisors of Mathematics
Conference Board of the Mathematical Sciences
Council of Presidential Awardees in Mathematics
Council of Scientific Society Presidents
Institute of Management Sciences
Mathematical Association of America
Mathematical Sciences Education Board
National Council of Supervisors of Mathematics
Operations Research Society of America
School Science and Mathematics Association
Society for Industrial and Applied Mathematics

SUPPORTERS

The professional organizations listed below have added their support for the quality mathematics curricula and assessment criteria provided by the *Curriculum and Evaluation Standards for School Mathematics*:

American Association of Physics Teachers
American Association of School Administrators
American Chemical Society
American Federation of Teachers
Association for Supervision and Curriculum Development
Council for Basic Education
Council for Exceptional Children
Council of Chief State School Officers
Council of the Great City Schools
International Reading Association
International Technology Education Association
Junior Engineering Technical Society
National Association for the Education of Young Children
National Association of Biology Teachers

Exhibit 3.3 (continued)

Curriculum and Evaluation Standards for School Mathematics
Endorsers, Supporters, and Allies

National Association of Elementary School Principals
National Association of Secondary School Principals
National Association of State Boards of Education
National Catholic Education Association
National Congress of Parents and Teachers
National Council for the Social Studies
National Council of Teachers of English
National Education Association
National School Boards Association
National Science Teachers Association
National Society of Professional Engineers

ALLIES

The organizations listed below have agreed to serve as allies in our effort to improve the teaching and learning of mathematics as described in the *Curriculum and Evaluation Standards for School Mathematics*:

American Association of Retired Persons
American Association of University Women
American Bankers Association
American Consulting Engineers Council
American Home Economics Council
American Indian Science and Engineering Society
American Institute of Certified Public Accountants
American Newspaper Publishers Association Foundation
Children's Television Workshop
Consumers Union
Indian Youth of America
Institute of Electrical and Electronics Engineers
Joint Council on Economic Education
Junior Achievement
National Coalition for Consumer Education
National Consumers League
National Council of LaRaza
National Council of Negro Women
National Federation of Business and Professional Women's Clubs
National Federation of Independent Business Foundation

Note: From *Curriculum and Evaluation Standards for School Mathematics* (pp. vi–viii), by the National Council of Teachers of Mathematics, 1989, Reston, VA: Author.

The national science standards document, *National Science Education Standards*, produced by the National Research Council (1996), lists the names and titles of over 100 science experts who reviewed the science standards. In addition, the following process is described:

> After the many suggestions for improving the predraft were collated and analyzed, an extensively revised standards document was prepared as a public document. This draft was released for nationwide review in December 1994. More than 40,000 copies of the draft *National Science Education Standards* were distributed to some 18,000 individuals and 250 groups. The comments of the many individuals and groups who reviewed this draft were again collated and analyzed; these were used to prepare the final *National Science Education Standards* that are presented here. (p. 15)

Similarly, the national geography standards document explicitly lists over 200 national and international reviewers. The document also provides a detailed description of the process that was used to design the standards:

> Further input was received from nine public hearings, each held in a different city. In addition to the more than 2,000 persons who were asked to review the standards, project administrators sent drafts for critique to a hundred state social studies and science coordinators, 750 geography teachers, all National Geographic Society Alliance network coordinators, legislative aides to state education committees, governors' aides to education, and stakeholders whose names were provided by the National Parent–Teachers Association, the Association for Supervision and Curriculum Development, state and local boards of education, the Business Roundtable, the American Geographical Society's business members, and teachers' unions. Project members met directors of other standards-writing projects and shared drafts among all the writing groups. Furthermore, the authors maintained close contact with the history and science groups—the disciplines with the strongest curriculum ties to geography.

> Along with the advice and counsel from these groups, the authors used materials from many national and international sources including *Guidelines for Geographic Education* (Joint Committee on Geographic Education 1984) and the *Geography Assessment Framework for the 1994 National Assessment of Educational Progress*. (p. 246)

In summary, the national standards documents taken as a group were produced through a process that pooled the cumulative wisdom and opinions of literally thousands of subject-matter experts, many of whom are explicitly identified, and scores of professional organizations, all of which are explicitly identified. The explicit identification of those who generated and reviewed the content in the national standards documents stands in stark contrast to Hirsch's vague references to "more than one hundred consultants" (*Cultural Literacy*, 1987, p. 146), "more than two hundred readers" (*Cultural Literacy*, 1988, p. xi), "hundreds of coeditors and coparticipants" (*Dictionary*, 1993, p. vii), and "about 150 teachers" (*Core Knowledge Sequence*, 1998, p. 1).

Problems with the National Documents

Given the apparent rigor with which the national standards documents were constructed, one might assume that the problems mentioned in Chapter 2 have been resolved. Americans now have a list of essential knowledge identified by experts in the various subject areas using a process that ensured an unbiased, valid accounting. Unfortunately, the national standards documents, taken as a group, present a number of challenges to educators who attempt to use standards as the cornerstone of their system redesign or reform initiatives: (1) differing approaches to standards development, (2) multiple perspectives on standards, and therefore, multiple documents within a subject area, and (3) too much content within and across content areas.

Differing Approaches to Standards

In order to see these national documents as the definitive listing of essential knowledge, one challenge that must be addressed is the variance in the levels of generality at which standards are stated. Even a cursory review of the standards listed in the various documents reveals very different perspectives on the level of generality at which standards should be stated. For example, the *National Standards for Arts Education* (Consortium of National Arts Education Associations, 1994) describes standards in relatively general terms, such as:

- Understanding the arts in relation to history and cultures

In contrast, a document from *National Standards for United States History: Exploring the American Experience* (NCHS, 1994b) describes standards in relatively specific terms, such as:

- Students should understand the causes of the Civil War.

The example from *National Standards for United States History* is obviously more specific than that from *National Standards for Arts Education*. In addition, the history document provides more detailed information for each of its standards than does the arts document. The degree to which standards are articulated in specific terms is critical especially if one looks to the national standards documents for explicit guidance as to what students should learn at specific grade levels. In *The Schools We Need and Why We Don't Have Them* (1996), Hirsch rightfully complained about the lack of specificity of the content listed in some of the national standards documents. Specifically, he objected to "the arbitrariness of the various conceptual schemes recently produced by curricular experts from the American Association for the Advancement of Science, the National Council of Teachers of Science [*sic*], and the National Academy of Science. These documents all follow different conceptual schemes" (p. 30).

The variance in the levels of specificity in the national standards documents was particularly vexing to Hirsch inasmuch as the hallmark of his approach is specificity. To illustrate, in its publicity materials the Core Knowledge Foundation (1998) notes:

> A typical state or district curriculum says, "Students will demonstrate knowledge of people, events, ideas, and movements that contributed to the development of the United States." But which people and events? What ideas and movements? In contrast, the Core Knowledge Sequence is distinguished by its specificity. By clearly specifying important knowledge in language arts, history and geography, math, science, and the fine arts, the Core Knowledge Sequence presents a practical answer to the question, "What do our children need to know?"

Multiple Documents in a Content Area

Although each of the primary subject areas has what might be called an official—or nationally recognized—standards document (see Table 3.1), a number of core subject areas have unofficial documents that should be consulted if a comprehensive analysis of the subject is sought. For example, *Curriculum and Evaluation Standards for School Mathematics*, published by NCTM (1989), is certainly considered the nationally accepted description of what students should know and be able to do in mathematics. However, mathematics standards and benchmarks also are explicitly and implicitly articulated in each of the following documents:

- *Benchmarks for Science Literacy* (1993). Project 2061, American Association for the Advancement of Science.

- *Mathematics Framework for the 1996 National Assessment of Educational Progress* (n.d.). National Assessment of Educational Progress.

- *Performance Standards: English Language Arts, Mathematics, Science, Applied Learning, Volume 1, Elementary School.* (1997). New Standards Project.

- *Performance Standards: English Language Arts, Mathematics, Science, Applied Learning, Volume 2, Middle School.* (1997). New Standards Project.

- *Performance Standards: English Language Arts, Mathematics, Science, Applied Learning, Volume 3, High School.* (1997). New Standards Project.

- *Group 5 Mathematics Guide* (Edition 1.2). (1993). International Baccalaureate.

- *Middle Years Programme: Mathematics* (Edition 1.1). (1995). International Baccalaureate.

Science offers another example of the problem of multiple documents. At least three documents have gained recognition as publications that provide worthwhile descriptions of what students should know and be able to do in science:

- *National Science Education Standards.* (1996). National Research Council.

- *Benchmarks for Science Literacy.* (1993). Project 2061, American Association for the Advancement of Science.

- *Scope, Sequence, and Coordination of Secondary School Science. Vol. 1. The Content Core: A Guide for Curriculum Designers.* (1993). Pearsall, M. K. (Ed).

In addition, 12 other documents offer useful support for developing standards and benchmarks in science. (For a list of these documents, see Kendall & Marzano, 1997.) In short, one would need to consult a number of documents to review mathematics and science comprehensively. We have reviewed the important text materials that address content information and skills and have concluded that a school or district would have to consult 116 documents to comprehensively review the arts, civics, economics, the English language arts, foreign languages, geography, health, history, mathematics, physical education, science, social studies, and technology. For example, one should review 12 documents in history, 8 documents in mathematics, and 25 documents in English language arts.

Too Much Content

In the early stages of the effort to develop national standards documents, it was assumed that the documents taken as a whole would present a concise, manageable list. However, as the standards drafts and final documents were produced, it became clear that the standards were far from concise. Commenting on the quality of the standards documents, Chester Finn asserted that "the professional associations, without exception, lacked discipline. They all demonstrated gluttonous and imperialistic tendencies" (in Diegmueller, 1995, p. 6).

At the time of Finn's statement in 1995, the standards documents, taken together, weighed about 14 pounds, stood six inches tall, and contained over 2,000 pages. Since then, more documents, more pounds, and more inches have been added to the total mass of standards. By contrast, the Japanese national curriculum fits into "three slender volumes, one for elementary schools, one for lower secondary schools, and one for upper secondary schools" (Ravitch, 1995, p. 15). Ron Brandt (1995), then executive editor of the Association for Supervision and Curriculum Development, acknowledged the problem of the sheer volume of the standards:

> I would describe them as an ambitious conception of what professional educators, most of whom are advocates or specialists in the various school subjects, want students to learn in those subjects. It's the classic curriculum dilemma faced by every principal, central administrator, and generalist teacher: specialists naturally expect a lot; they love their subject and they know its possibilities. Taken as a whole, however, such statements of aspirations are overwhelming. (p. 5)

In short, although the national standards documents identify important knowledge in the core subject areas, taken as a whole, they present far too much content to be effectively integrated into K–12 education. In fact, if implemented, the national standards documents would exacerbate one of the major problems currently plaguing American education: covering too much and, therefore, covering nothing in depth. This issue was dramatically illustrated in a major research undertaking, the Third International Mathematics and Science Study.

The TIMMS Findings

The Third International Mathematics and Science Study (TIMSS) was a large-scale, cross-national comparative study of the education systems in 41 countries. TIMSS researchers examined mathematics and science curricula, instructional practices, and school and social factors in all participating countries. Extensive achievement tests in mathematics and science also were given to students in the participating countries. In general, U.S. 4th-grade students did relatively well when compared to students of similar ages in other countries; 8th-grade students less so; and 12th-grade students performed quite poorly.[7] In a provocative *Wall Street Journal* article entitled "Why America Has the World's Dimmest Bright Kids," Chester Finn (1998) described the findings in the following way:

---

[7]Citation information for various reports about the TIMSS results can be found in footnote 2 in Chapter 1.

Today the U.S. Department of Education officially releases the damning data, which come from the Third International Mathematics and Science Study, a set of tests administered to half a million youngsters in 41 countries in 1995. But the results have trickled out. We learned that our fourth-graders do pretty well compared with the rest of the world, and our eighth-graders' performance is middling to poor. Today we learn that our 12th-graders occupy the international cellar. And that's not even counting the Asian lands like Singapore, Korea and Japan that trounced our kids in the younger grades. They chose not to participate in this study. (Sec. A, p. 22)

In an effort to determine how U.S. mathematics and science education might be improved, TIMSS researchers performed an in-depth comparison of educational practices in the United States and those in countries that consistently outperformed U.S. students. One of the key findings from this comparison was that both mathematics and science curricula in the United States tend to address many more topics than the mathematics and science curricula in other countries typically do.

In addition to trying to cover too much content, U.S. schools do not appear to make sound judgments regarding when to drop topics from the curriculum. Specifically, in both mathematics and science, topics remain in the U.S. curriculum for more grades than they do in other countries. For example, U.S. schools include more mathematics topics than schools in other countries in grades 1 and 2 and then keep repeating those topics until grade 7. However, in grades 9 and 11 the U.S. composite curriculum drops many more topics than do the curricula in other countries. The TIMSS researchers note, "On average, mathematical topics remain in the composite curriculum for two years longer than the international median" (Schmidt, McKnight, & Raizen, 1996, p. 5). The pattern is relatively the same in science.

The U.S. standards documents offer a comprehensive listing of important knowledge but encompass too much knowledge. Implementation of all of the content in the various standards documents would add to the already serious problem of an "overstuffed" U.S. curriculum. In short, when considered in light of the other challenges discussed in this section, one might easily conclude that in their current state, the national standards documents from the various subject areas are not useful tools for facilitating standards-based reform in American education.

State-Level Efforts

In spite of their imperfections, the national-level documents have some virtues. However, states determined that they needed to define—for their own communities— what students should know and be able to do. Thus, every state but one has identified standards or is in the process of identifying standards. State efforts to create standards were given an impressive endorsement at the second education summit in Palisades, New York, in March 1996 when the state governors committed to designing standards and sharing conceptual and technical information regarding their efforts (see National Governor's Association, 1996).

It is probably accurate to say that most states would prefer not to simply adopt standards set by national organizations. Yet, in spite of the efforts of individual states to design standards, their products frequently have not been well received. Beginning in 1995, a series of studies conducted by the American Federation of Teachers (AFT) (see Gandal, 1995a, 1996, 1997; AFT, 1998) has chronicled state-level efforts. When the first report (Gandal, 1995a) was published, virtually every state was in the process of developing academic standards; however, the majority of the standards were judged by AFT to be insufficiently clear and specific.

AFT's most recent report, *Making Standards Matter* 1998 (AFT, 1998), notes that the commitment to standards-based reform remains very strong in the states. However, the overall findings of the study indicate that the standards movement at the state level still leaves much to be accomplished.

The most damaging finding noted in all four AFT reports is that many state documents simply have weak standards—standards that do not clearly specify the information or skills that students should learn. For example, AFT's 1996 report (Gandal, 1996) offered the following as an example of a strong mathematics standard: "The student will differentiate between area and perimeter and identify whether the application of the concept of perimeter or area is appropriate for a given situation" (p. 16). Conversely, the 1996 report offered the following standard as an example of a weak mathematics standard from another state document: "Students should be able to represent and solve problems using geometric models" (p. 16). This lack of specificity in state documents has caused significant opposition to the state standards movement. For example, standards expert Matthew Gandal (1995b) explains that the 1992 Common Core of Learning standards in Virginia and the 1991 Student Learning Outcomes in Pennsylvania were so vague as to be judged nonacademic by the constituents of those states. This perception led to the defeat of the entire reform package and the redrafting of more specific standards in both states.

If one accepts the findings of the AFT reports, then it appears obvious that—to date, at least—the support and leadership that can be expected from state-level documents is relatively limited. For one thing, most state documents are presented as "guidelines" rather than as part of a system of accountability to ensure reform at the local level. As of 1998, only seven states have (or are developing) student promotion policies based on standards and less than half of the states require or plan to require students to pass high school graduation exams linked to their standards (AFT, 1998). Another concern is that most states have standards that are so vague that they probably will have to be reworked or perhaps totally rewritten by schools and districts in those states in order for them to be useful. Even in the 19 states whose standards were judged in the 1998 report to be specific enough, districts still most likely will have to supplement the state standards. For example, Colorado's standards were judged by the AFT to be specific enough for schools and districts to use. However, the Colorado standards are written at four levels: K–2, 3–5, 6–8, and 9–12. If educators at a Colorado school or district wish to identify what students should know at specific grade levels, they will have to extrapolate the four Colorado levels to 12 levels.

Other organizations also have reviewed the quality of state standards. For example, Education Week, with the support of the Pew Charitable Trusts, published reports in 1997 and in 1998 about the condition of public education in the United States. The 1998 report, *Quality Counts* 1998, noted:

> This edition of *Quality Counts* continues to chronicle the progress—or lack of progress—toward education reform in the 50 states. Last year, on average, the states received a solid C in academic standards and assessments, quality of teaching, school environment, and the equity, adequacy, and allocation of their education resources.
>
> One year later, the states still earn a C. But they are pushing ahead. Many are now working to align their student assessments with their standards, strengthen accountability, increase the choices available to students, and improve the preparation and licensing of new teachers. (Education Week on the Web, 1998)

Perhaps the bleakest perspective is found in a summary of a study undertaken by the Fordham Foundation (Finn, Petrilli, & Vanourek, 1998):

> In every subject, the number of states receiving D's or F's from our reviewers outnumbered those receiving A's or B's. When we aggregate the data across subjects, the picture is just as troubling. We have compiled a grade point average for each state. Using the traditional four-

point scale, no state earned an A average, only three (Arizona, California, and Texas) earned B averages, and nine flunked. The national cumulative GPA was 1.3, a D-plus. (p. 56)

Conclusion

In this chapter, we have described national- and state-level efforts to identify essential knowledge. These efforts, part of what is loosely referred to as "the standards movement," tapped the cumulative wisdom of tens of thousands of subject-matter experts and scores of professional organizations, resulting in standards documents in a variety of content areas. Although much effort has been devoted to the development and implementation of standards, no consensus has emerged as to what form "standards" should take or how they should be used. The result is that the character, scope, and level of detail provided in standards often vary significantly from one subject area to another. Thus, as a group, these documents do not constitute a useable accounting of core knowledge to educators who wish to use them in classrooms across the country. Problems with the documents range from a lack of specificity to an overabundance of content. What is needed is some form of secondary analysis of these standards documents so that their content may be more useful to educators and the general public. Fortunately, such an analysis has been undertaken.

Chapter 4

Toward a More Defensible Solution

In Chapter 3 we saw that the standards movement has produced, for the first time, a number of documents that together are an invaluable resource for what K–12 students should know and be able to do in all major subject areas. However, although these standards documents are quite extensive and detailed, as a group they are difficult for educators and noneducators to use. In this chapter we describe a major research effort that has been conducted to address the first two problems: that there are competing approaches to developing standards and that there are multiple documents within a content area. In later chapters we discuss how the last concern—too much content—might be addressed at the local, school, or district levels.

Some subject-area groups have argued that the disciplines are so inherently different that a common approach to standards is not possible (Viadero, 1993). However, as this section will show, a number of basic techniques can be successfully applied to describe content knowledge regardless of the domain. The application of this process results in content knowledge expressed in a roughly equivalent format across subject areas, which should facilitate communication of and about standards. Clear standards provide clearer expectations for students and the possibility of better communication among teachers, administrators, parents, and the larger community.

The McREL Standards Database: A Research Perspective

The first two problems with the national documents were addressed by researchers at the Mid-continent Regional Educational Laboratory (McREL), a nonprofit organization specializing in applied educational research and development. In part through its funding from the U.S. Office of Educational Research and Improvement (OERI), McREL researchers analyzed all of the relevant national and state standards documents. To illustrate how efforts undertaken by McREL researchers have addressed the first two concerns outlined in Chapter 3, we consider the field of mathematics.

Recall from the discussion in Chapter 3 that the nationally accepted standards document for mathematics is *Curriculum and Evaluation Standards for School Mathematics*, published in 1989 by the National Council of Teachers of Mathematics. However, there are a number of other documents that identify what students should know and be able to do in mathematics. As mentioned in Chapter 3, these include the following:

- *Benchmarks for Science Literacy*. (1993). Project 2061, American Association for the Advancement of Science.

- *Mathematics Framework for the 1996 National Assessment of Educational Progress*. (n.d.) National Assessment of Educational Progress.

- *Performance Standards: English Language Arts, Mathematics, Science, Applied Learning, Volume 1, Elementary School*. (1997). New Standards Project.

- *Performance Standards: English Language Arts, Mathematics, Science, Applied Learning, Volume 2, Middle School*. (1997). New Standards Project.

- *Performance Standards: English Language Arts, Mathematics, Science, Applied Learning, Volume 3, High School*. (1997). New Standards Project.

- *Group 5 Mathematics Guide (Edition 1.2)*. (1993). International Baccalaureate.

- *Middle Years Programme: Mathematics (Edition 1.1)*. (1995). International Baccalaureate.

All of these documents were produced by teams of experts who attempted to identify the mathematics information and skills that students should learn from kindergarten through 12th grade. One might assume that it would be necessary to survey all of these documents to gain a comprehensive view of what mathematics specialists say students should learn prior to high school graduation. In fact, this is precisely what McREL researchers did. Specifically, we developed a composite list of what students should know and be able to do in various subject matters by analyzing all important standards documents for those subject areas.

An obvious question that arises is, What criteria were used to determine a document's "importance"? Documents used for each content area were selected based on three criteria: (a) completeness, (b) perceived acceptance by the subject-discipline community, and (c) level of specificity and scope congruent with the perspective on standards and benchmarks taken by McREL researchers. Inasmuch as there was more than one document within many of the domains considered, a reference report was selected for each domain. Documents selected as reference documents were those that best met the three identified criteria.

Once a reference document was selected, it was analyzed to identify standards and related benchmarks. (A detailed description of this process can be found in Kendall & Marzano, 1997, pp. 37–38.) When the analysis of the reference document was complete, information from the other documents was integrated into the standards and benchmarks identified from the reference document. On some occasions, the analysis of secondary documents within a domain revealed a need to create new standards for information or skills that were neither explicitly or implicitly stated in the reference document.

In all, McREL researchers analyzed 116 unique documents. Appendix A lists all of the documents analyzed for each subject area. Table 4.1 reports the number of documents analyzed for each subject area.

Table 4.1

Number of Documents Analyzed by McREL Researchers for Each Subject Area

Subject Area	Number of Documents Analyzed
Mathematics	8
Science	15
History	12
Language Arts	32
Geography	6
The Arts	6
Civics	9
Economics	6
Foreign Language	3
Health	6
Physical Education	3
Technology	14
Behavioral Studies	4
Life Skills	18
TOTAL	**142***

*The total number of documents analyzed is 142, as opposed to 116, because some documents address more than one subject area.

In conducting this study, McREL researchers had to address the issue of differing levels of specificity. Recall from Chapter 3 that some national documents describe standards in very general terms, whereas other documents describe them in very specific terms. McREL researchers concluded that it was most useful to think of a standard as described in the national documents as a general category of information and skill. For example, Exhibit 4.1 lists the composite standards in mathematics that McREL researchers constructed after analyzing eight different documents, all of which were designed to identify what students should know and be able to do over the course of a K–12 education. These topics will come as no surprise to those familiar with mathematics instruction in school. Number sense, computation, measurement, functions, and so on are the basic categories into which mathematics educators have organized their subject matter for decades.

Exhibit 4.1

Mathematics Standards Constructed by McREL Researchers
Based on Analysis of Standards Documents

1. Uses a variety of strategies in the problem-solving process

2. Understands and applies basic and advanced properties of the concepts of numbers

3. Uses basic and advanced procedures while performing the processes of computation

4. Understands and applies basic and advanced properties of the concepts of measurement

5. Understands and applies basic and advanced properties of the concepts of geometry

6. Understands and applies basic and advanced concepts of statistics and data analysis

7. Understands and applies basic and advanced concepts of probability

8. Understands and applies basic and advanced properties of functions and algebra

9. Understands the general nature and uses of mathematics

To gain the specificity and detail that Hirsch rightfully argues for, McREL researchers listed specific elements of information and skill under each standard at specific grade-level intervals. These specific elements of information and skill are commonly referred to within the standards movement as *benchmarks*. To illustrate, Exhibit 4.2 lists the benchmarks for the third mathematics standard, which deals with computation.

Exhibit 4.2

Benchmarks Developed by McREL Researchers
for Mathematics Standard 3: Computation

GRADES K–2

- Adds and subtracts whole numbers
- Solves real-world problems involving addition and subtraction of whole numbers
- Understands common terms used with estimation
- Understands the inverse relationship between addition and subtraction

GRADES 3–5

- Adds, subtracts, multiplies, and divides whole numbers and decimals
- Adds and subtracts simple fractions
- Uses specific strategies to estimate computations and check the reasonableness of results
- Performs basic mental computations
- Determines the effects of arithmetic operations on size and order of numbers
- Understands the properties of and the relationship among arithmetic operations
- Solves real-world problems involving number operations
- Knows the language of basic operations

GRADES 6–8

- Adds, subtracts, multiplies, and divides fractions, integers, and rational numbers
- Understands exponentiation of rational numbers and root-extraction
- Selects and uses appropriate computational methods for a given situation
- Understands the correct order of operations for performing arithmetic computations
- Uses proportional reasoning to solve mathematical and real-world problems
- Understands the properties of operations with rational numbers
- Knows when an estimate is more appropriate than an exact answer
- Understands how different algorithms work for arithmetic computations and operations

GRADES 9–12

- Adds, subtracts, multiplies, divides, and simplifies rational expressions
- Performs operations on and simplifies radical expressions containing positive rational numbers
- Understands various sources of discrepancy between an estimate and a calculated answer
- Uses a variety of operations on expressions containing real numbers
- Understands basic applications of an operations on matrices
- Uses recurrence relations to model and to solve real-world problems
- Understands counting procedures and reasoning

Benchmarks specify the information or skills that students are expected to learn by the end of a designated grade level or span of grade levels. For example, the K–2 benchmarks listed in Table 4.3 indicate that by the end of second grade, students should be able to perform rudimentary computations such as adding and subtracting whole numbers; the 3–5 benchmarks indicate that by the end of fifth grade, students should be able to add, subtract, multiply, and divide whole numbers as well as add and subtract simple fractions. In all, McREL researchers identified 256 different standards and 3,968 benchmarks. These standards are organized into 14 major categories representing traditional subject areas (see Exhibit 4.3).

Exhibit 4.3
Number of Standards and Benchmarks by Subject Area
McREL Standards Database

MATHEMATICS: 9 standards, 226 benchmarks

SCIENCE: 16 standards, 265 benchmarks

HISTORY:

- *Historical Understanding*: 2 standards, 48 benchmarks
- *K–4 History*: 8 standards, 108 benchmarks
- *U.S. History*: 31 standards, 404 benchmarks
- *World History*: 46 standards, 722 benchmarks

LANGUAGE ARTS: 8 standards, 274 benchmarks

ARTS:

- *Art Connections*: 1 standard, 13 benchmarks
- *Dance*: 6 standards, 62 benchmarks
- *Music*: 7 standards, 80 benchmarks
- *Theatre*: 6 standards, 72 benchmarks
- *Visual Arts*: 5 standards, 42 benchmarks
  Civics: 29 standards, 427 benchmarks

ECONOMICS: 10 standards, 159 benchmarks

FOREIGN LANGUAGE: 5 standards, 84 benchmarks

GEOGRAPHY: 18 standards, 238 benchmarks

HEALTH: 10 standards, 136 benchmarks

PHYSICAL EDUCATION: 5 standards, 105 benchmarks

TECHNOLOGY: 5 standards, 94 benchmarks

BEHAVIORAL STUDIES: 4 standards, 100 benchmarks

LIFE SKILLS:

- *Thinking and Reasoning*: 6 standards, 121 benchmarks
- *Working with Others*: 5 standards, 51 benchmarks
- *Self-Regulation*: 6 standards, 59 benchmarks
- *Life Work*: 8 standards, 78 benchmarks

These 256 standards and their related benchmarks are published under the title *Content Knowledge: A Compendium of Standards and Benchmarks for K–12 Education* (2nd ed.), (Kendall & Marzano, 1997), which we hereinafter refer to as the "standards database." Given the number and quality of the documents that were used to construct this database, one might legitimately claim that it is the most valid and thorough accounting to date of what content-area specialists say students should know and be able to do across the most common subject areas. Indeed, the standards database synthesizes the intensive work of a group of researchers over a period of seven years. It is a resource that educators have had until now.

To convey a sense of the information that is available in the standards database, we consider the subject of geography. McREL researchers have identified 18 standards in geography and organized them into the six groupings, as reported in Exhibit 4.4. As noted in Chapter 3, benchmarks were identified for each of the 18 geography standards.

Appendix B lists the 256 standards and an abridged version of their related benchmarks. To illustrate, consider Exhibit 4.5, which compares the abbreviated benchmarks presented in Appendix B for grades 6–8 benchmarks for the fifth geography standard, "Understands the concept of regions," with their more detailed counterpart articulated in the *Compendium*, the standards database.

The standards database clearly provides much more detail than does Appendix B. For example, the first abbreviated benchmark listed in Exhibit 4.5 simply states that the student "knows regions at various spatial scales," whereas the complete benchmark from the standards database provides specific examples: hemispheres, regions, countries, cities.

It is also important to note that each benchmark in the standards database has a detailed code called a *citation log*. (For ease of discussion here, we have not included all of the information contained in the citation log for each benchmark. For a detailed discussion, see Kendall & Marzano, 1997.) The citations in the log specify the documents in which the knowledge identified in the benchmark appears and whether the knowledge is stated explicitly or implicitly within those documents. To illustrate, consider the citation log for the first benchmark: (GE,152;NI,45). The letter G indicates that the information (or skill) that is the substance of the benchmark is found in *Geography for Life: National Geography Standard* (Geography Education Standards Project, 1994). The letter E indicates that the information is explicitly stated, and the number *152* designates the page on which it is found. The letter N indicates that the information also is found in *Item Specifications: 1994 National Assessment of Educational Progress in Geography* (NAEP, 1992). The letter I indicates that it is implicit in that document, and the number *45* identifies the page number on which the information is implicitly stated.

Exhibit 4.4

Geography Standards by Topic
McREL *Compendium* (Standards Database)

THE WORLD IN SPATIAL TERMS

1. Understands the characteristics and uses of maps, globes, and other geographic tools and technologies

2. Knows the location of places, geographic features, and patterns of the environment

3. Understands the characteristics and uses of spatial organization of Earth's surface

PLACES AND REGIONS

4. Understands the physical and human characteristics of place

5. Understands the concept of regions

6. Understands that culture and experience influence people's perceptions of places and regions

PHYSICAL SYSTEMS

7. Knows the physical processes that shape patterns on Earth's surface

8. Understands the characteristics of ecosystems on Earth's surface

HUMAN SYSTEMS

9. Understands the nature, distribution, and migration of human populations on Earth's surface

10. Understands the nature and complexity of Earth's cultural mosaics

11. Understands the patterns and networks of economic interdependence on Earth's surface

12. Understands the patterns of human settlement and their causes

13. Understands the forces of cooperation and conflict that shape the divisions of Earth's surface

ENVIRONMENT AND SOCIETY

14. Understands how human actions modify the physical environment

15. Understands how physical systems affect human systems

16. Understands the changes that occur in the meaning, use, distribution, and importance of resources

USES OF GEOGRAPHY

17. Understands how geography is used to interpret the past

18. Understands global development and environmental issues

Note: From *Content Knowledge: A Compendium of Standards and Benchmarks for K–12 Education* (2nd ed.), by J. S. Kendall and R. J. Marzano, 1997, Aurora, CO: Mid-continent Regional Educational Laboratory.

Exhibit 4.5

Benchmark Comparison: Abbreviated Version and Full Version
Grades 6–8, Geography Standard 5: "Understands the Concept of Regions"

APPENDIX B ABBREVIATED VERSION
- Knows regions at various spatial scales
- Understands criteria that give a region identity
- Knows types of regions
- Knows factors that contribute to changing regional characteristics
- Understands the influences and effects of particular regional labels and images
- Understands ways regional systems are interconnected

STANDARDS DATABASE FULL VERSION

(GE,152;NI,45)

- Knows regions at various spatial scales (e.g., hemispheres, regions within continents, countries, cities)

(GE,152;NI,56–57)

- Understands criteria that give a region identity (e.g., its central focus, such as Amsterdam as a transportation center; relationships between physical and cultural characteristics, such as the Sunbelt's warm climate and popularity with retired people)

(GE,152)

- Knows types of regions such as formal regions (e.g., school districts, circuit-court districts, states of the United States), functional regions (e.g., the marketing area of a local newspaper, the "fanshed" of a professional sports team), and perceptual regions (e.g., the Bible Belt in the United States, the Riviera in southern France, the Great American Desert)

(GE,153;NE,64–65)

- Knows factors that contribute to changing regional characteristics (e.g., economic development, accessibility, migration, media image)

(GE,153;NI,56–57)

- Understands the influences and effects of particular regional labels and images (e.g., Twin Peaks in San Francisco; Capitol Hill in Washington, D.C.; the South; the rust belt; "developed" vs. "less-developed" regions)

(GE,153;NI,56–57)

- Understands ways regional systems are interconnected (e.g., watersheds and river systems, regional connections through trade, cultural ties between regions)

SOURCE CODES (*citation log*, right side of page):

1st letter of each code in parentheses	*2nd letter of code*
G = GESP: National Geography Standards	E = Explicitly stated in document
E = JCGE: Guidelines for Geographic Education	I = Implied in document
IE, IG = Int'l Bacc.:Environmental Systems, Geography	*Number*
N = NAEP: Item Specifications in Geography	Page number of cited document *or*,
T = GENIP: K–6 Geography: Themes, Key Ideas	*for duplicates,*
D = Duplicated in another standard	Standard number & level of duplicate

Note: The lower portion of this exhibit is adapted from *Content Knowledge: A Compendium of Standards and Benchmarks for K–12 Education* (2nd ed.) (pp. 516–517), by J. S. Kendall and R. J. Marzano, 1997, Aurora, CO: Mid-continent Regional Educational Laboratory.

The database constructed by McREL researchers reports what subject-matter experts have determined is important for students to know and be able to do across a wide range of subject matter. The credibility of the people and organizations whose work is represented in this database lends validity to the claim that it is a complete and credible basis from which to determine what legitimately comprises student literacy.

Even a cursory review of the documents that have been produced under the aegis of the standards movement (and synthesized in the McREL database) makes clear that students should not merely possess information and skill in traditional subject areas. Those scholars and teachers who contributed to the original reports that ultimately formed the database also identified other significant areas in which students should be competent. It is these areas that are the focus of the next section.

Life Skills: What Hirsch Left Out

Researchers at McREL, in their review of the many documents addressing content, have determined that it is most useful to conceptualize knowledge identified in the standards database as falling into two broad categories: (1) traditional subject-matter knowledge and (2) life skills. The general category we refer to as "life skills" addresses knowledge that has been identified as applicable not only to academics, but to life in general. We have organized life skills into two categories: thinking and reasoning, and work skills.

Those who have studied the *Dictionary of Cultural Literacy* and related works will quickly notice that although Hirsch and his colleagues appear to have gone to great lengths to identify specific subject-matter knowledge, they have focused little or no attention on identifying specific life skills. As the following sections will show, however, there is a great deal of support for the teaching of life skills, from both education and business leaders and from research findings.

Thinking and Reasoning

Over 80 years ago, John Dewey (1916) wrote, "The sole direct path to enduring improvement in the methods of instruction and learning consists in centering upon the conditions which exact, promote, and test thinking" (p. 6). Similarly, in 1961, a report sponsored by the National Education Association (See Educational Policies Commission, 1961) identified the improvement of thinking and reasoning as central to American education. More recently, calls for the enhancement of thinking and reasoning in American education have come from the National Science Board Commission on Precollege Education in Mathematics, Science and Technology (1983), the College Board (1983), the National Education Association (Futrell, 1987), and the American Federation of Teachers (1985).

In addition, the need to enhance students' abilities to think and reason is explicitly stated in Goal 3 of the six national education goals established at the first education summit in Charlottesville, Virginia. (See Chapter 3 for a discussion of the summit.) As mentioned previously, Goal 3 explicitly targeted the subjects of English, mathematics, science, history, and geography. In addition, it noted that "every school in America will ensure that all students learn to use their minds well so they may be prepared for responsible citizenship, further learning, and productive employment in our modern economy" (NEGP, 1991, p. ix).

The need for a greater emphasis on thinking and reasoning as a compliment to instruction in traditional subject-matter content is self-evident if one examines the current performance of U.S. students. To illustrate, consider the following problem, given by the National Assessment of Educational Progress (NAEP, a federally funded effort to measure the knowledge and basic skills of American students) to a representative sample of U.S. 13- and 17-year-olds:

Estimate the answer to 3.04 x 5.3:				
a. 1.6	b. 16	c. 160	d. 1,600	e. don't know

Twenty percent of the 13-year-olds and 40 percent of the 17-year-olds got the right answer (Silver, 1986). A logical conclusion might be that students simply did not know how to compute. However, when asked to compute the product of 3.04 x 5.3, 60 percent of the 13-year-olds and 80 percent of the 17-year-olds answered the problem correctly. In short, the students were quite capable of the basic mathematics skill of computation, but they did not perform well in the basic thinking skill of inference. Similarly, research has found that elementary students can pass chapter quizzes on photosynthesis and still not understand that plants make their own food (Anderson & Smith, 1984). Again, an understanding of the factual knowledge did not translate into an ability to think about the information.

Another example from NAEP further illustrates students' poor thinking skills. When U.S. students were asked to compare the food eaten by frontiersmen—*based on information given to them*—with the food they eat, only 16 percent of students in grade 8 and 27 percent of students in grade 12 provided an adequate or better than adequate response (Mullis, Owen, & Phillips, 1990). Again, subject-matter knowledge was not the issue; students were provided with a description of the food eaten by frontiersmen and certainly were aware of their own diet. They simply did not effectively use the thinking skill of comparison.

In spite of the rather strong evidence that U.S. students need instruction in thinking and reasoning, Hirsch clearly objects to such an instructional emphasis. For example, in *The Schools We Need and Why We Don't Have Them* (1996), Hirsch devotes a substantial part of one chapter to arguing against the teaching of thinking. Oddly enough, the argument is found in a chapter subtitled "Education and Mainstream Research." Hirsch's entire case against the teaching of thinking rests on his assertion that there is little or no research to support the direct teaching of thinking:

> The oft-repeated goal of the educational community—to inculcate general thinking skills—is not, then, soundly based in research. And that is stating the point too mildly. The idea that school can inculcate abstract, generalized skills for thinking, "accessing," and problem solving, and that these can be readily applied to the real world is, bluntly, a mirage. (p. 143)

To support his claims, Hirsch cites two studies that, he asserts, illustrate that thinking skills cannot be transferred. However, both of these studies focus on highly specific rules of logic and are not representative of the many and varied skills within the general category of thinking and reasoning. In addition, Hirsch fails to mention the vast amount of research that supports the teaching of thinking. For example, in their review of research on the teaching of thinking, Nickerson, Perkins, and Smith (1985) identify over 25 programs that have consistently illustrated their effectiveness at improving the thinking of K–12 students. Similarly, Costa (1985) lists over 30 programs that have proven records of enhancing students' thinking. Ross (1988) lists over 45 studies that have demonstrated the positive effects of teaching thinking. Additional reviews have been conducted by Marzano (1991), Nickerson (1988), and Segal, Chipman, and Glaser (1985). In short, Hirsch's assertion that research does not support the teaching of thinking is simply and unequivocally false.

Although researchers in education and psychology agree on the importance of teaching thinking and reasoning, they do not agree on the specific thinking and reasoning skills that should be taught. In fact, a number of education researchers and program developers have independently developed lists of thinking and reasoning skills that are quite different in nature (see Beyer, 1988; de Bono, 1985; Marzano, 1992; Quellmalz, 1987). One can assume, however, that if general thinking and reasoning skills do, in fact, exist, they should be referred to in the national standards documents described in Chapter 3 and earlier in this chapter. To illustrate, if the standards documents in mathematics, science, and history all highlight the thinking and reasoning skill of problem solving, then one might conclude that problem solving is a general thinking and reasoning skill that cuts across these subject areas. The national standards documents, then, represent a source from which general thinking and reasoning skills can be gleaned. To study thinking and reasoning in the national documents, McREL researchers focused their attention on the documents listed in Exhibit 4.6.

Exhibit 4.6

Documents that Reference Thinking and Reasoning Skills by Subject Area

1. **Mathematics**
   - *Curriculum and Evaluation Standards for School Mathematics* (1989). National Council of Teachers of Mathematics.
2. **Science**
   - *Benchmarks for Science Literacy.* (1993). Project 2061, American Association for the Advancement of Science.
   - *National Science Education Standards.* (1996). National Research Council.
3. **History**
   - *National Standards for History: Basic Edition.* (1996). National Center for History in the Schools.
4. **Language Arts**
   - *Standards in Practice: Grades K–2.* (1996). L. K. Crafton.
   - *Standards in Practice: Grades 3–5.* (1996). M. Sierra-Perry.
   - *Standards in Practice: Grades 6–8.* (1996). J. D. Wilhelm.
   - *Standards in Practice: Grades 9–12.* (1996). P. Smagorinski.
5. **Geography**
   - *Geography for Life: National Geography Standards.* (1994). Geography Education Standards Project.
6. **Social Studies**
   - *Expectations of Excellence: Curriculum Standards for Social Studies.* (1994). National Council for the Social Studies.
7. **The Arts**
   - *National Standards for Arts Education: What Every Young American Should Know and Be Able to Do in the Arts.* (1994). Consortium of National Arts Education Associations.
8. **Civics**
   - *National Standards for Civics and Government.* (1994). Center for Civic Education.
9. **Foreign Language**
   - *Standards for Foreign Language Learning: Preparing for the 21st Century.* (1996). National Standards in Foreign Language Education Project.
10. **Health**
    - *National Health Education Standards: Achieving Health Literacy.* (1995). Joint Committee on National Health Education Standards.
11. **Physical Education**
    - *Moving into the Future: National Standards for Physical Education: A Guide to Content and Assessment.* (1995). National Association for Sport and Physical Education.
12. **The World of Work**
    - *What Work Requires of Schools: A SCANS Report for America 2000.* (1991). The Secretary's Commission on Achieving Necessary Skills.
    - *Workplace Basics: The Essential Skills Employers Want.* (1990). A. P. Carnevale, L. J. Gainer, & A. S. Meltzer.

Note: From *Content Knowledge: A Compendium of Standards and Benchmarks for K–12 Education* (2nd ed.), by J. S. Kendall and R. J. Marzano, 1997, Aurora, CO: Mid-continent Regional Educational Laboratory.

Content areas 1 through 11 listed in Exhibit 4.6 are traditionally considered basic by most state departments of education, as evidenced by the fact that most states have identified, or are in the process of identifying, standards in these specific areas or combinations of these areas (e.g., civics, history, and geography are sometimes combined into one subject area). In addition to the documents that address the core subject areas, McREL researchers analyzed two documents that identify the skills that employers (i.e., the "world of work") think should be enhanced in K–12 education. (See item 12 in Exhibit 4.6.)

Note that multiple documents were identified for two subject areas (in addition to the world of work). Specifically, in science the official standards document is certainly the *National Science Education Standards*, published by the National Research Council. However, *Benchmarks for Science Literacy* also was analyzed because of its wide acceptance as a reference document in the field of science. For the English language arts, four grade-interval-specific documents were analyzed in place of *Standards for the English Language Arts*, the more general document published in 1996 by the National Council of Teachers of English (NCTE) and the International Reading Association (IRA). (This was done at the recommendation of NCTE [Myers, 1997] since the more specific documents were designed to articulate benchmarked skills and abilities, whereas the general document was not.)

All of the documents listed in Exhibit 4.6 were analyzed for thinking and reasoning skills, whether stated explicitly or implicitly. In all, six general thinking and reasoning skills were identified and written as standards. These standards are listed below, along with the percentage of subject areas in which the essential skill is cited:

1. Utilizes mental processes that are based on identifying similarities and differences (100%)
2. Applies problem-solving and troubleshooting techniques (83%)
3. Understands and applies basic principles of argumentation (83%)
4. Applies decision-making techniques (75%)
5. Understands and applies basic principles of hypothesis testing and scientific inquiry (58%)
6. Understands and applies basic principles of logic and reasoning (50%)

As indicated above, the extent to which the thinking and reasoning processes are addressed across the twelve subject areas ranges from a low of 50% to a high of 100%. For each of these thinking and reasoning skill areas (as for all subject-area standards), specific benchmarks were identified for each of the four grade-level intervals: grades

K–2, 3–5, 6–8, and 9–12. To illustrate, Exhibit 4.7 presents the 6–8 benchmarks for the thinking and reasoning skill of "understanding and applying basic principles of hypothesis testing and scientific inquiry."

Exhibit 4.7

Grades 6–8 Benchmarks for Hypothesis Testing and Scientific Inquiry
McREL *Compendium* (Standards Database)

(2I,233;NHI,66;NSI,145)

- Understands that there are a variety of ways people can form hypotheses, including basing them on many observations, basing them on very few observations, and constructing them on only one or two observations

(MI,75;NSI,148,171)

- Verifies results of experiments

(2E,299;NHI,66;NSI,145)

- Understands that there may be more than one valid way to interpret a set of findings

(2E,299;NSI,171)

- Questions findings in which no mention is made of whether the control group is very similar to the experimental group

(SSE,149;NSE,145;NSI,171)

- Reformulates a new hypothesis for study after an old hypothesis has been eliminated

(MI,78,81,143;NSI,145,171)

- Makes and validates conjectures about outcomes of specific alternatives or events regarding an experiment

---

SOURCE CODE (*citation log*, right side of page)

1st letter(s) of each code in parentheses

2 = Project 2061: Benchmarks for Science Literacy
A = CNAEA: National Standards for Arts Education
C = CCE: National Standards for Civics and Govt.
F = ACTFL: Standards for Foreign Lang. Learning
G = GESP: National Geography Standards
H = JHESC: National Health Education Standards
M = NCTM: Curric. & Eval. Stan. for School Math
NH = NCHS: Nat'l Standards for History: Basic Ed
NS = NRC: National Science Education Standards

2nd letter of code
E = Explicitly stated in document
I = Implied in document

Number
Page number of cited document

P = NASPE: National Standards for Physical Education
S = SCANS: Report for America 2000
SP 1,2,3,4 = NCTE: Standards in Practice
SS = NCSS: Curriculum Standards for Social Studies
W = Carnevale: Workplace Basics

Note: Adapted from *Content Knowledge: A Compendium of Standards and Benchmarks for K–12 Education* (2nd ed.), pp. 613–614, by J. S. Kendall and R. J. Marzano, 1997, Aurora, CO: Mid-continent Regional Educational Laboratory.

Again, these benchmarks are found in McREL's standards database, *Content Knowledge: A Compendium of Standards and Benchmarks for K–12 Education* (2nd ed.) (Kendall & Marzano, 1997), and in Appendix B in a simplified version. Note that each benchmark listed in Exhibit 4.7 is accompanied by a citation log, which identifies the documents and page numbers for each citation along with information about the implicitness or explicitness of the citation. (See the first part of this chapter for a discussion of the citation log.)

This level of detailed analysis allowed McREL researchers to answer the question, To what extent do different subject areas emphasize these various thinking and reasoning skills? Table 4.2 presents the results of our analysis.

Table 4.2

Emphases on Various Critical Thinking and Reasoning Skills by Subject Matter

Subject Matter	Similarities & Differences	Problem Solving	Argumen- tation	Decision Making	Hypothesis Testing	Logic
Science (27.2%)*	8.3%	11.5%	22.9%	3.1%	32.3%	21.8%
History (13.0%)	32.6%	26.1%	15.2%	15.2%	8.7%	2.2%
Mathematics (11.3%)	17.5%	50.0%	7.5%	0.0%	20.0%	5.0%
Social Studies (9.1%)	28.1%	6.3%	28.1%	28.1%	3.1%	6.3%
The Arts (8.2%)	46.4%	32.1%	7.1%	14.3%	0.0%	0.0%
Civics (7.4%)	23.1%	38.5%	7.7%	30.8%	0.0%	0.0%
Work (6.8%)	12.5%	54.2%	20.8%	0.0%	4.2%	8.3%
Foreign Language (4.0%)	92.9%	0.0%	7.1%	0.0%	0.0%	0.0%
Geography (3.7%)	30.8%	7.7%	7.7%	30.8%	23.1%	0.0%
Health (3.7%)	46.2%	15.4%	7.7%	30.8%	0.0%	0.0%
Physical Education (3.1%)	45.5%	18.2%	0.0%	36.4%	0.0%	0.0%
Language Arts (2.8%)	50.0%	0.0%	0.0%	10.0%	20.0%	20.0%

*The number in parentheses after each subject area is the percentage of total references to thinking and reasoning skills that were found in the documents in that subject area. For example, 27.2% of all of the references to thinking and reasoning were found in the science documents analyzed by McREL researchers.

The twelve subject areas reviewed are listed in the first column of Table 4.2, ranked in order of the percentage of total number of references to thinking and reasoning attributed to that subject area. For example, references to thinking and reasoning skills in the science documents account for 27.2 percent of the total number of references to thinking and reasoning across all of the documents analyzed; history accounts for 13 percent; mathematics, 11.3 percent; and so on. We caution readers against assigning too much importance to these percentages, since the number of references to thinking and reasoning skills was influenced, at least in part, by the number and length of documents analyzed. (For example, only one comparatively short document was analyzed for health, whereas two comparatively lengthy documents were analyzed for science.) Nonetheless, a number of findings are worth highlighting.

Language arts, for which the highest number of documents were reviewed (four), accounts for the lowest percentage of references to thinking and reasoning. In addition, three subject areas (science, history, and mathematics) account for over half (51.5 percent) of all references made to thinking and reasoning.

Another finding worth highlighting is based on the patterns of emphasis within individual subject areas. For example, one can see that the field of science heavily emphasizes hypothesis testing and scientific inquiry since 32.3 percent of the references to thinking and reasoning in the science documents were to this one specific thinking skill area. In addition, the study of science emphasizes argumentation and the use of logic, and, to a lesser extent, problem solving and identifying similarities and differences. However, little emphasis is placed on decision making as a thinking skill. The percentages reported in Table 4.2 reflect what content-area experts think are important thinking and reasoning skills for their areas. Thus, these findings suggest that as educators deliver content, they might select the critical thinking and reasoning skills they teach on the basis of where content experts place their emphasis.

Work Skills

As their name indicates, work skills are commonly associated with the world of work. Work skills gained national prominence when the Secretary's Commission on Achieving Necessary Skills (SCANS) published the report *What Work Requires of Schools: A SCANS Report for America 2000* (1991). The commission spent 12 months "talking to business owners, to public employees, to the people who manage employees daily, to union officials, and to workers on the line and at their desks. We have talked to them in their stores, shops, government offices, and manufacturing facilities" (p. v). The strong message from all quarters was that American students must be taught a variety of skills and abilities to be productive members of the work force. Many of these skills and abilities went beyond the traditional academic subjects commonly found in the curriculum. For example, the SCANS report identified a "three-part foundation of skills and personal qualities" (p. vii). The first part of the foundation involved traditional academic content, such as reading, writing, arithmetic and mathematics, speaking and listening. The second part of the foundation involved the thinking skills of "thinking creatively, making decisions, solving problems, seeing things in the mind's eye, knowing how to learn, and reasoning" (p. vii). The third part of the foundation involved work skills, such as individual responsibility, self-esteem, sociability, self-management, and integrity.

Workplace Basics: The Essential Skills Employers Want (Carnevale, Gainer, & Meltzer, 1990), a complimentary work to the SCANS report, was published by the American Society for Training and Development (ASTD), which represents some 50,000 people who work in the field of human resource development. The set of skills identified in this document was almost identical to that articulated in the SCANS report. From these two reports, one can infer that American employers are giving American educators a strong message: Teach and reinforce work-related skills.

This same message also has been heard from parents and educators. The polling firm Public Agenda surveyed a representative sample of parents regarding what should be taught in the schools. Public Agenda's report, entitled *First Things First: What Americans Expect from Public Schools* (Farkas, Friedman, Boese, & Shaw, 1994), noted that 88% of those surveyed said, among other things, that schools should teach and reinforce work-related competencies such as punctuality, dependability, and self-discipline. The American Association of School Administrators polled 55 noted educators, referred to as the "Council of 55," regarding what schools should teach to prepare students for the 21st century. The council identified interpersonal skills, such as being part of a team, as critical to success in the next century (Uchida, Cetron, & McKenzie, 1996).

In our analysis of the standards documents, we found that work skills could be organized into three subcategories: (1) working with others, (2) self-regulation, and (3) life work. The category of skills entitled *working with others* deals with skills and abilities that are associated with working in groups and with those skills and abilities associated with effective interpersonal communications. *Self-regulation* skills generally address the ability to monitor one's own thinking; this set of skills is commonly referred to as "metacognition" by psychologists. *Life work* skills deal with those competencies that are directly related to acquiring or maintaining a job; these skills address areas such as becoming familiar with and using different information sources to accomplish specific tasks, readying oneself to pursue and acquire specific jobs, developing a strong work ethic, and the like.

Hirsch (1996) takes exception to emphasizing what we call self-regulation skills. He gives four primary reasons that an "Emphasis on Metacognition" (which he refers to as EOM) is problematic:

- EOM may interfere with the orderly development of adaptive problem-solving strategies.

- EOM may carry severe opportunity costs by usurping subject matter instruction.

- EOM may overload working memory and thus impair rather than help learning.

- All of these potential drawbacks may have the most adverse effects on slow or disadvantaged learners. (p. 139)

In his critique of metacognitive instruction, Hirsch does not cite a single study that directly supports his position. In addition, he ignores a series of research reviews, conducted by Wang, Haertel, and Walberg (1993), which concluded that out of 30 categories of instructional innovations, those that focus on meta-cognition were second in terms of their impact on student achievement.[8] Wang, Haertel, and Walberg's syntheses (called a *meta-analysis*) covered more than 22,000 studies and nearly 15 million students (see Marzano, 1998a for a discussion).

Some critics also discount the teaching of skills related to working with others. Specifically, those who ascribe to the content-heavy focus advocated by Hirsch and his colleagues object to the notion that students should be taught skills that improve their ability to work in cooperative situations. Hirsch (1996) himself decries the overuse of cooperative learning strategies, while giving some approval to its restrained use:

> The method still retains vestiges of its historical origins in progressivist practices, when group cooperation was elevated above competition and individual achievement. . . . Cooperative learning, used with restraint, can be an excellent method of instruction when used in conjunction with whole-class instruction. It has not been effective when used as the principal or exclusive means of instruction. (pp. 246–247)

To the extent that Hirsch supports cooperative learning, his support is well founded. Cooperative learning has been proven consistently to enhance both achievement and cooperation. Specifically, over 286 studies have demonstrated that cooperative learning will increase student achievement by about 27 percentile points (Johnson, Maruyama,

---

[8]Strategies that focus on classroom management had the greatest impact on student achievement. See Wang, Haertel, and Walberg (1993), pp. 272–273, Table 4.

Johnson, Nelson, & Skon, 1981). Stated differently, if cooperative learning is used as an instructional strategy, an average student will increase his or her performance on a test of academic achievement from the 50th percentile to the 77th percentile.

Hirsch is relatively silent on life-work competencies. Although there is no reason to conclude that Hirsch would not be in favor of them, it is safe to assume that he would want schools to heavily emphasize the information and skills associated with traditional subject areas.

Conclusion

In this chapter we have described the content that has been identified as important in the national- and state-level standards documents and summarized in the McREL database. A review of this content shows that in addition to traditional subject matter, an area of learning that we term *life skills* forms an important part of schooling. The skills of thinking and reasoning are of particular significance for two reasons. First, research shows that students tend to perform poorly in these areas. Second, subject-area specialists have consistently included thinking and reasoning skills in their descriptions of what students should know and be able to do.

The knowledge that has been summarized in the McREL standards database represents a significant step forward in the identification of what truly makes a student literate. Without such a common format for standards, even the basics of a school system can break down. When demands on schooling become more complex, as for example when teachers seek to design lesson plans that incorporate standards from more than one discipline, a lack of common language can overburden innovative work. Thus, the database remedies two difficult problems that we have identified as side effects of the standards movement: that of multiple documents that describe what is important in each subject area, and wide variation in the ways in which knowledge is identified and described in these documents. However, the third problem we identified—an overabundance of content—remains to be addressed. In addition to the sheer volume of the documents, the question arises, Is there enough time in the school day to teach the content these documents identify?

Chapter 5

The Problem of Time

As we have seen in previous chapters, the collective efforts of subject-matter specialists resulted in numerous documents identifying the information and skills that students should know prior to high school graduation. Yet, an important question is whether the amount of available instructional time is sufficient to cover all of the content identified by professionals in their respective areas of expertise. This chapter considers the problem of time and presents two broad approaches toward a solution.

Estimating How Much Time Is Required

To address the question of time, McREL researchers analyzed the standards and benchmarks in the McREL standards database. (These standards and benchmarks are described in Chapter 4 and reported in abbreviated form in Appendix B.) As we noted in Chapter 4, the standards database contains 256 standards and 3,968 benchmarks. With the exception of history, the standards in the content areas are articulated K–12. This means that all of the benchmarks for the different grade-level intervals (i.e., K–2, 3–5, 6–8, 9–12) are intended to be addressed. However, the history standards are written to be taught within one grade-level interval.[9] Thus, from the perspective of classroom teaching time, the database can be thought of as covering only 200 standards and 3,093 benchmarks. Table 5.1 shows how the 200 standards and 3,093 benchmarks are distributed across various subject areas.

---

[9]For example, if a history standard that addresses "how political institutions and religious freedom emerged in the North American colonies" (see U.S. history standard 4 in Appendix B) is addressed at grades 5–6, this content would not be repeated at other grades even though benchmarks have been identified under this standard for other grade levels. In addition, the content identified under the K–4 history standards is a simpler version of material covered in later grades. For a complete discussion of how the history standards are formatted, see Kendall & Marzano, 1997, pp. 105–109.

Table 5.1

Summary of Standards and Benchmarks by Subject Area
(Classroom Implementation Set)

Subject Area	Number of Standards	Number of Benchmarks	Number of Benchmarks per Standard
Mathematics	9	226	25.11
Science	16	265	16.56
History	31	407	13.13
Historical Understanding	2	48	24.00
K-4 History	4	54	13.50
U.S. History	10	135	13.50
World History	15	170	11.33
Language Arts	8	274	34.25
Geography	18	238	13.22
The Arts	25	269	10.76
Art Connections	1	13	13.00
Dance	6	62	10.33
Music	7	80	11.43
Theatre	6	72	12.00
Visual Arts	5	42	8.40
Civics	29	427	14.72
Economics	10	159	15.90
Foreign Language	5	84	16.80
Health	10	136	13.60
Physical Education	5	105	21.00
Technology	5	94	18.80
Behavioral Studies	4	100	25.00
Thinking & Reasoning	6	121	20.17
Work Skills	19	188	9.89
Working with Others	5	51	10.20
Self-Regulation	6	59	9.83
Life Work	8	78	9.75
TOTAL	200	3,093	15.47

As Table 5.1 shows, the 200 standards are not distributed evenly across the various subject areas. In addition, standards for different content areas vary in the number of benchmarks they encompass. Language arts has the highest number of benchmarks per standard (34.25); work skills has the fewest number of benchmarks per standard (9.89). Civics and history have the most benchmarks (427 and 407, respectively), and foreign language has the fewest (84). Because of the great variance in the number of benchmarks per standard, the number of *benchmarks* (as opposed to the number of standards) is the better measure of the amount of content identified in a given subject area.

What is the feasibility of addressing 3,093 benchmarks within the present education system? To answer this question, we first must determine how much time is currently available.

A number of studies have been conducted on how time is spent in American education, revealing some strong patterns. One of the most stable aspects of time usage is the number of days in the school year—probably because of state law mandates. Although it is commonly assumed that schools operate on a 180-day calendar, studies have found some significant variations. For example, a 1983 study (see Karweit) of United States schools found that the number of days scheduled for school ranged from 175 to 184 days, with an average of 179. A more recent study by the National Education Commission on Time and Learning, published as *Prisoners of Time* (1994), reported that as of 1994, 11 states permit school terms of 175 days or less and only one state requires more than 180 days.

A number of studies also have been conducted concerning the length of the school day. These studies found that, although fairly stable, the amount of time students spend in school each day also varies. A 1963 study (see Reuter) found that the length of the school day varied from four to six hours. In the late 1970s, a large-scale study known as the Beginning Teacher Evaluation Study (BTES) found that second graders were in school 5.5 hours, whereas fifth graders were in school for 6.0 hours (Fisher et al., 1978). Harnischfeger and Wiley (1978) found that the length of the school day within the same district could vary by as much as 45 minutes. A 1994 study by the National Education Commission on Time reported that, on the average, schools offer a six-period day with about 5.6 hours of classroom time per day.

If we accept the estimate of 5.6 hours of classroom time per day and assume that the school year is 180 days in length, simple arithmetic tells us that about 1,008 hours (5.6 x 180) of classroom time are available in a school year, and 13,104 hours (13 x 1,008) are available over 13 years of schooling—grades K–12. In all, teachers have a maximum of 13,104 hours to teach and reinforce the knowledge identified in the 200 standards and 3,093 benchmarks.

One might assume that 3,093 benchmarks can easily be covered in 13,104 hours. However, those who study the use of classroom time have noted that not all of the time that is *available* for instruction is necessarily *used* for instruction. Activities such as breaks between activities, disruptions, socializing, and other noninstructional activities use up some of the classroom time. Estimates of how much time is actually devoted to instruction vary widely, from 21 percent to 69 percent (see Conant, 1973; Park, 1976; Marzano & Riley, 1984; and National Education Commission on Time and Learning, 1994). If we take the highest estimate of 69 percent as the upper boundary of the percentage of time that typically is devoted to instruction within the current system, then we can conclude that of the 13,104 classroom hours theoretically available in K–12 education, in fact only 9,042 hours (.69 x 13,104) are actually used for instruction in the best of circumstances—about 695.6 hours per year (or about 3.9 hours per day). In the most optimistic scenario, then, educators have a total of 9,042 hours, spanning kindergarten through grade 12, within which to teach and reinforce the 200 standards and 3,093 benchmarks. The next critical question is, How much time would it take to cover those standards and benchmarks?

Although there is a wealth of research one can access to answer the question of how much time is available in K–12 education, there is little, if any, research that directly addresses how much time it takes to teach specific standards and benchmarks. To informally address this question, McREL researchers asked 350 practicing teachers to estimate the amount of time (rounded to the nearest hour) it would take to "adequately address" the content in a representative sample of benchmarks from the database (Marzano, 1998).

At least two estimates of time were obtained for each benchmark. The average number of hours estimated across all sample benchmarks was computed to be approximately five hours.[10] This overall mean was considered an estimate of the average number of hours it would take to address any given benchmark in the McREL standards database. The estimated hours necessary to address each *standard* was computed by multiplying the number of benchmarks by the five hours estimated to teach each benchmark. Although we recognize that this crude method of estimation can result in a fair amount of error in the estimates of time, nonetheless it illustrates the general magnitude of the content volume issue. Estimates of the amount of time required to address the standards in the various subject areas are reported in Table 5.2.

---

[10]We wish to stress that the estimate of five hours per benchmark is an average and that the time required to adequately address various benchmarks will vary widely across subject areas. We also think it worth remarking that some have argued that the average required time is less if information and skills are taught together, either in an interdisciplinary fashion or within the same content area. Our analysis suggests that this approach might reduce the time required for instruction, but that the reduction is minimal.

Table 5.2

Time Required to Address Subject-Area Standards and Benchmarks

Subject Area (Number of Benchmarks)	Time in Hours*	
1. Civics (427)	2,135	
2. History (407)	2,035	
Historical Understanding (48)		240
K–4 History (54)		270
U.S. History (135)		675
World History (170)		850
3. Language Arts (274)	1,370	
4. The Arts (269)	1,345	
Art Connections (13)		65
Dance (62)		310
Music (80)		400
Theatre (72)		360
Visual Arts (42)		210
5. Science (265)	1,325	
6. Geography (238)	1,190	
7. Mathematics (226)	1,130	
8. Economics (159)	795	
9. Work Skills (188)	940	
Working with Others (51)		255
Self-Regulation (59)		295
Life Work (78)		390
10. Health (136)	680	
11. Thinking and Reasoning (121)	605	
12. Physical Education (105)	525	
13. Behavioral Studies (100)	500	
14. Technology (94)	470	
15. Foreign Language (84)	420	
TOTAL (3,093 benchmarks)	15,465	

*The total number of hours estimated to teach the benchmarks in each subject area was calculated by multiplying the number of benchmarks by the five hours estimated to teach each benchmark.

As Table 5.2 shows, using our estimate of five hours per benchmark, it would take 15,465 hours to cover all 3,093 benchmarks. Obviously, the 15,465 hours of time necessary for instruction do not fit into the estimated 9,042 hours of instructional time across the K–12 years. In other words, educators would have to increase the amount of instructional time by about 71 percent in order to cover all of the benchmarks identified in the McREL standards database. This means that, as currently structured, schooling would have to be extended from kindergarten to grade 21, or 22 years of schooling. It is doubtful that even the most devoted teachers and enthusiastic students would sign on for an additional four years of K–12 education, let alone nine. In short, the answer to the question of whether the standards documents considered as a group contain too much content from an instructional perspective, based on even the rough estimates used here, is an unqualified "yes."

Addressing the Problem

There appear to be two primary options for addressing the problem of too much content: (1) increase the amount of instructional time or (2) decrease the number of standards that must be addressed.

Increase the Amount of Instructional Time

As we have seen, to cover all of the standards and benchmarks identified by subject-matter specialists, schools would have to significantly increase the amount of instructional time. In fact, from the beginning of the standards movement, professionals from the various content areas assumed that more time for instruction would be needed. For example, when the National Education Commission on Time and Learning (1994) held a hearing to discuss the needed changes in instructional time, the following comments were recorded by representatives from various subject-matter organizations:

- **Arts.** "I am here to pound the table for 15 percent of school time devoted to arts instruction," declared Paul Lehman of the Consortium of National Arts Education Association.

- **English.** "These standards will require a huge amount of time, for both students and teachers," Miles Myers of the National Council of Teachers of English told the Commission.

- **Geography.** "Implementing our standards will require more time. Geography is hardly taught at all in American schools today," was the conclusion of Anthony DeSouza of the National Geographic Society.

- **Science.** "There is a consensus view that new standards will require more time," said David Florio of the National Academy of Sciences. (p. 21)

Perhaps heeding the assertions of these subject-matter representatives, the National Education Commission on Time and Learning (1994) strongly recommended that schools across the country allocate at least 990 hours per year of instructional time to core academic subjects. This would represent an increase of 42 percent from the 695.6 hours per year currently dedicated to instruction on average in schools across the country. One way to gain this additional instructional time is to lengthen the school day. The commission offered the Thomas Jefferson High School for Science and Technology in Alexandria, Virginia, as an example of the potential benefits of this option (see Exhibit 5.1).

Exhibit 5.1
Thomas Jefferson High School
Using Time Effectively

No one can visit the Thomas Jefferson High School for Science and Technology, Alexandria, Virginia, without realizing it is one of the most remarkable public schools in the United States—remarkable for the wealth of the suburban school district that supports it, the talents of its selected students, the skill of its staff, the technologies it employs, and the support it receives from the business community.

It is remarkable for something else as well. Its schedule is different; every school day at Thomas Jefferson is lengthened by one period, during which every one of its 1,600 9th to 12th graders is required to participate in a student activity or related course-work such as tutoring, laboratories, or guidance activities. Daily schedules are also flexible enough to let every class meet for at least one double-period every week.

The selectivity of the school—and corporate sponsorship of state-of-the-art technological environments in areas such as optics, energy systems, telecommunications, biotechnology, and industrial robotics— makes it easy to overlook the school's schedule as a factor in its success.

What does the extra period mean in practice? According to sophomore Paul Helms, "It is one of the most important things in the school. I use it to go to a Latin Honors class." Senior Seth Mitcho: "Eighth period has helped make this school the center of our lives and often of our families."

A schedule that helps make school the center of the lives of students and families may be the most remarkable thing about the Thomas Jefferson High School for Science and Technology.

Note: From *Prisoners of Time* (p. 33), by the National Education Commission on Time and Learning, 1994, Washington, DC: U.S. Department of Education.

Another option is to lengthen the school year. As an illustration of this option, the National Education Commission on Time and Learning (1994) described how the Beacon Day elementary and high schools in Oakland, California, use time:

> At Beacon Day School (elementary) and Beacon High School in Oakland, California, the school year never really ends. At these private schools, the school day is over ten hours long. There is no set vacation period; parents plan vacations to fit family needs; students work in teams by achievement level, not age; letter grades are unknown in the elementary school; and students spend six to eight hours a week on art, music, dance, drama, or martial arts. "There's no summer vacation, so there's extra time to learn," 10-year-old Colin Gage told the commission. (p. 16)

As straightforward as it might seem for a school or district to increase the amount of instructional time, there appears to be no widespread support for doing so. For example, a 1997 poll of American adults found that only 25 percent of those surveyed favored increasing the amount of time students spend in school (see Sadowski, 1998). In addition, when Virginia legislators found that each day added to the school year would cost an additional $13.6 million in state and local funds, support for increasing the length of the school year quickly vanished (see Sadowski, 1998).

Conducting a Time Audit

In lieu of lengthening the school day or school year, a school or district could find ways to use time more efficiently. Toward this end, one of the more useful activities a school or district can engage in is to perform a time audit, a form of self-study. The purpose of conducting this study is to give educators in a school community a sense of the degree to which they use time efficiently and then to use the results to enhance the way they use time.

During the process of conducting a time audit, a school or district estimates a number of time-related quantities, including the following, to arrive at an academic efficiency index: (1) total school time, (2) noninstructional school time, (3) noninstructional class time, (4) nonengaged time, and (5) absenteeism. In short, a school estimates its academic efficiency using the following formula:

> Total School Time
> — noninstructional school time
> — noninstructional class time
> — nonengaged time
> — absenteeism
> _____
> Academic Efficiency

The following pages briefly review the process of conducting a time audit. (A detailed description of the process, along with the necessary worksheets for conducting an audit, are offered in Appendix C.)

Total School Time: Total school time is simply the amount of time per day a student is expected to be in school.

Noninstructional School Time: Noninstructional school time is the time that a school or district dedicates to activities such as the following:

- lunch period
- homeroom
- breaks between classes
- recess
- announcements
- other noninstructional activities (such as fire drills and assemblies)

The difference between total school time and noninstructional school time is class time. This relationship might be graphically depicted as shown in Figure 5.1. The shaded portion of Figure 5.1 represents the proportion of the school day allocated for classes, the time during which students have the opportunity to receive instruction.

Figure 5.1
Class Time

Noninstructional Class Time: As discussed previously, not all of class time that is available for instruction is used for instruction. Indeed, students are not receiving instruction while teachers are engaged in activities like these:

- taking attendance
- passing out papers
- disciplining students
- listening to or making announcements from the office
- socializing with students
- working with one or two students while other students wait

The total time devoted to noninstructional class activities such as these must be subtracted from total class time. The remaining time is instructional class time. The relationship between the time quantities we have discussed so far is depicted in Figure 5.2.

Figure 5.2

Instructional Time

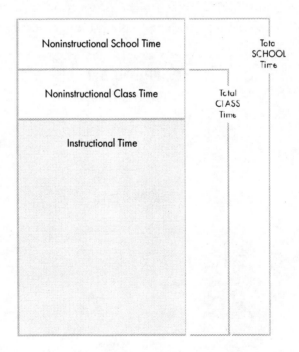

Nonengaged Time: While instruction is occurring, students are either engaged in instructional activities or not. During *engaged time*, students are actively involved in relevant learning tasks. During *nonengaged time*, students are involved in activities such as making transitions to new activities, waiting for help, socializing, or daydreaming. The amount of time students are engaged in academic work has been shown to be significantly related to academic achievement (see Walberg, 1997). This is particularly true for lower-ability students. To illustrate, consider Table 5.3, which highlights the relationship between engaged time and reading achievement for students of differing abilities.

Table 5.3

Correlation Between Engaged Time and Reading Achievement

Lowest 25% In Reading Ability	Middle 50% In Reading Ability	Highest 25% In Reading Ability
Correlation = .70	Correlation = .31	Correlation = .32

Note: Data from *Managing School Resources to Improve Student Achievement*, by R. A. Rossmiller, 1982. Paper presented at the State Superintendent's Conference, Madison, WI.

The correlation (i.e., the relationship) between engaged time and reading achievement for students in the lowest 25 percent in reading was .70, whereas the correlation was .31 and .32 for students in the middle 50 percent and highest 25 percent, respectively. This implies that lower ability students benefit the most from engaged time and are hurt the most when their engaged time is low.

Calculating the average amount of engaged time in a school day helps educators to determine even more precisely the percentage of the school day truly available for student learning. The relationship between the various time estimates calculated thus far is depicted in Figure 5.3.

Absenteeism: The final quantity that a school or district must estimate is the average proportion of absenteeism among students. Obviously, students cannot be engaged in instructional activities (or any other school activities) if they are absent from school. Subtracting this quantity from the total amount of time available in the school results in an estimate of the percentage of time in a school day during which students actually have the opportunity to learn. This is depicted in Figure 5.4.

Figure 5.3
Engaged Time

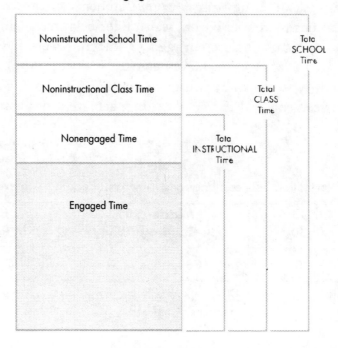

Figure 5.4
Academic Efficiency

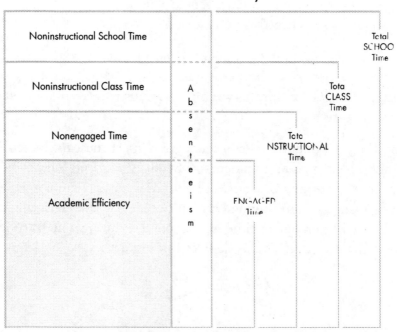

Note that absenteeism cuts across all other factors. Again, this is because students cannot participate in any school activity (instructional or otherwise) if they are absent. The shaded area in Figure 5.4 represents the proportion of time actually available for student learning. As a percentage of the total time, this time has been referred to as the *academic efficiency index* of a school or district (Marzano & Hutchins, 1983).

Over the years, McREL researchers have been able to determine the average values of the academic efficiency index for various levels of schooling. These average values are reported in Table 5.4. As Table 5.4 indicates, high schools have an academic efficiency index of .514, on the average, indicating that 51.4% of the school day is available for student learning.

Table 5.4
Average Academic Efficiency Index Values

High School	.514
Middle School/Junior High	.577
Elementary School	.551

Note: Data from *A+: Achieving Excellence: An Educational Decision-Making and Management System for Leadership, Efficiency, Effectiveness, Excellence,* by the Mid-continent Regional Educational Laboratory, 1991, Aurora, CO: Author.

To illustrate how a school might use the academic efficiency index, assume that a high school has determined that its total school time—from the perspective of an individual student—is 6.0 hours and that its academic efficiency index is 51.4. This school knows that, on the average, only 3.08 hours a day are truly available for student learning. Viewed from this perspective, it seems clear that the effective use of time during a school day can positively impact student learning. Consequently, we recommend that schools and districts engage in a thorough audit of their use of time and then use the results to enhance the way that time is used as much as possible.

Decrease the Number of Standards

Another option for addressing the issue of too much content is to decrease the number of topics that students are expected to master. As described in Chapter 4, this option is strongly suggested by the Third International Mathematics and Science Study (TIMSS), which found that U.S. schools try to cover too much content when compared with schools in other countries. To illustrate the differences in the number of topics addressed by U.S. schools when compared to schools in other countries, consider Table 5.5.

Table 5.5

Number of Topics in Textbooks by Country

Country	Mathematics	
	Grade 4	Grade 8
United States	30 to 35	30 to 35
Germany	20	20
Japan	10	10

Country	Science		
	Grade 4	Grade 8	Grade 12
United States	50 to 65	50 to 65	50 to 65
Germany		7	
Japan	5 to 15	5 to 15	5 to 15

Note: Data taken from *Splintered Vision: An Investigation of U.S. Science and Mathematics Education: Executive Summary* (p. 6), by W. H. Schmidt, C. C. McKnight, and S. A. Raizen, 1996, Lansing, MI: U.S. National Research Center for the Third International Mathematics and Science Study, Michigan State University.

As shown in Table 5.5, U.S. fourth- and eighth-grade mathematics textbooks cover between 30 to 35 topics, whereas textbooks in Germany and Japan cover 20 and 10 topics, respectively. Similarly, whereas U.S. fourth-, eighth-, and twelfth-grade science textbooks address between 50 and 65 topics, Japanese textbooks cover between 5 and 15 topics, and German textbooks cover 7 topics (at least at the eighth grade). In short, the TIMSS study indicates that although U.S. mathematics textbooks address nearly 175 percent as many topics as do German textbooks and 350 percent as many topics than do Japanese textbooks, both German and Japanese students performed better than U.S. students in mathematics. Similarly, although U.S. science textbooks cover more than nine times as many topics than German textbooks and more than four times as many topics than Japanese textbooks, both German and Japanese students significantly outperform U.S. students in their understanding and use of science knowledge. Although other factors may affect test scores, if we accept the findings of the TIMSS researchers, clearly it would benefit U.S. schools to decrease the amount of content they try to cover.

But how is a school district to approach the elimination of content? Asking subject-matter experts to rate or rank the importance or necessity of standards in these content areas might be one strategy for gaining insight into which standards to choose. (McREL is considering initiating a study to implement this approach.) For example, one approach might be to convene a group of subject-matter experts—within a school community or at the state level—and ask them to identify the knowledge in their respective content areas that should be covered given a specified number of hours per day or year during which the content can be taught.

Another option is to ask educators in a community or state to rank order the knowledge that should be taught given a set of time constraints. Still another option is to poll a wider group—parents, citizens and other community members, as well as educators—about what should and should not be included in a K–12 educational experience to determine the information and skills that they consider to be "essential."

Such a strategy would operationalize the historical role of the local community to set policy and establish curriculum. Ravitch (1983) notes that local control traditionally has been a centerpiece of American education. Pulliam (1987) echoes Ravitch's comments, noting that strong involvement of the local community in policy and curricular issues is imperative to effective education. Obviously, allowing teachers and community members to play a role in the process of identifying those standards that are most essential—and by default, those standards that will not be addressed—is probably the ultimate manifestation of local control.

Conclusion

In this chapter, we have reviewed two broad approaches to the complex problem of time that schools and districts might wish to consider further: increasing the amount of time devoted to instruction, and decreasing the number of standards that students are expected to learn across the K–12 years. Educators concerned about the volume of content they are being urged to teach will perhaps be disheartened by the time estimates we present in this chapter. As we demonstrated, by our estimates, a significant increase in the instructional time available in most schools would be needed to teach all of the standards and benchmarks identified as imperative for students to master prior to high school graduation—a challenging undertaking, to say the least.

The second option we introduced in this chapter is to decrease the amount of content that is covered over the course of a K–12 education. We anticipate that the question of how to approach this task will require several years of study to address. Nonetheless, in the next chapter we consider one approach: Of all the content that subject-area experts have identified, what do American adults recognize as information and skills that have been essential in their own lives and that they believe students should learn prior to high school graduation?

Chapter 6

The McREL Standards Survey

As our discussions thus far have shown, there simply is not enough time available over the course of a K–12 education—at least as presently structured—to address all of the knowledge identified in the national standards documents. One way to deal with this problem is to use time more efficiently. Another option is to decrease the number of standards that are addressed by prioritizing standards. As a school or district approaches this second option, at least two critical questions immediately arise: Which standards should we teach? and Who should decide?

One approach is to survey constituent groups about their preferences and then use those preferences to inform the decision-making process. In this chapter, we discuss a survey of U.S. adults that McREL undertook to determine which standards they consider essential for a K–12 education. Schools and districts wrestling with the problem of time might use the results we present here to guide their curricular decisions. They also might undertake their own survey of content and education experts as well as community constituent groups. Either way, it is our hope that these findings will stimulate the thinking of America's educators relative to the issue of how to address content-area standards within the time currently available.

Survey Design and Overview

In an effort to offer a prototype of how a school or district might approach local community members relative to the issue of which standards should be addressed in the curriculum, we developed a set of questionnaires that cover all of the standards in the McREL standards database—those standards that emerged from McREL's previous analysis of 116 national- and state-level standards documents. The questionnaires are reported in their entirety in Appendix D.[11] As shown in Table 6.1, there are four questionnaires in all, each addressing different subject areas.

---

[11]If a school or district wishes to use these questionnaires to conduct a survey at the local level, permission may be obtained by contacting McREL in Aurora, Colorado.

Table 6.1

Subject Areas Covered by the Questionnaires

QUESTIONNAIRE	SUBJECT AREAS COVERED
Questionnaire #1	World History, Health, Mathematics, Foreign Language
Questionnaire #2	U.S. History, Physical Education, Science, Behavioral Studies, Technology
Questionnaire #3	Civics, Language Arts, Life Skills, Economics
Questionnaire #4	Geography, The Arts, Historical Understanding

McREL contracted with the Gallup Organization to administer these questionnaires to a representative sample of U.S. adults regarding the relative importance of the standards in the McREL database.[12] In all, over 2,400 adults responded to the four questionnaires. (To limit the number of standards any one respondent would have to rate, a four-questionnaire design was used, with respondents randomly receiving one of the surveys.) Respondents were asked to consider the following scale relative to each topic, or standard:

- *definitely* necessary for students to learn prior to high school graduation

- *probably* necessary for students to learn prior to high school graduation

- *probably not* necessary for students to learn prior to high school graduation

- *definitely not* necessary for students to learn prior to high school graduation

Using this scale, we rank-ordered the standards in the McREL database relative to their perceived importance by American adults. Specifically, our criterion for ranking was the percentage of respondents who considered the standard definitely necessary for students to learn prior to high school graduation. Each standard was rated independently of the others; respondents were not asked to consider the standards collectively. (Owing to the size of the database, respondents could not be asked to review the standards as a whole and to select what they believed to be an ideal curriculum.)

---

[12]For a comprehensive, technical discussion of the results of the McREL standards survey, see Marzano, Kendall, & Cicchinelli, 1998.

Implications of the Results

The results of this survey offer a way to rank-order subject-area standards in terms of the preferences of the American public. When these findings are considered in light of what is known about the amount of time available in school and estimates of the amount of time necessary to adequately teach the content in each standard (see discussion in Chapter 5), one has a method for determining which standards might be addressed within the time currently available for instruction in the education system and, thus, which standards might be excluded.

The information derived from this study, along with estimates of how long it takes to address the content inherent in each standard, allows for the identification of a "cut-point" for selecting the standards that might be included (and not included) in a K–12 curriculum. To illustrate how such a cut-point could be established, consider the following process.

As discussed in Chapter 5, research indicates that, in general, schools and districts have about 9,042 hours available for instruction over 13 years of schooling (i.e., kindergarten through grade 12). In addition, McREL researchers estimate that five hours are required to teach the content within each benchmark. If we keep a running total of the amount of time it takes to teach each standard beginning with the top-ranked standard, the 9,042-hour limit is reached at the 133rd standard.

Recall from the discussion in Chapter 5 that the estimated number of hours necessary to address each *standard* was computed by multiplying the number of benchmarks by the five hours estimated to teach each benchmark. For example, there are 13 benchmarks identified under Health Standard 9: Understands aspects of substance use and abuse. These benchmarks are reported in Table 6.2.

Table 6.2

Benchmarks for Health Standard 9:
"Understands Aspects of Substance Use and Abuse"
from McREL Standards Database
by Level

LEVEL	BENCHMARK(S)
K–2	1. Knows how to distinguish between helpful and harmful substances
3–5	2. Differentiates between the use and misuse of prescription and nonprescription drugs
	3. Knows influences that promote alcohol, tobacco, and other drug use
	4. Recognizes high-risk substance abuse situations that pose a threat to oneself or others
	5. Knows ways to avoid, recognize, and respond to negative social influences and pressure
6–8	6. Knows conditions that may put people at higher risk for substance abuse problems
	7. Knows factors, signs, and symptoms involved in the development of a drug dependency
	8. Knows the short- and long-term consequences of the use of alcohol, tobacco, and other drugs
	9. Knows public policy approaches to substance abuse control and prevention
	10. Knows community resources that are available to assist people with substance problems
9–12	11. Knows the effects associated with the use of drugs on reproduction and children
	12. Knows how substance abuse often plays a role in dangerous behavior and effects the community
	13. Understands that drug dependencies are treatable diseases/conditions

Note: The benchmarks reported in this table are the abbreviated version, which can be found in Appendix B. The full version can be found in *Content Knowledge: A Compendium of Standards and Benchmarks for K–12 Education* (2nd ed.), by J. S. Kendall & R. J. Marzano, 1997, Aurora, CO: Mid-continent Regional Educational Laboratory.

To determine roughly how much time it would take to teach the content identified under this health standard, we multiplied 13 (the number of benchmarks under this standard) by 5 (the average estimated number of hours needed to adequately address the content in a benchmark). Using this method, we found that the top 133 standards could be addressed within the estimated 9,042 hours of instructional time available across a K–12 education. These 133 standards are listed in Table 6.3.

Table 6.3

Standards that Can Be Addressed in the Time Available
Based on Answers of All Respondents
(Ranked by Highest Percentage of "Definitely" Responses to Survey)

SUBJECT AREA	STANDARD (The number in parentheses is the standard number as reported in Appendix B)	
1. Health	(9)	Understands aspects of substance use and abuse
2. Language Arts	(3)	Uses grammatical and mechanical conventions in written compositions
3. Health	(3)	Understands the relationship of family health to individual health
4. Health	(8)	Knows essential concepts about the prevention and control of disease
5. Technology	(2)	Knows the characteristics and uses of computer software programs
6. Health	(4)	Knows how to maintain mental and emotional health
7. Geography	(1)	Understands the characteristics and uses of maps, globes, and other geographic tools and technologies
8. World History	(41)	Understands the causes and global consequences of World War II
9. Life Work	(7)	Displays reliability and a basic work ethic
10. Life Work	(8)	Operates effectively within organizations
11. Health	(1)	Knows the availability and effective use of health services, products, and information
12. Health	(6)	Understands essential concepts about nutrition and diet
13. U.S. History	(6)	Understands the causes of the American Revolution, the ideas and interests involved in shaping the revolutionary movement, and reasons for the American victory
14. Life Work	(3)	Manages money effectively
15. U.S. History	(13)	Understands the causes of the Civil War
16. Health	(5)	Knows essential concepts and practices concerning injury prevention and safety
17. Life Work	(5)	Makes general preparation for entering the work force
18. Technology	(1)	Knows the characteristics and uses of computer hardware and operating systems
19. Health	(10)	Understands the fundamental concepts of growth and development
20. Mathematics	(9)	Understands the general nature and uses of mathematics
21. Mathematics	(4)	Understands and applies basic and advanced properties of the concepts of measurement
22. Life Work	(4)	Pursues specific jobs

Table 6.3 (continued)
Standards that Can Be Addressed in the Time Available
Based on Answers of All Respondents
(Ranked by Highest Percentage of "Definitely" Responses to Survey)

23. Science	(1)	Understands basic features of the Earth
24. Health	(7)	Knows how to maintain and promote personal health
25. Civics	(24)	Understands the meaning of citizenship in the United States, and knows the requirements for citizenship and naturalization
26. World History	(40)	Understands the search for peace and stability throughout the world in the 1920s and 1930s
27. Civics	(3)	Understands the sources, purposes, and functions of law and the importance of the rule of law for the protection of individual rights and the common good
28. Life Work	(6)	Makes effective use of basic life skills
29. U.S. History	(23)	Understands the causes of the Great Depression and how it affected American society
30. Self-Regulation	(3)	Considers risks
31. Working with Others	(3)	Works well with diverse individuals and in diverse situations
32. Science	(7)	Understands how species depend on one another and on the environment for survival
33. Mathematics	(3)	Uses basic and advanced procedures while performing the processes of computation
34. U.S. History	(25)	Understands the causes and course of World War II, the character of the war at home and abroad, and its reshaping of the U.S. role in world affairs
35. Working with Others	(4)	Displays effective interpersonal communication skills
36. Civics	(4)	Understands the concept of a constitution, the various purposes that constitutions serve, and the conditions that contribute to the establishment and maintenance of constitutional government
37. Language Arts	(7)	Demonstrates competence in the general skills and strategies for reading a variety of informational texts
38. Civics	(1)	Understands ideas about civic life, politics, and government
39. Civics	(8)	Understands the central ideas of American constitutional government and how this form of government has shaped the character of American society
40. World History	(45)	Understands major global trends since Word War II
41. U.S. History	(7)	Understands the impact of the American Revolution on politics, economy, and society

Table 6.3 (continued)
Standards that Can Be Addressed in the Time Available
Based on Answers of All Respondents
(Ranked by Highest Percentage of "Definitely" Responses to Survey)

42. Thinking and Reasoning	(5)	Applies basic trouble-shooting and problem-solving techniques
43. Language Arts	(1)	Demonstrates competence in the general skills and strategies of the writing process
44. Civics	(15)	Understands how the United States Constitution grants and distributes power and responsibilities to national and state government and how it seeks to prevent the abuse of power
45. Civics	(9)	Understands the importance of Americans sharing and supporting certain values, beliefs, and principles of American constitutional democracy
46. Geography	(8)	Understands the characteristics of ecosystems on Earth's surface
47. Language Arts	(4)	Gathers and uses information for research purposes
48. World History	(43)	Understands how post-World War II reconstruction occurred, new international power relations took shape, and colonial empires broke up
49. Self-Regulation	(5)	Maintains a healthy self-concept
50. Health	(2)	Knows environmental and external factors that affect individual and community health
51. Mathematics	(1)	Uses a variety of strategies in the problem-solving process
52. World History	(44)	Understands the search for community, stability, and peace in an interdependent world
53. Language Arts	(2)	Demonstrates competence in the stylistic and rhetorical aspects of writing
54. Physical Education	(4)	Understands how to monitor and maintain a health-enhancing level of physical fitness
55. Self-Regulation	(6)	Restrains impulsivity
56. Working with Others	(1)	Contributes to the overall effort of a group
57. Self-Regulation	(1)	Sets and manages goals
58. U.S. History	(2)	Understands cultural and ecological interactions among previously unconnected people resulting from early European exploration and colonization
59. Self-Regulation	(2)	Performs self-appraisal
60. Thinking and Reasoning	(1)	Understands and applies the basic principles of presenting an argument

Table 6.3 (continued)

Standards that Can Be Addressed in the Time Available
Based on Answers of All Respondents
(Ranked by Highest Percentage of "Definitely" Responses to Survey)

61. U.S. History	(22)	Understands how the United States changed between the post-World War I years and the eve of the Great Depression
62. Physical Education	(5)	Understands the social and personal responsibility associated with participation in physical activity
63. Thinking and Reasoning	(3)	Effectively uses mental processes that are based on identifying similarities and differences (compares, contrasts, classifies)
64. Economics	(6)	Understands the roles government plays in the United States economy
65. World History	(46)	Understands long-term changes and recurring patterns in world history
66. Geography	(7)	Knows the physical processes that shape patterns on Earth's surface
67. World History	(42)	Understands major global trends from 1900 to the end of World War II
68. World History	(39)	Understands the causes and global consequences of World War I
69. U.S. History	(4)	Understands how political, religious, and social institutions emerged in the North American colonies
70. Civics	(18)	Understands the role and importance of law in the American constitutional system and issues regarding the judicial protection of individual rights
71. Science	(5)	Understands the genetic basis for the transfer of biological characteristics from one generation to the next
72. Civics	(11)	Understands the role of diversity in American life and the importance of shared values, political beliefs, and civic beliefs in an increasingly diverse American society
73. Civics	(16)	Understands the major responsibilities of the national government for domestic and foreign policy, and understands how government is financed through taxation
74. Science	(8)	Understands the cycling of matter and flow of energy through the living environment
75. Self-Regulation	(4)	Demonstrates perseverance
76. Science	(16)	Understands the scientific enterprise
77. Working with Others	(2)	Uses conflict-resolution techniques
78. U.S. History	(14)	Understands the course and character of the Civil War and its effects on the American people
79. U.S. History	(24)	Understands how the New Deal addressed the Great Depression, transformed American federalism, and initiated the welfare state

Table 6.3 (continued)
Standards that Can Be Addressed in the Time Available
Based on Answers of All Respondents
(Ranked by Highest Percentage of "Definitely" Responses to Survey)

80. U.S. History	(10)	Understands how the industrial revolution, increasing immigration, the rapid expansion of slavery, and the westward movement changed American lives and led to regional tensions
81. Civics	(2)	Understands the essential characteristics of limited and unlimited governments
82. Working with Others	(5)	Demonstrates leadership skills
83. Behavioral Studies	(1)	Understands that group and cultural influences contribute to human development, identity, and behavior
84. U.S. History	(8)	Understands the institutions and practices of government created during the revolution and how these elements were revised between 1787 and 1815 to create the foundation of the American political system based on the U.S. Constitution and the Bill of Rights
85. U.S. History	(29)	Understands the struggle for racial and gender equality and for the extension of civil liberties
86. Life Work	(2)	Uses various information sources, including those of a technical nature, to accomplish specific tasks
87. Language Arts	(5)	Demonstrates competence in the general skills and strategies of the reading process
88. Science	(14)	Understands the nature of scientific knowledge
89. U.S. History	(16)	Understands how the rise of corporations, heavy industry, and mechanized farming transformed American society
90. U.S. History	(27)	Understands how the Cold War and conflicts in Korea and Vietnam influenced domestic and international politics
91. Economics	(3)	Understands the concept of prices and the interaction of supply and demand in a market economy
92. Life Work	(1)	Makes effective use of basic tools
93. U.S. History	(21)	Understands the changing role of the United States in world affairs through World War I
94. World History	(35)	Understands patterns of nationalism, state-building, and social reform in Europe and the Americas from 1830 to 1914
95. Civics	(20)	Understands the roles of political parties, campaigns, elections, and associations and groups in American politics
96. U.S. History	(5)	Understands how the values and institutions of European economic life took root in the colonies and how slavery reshaped European and African life in the Americas

Table 6.3 (continued)
Standards that Can Be Addressed in the Time Available
Based on Answers of All Respondents
(Ranked by Highest Percentage of "Definitely" Responses to Survey)

97. Civics	(5)	Understands the major characteristics of systems of shared powers and of parliamentary systems
98. Science	(3)	Understands essential ideas about the composition and structure of the universe and the Earth's place in it
99. Science	(11)	Understands energy types, sources, and conversions, and their relationship to heat and temperature
100. Geography	(16)	Understands the changes that occur in the meaning, use, distribution, and importance of resources
101. World History	(26)	Understands how the transoceanic interlinking of all major regions of the world between 1450 and 1600 led to global transformations
102. U.S. History	(3)	Understands why the Americas attracted Europeans, why they brought enslaved Africans to their colonies, and how Europeans struggled for control of North America and the Caribbean
103. Technology	(4)	Understands the nature of technological design
104. Civics	(17)	Understands issues concerning the relationship between state and local governments and the national government and issues pertaining to representation at all three levels of government
105. Civics	(29)	Understands the importance of political leadership, public service, and a knowledgeable citizenry in American constitutional democracy
106. Civics	(28)	Understands how participation in civic and political life can help citizens attain individual and public goals
107. Economics	(5)	Understands unemployment, income, and income distribution in a market economy
108. Behavioral Studies	(2)	Understands various meanings of social group, general implications of group membership, and different ways that groups function
109. Geography	(14)	Understands how human actions modify the physical environment
110. U.S. History	(18)	Understands the rise of the American labor movement and how political issues reflected social and economic changes
111. U.S. History	(26)	Understands the economic boom and social transformation of post-World War II United States
112. World History	(33)	Understands the causes and consequences of the agricultural and industrial revolutions from 1700 to 1850
113. U.S. History	(12)	Understands the sources and character of cultural, religious, and social reform movements in the antebellum period

Table 6.3 (continued)
Standards that Can Be Addressed in the Time Available
Based on Answers of All Respondents
(Ranked by Highest Percentage of "Definitely" Responses to Survey)

114. World History	(29)	Understands the economic, political, and cultural interrelations among peoples of Africa, Europe, and the Americas between 1500 and 1750
115. Economics	(7)	Understands savings, investment, and interest rates
116. World History	(36)	Understands patterns of global change in the era of Western military and economic domination from 1850 to 1914
117. Behavioral Studies	(3)	Understands that interactions among learning, inheritance, and physical development affect human behavior
118. U.S. History	(9)	Understands the United States territorial expansion between 1801 and 1861, and how it affected relations with external powers and Native Americans
119. Mathematics	(6)	Understands and applies basic and advanced concepts of statistics and data analysis
120. Science	(6)	Knows the general structure and functions of cells in organisms
121. Science	(15)	Understands the nature of scientific inquiry
122. U.S. History	(31)	Understands economic, social, and cultural developments in the contemporary United States
123. U.S. History	(15)	Understands how various reconstruction plans succeeded or failed
124. Science	(2)	Understands basic Earth processes
125. U.S. History	(30)	Understands developments in foreign and domestic policies between the Nixon and Clinton presidencies
126. Technology	(3)	Understands relationships among science, technology, society, and the individual
127. U.S. History	(11)	Understands the extension, restriction, and reorganization of political democracy after 1800
128. Geography	(15)	Understands how physical systems affect human systems
129. Language Arts	(8)	Demonstrates competence in speaking and listening as tools for learning
130. Civics	(26)	Understands issues regarding the proper scope and limits of rights and the relationships among personal, political, and economic rights
131. Civics	(25)	Understands issues regarding personal, political, and economic rights
132. Technology	(5)	Understands the nature and operation of systems
133. World History	(38)	Understands reform, revolution, and social change in the world economy in the early century

The K–12 curriculum that would result from a process such as this would have some interesting characteristics. Table 6.4 reports the comparative influence of the various subject-matter areas on the curriculum if a school or district were to use the results of the McREL standards survey to inform its decision-making process relative to curriculum.

Table 6.4

Comparative Influence of Various Subjects on a Curriculum Designed
Using McREL Survey Results (Ranked by Impact on the Curriculum)

Subject Area	Number of Standards in the Standards Database	Number of Standards that Would Be Included in the Curriculum	Number of Standards as a Percentage of the Curriculum*	Percentage of Standards in the Standards Database that Would Be Included in the Curriculum
U.S. History	31	26	19.5%	83.9%
Work Skills†	19	19	14.3%	100.0%
Civics	29	18	13.5%	62.1%
World History	46	14	10.5%	30.4%
Science	16	11	8.3%	68.8%
Health	10	10	7.5%	100.0%
Language Arts	8	7	5.3%	87.5%
Geography	18	6	4.5%	33.3%
Mathematics	9	5	3.8%	55.6%
Technology	5	5	3.8%	100.0%
Economics	10	4	3.0%	40.0%
Behavioral Studies	4	3	2.3%	75.0%
Thinking & Reasoning	6	3	2.3%	50.0%
Physical Education	5	2	1.5%	40.0%
The Arts (Dance, Music, Theatre, Visual Arts)	25	0	0.0%	0.0%
Foreign Language	5	0	0.0%	0.0%
Historical Understanding	2	0	0.0%	0.0%
TOTAL	248**	133	100.1%***	Average: 53.6%

†The 19 work skills standards include standards for the subcategories of working with others (5 standards), self-regulation (6 standards), and life work (8 standards). See Chapter 4 for discussion of these standards.

*The percentages in column 4 were calculated by dividing the number of standards that would be included in the curriculum for each content area (column 3) by 133.

**This number does not include the eight K–4 history standards because the McREL standards survey focused on content that students must know by the end of 12th grade. The content identified under the K–4 history standards is a simpler version of material covered in later grades. Thus, it would have been redundant to include these standards in the survey.

***The result is greater than 100% due to rounding.

There are a number of implications of relying on the results presented in Table 6.4 in terms of content that would—and would not—be included in the curriculum. History standards (U.S. history and world history) would account for 30 percent of the curriculum. Life skills (thinking and reasoning plus the work skills of working with others, self-regulation, and life work) would account for 16.6 percent of the curriculum; civics, for 13.5 percent; and science and mathematics together, for 12.1 percent. Yet, the curriculum would not include a single standard in the arts or foreign languages.

Equally noteworthy is the percentage of the standards in the McREL standards database that would be included in the curriculum. These results are presented in the last column of Table 6.4. For example, 100% of the standards related to work skills (i.e., working with others, self-regulation, and life work), health, and technology would be included in the curriculum. In addition, anywhere from 50 to 87.5% of the standards in U.S. history, civics, science, language arts, mathematics, behavioral studies, and thinking and reasoning would be included in the curriculum. On the other hand, a number of subject areas would have no standards, or very few standards, included in a curriculum designed using the assumptions we have discussed and the preferences for standards identified via the standards survey. Specifically, less than 50 percent of the standards in world history, economics, geography, and physical education would be included and, as we already noted, the curriculum would be devoid of foreign language standards and standards in dance, music, theatre, and the visual arts.

The Problems of Basing a Curriculum Solely on Public Opinion

Clearly, the K–12 curriculum produced if one relies solely on the opinions of the general public would have some strong, unintended, negative consequences. This study indicates that in addition to lacking arts or foreign language standards, important standards in traditionally core subject areas would be excluded from the curriculum. To illustrate, consider the areas of mathematics and science.

The Third International Mathematics and Science Study (TIMSS) (which we briefly discussed in previous chapters) generally is considered the most comprehensive comparison ever conducted of the achievement of U.S. students with that of students in other countries. In fact, according to Pascal Forgione (1998), Commissioner of Educational Statistics, the TIMSS study represents the "most rigorous international study of schools and student achievement ever conducted. . . .The scope of TIMSS is unprecedented in the annals of education research. The international project involved the testing of more than one-half million students in mathematics and science at three grade levels in 41 countries" (p. 5).

In addition to revealing that U.S. mathematics and science curricula cover more topics in less depth than those in other countries, the achievement of U.S. 8th-grade students in mathematics and U.S. 12th-grade students in mathematics and science ranked among the lowest across the countries compared. In particular, the TIMSS report on the twelfth-grade results (U.S. Department of Education, 1998) notes:

> U.S. twelfth graders performed below the international average and among the lowest of the 21 TIMSS countries on the assessment of mathematics general knowledge. U.S. students were outperformed by those in 14 countries, and outperformed those in 2 countries. Among the 21 TIMSS nations, our students' scores were not significantly different from those in 4 countries.
>
> U.S. twelfth graders also performed below the international average and among the lowest of the 21 TIMSS countries on the assessment of science general knowledge. U.S. students were outperformed by students in 11 countries. U.S. students outperformed students in 2 countries. Our students' scores were not significantly different from those of 7 countries. . . .
>
> In all three content areas of advanced mathematics and in all five content areas of physics, U.S. physics and advanced mathematics students' performance was among the lowest of the TIMSS nations. (pp. 13–14)

Although mathematics and science educators across the country have used the TIMSS findings as a mandate to increase the rigor of the U.S. K–12 mathematics and science curriculums, some of the very topics that the TIMSS study suggests emphasizing would be excluded if the results of the McREL standards survey were the primary guide to curriculum design. To illustrate, Table 6.5 lists the "advanced" mathematics topics and science topics on which U.S. students scored unfavorably when compared with students in other countries. Much of the content covered by the topics listed in Table 6.5 relate to standards that would not be included in the curriculum using the assumptions discussed thus far in this section.

Some of the advanced topics listed in Table 6.5 would not be included in the curriculum if one were to strictly follow the results of the McREL standards survey. For example, the advanced mathematics topics of basic geometry, coordinate geometry, polygons and circles, and three-dimensional geometry all belong to mathematics standard 5, "Understands and applies basic and advanced properties of the concepts of geometry." This standard would not be included in a curriculum using the assumptions discussed in this chapter.

Table 6.5

TIMSS Advanced Mathematics and Science Topics
with Poor U.S. Student Performances

ADVANCED MATHEMATICS TOPICS
Numbers, Equations, and Functions: Complex numbers and their properties, permutations and combinations; equations and formulas, and patterns, relations and functions **Calculus:** Infinite processes, and change **Geometry:** Basic geometry, coordinate geometry, polygons and circles, and three-dimensional geometry
ADVANCED SCIENCE TOPICS (Physics)
Mechanics: Dynamics of motion; time, space and motion, types of forces; and fluid behavior **Electricity/Magnetism:** Electricity; and magnetism **Heat:** Physical changes; energy types, sources and conversions; heat and temperature; and kinetic theory **Wave Phenomena:** Sound and vibration; light; and wave phenomena **Modern Physics:** Nuclear chemistry; quantum theory and fundamental particles; beyond the solar system; subatomic particles; and relativity theory

Note: From *Pursuing Excellence: A Study of U.S. Twelfth-Grade Mathematics and Science Achievement in International Context* (pp. 40 and 48) by the U.S. Department of Education, National Center for Education Statistics, 1998, Washington, DC: U.S. Government Printing Office.

Findings and observations such as these call into question the advisability of using the opinions of the American public at large as the primary determiner of what should be included in the K–12 curriculum. A more prudent strategy might be to devise a strategy for striking a balance between the suggestions of the general public and the guidance of the nation's subject-matter specialists.

Differences Between Groups of Respondents

Thus far this chapter has focused on the overall results of the McREL standards survey. This section highlights particularly noteworthy findings relative to differences in responses based on respondent education level.

To determine whether answers varied among different groups of respondents, each questionnaire sought demographic data about respondents. The questions posed are reprinted in Exhibit 6.1. Not all of the demographic variables produced findings that were significant in a practical sense in terms of differences among respondents. Of the questions listed in Exhibit 6.1, education level presented the most interpretable results.

Exhibit 6.1

Demographic Questions

These last questions are for classification purposes. As with the other responses you have given, there will be no linkage of your answers to you personally. Gallup will keep all of your answers strictly confidential.

1. Please mark the box that corresponds to your age:
   - ❑ 18–24   ❑ 55–64
   - ❑ 25–34   ❑ 65–74
   - ❑ 35–44   ❑ 75 or older
   - ❑ 45–54

2. Please mark the highest level of formal education you have completed:
   - ❑ 8th grade or less
   - ❑ Some high school
   - ❑ High school graduate
   - ❑ Trade, Technical or Vocational Training Beyond High School
   - ❑ Some college, including Community or Junior College
   - ❑ Undergraduate College or University Degree
   - ❑ Graduate School Course Work or Degree

3. To which of the following race or ethnic groups do you <u>primarily</u> consider yourself to belong? (Please mark one box only.)
   - ❑ Black or African-American
   - ❑ Asian
   - ❑ Pacific Islander
   - ❑ Hispanic
   - ❑ Native American, including American Indian, Eskimo and Aleut
   - ❑ Origin in Indian sub-continent
   - ❑ Other

4. Currently, are you employed full-time, part-time, or not employed?
   - ❑ Full-time
   - ❑ Part-time
   - ❑ Not employed

5. Which of the following categories represents your total annual household income, before taxes:
   - ❑ Under $15,000 (Under $288 per week)
   - ❑ $15,000 to $24,999 ($289 to $480 per week)
   - ❑ $25,000 to $34,999 ($481 to $673 per week)
   - ❑ $35,000 to $39,999 ($674 to $769 per week)
   - ❑ $40,000 to $49,999 ($770 to $961 per week)
   - ❑ $50,000 to $59,999 ($962 to $1,154 per week)
   - ❑ $60,000 to $74,999
   - ❑ $75,000 to $99,999
   - ❑ $100,000 to $124,999
   - ❑ $125,000 or more

6. Are you male or female?
   - ❑ Male   ❑ Female

7. In which state do you have your main residence? ❑❑ (Example: "AZ" for Arizona)
   - ❑ Main residence is outside of the 50 U.S. States

For purposes of these analyses, responses to the education-level question were dichotomized into the following two categories: (1) respondents whose educational experience included some type of formal study beyond high school (i.e, trade school, technical, or vocational training beyond high school; some college, including community college or junior college; undergraduate college or university degree; graduate school course work or degree) and (2) respondents whose formal educational experience terminated at high school or below. When the differences between the two groups were analyzed in terms of the standards that would be included in the curriculum (considering the 9,042-hour limit on available instructional time), somewhat different patterns emerged. Table 6.6 presents an accounting of the number of standards from various subject areas that would be included in the curriculum for both groups.

Table 6.6

Standards that Would Be Included in the Curriculum
(Based on "Definitely" Responses by Respondent Education Level)

Subject Area	Number of Standards and Percentage of Curriculum Using Highest Percentage of "Definitely" Responses			
	Respondents with More Than a High School Education		Respondents with High School Education or Less	
	Number of Standards	Percentage of Curriculum	Number of Standards	Percentage of Curriculum
U.S. History	29	21.8%	19	15.1%
Civics	16	12.0%	18	14.3%
World History	14	10.5%	13	10.3%
Science	13	9.8%	10	7.9%
Health	10	7.5%	10	7.9%
Life Work	8	6.0%	8	6.3%
Language Arts	7	5.3%	7	5.6%
Self-Regulation	6	4.5%	6	4.8%
Geography	5	3.8%	6	4.8%
Mathematics	5	3.8%	4	3.2%
Working With Others	5	3.8%	5	4.0%
Economics	4	3.0%	5	4.0%
Thinking and Reasoning	4	3.0%	3	2.4%
Behavioral Studies	3	2.3%	4	3.2%
Physical Education	2	1.5%	3	2.4%
Technology	2	1.5%	5	4.0%
The Arts (Dance, Music, Theatre, Visual Arts)	0	0.0%	0	0.0%
Foreign Language	0	0.0%	0	0.0%
TOTAL	133*	100.1%**	126*	100.2%**

*The difference in the numbers of standards that would be included in the curriculum (assuming 9,042 hours available for instruction) is due to the differing amounts of time required to address individual standards given the varying number of benchmarks that different standards include. (See discussion of time in Chapter 5.)

**The result is greater than 100% due to rounding.

As Table 6.6 shows, a curriculum designed based on the opinions of Americans with an education background beyond high school would include more standards in mathematics, science, world history, and thinking and reasoning. Conversely, the curriculum would include fewer standards in civics, economics, geography, physical education, technology, and behavioral studies. These differences are more than cosmetic. Some interesting patterns also are found when the number of standards that would be included in the curriculum for the "core" subject areas (considering the limitation of time) are compared between the two education-level subgroups. Table 6.7 compares the relative emphasis on core subject areas—mathematics, science, history (U.S. and world), language arts, and geography—for these two groups.

Table 6.7

Comparison of Number of Core Subject-Area Standards
that Would Be Included in the Curriculum
(Based on "Definitely" Responses by Respondent Education Level)

Subject Area	Respondents with More Than High School Education	Respondents with High School Education or Less	All Respondents
History (U.S. & World)	43	32	39
Science	13	10	11
Language Arts	7	7	7
Mathematics	5	4	5
Geography	5	6	6
TOTAL	73	59	68

The number of standards from core subject areas that would be included in the curriculum, given assumptions about available time, ranges from a high of 73 to a low of 59. Table 6.7 shows that when standards were ranked based on the answers of U.S. adults with more than a high-school education, more standards were included from the core subject areas (i.e., mathematics, science, history, language arts, and geography) than when standards were ranked using the answers of U.S. adults with a high school diploma or less or using the answers of all survey respondents. For this reason, we recommend that a school or district wishing to factor these survey results into its decision-making process relative to curriculum emphases use the standards that the more highly educated respondents most often rated as definitely necessary for students to learn. The standards that can be addressed in the 9,042 hours available are listed in Table 6.8.

Table 6.8

Standards that Can Be Addressed in the Time Available
Based on Answers of Respondents with More Than a High School Education
(Ranked by Highest Percentage of "Definitely" Responses to Survey)

SUBJECT AREA	STANDARD (The number in parentheses is the standard number as reported in Appendix B)	
1. Health	(9)	Understands aspects of substance use and abuse
2. Language Arts	(3)	Uses grammatical and mechanical conventions in written compositions
3. Health	(3)	Understands the relationship of family health to individual health
4. U.S. History	(13)	Understands the causes of the Civil War
5. U.S. History	(6)	Understands the causes of the American Revolution, the ideas and interests involved in shaping the revolutionary movement, and reasons for the American victory
6. World History	(41)	Understands the causes and global consequences of World War II
7. Technology	(2)	Knows the characteristics and uses of computer software programs
8. Health	(8)	Knows essential concepts about the prevention and control of disease
9. Science	(1)	Understands basic features of the Earth
10. Geography	(1)	Understands the characteristics and uses of maps, globes, and other geographic tools and technologies
11. Health	(4)	Knows how to maintain mental and emotional health
12. Health	(1)	Knows the availability and effective use of health services, products, and information
13. Health	(6)	Understands essential concepts about nutrition and diet
14. U.S. History	(25)	Understands the causes and course of World War II, the character of the war at home and abroad, and its reshaping of the U.S. role in world affairs
15. Mathematics	(9)	Understands the general nature and uses of mathematics
16. World History	(40)	Understands the search for peace and stability throughout the world in the 1920s and 1930s
17. Civics	(1)	Understands ideas about civic life, politics, and government
18. Civics	(4)	Understands the concept of a constitution, the various purposes that constitutions serve, and the conditions that contribute to the establishment and maintenance of constitutional government
19. Language Arts	(7)	Demonstrates competence in the general skills and strategies for reading a variety of informational texts
20. U.S. History	(23)	Understands the causes of the Great Depression and how it affected American society

Table 6.8 (continued)

Standards that Can Be Addressed in the Time Available
Based on Answers of Respondents with More Than a High School Education
(Ranked by Highest Percentage of "Definitely" Responses to Survey)

21. Working with Others	(3)	Works well with diverse individuals and in diverse situations
22. Life Work	(4)	Pursues specific jobs
23. Science	(7)	Understands how species depend on one another and on the environment for survival
24. Mathematics	(3)	Uses basic and advanced procedures while performing the processes of computation
25. Civics	(8)	Understands the central ideas of American constitutional government and how this form of government has shaped the character of American society
26. Life Work	(8)	Operates effectively within organizations
27. Life Work	(7)	Displays reliability and a basic work ethic
28. Self-Regulation	(3)	Considers risks
29. Mathematics	(4)	Understands and applies basic and advanced properties of the concepts of measurement
30. Language Arts	(1)	Demonstrates competence in the general skills and strategies of the writing process
31. Technology	(1)	Knows the characteristics and uses of computer hardware and operating systems
32. Civics	(3)	Understands the sources, purposes, and functions of law and the importance of the rule of law for the protection of individual rights and the common good
33. Health	(5)	Knows essential concepts and practices concerning injury prevention and safety
34. U.S. History	(7)	Understands the impact of the American Revolution on politics, economy, and society
35. World History	(45)	Understands major global trends since Word War II
36. Thinking and Reasoning	(3)	Effectively uses mental processes that are based on identifying similarities and differences (compares, contrasts, classifies)
37. Health	(10)	Understands the fundamental concepts of growth and development
38. Life Work	(3)	Manages money effectively
39. Language Arts	(4)	Gathers and uses information for research purposes
40. Civics	(9)	Understands the importance of Americans sharing and supporting certain values, beliefs, and principles of American constitutional democracy

Table 6.8 (continued)

Standards that Can Be Addressed in the Time Available
Based on Answers of Respondents with More Than a High School Education
(Ranked by Highest Percentage of "Definitely" Responses to Survey)

41. Civics	(24)	Understands the meaning of citizenship in the United States, and knows the requirements for citizenship and naturalization
42. Working with Others	(4)	Displays effective interpersonal communication skills
43. Life Work	(5)	Makes general preparation for entering the work force
44. Health	(7)	Knows how to maintain and promote personal health
45. Language Arts	(2)	Demonstrates competence in the stylistic and rhetorical aspects of writing
46. Mathematics	(1)	Uses a variety of strategies in the problem-solving process
47. Working with Others	(1)	Contributes to the overall effort of a group
48. Civics	(15)	Understands how the United States Constitution grants and distributes power and responsibilities to national and state government and how it seeks to prevent the abuse of power
49. Thinking and Reasoning	(5)	Applies basic trouble-shooting and problem-solving techniques
50. U.S. History	(4)	Understands how political, religious, and social institutions emerged in the North American colonies
51. U.S. History	(2)	Understands cultural and ecological interactions among previously unconnected people resulting from early European exploration and colonization
52. U.S. History	(10)	Understands how the industrial revolution, increasing immigration, the rapid expansion of slavery, and the westward movement changed American lives and led to regional tensions
53. Self-Regulation	(1)	Sets and manages goals
54. World History	(43)	Understands how post-World War II reconstruction occurred, new international power relations took shape, and colonial empires broke up
55. U.S. History	(29)	Understands the struggle for racial and gender equality and for the extension of civil liberties
56. Geography	(8)	Understands the characteristics of ecosystems on Earth's surface
57. Science	(8)	Understands the cycling of matter and flow of energy through the living environment
58. U.S. History	(22)	Understands how the United States changed between the post-World War I years and the eve of the Great Depression
59. Life Work	(6)	Makes effective use of basic life skills
60. U.S. History	(24)	Understands how the New Deal addressed the Great Depression, transformed American federalism, and initiated the welfare state
61. Geography	(7)	Knows the physical processes that shape patterns on Earth's surface

Table 6.8 (continued)

Standards that Can Be Addressed in the Time Available
Based on Answers of Respondents with More Than a High School Education
(Ranked by Highest Percentage of "Definitely" Responses to Survey)

62. U.S. History	(5)	Understands how the values and institutions of European economic life took root in the colonies and how slavery reshaped European and African life in the Americas
63. Self-Regulation	(2)	Performs self-appraisal
64. Economics	(6)	Understands the roles government plays in the United States economy
65. World History	(44)	Understands the search for community, stability, and peace in an interdependent world
66. Behavioral Studies	(1)	Understands that group and cultural influences contribute to human development, identity, and behavior
67. Economics	(3)	Understands the concept of prices and the interaction of supply and demand in a market economy
68. Thinking and Reasoning	(1)	Understands and applies the basic principles of presenting an argument
69. Civics	(16)	Understands the major responsibilities of the national government for domestic and foreign policy, and understands how government is financed through taxation
70. Self-Regulation	(6)	Restrains impulsivity
71. Self-Regulation	(5)	Maintains a healthy self-concept
72. U.S. History	(8)	Understands the institutions and practices of government created during the revolution and how these elements were revised between 1787 and 1815 to create the foundation of the American political system based on the U.S. Constitution and the Bill of Rights
73. Civics	(11)	Understands the role of diversity in American life and the importance of shared values, political beliefs, and civic beliefs in an increasingly diverse American society
74. Science	(5)	Understands the genetic basis for the transfer of biological characteristics from one generation to the next
75. World History	(46)	Understands long-term changes and recurring patterns in world history
76. Physical Education	(4)	Understands how to monitor and maintain a health-enhancing level of physical fitness
77. Working with Others	(2)	Uses conflict-resolution techniques
78. Civics	(18)	Understands the role and importance of law in the American constitutional system and issues regarding the judicial protection of individual rights
79. World History	(42)	Understands major global trends from 1900 to the end of World War II
80. World History	(39)	Understands the causes and global consequences of World War I
81. Civics	(2)	Understands the essential characteristics of limited and unlimited governments

Table 6.8 (continued)

Standards that Can Be Addressed in the Time Available
Based on Answers of Respondents with More Than a High School Education
(Ranked by Highest Percentage of "Definitely" Responses to Survey)

82. U.S. History	(16)	Understands how the rise of corporations, heavy industry, and mechanized farming transformed American society
83. U.S. History	(14)	Understands the course and character of the Civil War and its effects on the American people
84. Physical Education	(5)	Understands the social and personal responsibility associated with participation in physical activity
85. U.S. History	(3)	Understands why the Americas attracted Europeans, why they brought enslaved Africans to their colonies, and how Europeans struggled for control of North America and the Caribbean
86. Science	(14)	Understands the nature of scientific knowledge
87. U.S. History	(27)	Understands how the Cold War and conflicts in Korea and Vietnam influenced domestic and international politics
88. Science	(16)	Understands the scientific enterprise
89. World History	(35)	Understands patterns of nationalism, state-building, and social reform in Europe and the Americas from 1830 to 1914
90. Science	(3)	Understands essential ideas about the composition and structure of the universe and the Earth's place in it
91. Civics	(5)	Understands the major characteristics of systems of shared powers and of parliamentary systems
92. U.S. History	(31)	Understands economic, social, and cultural developments in the contemporary United States
93. U.S. History	(21)	Understands the changing role of the United States in world affairs through World War I
94. Health	(2)	Knows environmental and external factors that affect individual and community health
95. U.S. History	(26)	Understands the economic boom and social transformation of post-World War II United States
96. World History	(26)	Understands how the transoceanic interlinking of all major regions of the world between 1450 and 1600 led to global transformations
97. Self-Regulation	(4)	Demonstrates perseverance
98. U.S. History	(9)	Understands the United States territorial expansion between 1801 and 1861, and how it affected relations with external powers and Native Americans
99. Behavioral Studies	(2)	Understands various meanings of social group, general implications of group membership, and different ways that groups function
100. U.S. History	(12)	Understands the sources and character of cultural, religious, and social reform movements in the antebellum period

Table 6.8 (continued)
Standards that Can Be Addressed in the Time Available
Based on Answers of Respondents with More Than a High School Education
(Ranked by Highest Percentage of "Definitely" Responses to Survey)

101. Science	(11)	Understands energy types, sources, and conversions, and their relationship to heat and temperature
102. Science	(6)	Knows the general structure and functions of cells in organisms
103. Language Arts	(5)	Demonstrates competence in the general skills and strategies of the reading process
104. U.S. History	(11)	Understands the extension, restriction, and reorganization of political democracy after 1800
105. Behavioral Studies	(3)	Understands that interactions among learning, inheritance, and physical development affect human behavior
106. Mathematics	(6)	Understands and applies basic and advanced concepts of statistics and data analysis
107. Economics	(5)	Understands unemployment, income, and income distribution in a market economy
108. Civics	(28)	Understands how participation in civic and political life can help citizens attain individual and public goals
109. Civics	(29)	Understands the importance of political leadership, public service, and a knowledgeable citizenry in American constitutional democracy
110. U.S. History	(15)	Understands how various reconstruction plans succeeded or failed
111. Civics	(17)	Understands issues concerning the relationship between state and local governments and the national government and issues pertaining to representation at all three levels of government
112. World History	(33)	Understands the causes and consequences of the agricultural and industrial revolutions from 1700 to 1850
113. Life Work	(1)	Makes effective use of basic tools
114. Working with Others	(5)	Demonstrates leadership skills
115. World History	(29)	Understands the economic, political, and cultural interrelations among peoples of Africa, Europe, and the Americas between 1500 and 1750
116. U.S. History	(28)	Understands domestic policies in the post-World War II period
117. Civics	(20)	Understands the roles of political parties, campaigns, elections, and associations and groups in American politics
118. Life Work	(2)	Uses various information sources, including those of a technical nature, to accomplish specific tasks
119. Geography	(14)	Understands how human actions modify the physical environment
120. Science	(10)	Understands basic concepts about the structure and properties of matter
121. World History	(36)	Understands patterns of global change in the era of Western military and economic domination from 1850 to 1914

Table 6.8 (continued)

Standards that Can Be Addressed in the Time Available
Based on Answers of Respondents with More Than a High School Education
(Ranked by Highest Percentage of "Definitely" Responses to Survey)

122. Science	(2)	Understands basic Earth processes
123. Science	(15)	Understands the nature of scientific inquiry
124. Science	(9)	Understands the basic concepts of the evolution of species
125. U.S. History	(18)	Understands the rise of the American labor movement and how political issues reflected social and economic changes
126. U.S. History	(17)	Understands massive immigration after 1870 and how new social patterns, conflicts, and ideas of national unity developed amid growing cultural diversity
127. Economics	(7)	Understands savings, investment, and interest rates
128. U.S. History	(30)	Understands developments in foreign and domestic policies between the Nixon and Clinton presidencies
129. Language Arts	(6)	Demonstrates competence in general skills and strategies for reading a variety of literary texts
130. U.S. History	(20)	Understands how Progressives and others addressed problems of industrial capitalism, urbanization, and political corruption
131. Geography	(16)	Understands the changes that occur in the meaning, use, distribution, and importance of resources
132. World History	(38)	Understands reform, revolution, and social change in the world economy in the early 20th century
133. Thinking and Reasoning	(2)	Understands and applies basic principles of logic and reasoning

Conclusion

The McREL standards survey results offer guidance in creating a comprehensive curriculum given the constraints of "available" instructional time in a typical K–12 education system. The findings suggest those content areas that might be emphasized as well as standards that might be selected within content areas. In addition, the survey results point to a number of standards that very few respondents rated as "definitely" necessary for students to learn prior to high school graduation.

This chapter also presents differences in preferences relative to specific standards and content areas for respondent subgroups created on the basis of education level. It appears that there are some significant differences in opinions between groups of respondents in terms of what is essential for students to know and be able to do as a result of K–12 education. This implies that schools and districts must determine if they will use the composite opinions of the members of their communities or weight the opinions of some groups within the community more heavily than those of others.

However, no matter how well a district reconciles the differences of opinions between the various groups within its community, the perplexing problem of time still remains: Within the current system, there is simply not enough time to cover in-depth all of the standards that have been identified as important by subject-matter experts. Fortunately, there is a way to address all of the knowledge deemed important by these specialists within the current structure of schooling. This solution is discussed in the next chapter.

Chapter 7

The Critical Role of Vocabulary: The Extensive Curriculum

If a school or district tries to solve the time problem by first prioritizing standards and then using that priority listing to determine which standards to teach, some subject-matter standards considered highly important by some groups invariably will be excluded. As we saw in Chapter 6, when the opinions of the public were used to rank the standards identified by specialists, none of the content in dance, music, theatre, visual arts, and foreign language was included in the curriculum, given considerations about time. In addition, important standards from core subject areas, such as mathematics and science, were excluded. A key issue, then, is whether a curriculum can be devised that at least exposes students to all of the content in the standards identified by subject-matter specialists. It was Hirsch who proposed a way out of this apparent dilemma.

Hirsch's Extensive and Intensive Curriculums

In his first book, *Cultural Literacy: What Every American Needs to Know* (1987/1988), Hirsch introduced the notion of a two-part curriculum: the extensive curriculum and the intensive curriculum. As described by Hirsch, the extensive curriculum is comprised of that knowledge about which all students should have a passing understanding; the intensive curriculum is comprised of that knowledge students should know in depth. A central feature of this two-part curriculum is that all students are exposed to a common extensive curriculum. However, the intensive curriculum to which students are exposed might differ significantly. Hirsch (1987/1988) explained this difference in the following way:

> The conception of a two-part curriculum avoids the idea that all children should study identical materials. It also resists the lure of a core curriculum, if that proposal is taken to mean that all high school graduates should study, say, *Romeo and Juliet*. A common extensive curriculum would ensure that students have some information about *Romeo and Juliet*, but in their intensive curriculum they might study *The Tempest* or *Twelfth Night* in detail. If a school decided that all its students

should read two Shakespeare plays in depth, even the most convinced traditionalists would find it hard to agree on which two plays they should be. Schools can find means of imparting extensive information side by side with an approach that conveys intensive knowledge as well, without imposing an arbitrary core curriculum. (p. 128)

Hirsch's recommendation for the content of the extensive curriculum was the list of 4,552 terms in his 1987 book and, subsequently, his 1988 revised list of 4,982 terms. As detailed in Chapter 2 of this work, we believe Hirsch's lists are flawed and do not offer an unbiased expert accounting of the content to which students should be exposed. Nonetheless, Hirsch's idea of an extensive curriculum has great merit for a number of reasons. First, it is based on sound research that indicates the importance of knowing basic terms, phrases, and events (see, e.g., Stitch et al., 1997; Anderson & Freebody, 1981; Nagy & Anderson, 1984; Nagy, 1988; McKeown & Curtis, 1987). Second, it provides a way for students to gain a general understanding of important content knowledge in a time-efficient manner. A general understanding benefits students in and of itself, but also provides useful "hooks" for students as they encounter the information later in more depth.

The Nature of Vocabulary

Hirsch's basic proposal was to teach his list of 4,552/4,982 terms and phrases as "vocabulary" items. In fact, Hirsch (1987/1988) initially referred to his list of terms and phrases as a "national vocabulary" (p. 139).

Hirsch's recognition of the singular importance of vocabulary was a powerful insight on his part. In terms of factors that enhance academic learning, vocabulary knowledge has few equals. This is because the words we use are indicators of the way we organize the world around us. In fact, linguists (see, e.g., Condon, 1968) explain that words provide us with new ways of perceiving the world. For example, before taking a course in astronomy, you might look at the night sky through a telescope and see only a sea of stars. After a few weeks of the course, however, you might begin to recognize the morning or evening star as a planet—a distinction you had not seen before. The creation of labels (words) is the tool we use to structure perceptions; new labels foster new perceptions. As linguist Condon (1968) notes, "when names are learned we see what we had not seen before, for we now know what to look for" (p. 31).

Given the nature of words, it is no wonder that sociologists commonly analyze the words used within a culture to determine what people consider important. The more important a phenomenon is within a society, the more words people will develop to represent that phenomenon. To illustrate, as far back as 1911, sociologist Boas (cited in Clark & Clark, 1977) noted that the Eskimo language has four words for snow, whereas English has only one. Similarly, in his study of the Garo of Burma, Burling (1970) concluded that since the Garo need to distinguish among more kinds of rice than other cultures do, their language has more words for rice. Clark and Clark (1977) explain that the Garo have created many distinctions about rice since it is so important to their culture. Consequently, they think about rice in ways other cultures do not, simply because Garo has more words. Similarly, Anderson (1990) noted that the Hanunoo people in the Philippines have 92 names for different varieties of rice because of its importance in their culture. Words, then, are the organizers for our experience of the world. They are pivotal to our ability to make sense of the world.

Hirsch expands the discussion of vocabulary, maintaining that these terms and phrases, which make up the content of shared background knowledge, are critical to reading comprehension. Discussing the findings of Jeanne Chall, Hirsch (1987/1988) notes:

> Professor Chall is one of several reading specialists who have observed that "world knowledge" is essential to the development of reading and writing skills. What she calls world knowledge I call cultural literacy, namely, the network of information that all competent readers possess. It is background knowledge, stored in their minds, that enables them to take up a newspaper and read it with an adequate level of comprehension. (p. 2)

The critical relationship vocabulary has to reading in particular, and learning in general, explains why some students have great difficulty in school from the day they first walk through the classroom door. For example, in 1941, Smith (cited in Nagy & Herman, 1984) found that for students in grades four through twelve, there was about a 6,000-word gap between students at the 25th and 50th percentiles on standardized tests. Using a more advanced method of calculating vocabulary size, Nagy and Herman (1984) estimated the difference to be anywhere between 4,500 and 5,400 words for low- versus high-achieving students. They also found a similar difference among students from different socioeconomic strata; specifically, they estimated a 4,700-word difference in vocabulary knowledge between upper- and lower-SES students. Similarly, they estimated that middle-class first graders know 50 percent more words than do lower-class first graders.

These findings have motivated some researchers to assert that vocabulary instruction should be a focal point of education, especially for students from more disadvantaged backgrounds (see, e.g., Marzano & Marzano, 1988). Indeed, after an extensive review of various programs designed for the educationally disadvantaged, researcher Becker (1977) recommended that intensive vocabulary training be a key aspect of all such programs.

Just as Hirsch's idea of vocabulary as a critical tool for enhancing student learning was a powerful insight, so, too, were his ideas about teaching vocabulary. His basic position was that students should be required to learn only very general knowledge regarding the terms and phrases he set forth in his books. Hirsch maintained that students should not be required to learn detailed definitions of each word or phrase; rather, they should be expected to possess relatively general—but commonly held—knowledge about each term or phrase.

To validate his position, Hirsch elaborated on a common theory of memory, technically referred to as *schema theory*. According to schema theory, when we read or hear a word, what we know about that word automatically comes to mind. For example, if you read or hear the words "civil war," characteristics such as the following may come to mind:

- conflict over slavery
- between the North and South
- in the mid-1800s
- Gettysburg was a major battle
- Abraham Lincoln
- General Grant

An individual's schema for any word or phrase, then, comprises those pieces of information that he or she associates with the word or phrase. A key aspect of schemata is that the information is stored in a hierarchic fashion, with the more common knowledge at the top, most accessible levels. To exemplify this idea, Hirsch related the findings of a study by psychologists Collins and Quillian (1969). Collins and Quillian posited that an individual's schema for the word *canary* might be depicted in a hierarchic fashion like the following:

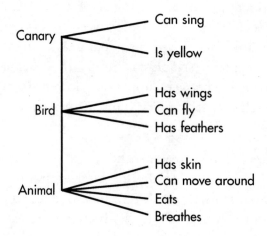

If it is true that information closest to the top of the hierarchy is most available, then people should remember the top-level information more quickly than the bottom-level information. Collins and Quillian's study tested this hypothesis by providing subjects with sentences like the following:

Canaries can move around.

Canaries are yellow.

Canaries can fly.

Subjects were asked to determine whether each sentence was true or false. According to schema theory, people should be able to verify the accuracy of sentences that come from the higher levels of the schema more quickly than sentences that come from the lower levels of the schema. The study's findings supported the hierarchic schema hypothesis. Hirsch (1988) made the following comments about the findings:

> Collins' and Quillian's observations suggest that the top portion of a schema is the important part to know. The schema canary can yield an indefinite number of facts and association [*sic*] by remote inference from knowledge of the world: canaries have backbones; canaries have their own special pattern of DNA; canaries are descended from reptiles; canaries must drink water; canaries mate; canaries die. One could go on this way for a long time, with specifications not only from biological but from physical knowledge: canaries obey the law of gravity and the laws of motion, and so on. But this secondary information about canaries is not important in communicating with fellow human beings. What is functional in reading, writing, and conversing is the distinctive system of traits in the schemata we use—the traits that differentiate canaries from other birds: their smallness, yellowness, ability to sing, use in human culture, being kept in cages, and so on. We need to know the primary traits commonly associated with canary in our culture in order to deploy the associations rapidly when we encounter the word *canary* in reading. (pp. 58–59)

Since the Collins and Quillian experiment, a number of other studies have demonstrated the hierarchic nature of human knowledge. (For a review of the research, see Anderson, 1990, 1995.)

Based on research evidence that top-level schema information is that which is necessary and sufficient for general literacy purposes, Hirsch (1987/1988) reasoned that schools should address the learning of his national vocabulary with a great deal of latitude and that students should be held accountable for only general knowledge of his 4,546/4,982 terms and phrases.

> The nature of this world knowledge as it exists in the minds of literate adults is typically elementary and incomplete. People reliably share just a few associations about canaries, such as yellow, sing, kept in cages, but not much more. Literate people know who Falstaff is, that he is fat, likes to eat and drink, but they can't reliably name the Shakespeare plays in which he appears. They know who Eisenhower was, and might recognize "military-industrial complex," but they can't be counted on to state anything else about Eisenhower's Farewell Address. In short, the information that literate people dependably share is extensive but limited—a characteristic central to this discussion. (p. 127)

Again, Hirsch's ideas have merit. Teaching vocabulary words and phrases at a relatively general level makes sound, cognitive sense.

Is Teaching Vocabulary a Practical Solution?

If Hirsch is correct in his assertion that learning important vocabulary terms and phrases is the cornerstone of understanding, how practical is his suggestion of trying to teach 4,982 terms? Research indicates that his idea is very practical. (For a comprehensive discussion of the research on vocabulary instruction, see Stahl & Fairbanks, 1986; and McKeown & Curtis, 1987.) Specifically, researchers have found that on average, vocabulary programs in schools attempt to teach students about 10 to 12 new words per week. Over an entire year, such a program would address 420 new words. However, year-long vocabulary programs are rare in education. This is because educators generally assume that there are simply too many words in the English language to teach. Specifically, it has been estimated that there are about 88,500 words students encounter in the print material they are exposed to in school. Even if 420 new words are taught each year, in thirteen years of schooling students would be taught only 5,460 words. Obviously, 5,460 words are only a small portion of the 88,500 words students will encounter. These figures have led some researchers (e.g., Nagy & Herman, 1984; Nagy, Herman, & Anderson, 1985; Beck, McKeown, & Omanson, 1984) to conclude that teaching vocabulary is an instructional activity that does not have a high enough payoff to warrant the effort it takes. Fortunately, this conclusion is not supported by the research.

Research (e.g., Stahl & Fairbanks, 1986) indicates that even when there is no attempt to ensure that the words students are taught are ones they will need to know when learning new content, the effect on their achievement is substantial. Specifically, teaching vocabulary has been shown to increase students' ability to understand new content by 12 percentile points (Stahl & Fairbanks, 1986). To illustrate, assume that two students of equal ability are asked to read and understand new information. However, student A is in a program where about 10 to 12 new vocabulary words are taught each week. Student B does not receive this instruction. Now assume that students A and B take a standardized test on the new content and that student B receives a score that places him at the 50th percentile relative to other students in the class. All else being equal, student A will receive a score that places her at the 62nd percentile on that same test simply because she received systematic vocabulary instruction. A 12 percentile point increase in achievement is not insignificant in a practical sense.

The effects of vocabulary instruction are even more powerful when the words selected are those that students most likely will need to know as they encounter new content. Specifically, research (Stahl & Fairbanks, 1986) indicates that student achievement will increase by 33 percentile points when vocabulary instruction focuses on specific words that are important to what they are learning. To illustrate, again consider students A and B, who have been asked to read and understand new content. Student B, who has not received systematic vocabulary instruction, receives a score on the test that puts him at the 50th percentile. Student A, who has received systematic instruction on words *that have been specifically selected because they are important to the new content*, will obtain a score that puts her at 83rd percentile.

Example

Given this rather dramatic potential gain for students in terms of their understanding of new content, it is hard to understand why some educators are reluctant to emphasize vocabulary. In fact, it is probably safe to say that few, if any, school districts in the country use systematic vocabulary programs designed for all students at all grade levels. One possible reason for the underuse of vocabulary instruction is that it is assumed to take too much time. Again, research findings provide some guidance here. Stahl and Fairbanks (1986) reviewed more than 50 controlled studies on vocabulary instruction and found that it generally takes about 1.5 minutes to introduce a new word to students. In addition, they found that the best results were obtained if the word were reviewed multiple times. If it takes about 1.5 minutes to review a word, then we can conclude that it will take students about 4.5 minutes to effectively learn a new word (1.5 minutes to be introduced to the new word, 1.5 minutes for the first review, and 1.5 minutes for the second review). Using these estimates, teaching 10 to 12 new words each week would take, at most, 54 minutes per week. If 10 to 12 words were systematically taught for 35 weeks of each school year, the total cost in time would be 31.5 hours. However, that 31.5 hours would help students learn 420 new terms each year. This effort would result in an average increase in achievement of 12 percentile points in terms of students' learning of new content that is related to words they have been learning. However, if the words were carefully selected so that they were ones students will most likely encounter when learning new content, student achievement could increase by as much as 33 percentile points. Again, this is not insignificant in a practical sense.

Which Words Should Be Taught?

The discussion above makes the case that teaching vocabulary provides educators with an efficient way to expose students to the content within all the standards and benchmarks identified by subject-matter experts. Thus, if the terms and phrases that are most important to the standards and benchmarks listed in Appendix B were identified, then students could be exposed to that content through a vocabulary approach. For example, if the important terms and phrases were identified relative to the mathematics standard and related benchmarks that deal with probability (see mathematics standard 7 in Appendix B), then all students could be taught this vocabulary—at a surface level at least—for the price of about 4.5 minutes per term, at least by one estimate. Obviously, learning these terms in this way would not result in students having an in-depth understanding of the topic of probability. However, all students would gain at least some understanding of the important concepts relative to the topic of probability, which would give them a foundation for learning these concepts at a deeper level should they encounter them as part of the intensive curriculum.

In fact, such a list of key concepts has been developed. In writing this book, we sought to identify the vocabulary words and phrases that represent expert opinion regarding the terms that are most important for students to know. To put together this list, McREL researchers used the McREL database of standards and benchmarks, described in Chapter 4, inasmuch as this database represents a synthesis of expert opinion. Researchers analyzed the information in each standard and benchmark to extract the key vocabulary terms and phrases. This process produced 6,710 words and phrases that represent the basic vocabulary of 14 content areas. These words and phrases are organized by grade-level bands (typically K–2, 3–5, 6–8, 9–12) and reported in Appendix E.[13] To illustrate the nature of these words and phrases, consider Table 7.1, which reports the mathematics vocabulary for the standards and benchmarks reported in the McREL *Compendium*.

---

[13] A more detailed description of the process used to develop the list of terms and phrases that appear in Appendix E can be found in the introduction to that appendix.

Table 7.1

Mathematics Vocabulary
McREL *Compendium* (Standards Database)

STANDARD	LEVEL 1: GRADES K-2	LEVEL 2: GRADES 3-5	LEVEL 3: GRADES 6-8	LEVEL 4: GRADES 9-12
1. Problem Solving	modeling problems numerical problem problem solving solve* table (data) whole number	counter example* diagram* invalid argument logic* method* process of elimination reasoning* solution* strategy* trial and error valid argument verify*	deductive reasoning graphical inductive reasoning pictorial symbol*	generalization* mathematical notation mathematical proof relationship theorem
2. Concept of Numbers	cardinal numbers counting number line ordinal numbers set unit	decimal equivalent even numbers fraction mixed numbers odd numbers percent place value relative magnitude three-dimensional two-dimensional	composite numbers divisibility exponent integer multiple negative (integers) positive (integers) prime numbers proportion ratio rational numbers Roman numerals root (square root, cube root) scientific notation square numbers subset	absolute value binary multiplication discrete mathematics finite graph irrational numbers logarithm matrices natural numbers real numbers remainder sequence*
3. Computation	addition estimation inverse relationship subtraction	addends computation division factor multiplication operation product rounding sum	algorithm associative property commutative property computational methods distributive property identity property order of operations rate root-extraction squares and cubes	Fibonacci sequence permutations and combinations power (exponentiation) radical expression reciprocal recurrence relation simplify

*Word or phrase appears more than once across the content areas included in Appendix E. For a more detailed explanation, see the introduction to Appendix E.

Table 7.1 (continued)

Mathematics Vocabulary
McREL *Compendium* (Standards Database)

STANDARD	LEVEL 1: GRADES K-2	LEVEL 2: GRADES 3-5	LEVEL 3: GRADES 6-8	LEVEL 4: GRADES 9-12
4. Measurement	distance height* length* measure* nonstandard unit standard unit temperature* time* weight*	angle area capacity* circumference mass* measurement tool metric unit perimeter protractor ruler* volume*	cubic unit degree of accuracy formula* grid* indirect measurement parallelogram precision significant digit square unit	absolute error acceleration relative error surface area* velocity*
5. Geometry	above behind below between corner geometric shape inside outside side	acute angle congruence cube dimensionality intersecting motion geometry obtuse angle parallel perpendicular polygon right angle similarity sphere symmetry	angle bisector compass* dilation geometric construction line segment perpendicular bisector planar cross section Pythagorean Theorem rotation scale drawing straightedge tessellation translation	arc chord cosine force* interior angle midpoint ordered pair polar coordinates proof scalar multiplication sine tangent transversal trigonometry vector vector addition velocity*
6. Statistics and Data Analysis	graph*	bar graph cluster data* extreme gap* line graph pie chart sample spread	bias* box-and-whisker plot central tendency circle graph conjectures* distribution (data) frequency* hypothesis* mean median mode outlier random sample range sampling error scatter plot statistic* stem-and-leaf plot	central limit theorem confidence interval correlation quartile deviation randomness regression line sampling distribution standard deviation two-way table variability

*Word or phrase appears more than once across the content areas included in Appendix E. For a more detailed explanation, see the introduction to Appendix E.

Table 7.1 (continued)

Mathematics Vocabulary
McREL *Compendium* (Standards Database)

STANDARD	LEVEL 1: GRADES K-2	LEVEL 2: GRADES 3-5	LEVEL 3: GRADES 6-8	LEVEL 4: GRADES 9-12

7. Probability	prediction*	certainty
		chance
		likely
		sample space
		uncertainty
		unlikely
			area model
			counting procedure
			experiment*
			experimental
			  probability
			odds
			probability*
			simulation*
			theoretical probability
			tree diagram
				compound event
				conditional probability
				dependent event
				discrete probability
				  distribution
				independent event
				normal curve
				random variable

8. Functions and Algebra	pattern* set of numbers	equation horizontal axis (X-axis) linear pattern number sentence open sentence rectangular coordinate system repeating pattern variable vertical axis (Y-axis)	expression* function inequality linear equation slope slope-intercept form substitution Venn diagram	direct variation domain inverse variation polynomial equation sigma notation sinusoidal function
9. Nature and Uses of Mathematics	no new vocabulary	no new vocabulary	abstract idea mathematician	natural science technology*

*Word or phrase appears more than once across the content areas included in Appendix E. For a more detailed explanation, see the introduction to Appendix E.

The words and phrases in Table 7.1 are highly content specific. Indeed, given the process that was used to identify them, we assert that the terms in Table 7.1 represent the core vocabulary of mathematics. If students have a general understanding of these words and phrases, they will have a sound foundation for learning the more detailed information and skills found in the benchmarks for this standard. In addition, even if a particular student never studies a specific mathematics standard in depth (i.e., never studies the standard as part of his intensive curriculum), he will have at least a general understanding of some of the important concepts within that topic. To illustrate, consider the terms and phrases appropriate for students in grades 6–8 for the standard on probability:

- experiment
- odds
- theoretical probability
- probability
- tree diagram
- simulation
- experimental probability

If all students were exposed to these words as part of a systematic program of vocabulary instruction, they would gain a general understanding of these concepts. Again, it is important to stress that the meaning of these words would be approached at a very general level—students would be presented with the top-level schema information only. For example, for the concepts of *simulation* and *area model*, students might be presented with simple descriptions like those below:

> **Simulation**: A way to experience what something is like without actually doing it. For example, a video game that allows you to pilot a jet fighter airplane is a simulation.

> **Area model**: A technique mathematicians use to represent the chances of something occurring. For example, below are area models for your chances of becoming a millionaire if you graduate from high school and if you graduate from college:

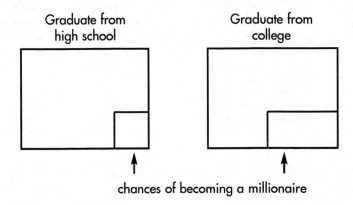

As the example illustrates, students would not be presented with technical definitions of the content vocabulary terms but, rather, with general descriptions that draw on experiences that might be familiar to them.

Implementing an Extensive Program of Vocabulary Instruction

How might educators go about teaching the 6,710 vocabulary terms presented in Appendix E? As described previously, at least one estimate is that, on average, it takes about 4.5 minutes for students to gain a general understanding of each new word or phrase. This means that to address all 6,710 terms, a district must set aside approximately 500 hours for vocabulary instruction over a 13-year period (i.e., grades K–12), or an average of about 39 hours per year. Fifteen minutes per day set aside for vocabulary instruction will be more than enough time to address all 6,710 terms[14]. This 15-minute instructional period could occur as an adjunct to "home room" period or be part of a class that all students take (e.g., language arts). During the daily 15 minutes of vocabulary instruction, we recommend the following process, or some adaptation of it.

Step 1: At the beginning of the school year, present students with all the words they will be expected to learn. Becoming familiar with the content vocabulary should be an ongoing task for students—a type of learning for which they will be somewhat, and perhaps primarily, responsibility. Thus, it is useful to present students with the words and phrases that make up the content vocabulary as soon as possible, preferably at the beginning of the school year. As previously described, the terms and phrases in Appendix E have been organized into grade-level bands (e.g., K–2, 3–5, 6–8, 9–12). A school or district might want to divide the words within these grade-level intervals into lists for specific grades. This can be accomplished by asking teachers within each grade-level interval (e.g., kindergarten teachers, first-grade teachers, and second-grade teachers for the K–2 interval) to work together to determine which words and phrases they will teach to students at each grade level.

Step 2: Provide students with an initial description of each new term. During each vocabulary instruction period, only two or three new terms should be presented. In addition, as illustrated previously, students should be presented with a general description of each new term, rather than a formal definition. The more examples that are used in these descriptions, the better. Ideally, examples should be drawn from experiences that are familiar to students.

Step 3: Ask students to elaborate on the initial description provided by the teacher. The next step in the process is for students to develop their own descriptions of the words or phrases they are learning. Students should be given the opportunity to do this during the same 15-minute instructional period in which the descriptions of the terms are initially presented. Research indicates that this is a key step in the process of learning new vocabulary items—students must "construct" their own descriptions of words to truly make them their own (see Stahl & Fairbanks, 1986). At this stage in the process, teachers should be very tolerant of differences among students, recognizing that people understand words in slightly different ways. For example, ask any two adults to explain what the word *measurement* means and undoubtedly somewhat different, though accurate, descriptions will be given. Students should be allowed the same degree of variance in the way they construct their individual descriptions of the terms or phrases.

---

[14]Some have suggested that an estimate of 4.5 minutes per term is not enough time. If we assume, instead, that 10 minutes per term is a more realistic figure, then 30 minutes per day would be needed across the K–12 years in order to help students gain a general understanding of the 6,710 terms and phrases found in Appendix E.

Although students should be granted the freedom to describe terms and phrases in individually meaningful ways, it is important for teachers to check the accuracy of students' descriptions. Obviously, student descriptions should not contain gross misconceptions. However, it is just as important not to be too rigid in what is expected of these descriptions. Again, as Hirsch notes, relative to the extensive curriculum, students should be expected to have an accurate, but very general and not necessarily complete, understanding of the words and phrases. (Note that we are assuming that there is a common, agreed-upon definition that teachers should hold students to, while allowing them to describe that understanding in ways that have meaning for them.)

Step 4: Have students keep a record of the words they are learning. Over time, the content vocabulary will provide a foundation for learning the intensive curriculum across all content areas. If students keep a cumulative record of what they have learned about the words on their lists, they can refer frequently to those words. This is easily done if students simply record in a spiral notebook the terms, the descriptions provided by the teacher, and their personal descriptions. (Obviously, locating entries in a notebook such as this is easier if the primary terms and phrases are alphabetized.)

Step 5: Encourage students to review and use the words and phrases. Students should be encouraged to periodically review the words they have recorded in their vocabulary notebooks. Recall that research indicates that multiple exposures to vocabulary words and phrases deepens students' understanding of them (Stahl & Fairbanks, 1986). Students also should be encouraged to use these terms and phrases as much as possible and to continue to refine their understanding of them. The following activities are suggested ways in which students might do this:

- Use the words and phrases in writing and speaking.

- Continually elaborate on the meaning of the word by
  - drawing a picture or symbol to represent a new understanding,
  - thinking of similar words,
  - creating a sentence that illustrates a new understanding, and
  - listing examples that reflect a new understanding.

Conclusion

In this chapter, we have continued our discussion of how to address the abundance of content identified in the national standards documents. Specifically, we have presented a case for teaching vocabulary as the extensive curriculum, a concept introduced by Hirsch in the 1987 and 1988 editions of *Cultural Literacy*, in which his national vocabulary was first presented. However, as we have made clear, it is our contention that such a list of terms and phrases should be built from a knowledge base that reflects expert opinion and that has been subject to wide public review. Although such an approach would be beneficial in priming students for more in-depth learning, it has been presented here primarily as a possible way of making the most of the minimal amount of instructional time available in the school day.

Chapter 8

Making It All Matter

The previous seven chapters have painted a complex picture relative to the design and implementation of a curriculum organized around essential knowledge. Such an endeavor raises troublesome issues, none of which is easily addressed. A knowledge base identified by subject-matter experts is an important foundation, but this research-based core of knowledge is just the beginning. Once content has been identified, a key issue is that there simply is not enough instructional time available in American schools to adequately address the content experts have identified as important. This topic was discussed in some detail in Chapter 5. Finding ways to address the problem of too little time has been one focus of this book. How might a school or district best address this problem?

Establishing Priorities

Seeking Community Input

If not everything that is important can be taught in depth, the question arises, What is most important to teach in depth? In other words, what is most important to include in the intensive curriculum? Answering this question is not a simple task. Chapter 6 provides an example of one approach to the problem: asking U.S. adults. As we discussed in that chapter, McREL surveyed a representative sample of U.S. adults to determine their opinions on the importance to a K–12 education of the information and skills in the McREL standards database. Similarly, a school or district could poll its local community members to ascertain which standards they believe are most important for students to master prior to high school graduation. One convenient option for a school or district wishing to undertake this process is to use the questionnaires reproduced in Appendix D because they address all of the standards in the McREL standards database, a comprehensive synthesis of the work of the national, professional subject-matter groups. Another option is for a school or district to design its own questionnaire, using selected items from the McREL questionnaires as well as newly constructed items.

Although designing a questionnaire is a relatively simple process, interpreting the results can be difficult. This is because it is likely that different constituent groups will have different opinions regarding what is most important and what is not. As we saw in Chapter 6, when the Gallup Organization polled a representative sample of American adults, the perspectives of those respondents who had more than a high school education differed from those who did not. A school or district will have to decide whether it will weight the opinions of some group or groups of respondents more heavily than those of another.

The task, of course, does not end there. Such a survey will not resolve more comprehensive questions, such as whether topics in mathematics are better taught in depth rather than breadth, or whether a liberal education requires that students study a foreign language or have some acquaintance with the arts. Though not the focus of this book, such questions form part of any curriculum decision-making process that a district undertakes and are not resolved through such surveys.

Matching State Goals

As we noted in Chapter 3, all states but one have published standards. Although the quality of many of these documents has been questioned, nonetheless some state standards are good and others are improving. A review of state standards is one step a district or school can take to aid its selection from the knowledge base (i.e., the McREL *Compendium*) of the content that should be part of the intensive curriculum—regardless of whether state standards must be adopted by schools and districts in a particular state or whether they are offered only as "guidelines." For many districts, such a choice is compelled (or, at minimum, strongly encouraged) when state assessments have been aligned to the information and skills described in state standards and when such assessments are a key component of a system of accountability.

A recent study by the regional educational laboratories notes that 28 states, or 55%, have tightly aligned their assessments with standards and that 45 states, or 88%, demonstrate some alignment of standards to state assessments (Regional Educational Laboratories, 1998). Thus, a district's selection of instructional content based on the appearance of that content in state standards should help ensure that students will be assessed on what they are taught. McREL's experience shows that districts and schools need not be concerned that including state standards within instruction will add content to the McREL standards database of essential knowledge. Through their work for a variety of clients, many of them school districts seeking to align their standards with state materials, McREL researchers have analyzed every major curriculum document published by the states and have found that state standards rarely include material that is not part of the knowledge base identified at the national level. For the most part, then, schools and districts can look to state standards to identify an important subset of essential knowledge and need not be concerned that such content is apart from or in addition to the information and skills identified at the national level.

Aligning Instruction and Assessments

Although assessment has not been the focus of this book, nonetheless it is an essential element of the process of instituting and successfully carrying out a standards-based approach to education.[15] In fact, assessments—from standardized tests to locally administered performance assessments—also can be used to determine what content would best form part of the intensive curriculum. Whether assessments are used to report the success of programs or the achievement of students, if they are valued and address content that is found in the knowledge base of standards and benchmarks, they should be used to select content that will be part of the intensive curriculum. This approach serves a dual purpose: It provides another means to prioritize content, and it furthers the alignment of curriculum with assessment.

Increasing Time for Instruction

It appears that the amount of time available for instruction is an insurmountable obstacle. One of the reports highlighted in Chapter 5 was *Prisoners of Time* by the National Education Commission on Time and Learning (1994). One of the more striking comparisons in that report was between the number of hours devoted to instruction in core academic subjects in American schools during the last four years of schooling versus the total in other countries. These differences are depicted in Figure 8.1.

It is difficult to reconcile these differences. American education simply does not devote the amount of time to instruction that other countries do. As explained by the National Education Commission on Time and Learning (1994):

> [Figure 8.1] speaks for itself. No matter how the assumptions underlying the figure are modified, the result is always the same— students abroad are required to work on demanding subject matter at least twice as long. In practical terms, this means that most foreign students are studying language, literature, science, and two or more languages, while many of our young people spend their time in study halls, pep rallies, driver education, and assemblies. (p. 25)

---

[15]For a detailed discussion of assessment in a standards-based system and other elements of implementing a standards-based approach, see *A Comprehensive Guide to Designing Standards-Based Districts, Schools, and Classrooms*, Marzano & Kendall, 1996.

Figure 8.1

The Final Four Years in Four Nations
Estimated Required Core Academic Time

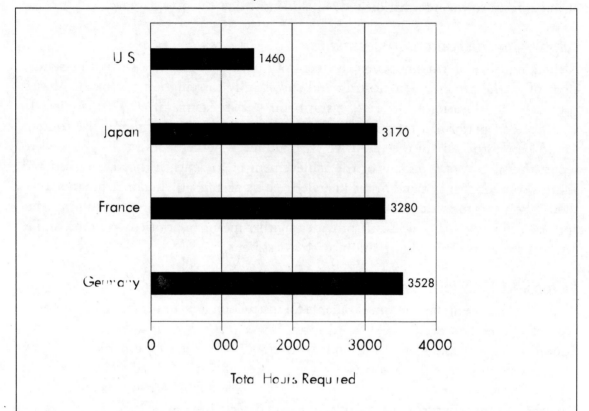

Source: United States estimate developed from *The Digest of Education Statistics* (NCES, 1992), State Education Indicators (Council of Chief State School Officers, 1990), and the Commission's review of academic requirements in 41 states and the District of Columbia. The estimate for Japan was developed from Monbusho (1993 publication of the Japanese Ministry of Education, Science and Culture) and site visits to Japanese secondary schools, and confirmed by senior Japanese ministry officials at a meeting in Washington. The estimate for France was developed from a French publication, Organization of the French Educational System Leading to the French Baccalaureat, and confirmed by French officials. The German estimate is actually the number of hours of required coursework for one state, Berlin.

Note: From *Prisoners of Time* (p. 24), by The National Education Commission on Time and Learning, 1994, Washington, DC: U.S. Department of Education.

It was findings such as these that led the Commission to recommend that American schools provide students with at least 5.5 hours daily instruction in academic subjects. As reported in Chapter 5, this would result in 990 hours of instruction per year, representing an increase of 42 percent over the estimated 695.6 hours of instructional time currently available.

The positive effects of increasing the amount of instructional time have been well established. For example, in a review of more than 130 studies, Walberg (1997) found that in 97 percent of these studies, there was a positive relationship between increased instructional time and learning. This is not to say that the simple act of increasing instructional time will dramatically increase the achievement of American students. As Sadowski (1998) notes, instructional time must be used effectively if substantial achievement gains are to be made. However, the limiting effects of the amount of time currently available in the U.S. education system are simply too prohibitive to ignore.

Redesigning the Curriculum

In Chapter 7 we reviewed the concepts of the intensive and extensive curriculums, which Hirsch introduced in his book *Cultural Literacy*. The intensive curriculum is comprised of those standards and their related benchmarks that a school or district has identified as most important for students to learn prior to high school graduation and that, thus, students will be exposed to in depth. The extensive curriculum is comprised of the content knowledge vocabulary—those terms and phrases (such as those that can be found in Appendix E) that students should gain at least a general understanding of over the K–12 years.

Once standards and benchmarks that should make up the intensive curriculum have been identified, then teachers should be expected to systematically address this content in their classrooms. Although this might seem obvious—surely teachers would teach the content specified by the school or district—recall from the discussion in Chapter 1 that teachers frequently make idiosyncratic decisions about what to address and what not to address. These decisions can result in huge gaps in the experiential base of students: They might not have the opportunity to learn important content because a specific teacher has decided not to cover it. To guard against these gaps in learning, we recommend that the content embedded in the standards and benchmarks that have been identified as most important—the intensive curriculum—be considered nonnegotiable in terms of what teachers cover in the classroom. The same should hold true for the extensive curriculum—the content vocabulary. Teachers should be expected to help students gain at least a general understanding of these terms and phrases for two reasons. First, if the benchmarks that the vocabulary was derived from are not covered in the intensive curriculum, then students will have at least some understanding of all of the key concepts and facts identified across the content areas. Second, if the benchmarks from which the vocabulary was derived are indeed covered in the intensive curriculum, then students will have a foundation of understanding that will facilitate more in-depth learning, the hallmark of the intensive curriculum. In short, the intensive and extensive curriculums should be the cornerstone of what a school or district offers to students and parents—a research-based core of knowledge that reflects a local perspective.

Conclusion

In this book we have sought to address the question that perhaps is most central to education—What should be taught? We have argued that analyzing the information and skills identified in the national standards documents should be the first step in answering this question. The resulting standards and benchmarks—synthesized in the McREL standards database—represent the essential knowledge that students should learn before graduating from high school.

Although we are not the first to note the problem of too much content given the instructional time available from kindergarten through grade 12, we have offered what we hope have been useful guidelines and suggestions for addressing the problem. Among other suggestions, we have advocated for increased instructional time as one means of easing the burden of an abundance of content, recognizing that such a suggestion is easier said than done and that, even so, it is doubtful that the increases that reasonably could be implemented would fully address the problem.

Recognizing this likely limitation, we have proposed additional solutions. Building on Hirsch's idea of the extensive and intensive curriculums, we have offered methods that can be helpful in selecting content that should be included in the intensive curriculum and a process for at least exposing students to all of the key concepts contained in the McREL *Compendium*, the knowledge base of standards and benchmarks.

Underlying the guidelines we have offered is the belief that local schools and districts must take the critical matter of curriculum into their own hands. No longer can American educators afford to have a laissez faire attitude about the content taught in schools. The public at large, parents, and local community members are demanding that schools provide a coherent and cohesive approach to content coverage. This book was written as a tool to be used by local schools and districts in that endeavor.

Documents to Consult for a Comprehensive Review of Subject Areas

Australian Education Council. (1994). *English: A Curriculum Profile for Australian Schools*. Commonwealth of Australia: Curriculum Corporation.

Australian Education Council. (1994). *Technology: A Curriculum Profile for Australian Schools*. Carlton, Victoria, Australia: Curriculum Corporation.

Board of Education, Commonwealth of Virginia. (1995, June). *Standards of Learning for Virginia Public Schools*. Richmond, VA: Author.

Bybee, R. W., Buchwald, C. E., Crissman, S., Heil, D. R., Kuerbis, P. J., Matsumoto, C., & McIreney, J. D. (1989). *Science and Technology Education for the Elementary Years: Frameworks for Curriculum and Instruction*. Andover, MA: National Center for Improving Science Education.

Bybee, R. W., Buchwald, C. E., Crissman, S., Heil, D. R., Kuerbis, P. J., Matsumoto, C., & McIreney, J. D. (1990). *Science and Technology Education for the Middle Years: Frameworks for Curriculum and Instruction*. Andover, MA: National Center for Improving Science Education.

California Department of Education. (1989). *Recommended Literature, Grades Nine Through Twelve*. Sacramento, CA: Author.

California Department of Education. (1989). *Visual and Performing Arts Framework for California Public Schools: Kindergarten Through Grade Twelve*. Sacramento, CA: Author.

California Department of Education. (1990). *Recommended Readings in Literature, Kindergarten Through Grade Eight*. Sacramento, CA: Author.

California Department of Education. (1990). *Science Framework for California Public Schools: Kindergarten Through Grade 12*. Sacramento, CA: Author.

California Department of Education. (1994). *Health Framework for California Public Schools: Kindergarten Through Grade 12*. Sacramento, CA: Author.

Carnevale, A. P., Gainer, L. J., & Meltzer, A. S. (1990). *Workplace Basics: The Essential Skills Employers Want*. San Francisco: Jossey-Bass.

Center for Civic Education. (1994). *National Standards for Civics and Government*. Calabasas, CA: Author.

Colorado Council on Economic Education. (1994). *Economics: Conceptual Content Standards, Grades K–12* (Draft). Denver: Author.

Colorado Department of Education (1996, June). *Content Standards for Foreign Language* (Second Draft). Denver, CO: Author.

Consortium of National Arts Education Associations. (1994). *National Standards for Arts Education: What Every Young American Should Know and Be Able to Do in the Arts*. Reston, VA: Music Educators National Conference.

Crabtree, C., Nash, G. B., Gagnon, P., & Waugh, S. (Eds.). (1992). *Lessons from History: Essential Understandings and Historical Perspectives Students Should Acquire*. Los Angeles: National Center for History in the Schools.

Crafton, L. K. (1996). *Standards in Practice: Grades K–2*. Urbana, IL: National Council of Teachers of English.

Edison Project. (1994a). *Student Standards for the Elementary Academy*. New York: Author.

Edison Project. (1994b). *Student Standards for the Junior Academy*. New York: Author.

Edison Project. (1994c). *Student Standards for the Primary Academy*. New York: Author.

Gagnon, P., & Bradley Commission on History in the Schools (Eds.). (1989). *Historical Literacy: The Case for History in American Education*. Boston: Houghton Mifflin.

Geographic Education National Implementations Project. (1987). *K–6 Geography: Themes, Key Ideas, and Learning Opportunities*. Washington, DC: Author.

Geography Education Standards Project. (1994). *Geography for Life: National Geography Standards*. Washington, DC: National Geographic Research and Exploration.

Gillespie, J. T. (Ed.) (1991a). *Best Books for Junior High Readers*. New Providence, NJ: Bowker.

Gillespie, J. T. (Ed.) (1991b). *Best Books for Senior High Readers*. New Providence, NJ: Bowker.

Gilliard, J. V., Caldwell, J., Dalgaard, B. R., Highsmith, R. J., Reinke, R., & Watts, M. (with Leet, D. R., Malone, M. G., & Ellington, L.). (1989). *Economics, What and When: Scope and Sequence Guidelines, K–12*. New York: Joint Council on Economic Education.

Hirsch, E. D., Jr. (1987). *Cultural Literacy: What Every American Needs to Know.* Boston: Houghton Mifflin.

Hirsch, E. D., Jr. (Ed.). (1991). *What Your First Grader Needs to Know: Fundamentals of a Good First-Grade Education.* New York: Delta.

Hirsch, E. D., Jr. (Ed.). (1991). *What Your Second Grader Needs to Know: Fundamentals of a Good Second-Grade Education.* New York: Delta.

Hirsch, E. D., Jr. (Ed.). (1992). *What Your Third Grader Needs to Know: Fundamentals of a Good Third-Grade Education.* New York: Delta.

Hirsch, E. D., Jr. (Ed.). (1992). *What Your Fourth Grader Needs to Know: Fundamentals of a Good Fourth-Grade Education.* New York: Delta.

Hirsch, E. D., Jr. (Ed.). (1993). *What Your Fifth Grader Needs to Know: Fundamentals of a Good Fifth-Grade Education.* New York: Delta.

Hirsch, E. D., Jr. (Ed.). (1993). *What Your Sixth Grader Needs to Know: Fundamentals of a Good Sixth-Grade Education.* New York: Delta.

Hirsch, E. D., Jr. (1996). *The Schools We Need and Why We Don't Have Them.* New York: Doubleday.

Hirsch, E. D., Jr., & Holdren, J. (Eds.) (1996). *What Your Kindergartner Needs to Know: Preparing Your Child for a Lifetime of Learning.* New York: Delta.

International Baccalaureate. (1992). *Language A1 Guide.* Geneva, Switzerland: Author.

International Baccalaureate. (1993). *Group 5 Mathematics Guide* (Edition 1.2). Geneva, Switzerland: Author.

International Baccalaureate (1995a). *Information Technology in a Global Society.* Geneva, Switzerland: Author.

International Baccalaureate. (1995b). *Middle Years Programme: Arts.* Geneva, Switzerland: Author.

International Baccalaureate. (1995c). *Middle Years Programme: Humanities* (Edition 1.1). Geneva, Switzerland: Author.

International Baccalaureate. (1995d). *Middle Years Programme: Language A.* Geneva, Switzerland: Author.

International Baccalaureate. (1995e). *Middle Years Programme: Mathematics* (Edition 1.1). Geneva, Switzerland: Author.

International Baccalaureate. (1995f). *Middle Years Programme: Sciences* (Edition 1.1). Geneva, Switzerland: Author.

International Baccalaureate. (1996a, May). *Language A1: World Literature List.* Geneva, Switzerland: Author.

International Baccalaureate. (1996b, May). *Prescribed Booklist: English A1.* Geneva, Switzerland: Author.

International Baccalaureate. (1996a). *Art/Design.* Geneva, Switzerland: Author.

International Baccalaureate. (1996b). *Biology.* Geneva, Switzerland: Author.

International Baccalaureate. (1996c). *Chemistry.* Geneva, Switzerland: Author.

International Baccalaureate. (1996d). *Design Technology.* Geneva, Switzerland: Author.

International Baccalaureate. (1996e). *Economics.* Geneva, Switzerland: Author.

International Baccalaureate. (1996f). *Environmental Systems.* Geneva, Switzerland: Author.

International Baccalaureate. (1996g). *Geography.* Geneva, Switzerland: Author.

International Baccalaureate. (1996h). *History.* Geneva, Switzerland: Author.

International Baccalaureate. (1996i). *Physics.* Geneva, Switzerland: Author.

International Baccalaureate. (1996j). *Psychology.* Geneva, Switzerland: Author.

International Baccalaureate. (1996k). *Social Anthropology.* Geneva, Switzerland: Author.

International Technology Education Association. (1996). *Technology for All Americans: A Rationale and Structure for the Study of Technology.* Reston, VA: Author.

Joint Committee on Geographic Education. (1984). *Guidelines for Geographic Education: Elementary and Secondary Schools.* Washington, DC: Association of American Geographers.

Joint Committee on Health Education Terminology. (1991). *Report of the 1990 Joint Committee on Health Education Terminology.* Journal of Health Education, 22(2), 97–107.

Joint Committee on National Health Education Standards. (1995). *National Health Education Standards: Achieving Health Literacy.* Reston, VA: Association for the Advancement of Health Education.

Law in a Free Society. (1977a). *Authority I (Elementary): A Civic Education Unit* (Teacher's ed.). Calabasas, CA: Author.

Law in a Free Society. (1977b). *Privacy I (Elementary): A Civic Education Unit* (Teacher's ed.). Calabasas, CA: Author.

Law in a Free Society. (1977c). *Privacy II (Elementary): A Civic Education Unit* (Teacher's ed.). Calabasas, CA: Author.

Law in a Free Society. (1979d). *Justice I (Elementary): A Civic Education Unit* (Teacher's ed.). Calabasas, CA: Author.

Law in a Free Society. (1983). *Responsibility I (Elementary): A Civic Education Unit* (Teacher's ed.). Calabasas, CA: Author.

Michigan Department of Education. (1996, September). *Physical Education: Content Standards and Benchmarks* (Draft). Lansing: Author.

Michigan State Board of Education. (1988). *Michigan Essential Goals and Objectives for Health Education*. Lansing, MI: Author.

Mississippi State Department of Education. (1994). *Mississippi Curriculum Structure: English Language Arts*. Jackson, MS: Author.

Music Educators National Conference. (1986). *The School Music Program: Description and Standards*. Reston, VA: Author.

Myers, M., & Spalding, E. (Eds.). (1997). *Exemplar Series: Grades 6–8*. Urbana, IL: National Council of Teachers of English.

Myers, M., & Spalding, E. (Eds.). (1997). *Standards Exemplar Series: Assessing Student Performance Grades 9–12*. Urbana, IL: National Council of Teachers of English.

National Assessment of Educational Progress. (1989). *Science Objectives: 1990 Assessment*. Princeton, NJ: Educational Testing Service.

National Assessment of Educational Progress. (1992a). *Description of Writing Achievement Levels-Setting Process and Proposed Achievement Level Definitions*. Iowa City, IA: American College Testing Program.

National Assessment of Educational Progress. (1992b). *Item Specifications: 1994 National Assessment of Educational Progress in Geography*. Washington, DC: National Assessment Governing Board.

National Assessment of Educational Progress. (1992c). *Provisional Item Specifications: 1994 National Assessment of Educational Progress in U.S. History*. Washington, DC: National Assessment Governing Board.

National Assessment of Educational Progress. (n.d.) *Mathematics Framework for the 1996 National Assessment of Educational Progress*. Washington, DC: Author.

National Assessment of Educational Progress Arts Education Consensus Project. (1994). *Arts Education Assessment Framework*. Washington, DC: National Assessment Governing Board.

National Assessment of Educational Progress Civics Consensus Project. (n.d.). *Civics Framework for the 1998 National Assessment of Educational Progress*. Washington, DC: National Assessment Governing Board.

National Assessment of Educational Progress Geography Consensus Project. (1992). *Geography Assessment Framework for the 1994 National Assessment of Educational Progress* (Draft). Washington, DC: National Assessment Governing Board.

National Assessment of Educational Progress in U.S. History. (1994). *Provisional Item Specifications*. Washington, DC: Council of Chief State School Officers.

National Assessment of Educational Progress Reading Consensus Project. (1990a). *Assessment and Exercise Specifications: 1992 NAEP Reading Assessment*. Washington, DC: National Assessment Governing Board.

National Assessment of Educational Progress Reading Consensus Project. (1990b). *Reading Assessment Framework for the 1992 National Assessment of Educational Progress*. Washington, DC: National Assessment Governing Board.

National Assessment of Educational Progress Science Consensus Project. (1993). *Science Assessment and Exercise Specifications for the 1994 National Assessment of Educational Progress*. Washington, DC: National Assessment Governing Board.

National Assessment of Educational Progress Science Consensus Project. (n.d.). *Science Framework for the 1996 National Assessment of Educational Progress*. Washington, DC: National Assessment Governing Board.

National Association for Sport and Physical Education. (1992). *Outcomes of Quality Physical Education Programs*. Reston, VA: Author.

National Association for Sport and Physical Education. (1995). *Moving into the Future, National Standards for Physical Education: A Guide to Content and Assessment*. St. Louis: Mosby.

National Business Education Association (1995). *National Standards for Business Education: What America's Students Should Know and Be Able to Do in Business*. Reston, VA: Author.

National Center for History in the Schools. (1994a). *National Standards for History for Grades K–4: Expanding Children's World in Time and Space*. (Expanded ed.). Los Angeles: Author.

National Center for History in the Schools. (1994b). *National Standards for United States History: Exploring the American Experience*. (Expanded ed.). Los Angeles: Author.

National Center for History in the Schools. (1994c). *National Standards for World History: Exploring Paths to the Present*. (Expanded ed.). Los Angeles: Author.

National Center for History in the Schools. (1996). *National Standards for History*. (Basic ed.). Los Angeles: Author.

National Council for the Social Studies. (1994). *Expectations of Excellence: Curriculum Standards for Social Studies*. Washington, DC: Author.

National Council of Teachers of English. (1989). *The English Coalition Conference: Democracy Through Language*. Urbana, IL: Author.

National Council of Teachers of English and the International Reading Association (October, 1995). *Standards for the English Language Arts* (Draft). Urbana, IL: National Council of Teachers of English.

National Council of Teachers of Mathematics. (1989). *Curriculum and Evaluation Standards for School Mathematics*. Reston, VA: Author.

National Council on Economic Education. (1997). *Voluntary National Content Standards in Economics*. NY: Author.

National Research Council. (1996). *National Science Education Standards*. Washington, DC: National Academy Press.

National Standards in Foreign Language Education. (1995, April). *Standards for Foreign Language Learning: Preparing for the 21st Century* (Draft). Yonkers, NY: Author.

National Standards in Foreign Language Education Project (1996). *Standards for Foreign Language Learning: Preparing for the 21st Century*. Lawrence, KS: Author.

New Standards Project. (1997a). *Performance Standards: English Language Arts, Mathematics, Science, Applied Learning: Volume 1: Elementary School*. Washington, DC: National Center on Education and the Economy, and the University of Pittsburgh.

New Standards Project. (1997b). *Performance Standards: English Language Arts, Mathematics, Science, Applied Learning: Volume 2: Middle School*. Washington, DC: National Center on Education and the Economy, and the University of Pittsburgh.

New Standards Project. (1997c). *Performance Standards: English Language Arts, Mathematics, Science, Applied Learning: Volume 3: High School*. Washington, DC: National Center on Education and the Economy, and the University of Pittsburgh.

North Carolina Department of Public Instruction (1992). *Teacher Handbook Component: Computer Skills*. Raleigh, NC: Author.

Pearsall, M. K. (Ed). (1993). *Scope, Sequence, and Coordination of Secondary School Science. Vol. 1. The Content Core: A Guide for Curriculum Designers*. Washington, DC: National Science Teachers Association.

Project 2061, American Association for the Advancement of Science. (1993). *Benchmarks for Science Literacy*. New York: Oxford University Press.

Quigley, C. N., & Bahmmeller, C. F. (Eds.). (1991). *Civitas: A Framework for Civic Education*. (National Council for Social Studies, Bulletin No. 86). Calabasas, CA: Center for Civic Education.

Saunders, P., & Gilliard, J. (Eds.). (1995). *A Framework for Teaching Basic Economic Concepts with Scope and Sequence Guidelines, K–12*. New York: National Council on Economic Education.

Secretary's Commission on Achieving Necessary Skills. (1991). *What Work Requires of Schools: A SCANS Report for America 2000*. Washington, DC: U.S. Department of Labor.

Sierra-Perry, Martha. (1996). *Standards in Practice: Grades 3–5*. Urbana, IL: National Council of Teachers of English.

Smagorinsky, Peter. (1996). *Standards in Practice: Grades 9–12*. Urbana, IL: National Council of Teachers of English.

Speech Communication Association. (1996). *Speaking, Listening, and Media Literacy Standards for K through 12 Education*. Annandale, VA: Author.

Stotsky, S., Anderson, P., & Beierl, D. (1989). *Variety and Individualism in the English Class: Teacher-Recommended Lists of Reading for Grades 7–12*. Boston, MA: New England Association of Teachers of English.

Texas Education Agency. (1996, February) *English Language Arts and Reading: Texas Essential Knowledge and Skills* (Draft). Austin, TX: Author.

Texas Education Agency. (1996). *Texas Essential Knowledge and Skills for Technology Applications* (Draft) (On-line). Available: http://www.tea.state.tx.us:70/sboe/schedule/9702/ch126.htm [1997, March 6].

Utah State Office of Education. (1993, August). *Core Curriculum: Language Arts* (On-line). Author. http://www.uen.org/utahlink/UtahCore/LangArts.html [1996, July 3].

Wilhelm, J. D. (1996). *Standards in Practice: Grades 6–8*. Urbana, IL: National Council of Teachers of English.

Standards and Benchmarks

Mathematics

1. Uses a variety of strategies in the problem-solving process

K-2
- Draws pictures to represent problems
- Uses discussions with others to understand problems
- Explains to others how numerical problem was solved
- Makes organized lists or tables of information necessary for solving a problem
- Uses whole number models

3-5
- Uses a variety of strategies to understand problem situations
- Represents problem situations in a variety of forms
- Understands that some ways of representing a problem are more helpful than others
- Uses trial and error and the process of elimination to solve problems
- Knows the difference between pertinent and irrelevant information when solving problems
- Understands the basic language of logic in mathematical situations
- Determines reasonableness and verifies results of problems
- Understands basic valid and invalid arguments

6-8
- Breaks complex problems into smaller parts or uses similar problem types to solve problems
- Uses a variety of strategies to understand problem-solving situations and processes
- Understands advantages and disadvantages of different methods used to solve problems
- Formulates a problem, determines information needed, chooses method for obtaining information
- Represents problems in and translates among graphical forms
- Uses inductive reasoning
- Uses informal deductive reasoning methods
- Understands special symbols of mathematics
- Uses a variety of reasoning processes to model and solve problems

9-12
- Uses a variety of strategies to understand new content and develop efficient solution methods
- Constructs algorithms for multi-step and non-routine problems
- Understands the concept of a mathematical proof
- Constructs logical verifications or counter examples to test conjectures and justify solutions
- Uses formal mathematical language and notation
- Understands the difference between a theorem and a statement that is verified empirically
- Understands connections between equivalent representations and similar problem situations
- Understands the components of mathematical modeling

2. Understands and applies basic and advanced properties of the concepts of numbers

K-2
- Understands that a number is a symbol of how much of something there is
- Counts whole numbers
- Understands symbolic, concrete, and pictorial representations of numbers
- Understands basic whole number relationships
- Understands the concept of a unit and its subdivision into equal parts

3-5
- Understands relationships among fractions, decimals, mixed numbers, and whole numbers
- Understands equivalent forms of percents, fractions, and decimals
- Understands the basic difference between odd and even numbers
- Understands the meaning of place value
- Understands relative magnitude of whole numbers, fractions, decimals, and mixed numbers
- Uses models to identify, order, and compare numbers

6-8
- Understands the relationships among equivalent number representations
- Understands the characteristics and properties of the set of rational numbers and its subsets
- Understands the role of positive and negative integers in the number system
- Understands basic number theory concepts

- Understands the characteristics and uses of exponents and scientific notation
- Understands the structure of numeration systems that are based on numbers other than ten
- Understands the concepts of ratio, proportion, and percent and the relationships among them

9-12
- Understands properties of the real number system and its subsystems
- Understands the properties and basic theorems of roots, exponents, and logarithms
- Understands that different mathematical systems may have the same underlying structure
- Uses number theory concepts to solve problems
- Uses discrete structures to represent and to solve problems

3. Uses basic and advanced procedures while performing the processes of computation

K-2
- Adds and subtracts whole numbers
- Solves real-world problems involving addition and subtraction of whole numbers
- Understands common terms used with estimation
- Understands the inverse relationship between addition and subtraction

3-5
- Adds, subtracts, multiplies, and divides whole numbers and decimals
- Adds and subtracts simple fractions
- Uses specific strategies to estimate computations and check the reasonableness of results
- Performs basic mental computations
- Determines the effects of arithmetic operations on size and order of numbers
- Understands the properties of and the relationships among arithmetic operations
- Solves real-world problems involving number operations
- Knows the language of basic operations

6-8
- Adds, subtracts, multiplies, and divides fractions, integers, and rational numbers
- Understands exponentiation of rational numbers and root-extraction
- Selects and uses appropriate computational methods for a given situation
- Understands the correct order of operations for performing arithmetic computations
- Uses proportional reasoning to solve mathematical and real-world problems
- Understands the properties of operations with rational numbers
- Knows when an estimate is more appropriate than an exact answer
- Understands how different algorithms work for arithmetic computations and operations

9-12
- Adds, subtracts, multiplies, divides, and simplifies rational expressions
- Performs operations on and simplifies radical expressions containing positive rational numbers
- Understands various sources of discrepancy between an estimate and a calculated answer
- Uses a variety of operations on expressions containing real numbers
- Understands basic applications of and operations on matrices
- Uses recurrence relations to model and to solve real-world problems
- Understands counting procedures and reasoning

4. Understands and applies basic and advanced properties of the concepts of measurement

K-2
- Understands the basic measures length, width, height, weight, and temperature
- Understands the concept of time and how it is measured
- Uses standard and non-standard units to tell time, count money, and make basic measures
- Makes estimates of familiar linear dimensions, weights, and time intervals and checks them

3-5
- Understands the measures perimeter, area, volume, capacity, mass, angle, and circumference
- Selects and uses appropriate tools for given measurement situations
- Knows approximate size of basic standard units
- Understands the relationships between measures
- Understands that measurement is not exact
- Uses specific strategies to estimate quantities and measurements
- Selects and uses appropriate units of measurement, according to type and size of unit

6-8   • Understand the basic concept of rate as a measure
        • Solves problems involving perimeter and area of various shapes
        • Understands the relationships among dimensions and corresponding units of measure
        • Solves problems involving units of measurement and converts same-system units as appropriate
        • Understands the concepts of precision and significant digits as they relate to measurement
        • Selects and uses appropriate units and tools to find measurements for real-world problems
        • Understands formulas for finding measures
        • Selects and uses appropriate estimation techniques to solve real-world problems
        • Understands procedures for basic indirect measurements

9-12   • Solves problems involving rate as a measure
        • Understands the concepts of absolute and relative errors in measurement
        • Selects and uses an appropriate direct or indirect method of measurement in a given situation
        • Solves real-world problems involving three-dimensional measures

5. Understands and applies basic and advanced properties of the concepts of geometry

K-2   • Understands basic properties of and similarities and differences between simple geometric shapes
        • Understands the common language of spatial sense
        • Understands that geometric shapes are useful for representing and describing real world problems
        • Understands that patterns can be made by putting different shapes together or taking them apart

3-5   • Knows basic geometric language for describing and naming shapes
        • Understands basic properties of figures
        • Predicts and verifies the effects of combining, subdividing, and changing basic shapes
        • Understands that shapes can be congruent or similar
        • Uses motion geometry to understand geometric relationships
        • Understands characteristics of lines
        • Understands how scale in maps and drawings shows relative size and distance

6-8   • Uses geometric methods to complete basic geometric constructions
        • Understands the defining properties of three-dimensional figures
        • Understands the defining properties of triangles
        • Understands geometric transformations of figures
        • Understands the relationships between two- and three-dimensional representations of a figure
        • Understands the mathematical concepts of similarity and congruency
        • Understands the concept of tessellation
        • Understands the basic concept of Pythagorean Theorem

9-12   • Understands that geometric objects/relations correspond directly to algebraic objects/ relations
        • Uses the Pythagorean Theorem and its converse and properties of special right triangles
        • Uses synthetic representations and analytic methods to solve geometric problems
        • Understands the characteristics and uses of vectors
        • Uses geometric constructions to complete simple proofs, to model, and to solve problems
        • Uses basic operations on vectors
        • Understands the basic concepts of right triangle trigonometry
        • Uses trigonometric ration methods to solve mathematical and real-world problems
        • Understands the basic properties and uses of polar coordinates
        • Uses inductive and deductive reasoning to verify properties of and relationships among figures
        • Uses properties of and relationships among figures to solve problems

6. Understands and applies basic and advanced concepts of statistics and data analysis

K-2   • Understands that observations about objects or events can be displayed in simple graphs
        • Understands that one can find out about a group of things by studying just a few of them

3-5   • Understands that data represent specific pieces of real-world information
        • Understands that spreading data out on a number line helps identify extremes, gaps, and clusters

- Understands that a summary of data should include where the middle is and the spread around it
- Organizes and displays data in simple bar graphs, pie charts, and line graphs
- Reads and interprets simple bar graphs, pie charts, and line graphs
- Understands that collecting, organizing, and displaying data can be done in many ways
- Understands the basic concept of a sample

6-8
- Understands basic characteristics of measures of central tendency
- Understands basic characteristics of frequency and distribution
- Understands the basic concepts of center and dispersion of data
- Reads and interprets data in charts, tables, plots, and graphs
- Uses data and statistical measures for a variety of purposes
- Organizes and displays data using tables, graphs, frequency distributions, and plots
- Understands faulty arguments, common errors, and misleading presentations of data
- Understands that the same set of data can be represented in a variety of ways
- Understands the basic concept of outliers
- Understands basic concepts about how samples are chosen

9-12
- Selects and uses the best method of representing and describing a set of data
- Understands measures of central tendency and variability and their applications
- Understands the concept of correlation
- Understands different methods of curve-fitting and various applications of these methods
- Understands how outliers may affect various representations of data
- Understands the factors that can affect the interpretation of data
- Understands sampling distributions, the central limit theorem, and confidence intervals
- Understands how sampling representativeness, randomness, and bias can affect outcomes
- Understands that the role of statistics is to estimate the size of uncertainty in making an inference

7. Understands and applies basic and advanced concepts of probability

K-2
- Understands that some events are more likely to happen than others
- Understands why some events can be predicted fairly well while others cannot

3-5
- Understands that the word "chance" refers to the likelihood of an event
- Recognizes events that are sure to happen, sure not to happen, and may or may not happen
- Understands what must be assumed when predictions are based on what is known about the past
- Understands that statistical predictions are better for describing some types of events than others
- Uses basic sample spaces to describe events

6-8
- Determines probability using mathematical/theoretical models
- Determines probability using simulations or experiments
- Understands how predictions are based on data and probabilities
- Understands that the measure of certainty in a given situation depends on a number of factors
- Understands the relationship between the expression of a probability and the events producing it

9-12
- Understands the concept of a random variable
- Understands conditional probability and independent, dependent, and compound events
- Uses a variety of experimental, simulation, and theoretical methods to determine probabilities
- Understands the differences among experimental, simulation, and theoretical probability
- Understands the properties of the normal curve and how it is used
- Understands the concept of discrete probability distribution

8. Understands and applies basic and advanced properties of functions and algebra

K-2
- Recognizes regularities in a variety of contexts
- Extends simple patterns

3-5
- Recognizes a wide variety of patterns and the rules that explain them
- Understands that the same pattern can be represented in different ways

- Knows that a variable is a letter or symbol that stands for one or more numbers
- Understands the basic concept of an equality relationship
- Solves simple open sentences
- Knows basic characteristics and features of the rectangular coordinate system

6-8
- Knows what a mathematical expression is
- Understands that a variable can be used in many ways
- Understands various representations of patterns and functions and the relationships among them
- Understands the basic concept of a function
- Solves linear equations using concrete, informal, and formal methods
- Solves simple inequalities and non-linear equations with rational number solutions
- Understands special values of patterns, relationships, and functions
- Understands basic operations on algebraic expressions
- Uses the rectangular coordinate system to model and to solve problems
- Solves simple systems of equations graphically
- Understands the properties of arithmetic and geometric sequences

9-12
- Understands appropriate terminology and notation used to define functions and their properties
- Uses expressions, equations, inequalities, and matrices to represent variable quantity situations
- Understands characteristics and uses of basic trigonometric functions
- Understands properties of graphs
- Understands basic concepts and applications of polynomial equations
- Understands the concept of a function as the correspondence between the elements of two sets
- Uses a variety of models to represent functions, patterns, and relationships
- Understands the general properties and characteristics of many types of functions
- Understands the effects of parameter changes on functions and their graphs
- Understands the basic concept of inverse function and the corresponding graph
- Uses a variety of methods to solve systems of equations and inequalities
- Understands formal notation and various applications of sequences and series
- Uses a variety of methods to solve complex equations

9. Understands the general nature and uses of mathematics

K-2
- no benchmarks at this level

3-5
- Understands that numbers and operations can be used for real-world descriptions and predictions
- Understands that mathematical ideas can be represented concretely, graphically, and symbolically

6-8
- Understands that mathematics has been helpful in practical ways for many centuries
- Understands that real things are often represented using abstract ideas like numbers or lines

9-12
- Understands the relationship between the study of mathematics and the study of natural science
- Understands the original purpose of mathematics and how it has evolved
- Understands the importance of simplicity in mathematics
- Understands the influence of practical issues on mathematical theories
- Understands that new mathematics and mathematical connections continue to be invented today
- Understands that science and mathematics operate under common principles
- Understands that mathematics provides a precise system to describe objects and events
- Understands that technology opens many new doors to mathematics
- Understands that mathematics often stimulates innovations in science and technology
- Understands that mathematicians follow various sets of rules which do not contradict each other

Science

1. Understands basic features of the Earth

K-2
- Knows that Earth materials consist of solids, liquids, and gases
- Knows that water can change from one form to another, but the amount of water stays the same
- Knows that weather conditions change daily and weather patterns change over the seasons

3-5
- Knows that water can change from one state to another through various processes
- Knows the major differences between fresh and ocean waters
- Knows that clouds and fog are made of tiny droplets of water
- Knows that air is a substance that surrounds us, takes up space, and moves around us as wind
- Knows that night and day are caused by the Earth's rotation on its axis
- Knows that the Sun provides the light and heat necessary to maintain the Earth's temperature

6-8
- Knows that the Earth is the only body in our solar system that appears able to support life
- Knows that the Earth is comprised of layers
- Knows the composition and structure of the Earth's atmosphere
- Knows ways in which clouds affect weather and climate
- Knows how the Earth's movement and position to the Sun affect seasons and weather patterns
- Knows factors that can impact the Earth's climate
- Knows the processes involved in the water cycle
- Knows the properties that make water an essential component of the Earth system
- Knows that the Sun is the principle energy source for phenomena on the Earth's surface

9-12
- Knows the major external and internal sources of energy on Earth
- Knows that weather and climate involve the transfer of energy in and out of the atmosphere
- Knows how winds and ocean currents are produced on the Earth's surface
- Knows how life is adapted to conditions on the Earth

2. Understands basic Earth processes

K-2
- Knows that rocks come in many different shapes and sizes

3-5
- Knows that smaller rocks come from the breakage and weathering of bedrock and larger rocks
- Knows that rock is composed of different combinations of minerals
- Knows the composition and properties of soils
- Knows how slow and rapid processes constantly change features on the Earth's surface
- Knows that fossils provide evidence about the Earth's past

6-8
- Knows factors that influence soil texture, fertility, and resistance to erosion
- Knows that rocks contain evidence of the minerals, temperatures, and forces that created them
- Knows processes involved in the rock cycle
- Knows that the Earth's crust is divided into plates that move at extremely slow rates
- Knows how land forms are created through constructive and destructive forces
- Knows methods used to confirm the age, history, and changing life forms of the Earth
- Knows that fossils provide evidence of how life and conditions on Earth have changed

9-12
- Understands geochemical cycles
- Knows that throughout the rock cycle, the total amount of material remains constant
- Understands the concept of plate tectonics
- Knows effects of the movement of crustal plates
- Knows methods used to estimate geologic time
- Knows how the evolution of life on Earth has changed the composition of the Earth's atmosphere

3. **Understands essential ideas about the composition and structure of the universe and the Earth's place in it**

K-2
- Knows that the stars are innumerable, unevenly dispersed, and of unequal brightness
- Knows basic patterns of the Sun and Moon

3-5
- Knows that the Earth orbits the Sun, and the Moon orbits the Earth
- Knows patterns of stars in the sky and how these patterns change nightly and seasonally
- Knows that planets look like stars but over time they appear to wander among the constellations
- Knows that telescopes magnify distant objects and increase the number of stars we can see
- Knows that astronomical objects are massive and separated from one another by vast distances

6-8
- Knows characteristics of our Sun and its position in the universe
- Knows characteristics and movement patterns of the nine planets in our Solar System
- Knows that the planet Earth and our Solar System appear to be somewhat unique
- Knows characteristics and movement patterns of asteroids, comets, and meteoroids
- Knows how the motions of the Sun and Moon explain phenomena on Earth
- Knows that the universe contains billions of stars and galaxies

9-12
- Understands general concepts related to the "big bang" theory of the origin of the universe
- Knows the ongoing processes involved in star formation and destruction
- Knows common characteristics of stars in the universe
- Knows ways in which technology has increased our understanding of the universe
- Knows that evidence suggests that our universe is expanding

4. **Knows about the diversity and unity that characterize life**

K-2
- Knows that plants and animals have features that help them live in different environments

3-5
- Knows different ways in which living things can be grouped and purposes of different groupings
- Knows that plants and animals progress through life cycles

6-8
- Knows ways in which living things can be classified
- Knows that animals and plants have different structures that serve different functions for survival
- Knows characteristics that unify a species of sexually reproducing organisms
- Knows evidence that supports the idea that there is unity among organisms

9-12
- Knows how organisms are classified into groups based on evolutionary relationships
- Knows how variation increases chance of survival of a species and of life

5. **Understands the genetic basis for the transfer of biological characteristics from one generation to the next**

K-2
- Knows that plants and animals closely resemble their parents
- Knows that differences exist among individuals of the same kind of plant or animal

3-5
- Knows that an organism's characteristics can be inherited or learned

6-8
- Knows that reproduction is essential to the continuation of a species
- Understands asexual and sexual reproduction
- Knows that the characteristics of an organism can be described in terms of a combination of traits
- Knows that hereditary information is carried in genes
- Knows how dominant and recessive traits contribute to genetic variation within a species

9-12
- Knows the properties of DNA and its role in specifying the characteristics of an organism
- Knows that genes may be altered or combined to create genetic variation within a species
- Knows that heritable characteristics can only be passed on through an organism's sex cells
- Knows that mutations and new gene combinations may have positive, negative, or no effects on the organism
- Knows characteristics of human genetics

6. Knows the general structure and functions of cells in organisms

K-2 • Knows basic life requirements of plants and animals

3-5 • Knows that plants and animals have structures that perform various functions

6-8 • Knows that cells are the fundamental units of life
• Knows that cells convert energy obtained from food to carry on life functions
• Knows the levels of organization in living systems (e.g., cells, tissues, organs, organ systems)
• Knows that specialized systems in multicellular organisms perform specialized functions
• Knows causes of disease in organisms

9-12 • Knows the structures of different types of cell parts and the functions they perform
• Understands the chemical reactions involved in cell functions
• Understands cell differentiation
• Knows how cell functions are regulated
• Knows that genetic information stored in DNA provides instructions for protein synthesis in cells
• Knows the structures of proteins and the role of proteins in cell function
• Understands the structure and functions of nervous systems in multicellular animals

7. Understands how species depend on one another and on the environment for survival

K-2 • Knows that living things are found almost everywhere in the world

3-5 • Knows that organisms' behavior is influenced by internal cues and external cues
• Knows that environmental factors influence organisms' patterns of behavior
• Knows that changes in the environment can have different effects on different organisms
• Knows that all organisms cause beneficial and detrimental changes in their environments

6-8 • Knows how organisms regulate and maintain life functions in a constantly changing environment
• Knows that organisms react to internal and environmental stimuli through behavioral response
• Knows ways in which species interact and depend on one another in an ecosystem
• Knows components of populations and ecosystems
• Knows factors that affect the number and types of organisms an ecosystem can support
• Knows relationships that exist among organisms in food chains and food webs

9-12 • Knows how the interrelationships among organisms generate and maintain stable ecosystems
• Knows ways in which humans can modify ecosystems and cause irreversible effects

8. Understands the cycling of matter and flow of energy through the living environment

K-2 • Knows resources that plants and animals require for energy and growth

3-5 • Knows that energy transfer is essential to all living organisms
• Knows the organization of simple food chains and food webs

6-8 • Knows how energy is transferred through food webs in an ecosystem
• Knows how matter is recycled within ecosystems

9-12 • Knows how chemical elements cycle through living systems and the physical environment
• Knows that living systems require a continuous input of energy
• Understands how plants transfer energy from the Sun to living systems
• Knows how organisms are designed to obtain, transport, release, and eliminate matter and energy
• Knows factors that limit the amount of life an environment can support

9. Understands the basic concepts of the evolution of species

K-2 • Knows that some kinds of organisms that once lived on Earth have completely disappeared

3-5 • Knows similarities and differences that exist among fossils of past life and existing organisms

6-8
- Knows that fossils document the appearance, diversification, and extinction of many life forms
- Knows basic ideas related to biological evolution
- Understands the concept of extinction and its importance in biological evolution

9-12
- Knows that heritable characteristics largely influence organisms' chances for survival
- Understands the concept of natural selection
- Knows how natural selection explains the diversity and unity of past and present life forms
- Knows the theory of evolution
- Knows the history of the origin and evolution of life on Earth

10. Understands basic concepts about the structure and properties of matter

K-2
- Knows that different objects are made up of different materials and have different properties
- Knows that the properties of different materials can be changed in different ways

3-5
- Knows that objects can be classified according to their properties
- Knows that materials may be composed of parts that cannot be seen without magnification
- Knows that tools can be used to measure properties such as length, weight, and volume
- Knows that materials have different states and can be changed from one state to another
- Knows that the mass of a material remains constant

6-8
- Knows that all matter is made up of atoms
- Knows that a molecule (or crystal) is the smallest particle of a substance that retains its properties
- Knows that atoms in solids, liquids, and gas are in constant, random motion
- Knows that pure elements contain only one kind of atom, and over 100 elements exist
- Knows that many elements can be grouped according to similar properties
- Knows that substances can react chemically to form new substances with different properties
- Understands the conservation of matter in physical and chemical change
- Knows methods used to separate mixtures into their component parts
- Knows factors that influence reaction rates
- Knows that oxidation involves the combining of oxygen with another substance

9-12
- Understands the arrangement of the periodic table
- Knows how the electron configuration of atoms governs the chemical properties of an element
- Knows that atoms can be bonded together to form molecules and compounds
- Knows factors that determine the physical properties of a compound
- Knows the structure of an atom
- Knows that the number of electrons in an atom determines whether the atom is electrically neutral or an ion
- Knows that most elements have two or more isotopes
- Knows how radioactive isotopes can be used to estimate the age of materials that contain them
- Knows that electrons, neutrons, and protons are made up of even smaller constituents
- Knows factors that affect the rate at which chemical reactions can take place
- Understands the complete mole concept and ways in which it can be used
- Knows that chemical reactions can be accelerated by catalysts
- Knows structures that may be formed from the bonding of carbon atoms and their roles in various chemical reactions
- Understands oxidation/reduction reactions and acid/base reactions
- Understands radical reactions and their role in natural and human processes

11. Understands energy types, sources, and conversions, and their relationship to heat and temperature

K-2
- Knows that the Sun supplies heat and light to Earth
- Knows ways in which heat can be produced
- Knows that electricity in circuits can produce light, heat, sound, and magnetic effects

3-5
- Knows that heat is often produced as a byproduct when one form of energy is converted to another form
- Knows that some materials conduct heat better than others
- Knows the organization of a simple electrical circuit

6-8
- Knows that energy is a property of many substances
- Understands that energy cannot be created or destroyed
- Knows how the Sun acts as a major source of energy for changes on the Earth's surface
- Knows that heat can be transferred through conduction, convection, and radiation
- Knows that electrical circuits are used to transfer electrical energy
- Knows that most chemical and nuclear reactions involve a transfer of energy

9-12
- Knows that although the total energy of the universe remains constant, it tends to spread out uniformly
- Knows that all energy can be considered to be kinetic, potential, or energy contained by a field
- Understands the relationship between heat and temperature
- Understands that chemical reactions either release or consume energy
- Knows how the energy associated with individual atoms and molecules can be used to identify the substances they comprise
- Understands processes involved in nuclear reactions

12. Understands motion and the principles that explain it

K-2
- Knows that vibrating objects produce sound
- Knows that light travels in a straight line until it strikes an object
- Knows that an object's position can be described by locating it relative to another object or the background
- Knows that things move in many different ways
- Knows that the position and motion of an object can be changed by pushing or pulling

3-5
- Knows that the pitch of a sound depends on the frequency of the vibration producing it
- Knows that light can be reflected, refracted, or absorbed
- Knows that an object's motion can be described by tracing and measuring its position over time
- Knows effects of applying a force to an object
- Knows the relationship between the strength of a force and its effect on an object

6-8
- Knows characteristics of vibrations
- Knows that light interacts with matter through transmission, absorption, and scattering
- Knows that visible light makes up only a narrow range of wavelengths of electromagnetic radiation
- Knows how an object's motion can be described and represented graphically
- Understands effects of balanced and unbalanced forces on an object's motion
- Knows that an object that is not being subjected to a force will continue to move at a constant speed and in a straight line

9-12
- Knows that waves have energy and can transfer energy when they interact with matter
- Knows the range of the electromagnetic spectrum and characteristics of electromagnetic waves
- Knows that apparent changes in wavelength can provide information about changes in motion
- Understands general concepts related to the theory of special relativity
- Knows how the laws of motion can be used to determine the effects of forces on the motion of objects

13. Knows the kinds of forces that exist between objects and within atoms

K-2
- Knows that magnets can be used to make some things move without being touched
- Knows that things near the Earth fall to the ground unless something holds them up

3-5
- Knows effects of electrically charged material on other charged and uncharged materials
- Knows that magnets attract and repel each other and attract certain kinds of other materials
- Knows that the Earth's gravity pulls any object toward it without touching it

6-8
- Knows that electric currents can produce magnetic forces and magnets can cause electric currents
- Understands general concepts related to gravitational force

9-12 • Knows how insulators, semiconductors, conductors, and superconductors respond to electric forces
• Knows how an excess or deficit of negative charges in a material affects the material
• Knows that magnetic and electric forces are different aspects of a single electromagnetic force
• Knows that electromagnetic forces exist within and between atoms
• Understands the relative strength of nuclear, electromagnetic, and gravitational forces
• Knows how to calculate the strength of the gravitational force between two masses
• Knows how to calculate the strength of the electric force between two charged objects

14. Understands the nature of scientific knowledge

K-2 • Knows that scientific investigations generally work the same way in different places

3-5 • Knows that the general evidence collected from an investigation should be replicable by others

6-8 • Knows that experiments should yield consistent results before the results are accepted as correct
• Knows that most core ideas in science are supported by much experimental and observational evidence
• Knows that the work of science requires questioning, response to criticism, and open communication

9-12 • Knows ways in which science distinguishes itself from other bodies of knowledge
• Knows that scientific explanations must meet certain criteria to be considered valid
• Understands how scientific knowledge changes and accumulates over time
• Knows that most changes to the body of scientific knowledge are small modifications

15. Understands the nature of scientific inquiry

K-2 • Knows that learning can come from careful observations and simple experiments
• Knows that tools can be used to gather information and extend the senses

3-5 • Knows the basic purposes and functions of scientific investigations
• Knows that scientists use different kinds of investigations to answer different questions
• Plans and conducts simple investigations
• Uses simple equipment and tools to gather scientific data and extend the senses
• Knows that good scientific explanations are based on evidence and scientific knowledge
• Knows that scientists make the results of their investigations public
• Knows that scientists review and ask questions about the results of other scientists' work
• Knows that different people may interpret the same set of observations differently

6-8 • Knows general methods used to conduct scientific investigations
• Designs and conducts a scientific investigation
• Knows that observations can be affected by bias
• Uses appropriate tools and techniques to gather, analyze, and interpret scientific data
• Establishes relationships based on evidence and logical argument
• Understands the nature of scientific explanations
• Knows that scientific inquiry involves evaluating models, explanations, and results of experiments
• Knows possible outcomes of scientific investigations

9-12 • Understands the use of hypotheses in science
• Uses scientific procedures to design and conduct scientific investigations
• Knows that observation may be used when conditions of an investigation cannot be controlled
• Uses technology and mathematics to perform scientific investigations and communications
• Knows that conceptual principles and historical and current knowledge guide scientific inquiries
• Knows that scientists conduct investigations for a variety of reasons
• Knows that scientific investigations and communications must meet certain criteria to be valid

16. Understands the scientific enterprise

K-2 • Knows that in science it is helpful to work with a team and share findings with others

3-5 • Knows that people of all ages, backgrounds, and groups have contributed to science

- Knows that science is an ongoing process and will never be finished
- Knows that scientists and engineers often work in teams to accomplish a task

6-8
- Knows that people of diverse backgrounds and interests engage in fields of science
- Knows that the work of science requires various human abilities, qualities, and habits of mind
- Knows various settings in which scientists and engineers may work
- Understands ethics associated with scientific study
- Knows that much of current scientific knowledge is based on ideas that were not accepted in earlier periods of history
- Knows ways in which science and society influence one another

9-12
- Knows that throughout history, diverse cultures have developed scientific ideas
- Knows that individuals and teams contribute to science at different levels of complexity
- Understands the ethical traditions associated with the scientific enterprise
- Knows that science and technology only indicate what can happen in society, not what should happen
- Understands that science involves different types of work in many different disciplines
- Knows that creativity, imagination, and a good knowledge base are required in scientific work

History: Historical Understanding

1. Understands and knows how to analyze chronological relationships and patterns

K-2
- Knows how to identify the beginning, middle, and end of historical stories, myths, and narratives
- Knows how to develop picture time lines
- Distinguishes among broad categories of historical time
- Understands calendar time in days, weeks, and months

3-5
- Understands calendar time in years, decades, and centuries
- Knows how to construct time lines
- Knows how to interpret data presented in time lines
- Knows how to identify patterns of change and continuity
- Distinguishes between past, present, and future time
- Understands the broadly defined eras of state and local historical events

6-8
- Understands how to diagram the temporal structure of events in various sources
- Knows how to construct and interpret multiple tier time lines
- Know how to calculate calendar time
- Understands patterns of change and continuity in the historical succession of related events
- Knows how to impose temporal structure on their historical narratives
- Knows how to periodize events of the nation into broadly defined eras

9-12
- Knows how to identify the temporal structure and connections disclosed in historical narratives
- Understands historical continuity and change related to a particular development or theme
- Understands the organizing principles of alternative models of historical periodization
- Understands systems of recording time and the astronomical systems on which they are based

2. Understands the historical perspective

5-6
- Knows how to view the past in terms of the norms and values of the time
- Understands that specific individuals had a great impact on history
- Understands that specific ideas had an impact on history
- Understands that "chance events" had an impact on history
- Understands that specific decisions and events had an impact on history
- Evaluates historical fiction according to the accuracy of its content and the author's interpretation
- Predicts how events might have turned out differently if different courses of action were chosen

7-8
- Understands that specific individuals and their values had an impact on history
- Analyzes the influence specific ideas and beliefs had on a period of history

- Analyzes the effect that specific "chance events" had on history
- Analyzes the effects specific decisions had on history
- Understands that historical accounts are subject to change based on newly uncovered records
- Knows different types of primary and secondary sources

9-12
- Analyzes the values held by specific people who influenced history
- Analyzes how things might have been different in the absence of specific ideas and beliefs
- Analyzes how things might have been different in the absence of specific "chance events"
- Analyzes how things might have been different in the absence of specific decisions
- Knows that the consequences of human intentions are influenced by the means of carrying them out
- Understands that change and continuity are equally probable and natural
- Knows how to avoid seizing upon particular lessons of history as cures for present ills
- Understands how past events are affected by the irrational and the accidental
- Analyzes how historical interpretations are influenced by newly uncovered records
- Understands how the past affects our private lives and society in general
- Knows how to perceive past events with historical empathy
- Knows how to evaluate the credibility and authenticity of historical sources
- Evaluates the validity and credibility of different historical interpretations
- Uses historical maps to understand the relationship between historical events and geography

History: K-4 History

1. Understands family life now and in the past, and family life in various places long ago

K-2
- Knows a family history through two generations
- Understands family life today and how it compares to family life in the recent past and long ago
- Knows the cultural similarities and differences between families now and in the past
- Understands family life in a community of the past and a community of the present
- Understands personal family or cultural heritage through stories, songs, and celebrations
- Knows ways in which people share family beliefs and values

3-4
- Knows the ways that families long ago expressed and transmitted their beliefs and values
- Understands the dreams, ideals, and problems of various groups of people
- Understands the daily life of a farm family from long ago

2. Understands the history of the local community and how communities in North America varied long ago

K-2
- Understands changes in community life over time
- Understands the contributions and significance of historical figures of the community
- Understands the daily life and values of early Hawaiians or Native American cultures
- Understands the daily life of a colonial community
- Understands life in a pioneer farming community

3-4
- Knows of problems, different perspectives, choices, and solutions in the community's past
- Knows characteristics of Native American societies long ago
- Understands the historical development and daily life of a colonial community
- Understands the challenges and difficulties encountered by people in pioneer farming communities
- Understands how geographical features contributed to the establishment and growth of communities
- Understands daily life in ethnically diverse urban communities long ago
- Knows the history of the local community since its founding
- Understands changes in land use and economic activities in the local community since its founding

3. **Understands the people, events, problems, and ideas that were significant in creating the history of their state**

K-2
- Understands the origins and culture of different groups who lived in the state or region
- Knows the impact of early explorers and settlers on the environment of the state or region
- Understands the reasons different groups came to the state or region
- Understands the different lives, plans, and dreams of various racial and ethnic groups in the state
- Understands how symbols, slogans, and mottoes represent the state
- Knows important buildings, statues, and monuments in the state's history

3-4
- Understands differences between the lives of Native Americans or Hawaiians today and in the past
- Understands reasons the first explorers and settlers came to the state or region
- Knows about the first and successive groups of inhabitants in the state or region
- Understands the reasons recent immigrants came to the state and their experiences
- Understands population patterns and changes over a period of time in a city or town in the state
- Knows the order of major events in state history, their impact on people, and how they relate to national history
- Understands major historical events that involved interaction among various groups in the state
- Understands the influence of geography on the history of the state or region
- Understands how the ideas of significant people affected the history of the state
- Understands the unique historical conditions that led to statehood
- Knows the origin of the names of places, rivers, cities, and counties in the state

4. **Understands how democratic values came to be, and how they have been exemplified by people, events, and symbols**

K-2
- Knows the English colonists who became revolutionary leaders and fought for independence
- Understands how individuals worked to achieve the liberties and equality associated with the principles of American democracy
- Understands ways in which fundamental values have been applied by different groups of people
- Knows how people in the community have taken responsibility for the common good
- Understands the significance of important figures to the history of our democracy
- Understands the ways in which people in a variety of fields have advanced various causes
- Understands the reasons that Americans celebrate certain national holidays
- Knows the history of American symbols
- Knows why important buildings, statues, and monuments are associated with state and national history
- Understands how people have helped newcomers get settled and learn the ways of the new country

3-4
- Understands the ideas of important national documents and the people responsible for them
- Understands the basic principles of American democracy
- Understands how people over the last 200 years have struggled to bring the basic principles of American democracy to different groups of people
- Understands the accomplishments of ordinary people in historical situations and how they struggled for the common good
- Understands how people in the local community displayed courage in helping the common good
- Understands historical figures who believed in the fundamental democratic values
- Understands the character traits of historical figures who have advanced individual rights and the common good
- Understands the historical events and democratic values commemorated by national holidays
- Knows the history of events and figures responsible for historical documents
- Knows the significance of the Pledge of Allegiance and other patriotic songs, sayings, and poems
- Understands how songs, symbols, and slogans reflect freedom of expression and the role of protest in democracy
- Understands why Americans went to war to win independence from England
- Understands how ordinary people have worked to create or enhance our national symbols
- Understands how people have helped to make the community a better place to live

5. **Understands the causes and nature of movements of large groups of people into and within the United States, now and long ago**

K-2 • Understands what life was like for children and families "on the trail"

3-4 • Knows the various movements of large groups of people in the history of the U.S.
 • Knows how Native Americans were affected by European colonization and expansion of the U.S.
 • Understands the experience of immigrant groups
 • Knows the reasons various groups migrated to different parts of the U.S.
 • Understands the experiences of those who moved from farm to city during the time when cities grew

6. **Understands the folklore and other cultural contributions from various regions of the United States and how they helped to form a national heritage**

K-2 • Knows regional folk heroes, stories, or songs that contribute to the cultural history of the U.S.
 • Knows the differences between toys and games children played long ago and those of today

3-4 • Understands the contributions of regional folk heroes and popular figures to the cultural history of the U.S.
 • Understands how stories, legends, songs, ballads, and tall tales describe people's lives
 • Understands how arts, crafts, music, and language of people from various regions influenced the nation

7. **Understands selected attributes and historical developments of societies in Africa, the Americas, Asia, and Europe**

K-2 • Understands the main ideas in stories, songs, and other traditional literature that reflect different cultures
 • Knows the holidays and ceremonies of different societies
 • Understands the daily life, history, and beliefs of a country as reflected in various art forms
 • Knows the journeys of Marco Polo and Christopher Columbus

3-4 • Understands how historians learn about the past if there are no written records
 • Knows the effects geography has had on different aspects of societies
 • Knows various aspects of family life, structures, and roles in different cultures and eras
 • Knows about life in urban areas and communities of various cultures of the world
 • Knows significant historical achievements of various cultures of the world
 • Knows about the migrations of large groups in the past and recently
 • Knows about European explorers of the 15th and 16th centuries
 • Knows about the various items transported during the "Columbian Exchange"
 • Understands the different perspectives and major arguments surrounding the Columbian encounter

8. **Understands major discoveries in science and technology, some of their social and economic effects, and the major scientists and inventors responsible for them**

K-2 • Understands differences between hunters and gatherers and people who cultivate food
 • Knows the accomplishments of major scientists and inventors
 • Knows basic information about marine transportation
 • Knows the ways people communicate with each other and technology that facilitated communication
 • Knows various systems of long-distance communication and their effects
 • Understands differences in the methods of travel from various times in human history

3-4 • Knows about the development of the wheel and its early uses in ancient societies
 • Understands the development and the influence of basic tools on work and behavior
 • Knows various technological developments to control fire, water, wind, and soil and natural resources
 • Knows about technological inventions and developments that evolved during the 19th century
 • Knows the different forms of transportation and their developments over time
 • Understands the development of marine vessels
 • Understands the development of extensive road systems
 • Knows the developments of rail transportation in the 19th century
 • Understands the design and development of aircraft and rocketry
 • Knows about people who have made significant contributions in the field of transportation

- Understands the origins and changes in methods of writing over time
- Understands the significance of electronic developments in communication and their impact on the spread of ideas
- Knows about people who have made significant contributions in the field of communications
- Knows the significant scientific and technological achievements of various societies

History: United States History

1. Understands the characteristics of societies in the Americas, Western Europe, and Western Africa that increasingly interacted after 1450

5-6
- Understands the migration and settlement patterns of peoples in the Americas
- Understands the significance of beliefs held by both Native Americans and Europeans
- Understands social, economic, and cultural characteristics of European society
- Knows the impact of geography on the development of Western and Central Africa
- Understands characteristics of African, European, and Native American societies who converged in the western hemisphere after 1492
- Understands the impact of location and physical geography on different Native American societies
- Understands how various tribes united to form the Iroquois nation
- Knows factors that led to the age of exploration in the Americas

7-8
- Understands the rise and decline of the Mississippian mound-building society
- Understands the role of religion in Western Europe during the age of exploration
- Understands Islamic influences on Western Africa in the 15th and 16th centuries
- Knows factors that contributed to European exploration and settlement of the Americas
- Knows European perspectives of different cultures during the age of exploration and settlement

9-12
- Understands economic changes in Western Europe during the age of exploration
- Understands the similarities and differences among Native American societies
- Understands factors that stimulated overseas exploration
- Understands characteristics of Western African societies in the 15th and 16th centuries
- Understands facets of Native American culture
- Understands European perceptions of Native American societies during exploration

2. Understands cultural and ecological interactions among previously unconnected people resulting from early European exploration and colonization

5-6
- Knows the features of major European explorations between the 15th and 17th centuries
- Understands aspects of Spanish exploration, conquest, and immigration to the Americas

7-8
- Understands immediate and long-term impacts of Columbus' voyages on Native Americans
- Understands characteristics of Spanish and Portuguese exploration and conquest
- Understands differing motives among English, Spanish, French, and Dutch colonizers

9-12
- Understands political and religious factors that influenced colonization in the Americas
- Understands economic characteristics of the early Spanish and Portuguese empires in the Americas
- Understands ways in which historical interpretations of Columbus' voyages have changed
- Understands the long-term social and ecological impacts of the Columbian Exchange
- Understands characteristics of Spanish conquest and settlement in the Americas

3. Understands why the Americas attracted Europeans, why they brought enslaved Africans to their colonies, and how Europeans struggled for control of North America and the Caribbean

5-6
- Understands the lives of free and indentured immigrants who came to the Americas from Europe
- Understands changes in the European colonies in the centuries following their founding
- Understands the interaction between English settlers and Native Americans
- Knows similarities and differences among people in English, Spanish, and French settlements

7-8 • Understands cultural and environmental impacts of European settlement in North America
• Understands events that led to English victory over the French in the Seven Years War

9-12 • Understands characteristics of European colonization in the 17th and 18th centuries
• Understands the events and consequences of the Seven Years War
• Understands the nature of interaction between Native Americans and settlers

4. Understands how political, religious, and social institutions emerged in the North American colonies

5-6 • Understands the influence of Enlightenment ideas on American society
• Understands the development of colonial governments
• Understands Puritanism in colonial America
• Understands ways family and community life differed in regions of colonial North America

7-8 • Understand ideas that influenced religious and political aspects of colonial America
• Understands the concepts that contributed to the "rights of Englishmen"
• Understands the impact of the Civil War and the Glorious Revolution on the colonies
• Understands the tensions that led to violent conflict between colonists and their governments
• Understands the role of religion in the English colonies
• Understands how family and gender roles of different colonial regions changed over time

9-12 • Understands the development of representative government in colonial America
• Understands how gender, property ownership, religion, and legal status affected political rights
• Understands characteristics of religious development in colonial America
• Understands characteristics of the social structure of colonial America
• Understands the similarities and differences in colonial concepts of community
• Understands the elements of ethnic, class, and race relations in conflicts of colonial America

5. Understands how the values and institutions of European economic life took root in the colonies and how slavery reshaped European and African life in the Americas

5-6 • Understands the factors that shaped the economic system in the colonies and the Americas
• Understands economic life in the New England, Chesapeake, and southern colonies
• Understands elements of African slavery during the colonial period in North America

7-8 • Understands mercantilism and how it influenced patterns of economic activity
• Understands the environmental and legislative impacts on economic growth in the colonies
• Understands patterns of indentured servitude and influences on slavery
• Understands events that shaped African slavery in colonial America

9-12 • Understands the characteristics of mercantilism in colonial America
• Understands factors that influenced economic life in North American and West Indian colonies
• Understands elements of slavery in the colonies in the 17th century
• Understands the contributions of African slaves

6. Understands the causes of the American Revolution, the ideas and interests involved in shaping the revolutionary movement, and reasons for the American victory

5-6 • Understands the major consequences of the Seven Years War
• Knows events that led to the outbreak of the American Revolution and the Revolutionary War
• Understands the major ideas of the Declaration of Independence
• Understands the major developments and chronology of the Revolutionary War
• Understands perspectives of and roles played in the American Revolution by various groups
• Understands the contributions of each European power to the outcome of the Revolution

7-8 • Understands events that contributed to the "shot heard 'round the world"
• Understands contradictions between the Declaration of Independence and chattel slavery
• Understands the strategic elements of the Revolutionary War

- Understands the impact of European countries and individual Europeans on the American victory
- Understands the terms and implications of the Treaty of Paris
- Understands the creation of the Declaration of Independence

9-12
- Understands the social, political, and religious aspects of the American Revolution
- Understands how the ideas of the Declaration of Independence justified American independence
- Understands how the Declaration of Independence compares to other documents
- Understands the factors that led to the American victory in the Revolutionary War
- Understands the social and economic impact of the Revolutionary War
- Understands contributions of European nations during the American Revolution
- Understands how the Treaty of Paris influenced U.S. relations with other countries and Native Americans
- Understands the arguments of advocates and opponents of slavery in the revolutionary period
- Understands the military and diplomatic factors that helped produce the Treaty of Paris

7. Understands the impact of the American Revolution on politics, economy, and society

5-6
- Understands the major political issues in the thirteen colonies after their independence
- Understands the factors that led to Shay's Rebellion
- Understands the impact of the American revolutionary victory on different groups

7-8
- Understands political and economic issues addressed by the Continental Congress
- Understands how the ideals of the American Revolution influenced the goals of various groups

9-12
- Understands the differences among various state constitutions
- Understands efforts to rebuild the economy after the American Revolution
- Understands the goals of different groups of people after the American Revolution

8. Understands the institutions and practices of government created during the revolution and how these elements were revised between 1787 and 1815 to create the foundation of the American political system based on the U.S. Constitution and the Bill of Rights

5-6
- Understands events leading to the Constitutional Convention
- Understands the issues and ideas raised at the Constitutional Convention
- Understands the significance of the Bill of Rights and its specific guarantees
- Understands differences in early leaders and social and economic composition of the 1790s
- Understands the impact of the Whiskey Rebellion

7-8
- Understands events that led to and shaped the Constitutional Convention
- Understands arguments over the necessity of a Bill of Rights
- Understands events in the development of the U.S. Supreme Court
- Understands the development and impact of the American party system
- Understands the role of ordinary people in the Whiskey Rebellion

9-12
- Understands influences on the ideas established by the Constitution
- Understands how the Federalists and Anti-Federalists differed
- Understands the Bill of Rights and various challenges to it
- Understands the impact of Chief Justice Marshall's decisions
- Understands how the federal judiciary changed between the 1790s and the 19th century
- Understands the factors that led to the development of the two-party system
- Understands the factors that led to the Whiskey Rebellion

9. Understands the United States territorial expansion between 1801 and 1861, and how it affected relations with external powers and Native Americans

5-6
- Understands the factors that led to U.S. territorial expansion in the Western Hemisphere
- Understands the War of 1812
- Knows the foreign territorial claims in the Western Hemisphere in 1800
- Understands the impact of territorial expansion on Native American tribes

- Understands the origins and impact of Manifest Destiny
- Understands elements of the relationship between Texas and Mexico in the mid-19th century
- Understands events that led to the Mexican-American War

7-8
- Understands the short-term political and long-term cultural impacts of the Louisiana Purchase
- Understands how early state and federal policy influenced various Native American tribes
- Understands the social and political impact of the idea of Manifest Destiny
- Understands how various conflicts with Britain and Russia were resolved from 1815-1850
- Understands the significance of the Lewis and Clark expedition
- Understands the major events of U.S. foreign policy during the early 19th century

9-12
- Understands the impact of the Louisiana Purchase
- Understands the major provisions of the Monroe Doctrine
- Understands shifts in government policies toward Native Americans in the early 19th century
- Understands the initiating factors and outcomes of the Mexican-American War
- Understands different perspectives of events leading to the Mexican-American War
- Understands political interests and views regarding the War of 1812

10. Understands how the industrial revolution, increasing immigration, the rapid expansion of slavery, and the westward movement changed American lives and led to regional tensions

5-6
- Understands the lives of immigrants in American society during the antebellum period
- Understands the impact of major technological developments between 1801 and 1860
- Understands social and economic elements of urban and rural life in the early 19th century
- Understands popular and high culture in growing urban areas during the 19th century
- Understands how slavery shaped social and economic life in the South after 1800
- Understands elements of early western migration

7-8
- Understands how immigration affected American society in the antebellum period
- Understands the role of government in various areas of public service in the early 1800s
- Understands the social and economic impacts of the factory system
- Understands influences on urban life in the early and late 19th century
- Understands different economic, cultural, and social characteristics of slavery after 1800
- Understands characteristics of life on the western frontier in the 19th century
- Understands how major technological and economic developments influenced various groups

9-12
- Understands policies affecting regional and national interests during the early 19th century
- Understands characteristics of economic development during the 19th century
- Understands how slavery influenced economic and social elements of Southern society
- Understands significant religious, cultural, and social changes in the American West
- Understands the impact of the Industrial Revolution during the early and later 19th century
- Understands the social and cultural influence of former slaves in cities of the North

11. Understands the extension, restriction, and reorganization of political democracy after 1800

5-6
- Understands elements of suffrage in the antebellum years
- Understands why the election of Andrew Jackson was known as a victory for the "common man"
- Understands divisive issues prior to the Civil War

7-8
- Understands political influences and views after 1800
- Understands events that promoted sectional conflicts in the antebellum period
- Understands issues that influenced party development and promoted sectional differences

9-12
- Understands increased political activity in the first half of the 19th century
- Understands the positions of northern antislavery advocates and southern proslavery spokesmen

12. **Understands the sources and character of cultural, religious, and social reform movements in the antebellum period**

5-6
- Understands how literary and artistic movements fostered a distinct American identity
- Understands the major characteristics of the abolition movement in the antebellum period
- Understands the religious revivals that swept the nation in the early 19th century
- Understands the role of women in the reform movements in antebellum America

7-8
- Understands perspectives that influenced slavery in the antebellum period
- Understands the significant religious, philosophical, and social movements of the 19th century
- Understands how women influenced American society during the antebellum period

9-12
- Understands elements of slavery in both the North and South during the antebellum period
- Understands the social impact of the Second Great Awakening
- Understands the ideas of Transcendentalism
- Understands the development of Utopian communities
- Understands changing gender roles in the antebellum period
- Understands the ideas associated with women's rights during the antebellum period

13. **Understands the causes of the Civil War**

5-6
- Understands slavery prior to the Civil War
- Knows the locations of the southern and northern states and their economic resources

7-8
- Understands the economic, social, and cultural differences between the North and the South
- Understands the development of sectional polarization and secession prior to the Civil War
- Understands issues other than slavery that led to the Civil War

9-12
- Understands the reasons for the disruption of the second American party system
- Understands events that fueled the political and sectional conflicts over slavery

14. **Understands the course and character of the Civil War and its effects on the American people**

5-6
- Understands the technological, social, and strategic aspects of the Civil War
- Understands the provisions and significance of the Emancipation Proclamation
- Understands the impact of the Civil War on social and gender issues

7-8
- Understands the circumstances that shaped the Civil War and its outcome
- Understands how different groups of people shaped the Civil War

9-12
- Understands military events that influenced the outcome of the Civil War
- Understands the influence of Abraham Lincoln's ideas on the Civil War
- Understands the impact of the Civil War on Native Americans
- Understands how the Civil War influenced Northern and Southern society on the home front
- Understands how the Civil War influenced both military personnel and civilians

15. **Understands how various reconstruction plans succeeded or failed**

5-6
- Understands military, political, and social factors affecting the post-Civil War period
- Understands changes in social relations in the South during Reconstruction
- Understands the lives of African Americans during the Reconstruction era
- Understands the impact of the Reconstruction period on politics in the South
- Understands how the economy and life in the North and South changed over the war years

7-8
- Understands the effect of differing Reconstruction policies and how they were perceived
- Understands the reasons for and consequences of President Johnson's impeachment and trial
- Understands the economic and social problems facing the South
- Understands attempts to improve African American lives during Reconstruction
- Understands changes in different regions during Reconstruction

9-12 • Understands the elements of different plans for Reconstruction
• Understands the 14th and 15th amendments to the Constitution
• Understands events leading to the formation of the Compromise of 1877
• Understands impacts on African American attempts to improve their lives during Reconstruction
• Understands social and economic factors during and toward the end of Reconstruction
• Understands different perspectives of Reconstruction
• Understands the extent to which social and political issues were influenced by the Civil War

16. **Understands how the rise of corporations, heavy industry, and mechanized farming transformed American society**

5-6 • Understands the impact of significant achievements and individuals in the late 19th century
• Understands the economic and social changes that occurred in late 19th century American cities
• Understands social development and labor patterns in the late 19th century West
• Understands the environmental issues of the 19th century

7-8 • Understands influences on business and industry in the 19th century
• Understands responses to the challenges of rapid urbanization in the late 19th century
• Understands influences on the development of the American West
• Understands differences in commercial farming in various regions of the United States
• Understands various influences on the scenic and urban environment

9-12 • Understands the development of business in the late 19th century
• Understands issues associated with urban growth in the late 19th century
• Understands influences on economic conditions in various regions of the country
• Understands factors leading to the conservation movement of the late 19th century
• Understands how urban population and industrial growth influenced the environment
• Understands the role of class, race, gender, and religion in western communities

17. **Understands massive immigration after 1870 and how new social patterns, conflicts, and ideas of national unity developed amid growing cultural diversity**

5-6 • Understand patterns of immigrant life after 1870
• Understands the experiences of diverse groups and minorities in different regions of the country
• Understands social activities in the late 19th century

7-8 • Understands the background and experiences of immigrants of the late 19th century
• Understands the scientific theories of race and their application to society and politics
• Understands changes in American life in the late 19th century
• Understands opposition to discrimination in the late 19th century

9-12 • Understands challenges immigrants faced in society in the late 19th century
• Understands the influence of public education on American society after 1870
• Understands how scientific theories of race affected society in the late 19th century
• Understands the challenges diverse people encountered in late 19th century American society
• Understands changes in social and class development in late 19th century

18. **Understands the rise of the American labor movement and how political issues reflected social and economic changes**

5-6 • Understands changes in business and labor practices during the late 19th century
• Understands characteristics of labor conflicts of the late 19th century
• Understands major political issues and events of the late 19th century

7-8 • Understands conditions affecting employment and labor in the late 19th century
• Understands reactions to developments in labor in late 19th century America
• Understands the goals of political parties and individuals in the late 19th century

9-12 • Understands influences on the workforce during the late 19th century
• Understands labor issues of the late 19th century
• Understands the appeal of various political parties and the positions they took
• Understands how economic issues influenced American society
• Understands the issues and results of the 1896 election

19. Understands federal Indian policy and United States foreign policy after the Civil War

5-6 • Understands significant events for Native American tribes in the late 19th century
• Understands the expansion of the U.S. territories in the post-Civil War era
• Understands critical features of the Spanish-American War

7-8 • Understands interaction between Native Americans and white society
• Understands the causes and consequences of the Spanish-American War
• Understands factors that influenced U.S. expansionism in the late 19th century

9-12 • Understands factors in the outbreak and outcome of the Spanish-American War
• Understands elements that contributed to late 19th century expansionist foreign policy
• Understands influences on and perspectives of Native American life in the late 19th century

20. Understands how Progressives and others addressed problems of industrial capitalism, urbanization, and political corruption

5-6 • Understands Progressive ideas and reform efforts
• Understands political and legislative elements of the Progressive movement
• Understands issues and perspectives of different groups during the Progressive era
• Understands the experiences of migrants and immigrants in growing urban centers

7-8 • Understands the spread of Progressive ideas and successes of the Progressive movement
• Understands the influence of events and individuals on the Progressive movement
• Understands the New Nationalism, New Freedom, and Socialist agendas for change
• Understands the issues of those groups who supported and rejected the goals of Progressivism

9-12 • Understands the origins and impact of the Progressive movement
• Understands major social and political issues of the Progressive era
• Understands how the Progressive movement influenced different groups in American society
• Understands how racial and ethnic events influenced American society during the Progressive era
• Understands efforts to achieve women's suffrage in the early twentieth century

21. Understands the changing role of the United States in world affairs through World War I

5-6 • Understands various U.S. foreign policies in the early part of the 20th century
• Understands World War I prior to U.S. intervention
• Understands U.S. involvement in World War I

7-8 • Understands different types of U.S. diplomacy in the early 20th century
• Understands the development of World War I
• Understands the United States' intervention in World War I
• Understands the impact of the United States involvement in World War I
• Understands the significance of the Russian Revolution

9-12 • Understands U.S. foreign policy and involvement in foreign countries in the early 20th century
• Understands the causes, course, and impact of World War I prior to U.S. entry
• Understands how the home front influenced and was influenced by U.S. involvement in World War I
• Understands influences on the outcome of World War I

22. **Understands how the United States changed between the post-World War I years and the eve of the Great Depression**

5-6
- Understands efforts to restrict different groups of people in the post-World War I era
- Understands how urban life changed in the 1920s
- Understands the rise of a mass culture in the 1920s
- Understands influences on African American culture during the 1920s
- Understands the effects of women's suffrage on politics
- Understands how women's lives changed after World War I
- Understands aspects of prohibition

7-8
- Understands the various social conflicts that took place in the early 1920s
- Understands elements that contributed to the rise of a modern capitalist economy
- Understands changes in the social and cultural life of American society in the 1920s
- Understands events that shaped the political structure of América in the 1920s
- Understands changing attitudes toward women in the post-World War I era

9-12
- Understands the major social issues of 1920s America
- Understands factors that led to changes in work, production, and the rise of a consumer culture
- Understands influences on urban life in America during the 1920s
- Understands the impact of new cultural movements on American society in the 1920s
- Understands how political issues in the 1920s influenced American society

23. **Understands the causes of the Great Depression and how it affected American society**

5-6
- Understands economic aspects of the Great Depression
- Understands the environmental and social impact of the Great Depression

7-8
- Understands various political influences on the Great Depression
- Understands the social and economic impact of the Great Depression

9-12
- Understands influences on the national and global economy
- Understands the impact of the Great Depression on American culture
- Understands how the Great Depression influenced local, state, and charitable resources in the period from 1930-1938

24. **Understands how the New Deal addressed the Great Depression, transformed American federalism, and initiated the welfare state**

5-6
- Understands the background and leadership styles of depression-era presidents
- Understands the influences on and impact of the New Deal
- Understands the significance and legacy of the New Deal

7-8
- Understands renewed efforts to protect the environment during the Great Depression
- Understands the link between Progressivism and the New Deal
- Understands the factors contributing to the forging of the Roosevelt coalition in 1936
- Understands the labor movement during the New Deal era
- Understands various challenges to the New Deal
- Understands Herbert Hoover's and Franklin D. Roosevelt's responses to the Depression
- Understands the contributions of Eleanor Roosevelt to the New Deal
- Understands how the New Deal influenced public opinion

9-12
- Understands the first and second New Deals
- Understands how the New Deal influenced the civil and political rights of diverse groups
- Understands how the New Deal influenced labor and employment
- Understands influences on the New Deal
- Understands the significance and ideology of FDR and the New Deal
- Understands the proposals of Upton Sinclair's EPIC campaign in California

25. **Understands the causes and course of World War II, the character of the war at home and abroad, and its reshaping of the U.S. role in world affairs**

5-6 • Understands events leading to U.S. involvement in World War II
       • Understands significant military aspects of World War II
       • Understands events on the U.S. home front during World War II

7-8 • Understands new political thinking and forms of government between World Wars I and II
       • Understands how the outcome of World War contributed to the outbreak of World War II
       • Understands U.S. international relations prior to its entrance into World War II
       • Understands military strategies used during World War II
       • Understands the dimensions of Hitler's "final solution" and the Allies' response to the Holocaust
       • Understands the legacy of World War II
       • Understands how World War II influenced American society
       • Understands how minority groups were affected by World War II

9-12 • Understands the influence of international events on U.S. policies and political developments
       • Understands events that led to the Japanese attack on Pearl Harbor
       • Understands President Roosevelt's ideas and policies during World War II
       • Understands how World War II influenced the home front
       • Understands characteristics of the end of World War II

26. **Understands the economic boom and social transformation of post-World War II United States**

5-6 • Understands the impact of postwar scientific research on contemporary society
       • Understands how the American economy changed in the post-World War II period
       • Understands influences on American society during the post-World War II years

7-8 • Understands agricultural innovation and consolidation in the postwar period
       • Understands the immediate social, political, and economic impacts on America
       • Understands how American society changed after World War II

9-12 • Understands scientific and technological developments in America after World War II
       • Understands influences on the American economy after World War II
       • Understands the socioeconomic factors of the post-World War II period in America
       • Understands social, religious, cultural, and economic changes in the onset of the Cold War

27. **Understands how the Cold War and conflicts in Korea and Vietnam influenced domestic and international politics**

5-6 • Understands influences on international relations after World War II
       • Understands shifts in international relations after World War II
       • Understands the characteristics and impact of the Vietnam War

7-8 • Understands major events in U.S. foreign policy during the early Cold War period
       • Understands the difference between the foreign policies of Kennedy and Johnson
       • Understands political and social characteristics of the Vietnam War
       • Understands the Truman and Eisenhower doctrines of foreign policy

9-12 • Understands U.S. foreign policy from the Truman administration to the Johnson administration
       • Understands the political elements of the Vietnam War
       • Understands the social issues that resulted from U.S. involvement in the Vietnam War
       • Understands factors that contributed to the development of the Cold War

28. Understands domestic policies in the post-World War II period

5-6   • Understands the civil rights movement during President Truman's presidency
        • Understands the impact of the Kennedy and Johnson administrations on domestic affairs

7-8   • Understands the domestic policies of Presidents Truman and Eisenhower
        • Understands the role of McCarthyism in the early Cold War period
        • Understands the legacy of the New Frontier and Great Society domestic programs
        • Understands the major issues of the 1960 presidential campaign and Kennedy's stance on each

9-12   • Understands different elements of the Truman and Eisenhower administrations
        • Understands characteristics of the Kennedy presidency
        • Understands the various anti-communist movements after World War II
        • Understands characteristics of the Johnson presidency

29. Understands the struggle for racial and gender equality and for the extension of civil liberties

5-6   • Understands the development of the civil rights movement
        • Understands the involvement of diverse groups in the civil rights movement
        • Understands the development of the post-World War II women's movement
        • Understands the Warren Court's interpretation of freedom of religion

7-8   • Understands individual and institutional influences on the civil rights movement
        • Understands factors that shaped the women's rights movements after World War II
        • Understands conflicts raised by the Warren Court decisions

9-12   • Understands how diverse groups united during the civil rights movement
        • Understands conflicting perspectives on different issues addressed by the women's movement
        • Understands how various Warren Court decisions influenced society
        • Understands significant influences on the civil rights movement

30. Understands developments in foreign and domestic policies between the Nixon and Clinton presidencies

5-6   • Understands domestic politics from Nixon to Carter
        • Understands elements of both the Reagan and Bush presidencies
        • Understands the events that influenced U.S. foreign policy from Carter to Bush

7-8   • Understands the domestic problems facing Presidents Bush and Reagan
        • Understands the influence of major foreign policy events from Nixon to Clinton
        • Understands the impact of the Nixon administration ideas and policies
        • Understands key domestics issues of the post-Nixon years
        • Understands the issues and legislation affecting organized labor in the post-World War era

9-12   • Understands how the Nixon, Ford, and Carter administrations dealt with domestic issues
        • Understands the events and legacy of the Watergate break-in
        • Understands the impact of the Reagan presidency on relations with other countries
        • Understands the major economic issues from the Reagan through the Clinton presidencies
        • Understands the role of U.S. foreign policy on international events from Nixon to Clinton

31. Understands economic, social, and cultural developments in the contemporary United States

5-6   • Understands the changes in the contemporary workplace
        • Understands the factors that prompted new immigration in contemporary American society
        • Understands influences on religion in contemporary society
        • Understands aspects of contemporary American culture
        • Understands contemporary issues concerning gender and ethnicity

7-8   • Understands changes in the workplace and the economy in contemporary America
        • Understands demographic shifts and the influence on recent immigration patterns

- Understands the growth of religious issues in contemporary society
- Understands various influences on American culture
- Understands how different groups attempted to achieve their goals

9-12
- Understands how changes in the national and global economy have influenced the workplace
- Understands how recent immigration and migration patterns impact social and political issues
- Understands the impact of religious movements on political issues in contemporary America
- Understands influences on views of art, gender, and culture
- Understands major contemporary social issues and the groups involved

History: World History

1. Understands the biological and cultural processes that shaped the earliest human communities

5-6
- Understands scientific evidence regarding early hominid evolution in Africa
- Understands the social and cultural characteristics of hunter-gatherer communities

7-8
- Understands early hominid development and the evolution of different human communities
- Understands the role of the environment in the development of different human communities
- Understands how different human communities expressed their beliefs

9-12
- Understands methods used to study early human communities and what these studies reveal
- Understands how different kinds of evidence are used to determine the cultural characteristics of early human communities
- Understands physical, social, and cultural characteristics of different human communities
- Understands environmental, biological, and cultural influences on early human communities

2. Understands the processes that contributed to the emergence of agricultural societies around the world

5-6
- Understands the role of agriculture in early settled communities
- Understands the development of early agricultural communities in different regions of the world

7-8
- Understands immediate and long-term impacts and influences of early agricultural communities
- Understands influences on the spread of agricultural communities
- Understands what archaeological evidence reveals about the conditions of agricultural societies
- Understands inherent disadvantages and advantages of hunter-gatherer and early farming styles
- Understands the argument that agricultural life was an advance in human social development

9-12
- Understands how agricultural communities maintained their produce and livestock
- Understands what evidence has revealed about the cultural beliefs of early agricultural societies
- Understands social and cultural factors that define agricultural communities
- Understands what evidence reveals about different types of large agricultural communities
- Understands why some groups developed and accepted complete sedentary agriculture and others retained earlier subsistence methods

3. Understands the major characteristics of civilization and the development of civilizations in Mesopotamia, Egypt, and the Indus Valley

5-6
- Understands influences on the development of civilizations in the 4th and 3rd millennia BCE
- Understands the significance of writing in Mesopotamia, Egypt, and the Indus Valley
- Understands how economic, political, and environmental factors influenced the civilizations of Mesopotamia, Egypt, and the Indus Valley

7-8
- Understands factors that shaped the development of Mesopotamia, Egypt and the Indus Valley
- Understands the role of economics in the development of Mesopotamia, Egypt, and the Indus Valley

9-12 • Understands influences on the social and economic framework of Mesopotamia, Egypt, and the Indus Valley
• Understands how written codes and stories reflect social conditions in Mesopotamia, Egypt, and the Indus Valley
• Understands features of trading networks in Mesopotamia, Egypt, and the Indus

4. Understands how agrarian societies spread and new states emerged in the third and second millennia BCE

5-6 • Understands how the development of different types of tools influenced Chinese civilization
• Understands significant characteristics of early Chinese society and religion
• Understands the role of technology in early agrarian societies

7-8 • Understands the rise of urban and complex agrarian societies in the 3rd and 2nd millennium BCE
• Understands how the natural environment shaped Huang He civilization
• Understands what archaeological evidence reveals about the Shang Dynasty
• Understands the significance of advancements in tool and weapon technology

9-12 • Understands the social, cultural, and political characteristics of the Shang Dynasty
• Understands interaction between urban centers of Southwest Asia, Egypt, and the Aegean Basin, and the Eastern Mediterranean coast
• Understands how different agrarian societies developed
• Understands how the environment influenced civilizations in the Tigris, Nile, and Huang He valleys
• Understands cultural development of Chinese civilization in the 3rd and 2nd millennium BCE
• Understands the impact of various technologies (e.g., the wheel, pottery, the sail, the plow)
• Understands the cultural and economic conditions of Minoan and Egyptian civilizations

5. Understands the political, social, and cultural consequences of population movements and militarization in Eurasia in the second millennium BCE

5-6 • Understands the rise of pastoral societies in the Central Asian steppes
• Understands how the invention of the chariot affected Southwest Asian societies
• Understands characteristics of Mycenaean Greek society and culture
• Understands possible causes of the decline and collapse of Indus Valley civilization

7-8 • Understands the development of Indo-European language
• Understands the origins of the Hittite people and the major achievements of the Anatolia Empire
• Understands significant individuals and events in Egyptian civilization
• Understands significant events in the development of Mycenaean culture
• Understands characteristics of Aryan culture
• Understands reasons for the decline and collapse of Mohenjo-Daro and other Indus cities

9-12 • Understands characteristics of pastoral and agrarian societies
• Understands the beliefs and accomplishments of Mesopotamian and Egyptian rulers
• Understands characteristics of Mycenaean society
• Understands cultural elements of the Aryan civilization
• Knows the migration routes of Indo-European language speakers in the second millennium BCE
• Understands the emergence and militarization of new kingdoms
• Understands the decline of the Indus valley civilization
• Understands the reliability of epics as historic sources

6. Understands major trends in Eurasia and Africa from 4000 to 1000 BCE

5-6 • Knows areas of Eurasia and Africa where cities and dense farming populations appeared between 4000 and 1000 BCE
• Understands how new ideas, products, techniques, and institutions spread among regions

7-8 • Understands the emergence of civilizations in Southwest Asia, the Nile valley, India, China, and the Eastern Mediterranean

- Understands why in some places geographic, environmental, and economic conditions favored hunter-gatherer, pastoral, and small-scale agricultural ways of life rather than urban civilizations
- Knows important inventions, discoveries, and institutions that appeared from 4000 to 1000 BCE
- Understands the concept of a patriarchal society
- Understands the concept of "civilization" (e.g., the various criteria used to define "civilization")

9-12
- Understands the development of political and economic institutions
- Understands the role of pastoral peoples in Eurasia and Africa up to 1000 BCE

7. Understands technological and cultural innovation and change from 1000 to 600 BCE

5-6
- Understands patterns of Phoenician political organization, culture, and trade
- Understands the development of Greek city-states
- Understands elements of Judaism and how it compares to other religions
- Understands major events in the development of Kushite society
- Understands characteristics of pastoral nomadic societies
- Understands geographical and architectural features of Egypt and Kush

7-8
- Understands the role of technology in societies of Southwest Asia and the Mediterranean region
- Understands characteristics of the Assyrian and Babylonian Empires
- Knows the locations of significant Greek city-states and colonies
- Understands social development and religious beliefs of Jewish civilization
- Understands cultural elements of Kush society and their interaction with Egyptian civilization
- Understands the importance of maritime trade to the kingdom of Askum
- Understands elements of different pastoral nomadic peoples in Central Asia

9-12
- Understands how the implementation of laws and the spread of language influenced societies of the Mediterranean Basin and Southwest Asia
- Understands events that led to the spread of Judaism
- Understands how Kush culture interacted with or reflected characteristics of other civilizations
- Understands the emergence of states south of the Sahara desert and the influence of metal technology in Sub-Saharan and West Africa
- Understands the interaction between pastoral nomadic societies, warrior states, and agrarian states in Central Asia

8. Understands how Aegean civilization emerged and how interrelations developed among peoples of the eastern Mediterranean and Southwest Asia from 600 to 200 BCE

5-6
- Understands the social and political characteristics of Greek city-states
- Understands the major cultural elements of Greek society
- Understands significant military developments of the Persian Empire
- Understands Alexander's achievements as a military and political leader

7-8
- Understands the political framework of Athenian society
- Understands the role of art, literature, and mythology in Greek society
- Understands the characteristics of Persian founding, expansion, and political organization
- Understands elements of Alexander of Macedon's legacy
- Understands the impact and achievements of the Hellenistic period
- Understands the nature of major governmental systems in Greek city-states in the 6th and 5th centuries BCE
- Understands comparisons of the creation myths of Sumer, Babylon, Egypt, Greece, and nationalized China and the similarities and differences in world view they suggest

9-12
- Understands the legacy of Greek thought and government
- Knows significant Greek writings, literature, and mythology
- Understands the major events and the significance of the Persian Wars
- Understands Persian religious beliefs
- Understands how conquest influenced cultural life during the Hellenistic era

- Understands the characteristics of religion, gender, and philosophy in the Hellenistic era
- Understands how Sumerian, Egyptian, and Greek societies saw themselves in relation to their gods and how attitudes towards women are indicated in representations of their goddesses

9. **Understands how major religious and large-scale empires arose in the Mediterranean Basin, China, and India from 500 BCE to 300 CE**

5-6
- Understands the origins and social framework of Roman society
- Understands shifts in the political and social framework of Roman society
- Understands the significance of Jesus of Nazareth
- Understands events in the rise of Christianity
- Understands the fundamental elements of Chinese society under the early imperial dynasties
- Understands the commercial and cultural significance of the trans-Eurasian "silk roads"
- Understands the origins of Buddhism and fundamental Buddhist beliefs

7-8
- Understands the significant individuals and achievements of Roman society
- Understands influences on the economic and political framework of Roman society
- Understands fundamental characteristics of Chinese society under early imperial dynasties
- Understands the major religious beliefs and social framework in India during the Gangetic states and the Mauryan Empire
- Understands the status and role of women in Roman society
- Understands the influence of Christian beliefs on political, social, and cultural aspects of society

9-12
- Understands shifts in the political framework of Roman society
- Understands the spread of Christianity and how it related to other belief systems
- Understands the political and cultural characteristics of the Han Dynasty
- Understands how Buddhism and Brahmanism influenced one another and Indian society
- Understands the growth of the Mauryan Empire in the context of rivalries among Indian states
- Understands the cultural uses of Latin and Greek as universal languages of the Roman Empire
- Understands the political legacy of Roman society
- Understands the role and status of women in the Confucian tradition
- Understands how art and literature reflect different aspects of Indian society

10. **Understands how early agrarian civilizations arose in Mesoamerica**

5-6
- Understands the major characteristics and contributions of Olmec civilization

7-8
- Understands methods used to study Olmec civilization
- Understands characteristics of Olmec agriculture

9-12
- Understands the framework of Olmec society and its influence on other civilizations

11. **Understands major global trends from 1000 BCE to 300 CE**

5-6
- Knows the different forms of slavery or coerced labor in various empires
- Understands how new religious or ethical systems contributed to cultural integration of large regions of Afro-Eurasia

7-8
- Understands the concept and importance of "classical civilizations"
- Understands the development of large regional empires

9-12
- Understands the significance of iron technology in Eurasia and Africa
- Understands patterns of social and cultural continuity in various societies

12. **Understands the Imperial crises and their aftermath in various regions from 300 to 700 CE**

5-6
- Understands possible reasons for the decline of the Roman and Han Empires
- Understands various characteristics of Christianity and Buddhism
- Understands fundamental Hindu beliefs
- Understands significant religious and cultural features of the Gupta era
- Understands the influence of Hinduism and Buddhism in East and Southeast Asia

7-8
- Understands events that may have contributed to the decline of the Roman and Han Empires
- Understands how the spread of Buddhism and Christianity influenced different regions
- Understands political events that shaped the Gupta Empire
- Understands the basis of social relationships in India during the Gupta era
- Understands how the spread of trade and religion influenced Southeast Asia and Polynesian areas
- Understands the changing status of women in early Christian and Buddhist societies
- Understands major achievements in technology, astronomy, and medicine in the Gupta period

9-12
- Understands political and social elements during the decline of the Roman and Han Empires and the rise of the Byzantine Empire
- Understands the significant social, political, and cultural characteristics of Gupta society
- Understands Indian contributions to Southeast Asia
- Understands how the spread of different religions influenced conditions in various regions
- Understands shifts in the status of women from pagan Roman society to Christian society
- Understands the resurgence of Hinduism in India and its spread to South India
- Understands the significance of Pandyas and Pallavas

13. **Understands the causes and consequences of the development of Islamic civilization between the 7th and 10th centuries**

5-6
- Understands the spread of Islam in Southwest Asia and the Mediterranean region
- Understands the influence of Islamic ideas and practices on other cultures and social behavior
- Understands how the Byzantine state withstood attacks between the 8th and 10th centuries
- Understands the effect of geography on different groups and their trade practices
- Understands the significance of Baghdad (e.g., its role as a center of commerce)
- Understands the impact of the invention of paper on various cultures

7-8
- Understands how the Muslims spread Islamic beliefs and established their empire
- Understands significant aspects of Islamic civilization
- Understands significant aspects of Abbasid culture
- Understands how the Byzantine Empire defended itself against various invaders
- Understands the Byzantine role in preserving and transmitting ancient Greek learning

9-12
- Understands the problems facing the Byzantine and Sassanid Persian Empires in the 7th century
- Understands challenges to Muslim civilization
- Understands the nature of the Abbasid, Byzantine, and Sassanid Persian governments and military institutions
- Understands the social structure of the Abbasid Empire
- Understands political and economic systems of the Byzantine state
- Understands how the spread of Greek Orthodox Christianity affected different regions
- Understands significant changes in Islamic civilization between the 7th and 10th centuries
- Understands possible motivations behind the Byzantine preservation of ancient Greek and Hellenistic scholastic works

14. **Understands major developments in East Asia and Southeast Asia in the era of the Tang Dynasty from 600 to 900 CE**

5-6
- Understands geographic and political features of Tang China
- Understands characteristics of Japanese society through the imperial period
- Understands the importance of the commercial state of Srivijava and the Straits of Malacca in Southeast Asia as a trade link between India and China

7-8
- Understands China's influence on other cultures
- Understands how Buddhism was introduced from Tang China to Korea and Japan
- Understands the culture and technological achievements of Tang China
- Understands events that shaped Japanese culture
- Understands basic beliefs in Japanese culture

9-12
- Understands social and political characteristics of the reunification of China
- Understands features of cultural life in various regions of China
- Understands the influence of Chinese culture on different countries
- Understands the importance of women as authors at the Japanese court of the Heian period

15. **Understands the political, social, and cultural redefinitions in Europe from 500 to 1000 CE**

5-6
- Understands the influence of the monastery in European development
- Understands the development of the Merovingian and Carolingian states
- Understands the significance of Norse migrations and invasions
- Understands the significance of Charlemagne
- Knows the life story and major achievements of King Alfred of England ("Alfred the Great")

7-8
- Understands the importance of monasteries and convents as centers of political power, economic productivity, and communal life
- Understands the influence of the Carolingian Empire on the development of Europe
- Understands social class and gender roles in Medieval Europe
- Understands the significance of Clovis
- Understands the role of Norse peoples in the development of Europe

9-12
- Understands significant religious events that shaped medieval society
- Understands shifts in political power during 9th and 10th century Europe
- Understands the significance of different empires in Europe
- Understands reasons why the Carolingian Empire did not endure after Charlemagne's death

16. **Understands the development of agricultural societies and new states in tropical Africa and Oceania**

5-6
- Knows the routes by which migrants settled the Pacific Islands and New Zealand

7-8
- Understands influences on state-building in West Africa
- Understands the establishment of agricultural societies on the Pacific Islands and New Zealand
- Understands the role of oral history in understanding West African history

9-12
- Understands the origins and development of societies in Oceania
- Understands economic, social, and religious influences on Ghana society
- Understands settlement patterns in different regions of Africa

17. **Understands the rise of centers of civilization in Mesoamerica and Andean South America in the first millennium CE**

5-6
- Understands the significant features of Mayan civilization
- Understands different farming methods of Teotihuacan and Moche civilization
- Understands methods used to study Zapotec, Teotihuacan, and Moche civilizations

7-8
- Understands the economic and agricultural elements of Mayan society
- Understands social features of Mayan culture

- Understands what art and architecture reveal about early Mesoamerica and Andean societies
- Understands social features of Andean societies

9-12
- Understands ways in which the Mayan world view and cultural life were portrayed
- Understands Mayan achievements in astronomy, mathematics, and the development of a calendar
- Understands relationships between Mesoamerican and Andean societies
- Understands urban planning in Mayan culture

18. Understands major global trends from 300 to 1000 CE

5-6
- Understands major changes in the religious map of Eurasia and Africa between 300 and 1000 CE
- Understands the importance of international trade for African and Eurasian societies

7-8
- Understands the factors that contributed to the weakening of empires in world history from 300 to 1000 CE
- Understands the growth of economic and cultural exchanges among different regions from 300 to 1000 CE

19. Understands the maturation of an interregional system of communication, trade, and cultural exchange during a period of Chinese economic power and Islamic expansion

5-6
- Understands the impact of urbanization and commercial expansion on Chinese society between the 10th and 13th centuries
- Understands different elements of Japanese feudal society
- Understands the cultural characteristics of Islamic society
- Understands features of trade routes in Asia, Europe, and Africa

7-8
- Understands how Confucianism changed between the 10th and 13th centuries
- Understands the social and economic elements of Song China
- Understands government and politics of the Kamakura period
- Understands influences on the development of Buddhist sects in Japan
- Understands the development of Southeast Asian states
- Understands the expansion of Islam and daily life in Islamic regions
- Understands elements of trade in different regions

9-12
- Understands the struggle for Vietnamese independence from China and the subsequent reconstruction of Vietnamese society and government
- Understands religious, social, and political aspects of the Song Dynasty
- Understands how different religious movements influenced various cultures between the 11th and 13th centuries
- Understands the significance of Sufism
- Understands how interregional trade and communication affected Eurasia and Africa
- Understands significant religious and economic aspects of Chinese society between the 10th and 13th centuries
- Understands different social classes and gender roles in Japanese society
- Understands the significance of art and philosophy in Japanese and Cambodian society
- Understands how the wars with the Mongols influenced Japanese society
- Understands cultural and political aspects of the Turkic Empires

20. Understands the redefinition of European society and culture from 1000 to 1300 CE

5-6
- Understands significant developments in medieval English legal and constitutional practice and their importance for modern democratic thought and institutions
- Understands the systems of feudalism and manorialism
- Understands the influence of Christianity in Medieval Europe
- Understands the lives of different groups of people in Medieval Europe
- Understands the significance of the university in Medieval Europe

- Understands the significance of William the Conqueror in English society
- Understands aspects of the architecture of Medieval Europe

7-8
- Understands political events that shaped the development of European governments
- Understands the importance of inheritance laws, arranged marriages, dowries, and family alliances for dynastic and aristocratic politics
- Understands the connection between agricultural technology and increased agricultural production and population growth in Europe between 1000 and 1300 CE
- Understands Christian efforts for the Reconquest of Spain from Muslim powers
- Understands the consequences of German expansion into Poland and the Baltic region
- Understands art, architecture, and education in medieval Christian and Spanish Muslim society
- Understands the roles and motivations of squires, saints, and soldiers in Christian Europe

9-12
- Understands the role of feudalism and manorialism in European society
- Understands the development of English government and its legal and political system
- Understands the rise of the city-state in Italy and northern Europe
- Understands the effects of urbanization in Europe and the Mediterranean region
- Understands the spread of philosophy to Europe
- Understands comparisons of church-state relations and religious authority between Orthodox Christianity in the East and Latin Christianity in the West
- Understands the social elements of feudalism
- Understands how women influenced medieval politics
- Understands the influence of religious beliefs on various regions
- Understands the rise of guilds as economic and social institutions
- Understands how women's experiences in Europe were determined by social class, area, time, and stage of life and how these experiences are reflected in different types of literature

21. **Understands the rise of the Mongol empire and its consequences for Eurasian peoples from 1200 to 1350**

5-6
- Understands the significance of Chinggis Khan
- Understands Mongol interaction with different cultures

7-8
- Understands political, social, and cultural features of the Mongol Empire
- Understands the influence of the "Golden Horde" in various regions

9-12
- Understands the political features of the Mongol Empire and its influence on other regions
- Understands factors that led to the decline of the Mongol Empire after Ogodei Kahn's death
- Understands the interaction between the Mongols and cultures of Mongol domination
- Knows the trade routes that emerged under Mongol rule, and the goods traded along these routes
- Understands the usefulness of foreign sources in recording the history of areas under Mongol rule
- Knows the consequences of the death of the Great Khan Agate and the Great Khan Mongke

22. **Understands the growth of states, towns, and trade in Sub-Saharan Africa between the 11th and 15th centuries**

5-6
- Understands influences on the economic development of Sub-Saharan empires
- Understands social and religious features of West Africa
- Understands the emergence of commercial towns on the East African coast and the significance of Swahili as the language of trade

7-8
- Understands the development of the empires of Mali and Songhay
- Understands religious aspects of Ethiopian society
- Understands significant features of the major population centers of Bantu and the East African coastal region in the 2nd millennium CE
- Understands how architecture reveals the influence of foreign states

9-12
- Understands how art and architecture reveal elements of Ile-Ife, Benin, and other societies
- Understands the political, social, economic, and religious development of the West African Sudan and the East African coast between the 8th and 13th centuries
- Understands the influence of religion on African culture
- Understands the role of language in shaping African society
- Understands the network of trade between East Africa, Southeast Asia, and the Persian Gulf

23. Understands patterns of crisis and recovery in Afro-Eurasia between 1300 and 1450

5-6
- Understands the origins and impact of the plague
- Understands the social, political, and cultural characteristics of Europe after the 14th century
- Understands the origins and early expansion of the Ottoman Empire up to 1453

7-8
- Understands how the plague influenced economic, social, and political conditions
- Understands causes for changes in social, political, and religious events in Europe after the 14th century
- Understands the "humanism" that emerged in Italy in the 14th and 15th centuries
- Understands the Zheng He maritime expeditions of the early 15th century
- Understands the significance of Timur the Lame (Tamerlane)

9-12
- Knows ways in which long-term climatic change contributed to Europe's economic and social crisis in the 14th century
- Understands religious and political changes in post 14th-century Europe
- Understands characteristics of 15th century Italian humanism
- Understands shifts in the leadership and political climate in China
- Understands perceptions of the Black Death from diverse, contemporaneous sources
- Understands events and consequences of Jewish scapegoating in Europe during the Great Plague
- Understands immediate and long-term consequences of the plague on European society
- Understands how economic conditions influenced the political and social climate in post 14th- century Europe
- Understands the significance of Joan of Arc
- Understands Timur the Lame's patronage of scholars, artists, and scientists at Samarkand
- Understands what accounts for the success of the Ottoman empire

24. Understands the expansion of states and civilizations in the Americas between 1000 and 1500

5-6
- Understands how the Aztec Empire arose in the 14th century
- Understands social and political elements of Incan society
- Understands what various sources can illustrate about pre-European life in the Americas

7-8
- Understands social and cultural features of Aztec society
- Understands cultural and economic elements of North American and Mesoamerican civilizations
- Understands major political and social features of Incan society
- Understands the similarities and differences between Incan and Aztec society
- Understands how the natural environment affected the organization of developing societies of the North American plains, Southwestern deserts, and the tropical forests of the Yucatan

9-12
- Understands political, social, and economic features of Aztec society
- Understands the significance of the mound centers located in the Mississippi valley
- Understands gender roles in Caribbean, Mesoamerican, and Andean societies
- Knows the technology and urbanism of the Incas (in Cuzco), the Aztecs (in Tenochtitlan), and of North American mound-builders

25. **Understands major global trends from 1000 to 1500 CE**

5-6 • Understands influences on the growth of long-distance exchanges between different regions

7-8 • Understands how major migratory and military movements of pastoral peoples of Asia and Africa affected agrarian states and societies of Eurasia and Africa
• Understands economic, political, and cultural differences and similarities between Europe and Asia
• Understands the impact of interaction between Christians and Muslims in the Mediterranean region
• Understands the concept of capitalism and the emergence of capitalistic institutions and productive methods in Europe and other parts of Afro-Eurasia
• Understands differences and similarities between the Inca and Aztec empires and empires of Afro-Eurasia

9-12 • Understands demographic changes in various regions from 1000 to 1500 CE

26. **Understands how the transoceanic interlinking of all major regions of the world between 1450 and 1600 led to global transformations**

5-6 • Understands the interregional trading system that linked peoples of Africa, Asia, and Europe on the eve of the European overseas voyages
• Understands what contributed to increasing oceanic travel in the 15th and 16th centuries
• Understands the character and impact of Portuguese maritime expansion to Africa, India, and Southeast Asia upon local populations
• Understands features of Spanish exploration and conquest
• Understands the cultural and biological exchange between the Americas and Afro-Eurasia in the late 15th and 16th centuries
• Knows the major accomplishments of Columbus

7-8 • Understands the impact of the expeditions in the 15th and 16th centuries
• Understands how the Ottoman, Indian, Chinese, Japanese, Vietnamese, and Siamese powers restricted European commercial, military, and political penetration in the 16th century
• Understands cultural interaction between various societies in the late 15th and 16th centuries
• Understands the impact of the exchange of flora, fauna, and pathogens on the Americas and the global population
• Understands the impact of migrations of the Muslims and Jews after their expulsion from Spain
• Knows which crops in Spanish and Portuguese regions of the Americas were domestic and which were commercial, and knows what resources commercial crops demanded

9-12 • Understands features of Portuguese overseas trade and exploration
• Understands features of European society that stimulated exploration and conquest overseas
• Understands the consequences of Portuguese military conflicts and interaction with other cultures
• Understands the consequences of the spread of disease globally and regionally
• Understands how knowledge of the Americas affected European religious and intellectual life
• Knows the extent of Chinese activities in the Indian Ocean in the 15th century
• Understands measures that restricted Muslims and Jews in the 15th and 16th centuries
• Understands how various cultures responded to European presence in the 15th and 16th centuries
• Knows the dynamics of the encomienda system of colonial government and labor
• Knows the routes of exchange of specific flora and fauna between the 15th and 18th centuries, and the impact of these exchanges on the world economy

27. **Understands how European society experienced political, economic, and cultural transformations in an age of global intercommunication between 1450 and 1750**

5-6 • Understands the social characteristics of European society from 1450 to 1750
• Understands significant contributions of the Renaissance and Reformation to European society
• Understands the English civil war and the Revolution of 1688
• Understands the significance of the Scientific Revolution and the Age of Enlightenment
• Understands the role of gunpowder in changing European warfare

7-8
- Understands early influences on the Scientific Revolution and the Enlightenment
- Understands changes in urban and rural Europe between the 15th and 18th centuries
- Understands significant social and cultural changes that took place during the Renaissance
- Understands origins of the Reformation and Catholic Reformation
- Understands the emergence of strong individual leaders, monarchies, and states in Europe between the 16th and 18th centuries
- Understands contributions of the Scientific Revolution to European society
- Understands the short and long-term impact of Enlightenment ideas
- Understands the effects on world trade of the Spanish silver trade from America
- Understands the role of gunpowder in the development of strong European leadership
- Understands the long and short-term causes of the "Glorious" revolution of 1688

9-12
- Understands shifts in the European economy, trade, and labor systems in the 16th century
- Understands causes and consequences of the religious wars in Europe in the 16th and 17th centuries, and the legacy of these wars in modern Europe
- Understands the accomplishments of European leaders between the 16th and 18th centuries
- Understands influences on the spread of scientific ideas and Enlightenment thought
- Understands features of the conflict between religious beliefs and scientific thought during the Scientific Revolution
- Understands the role of the Enlightenment in shaping European society
- Understands individuals and ideologies that emerged during the Renaissance and Reformation
- Understands sources of military buildup of the 17th and 18th centuries
- Understands the goals and issues of the Cavaliers and Roundheads in the English Civil War
- Understands factors that influenced the development of the Dutch Republic, England, and France

28. **Understands how large territorial empires dominated much of Eurasia between the 16th and 18th centuries**

5-6
- Understands the power and limit of imperial absolutism under the Ming Dynasty
- Understands how China viewed its role in the world during the Ming Dynasty
- Understands political and cultural achievements of the Ottoman Empire
- Understands political achievements of the Safavid and Mughal Empires
- Understands the network of Afro-Eurasian trade in the 16th and 17th centuries

7-8
- Understands interactions between China and other countries during the Ming Dynasty
- Understands features of class structure and sources of social change in China
- Understands factors that influenced the development of the Ottoman Empire
- Understands political and religious influences on the development of the Mughal Empire
- Understands changes in the political structure of the Ming Dynasty
- Understands factors that influenced the development and expansion of the Safavid Empire
- Knows reasons why the East India Company had difficulty selling more British goods in India than it imported

9-12
- Understands influences on the Chinese economy and social structure
- Understands significant cultural and social features of the Ming Dynasty
- Understands the social, economic, and cultural features of the Ottoman Empire
- Understands cultural and religious influences on Mughal social and cultural conditions
- Understands major political events in the rise and decline of the Ottoman Empire
- Understands the origins and development of the Safavid Empire
- Knows similarities and differences between major empires and leaders

29. **Understands the economic, political, and cultural interrelations among peoples of Africa, Europe, and the Americas between 1500 and 1750**

5-6
- Understands European influence in the Americas between the 16th and 18th centuries
- Understands features of the labor system and economy in the Americas
- Understands elements of the trans-Atlantic African slave trade
- Understands elements of the slave trade in Africa

7-8
- Understands the consequences of European interaction with indigenous peoples of the Americas
- Understands features of and participants in the slave trade
- Understands factors that contributed to the development of various African societies
- Knows the causes and consequences of encounters among Khoisan groups, Bantu-speaking peoples, and European settlers in South Africa in the 17th and 18th centuries
- Understands the characteristics of various European colonies in the Western Hemisphere

9-12
- Understands economic and political features of various European colonies between the 16th and 18th centuries
- Knows reasons for the emergence of social hierarchies based on race and gender in both the Iberian Empire and the British colonies in the Americas
- Understands the development of different African societies
- Understands characteristics of the development of European colonies in the Americas
- Understands possible reasons why Catholics were generally more successful than Protestants in converting non-Europeans between the 16th and 18th centuries
- Understands the development of colonial labor systems and their impact on indigenous peoples
- Understands the "Black Legend" and how it helped build opposition toward Spain
- Understands how slavery was defined by different groups of people
- Understands how the African slave trade affected the lives of slaves in the Western Hemisphere

30. Understands transformations in Asian societies in the era of European expansion

5-6
- Understands the impact of European military and commercial involvement in Asia
- Understands social and political features of Japanese society under the Tokugawa shogunate
- Understands the role of art in conveying ideas in China and Japan
- Knows what groups of people in India most frequently converted to Islam between the 16th and 18th centuries, and the major vehicle for conversion

7-8
- Understands political, economic, and social aspects of Chinese society during the era of European expansion
- Understands trade patterns and relations between Europe and China
- Understands how the spread of different religions affected various Asian countries
- Understands features in the development of Korean and Japanese culture
- Understands the spread of Confucianism in various Asian cultures
- Understands the evolution, recurring themes, and foreign influence in Japanese art and artists

9-12
- Understands the economic and cultural consequences of European involvement in other countries
- Understands the impact of the Seven Years War on the power of Britain and France in Asia
- Knows the events that led to the demise of centralized control by the imperial Mughals and the ascent of Maratha and Sikh power in India
- Understands the structure of Chinese society during the period of European commercial expansion
- Understands the spread of different religions throughout the world
- Understands how art, literature, and architecture reflect aspects of different cultures and religions
- Understands Mughal responses to the expansion of European commercial power in Asia
- Understands foreign influences on Japanese and Chinese economies
- Understands how the unification of Japan and the centralization of feudalism under Tokugawa rule compared to the rise of nation states in early modern Europe

31. Understands major global trends from 1450 to 1770

5-6
- Understands major shifts in world demography and urbanization between 1450 and 1770
- Understands the changes in world political boundaries that took place between 1450 and 1770
- Understands how the acceleration of scientific and technological innovations between 1450 and 1770 affected social, economic, and cultural life in various parts of the world

7-8
- Knows ways in which expanding capitalistic enterprise and commercialization affected relations among states and contributed to changing class and race relations
- Understands the influence of technological advancements on society

- Knows how Buddhism, Islam, and Christianity spread between 1450 and 1750
- Understands patterns of social and cultural continuity in various societies

9-12
- Understands the catalysts behind the shift of economic power from the Mediterranean basin to Northern Europe during the 16th century
- Understands the emergence of capitalism in India and Europe
- Understands how the Ming and Qing rulers viewed the European merchants, Christian missionaries, and military personnel who sought trading privileges in China
- Understands how traditional Puritan and Confucian attitudes toward profit making affected commerce and trading practices in China and the early New England colonies

32. **Understands the causes and consequences of political revolutions in the late 18th and early 19th centuries**

5-6
- Understands the ideas and events that shaped the Revolution in France
- Understands the origins and development of Latin American independence movements

7-8
- Understands the diverse factors that affected conditions in Old Regime France
- Understands events and ideas that influenced the course of the French Revolution
- Understands how the French Revolution changed social conditions in France
- Knows the consequences of Napoleon's invasions
- Understands the political and ideological objectives of Latin American independence movements
- Knows the leading figures and issues of the Congress of Vienna
- Understands elements of the Haitian revolution

9-12
- Understands the impact of the Haitian Revolution
- Understands comparisons between the Latin American revolutions and those in America, France, and Haiti
- Understands the status of women and other social classes during and following the Latin American independence movements
- Understands the political beliefs and writings that emerged during the French Revolution
- Understands the ideas and issues during and after the Latin American independence movement

33. **Understands the causes and consequences of the agricultural and industrial revolutions from 1700 to 1850**

5-6
- Understands the emergence and impact of industrialism in 18th-century England
- Understands the impact of the industrial revolution in Europe and the Atlantic Basin
- Understands aspects of the abolition movement in the 18th and 19th centuries

7-8
- Understands why industrialization flourished in Britain
- Understands the effect of the industrial revolution on social and political conditions in various regions
- Understands the status of slavery and slaves throughout the 19th century
- Understands the importance and consequences of new technologies in the agricultural revolution
- Understands the impact of new technology that emerged during the industrial revolution
- Knows new patterns in world manufacturing production that developed among the nations of Great Britain, United States, Germany, France, Russia, and Italy between 1800 and 1900
- Understands the discourse surrounding the abolition of slavery
- Understands significant individuals in the abolition movement

9-12
- Understands the effect of economic conditions and theories on industrialization
- Understands how industrialization shaped social class and labor organizations
- Understands reasons why various countries abolished slavery
- Understands the realities and romanticized visions of pre-industrial England
- Understands the relationship between improvements in agriculture, population increase, the rise of the textile industry, the enclosure movement, urbanization, and industrialization in 18th century England
- Understands Adam Smith's analysis of capitalism in The Wealth of Nations
- Understands how industrialization developed differently in Britain than it did on the continent

- Understands different perspectives regarding the nature of the African slave trade
- Knows the extent of slave imports to Brazil, Spanish America, the West Indies, the French West, British North America, and the U.S.

34. Understands how Eurasian societies were transformed in an era of global trade and the emergence of European power from 1750 to 1870

5-6
- Understands changes in social and political elements of the Ottoman Empire during the 18th and 19th centuries
- Understands political characteristics of Egypt
- Understands aspects of Russian expansion and settlement in the late 18th and 19th centuries
- Understands the advance of British power in India up to 1850, its social and economic impact, and the efforts of Indians to resist European conquest and achieve cultural renewal
- Understands Chinese policies toward foreign trade and immigration to other countries
- Understands events and ideas that led to the modernization of Japan
- Understands the emergence of European trading companies and their impact on Indian culture

7-8
- Understands the decline of the Ottoman Empire in the 19th century
- Understands political conditions in Russia during the reign of Catherine the Great
- Understands the impact of foreign trade and politics on Indian culture
- Understands the effects of population growth in China between the 17th and 19th centuries
- Understands causes of political and social turmoil in China in the 18th and 19th centuries
- Understands the origins of Japanese modernization and Japan's changing policies toward Western influences
- Understands the general political, social, and economic structure of Russia in the 1800s
- Understands significant cultural and political changes in India in the 18th and 19th centuries
- Understands Dutch involvement in various regions

9-12
- Understands the social structure of the Ottoman Empire in the early and middle 19th century
- Understands events that shaped the social structure of Russia in the 19th century
- Understands how Western culture influenced Asian societies
- Understands causes and consequences of the Taiping Rebellion
- Understands China's relations with Western countries
- Understands Japan's political and social transformation in the 19th century
- Knows the individual motivations of the English, French, and Ottomans in the Crimean War, as well as the significance of the outcome of the war for each of these participants
- Understands the expansion and development of Russia in the 19th century and early 20th century
- Understands how the British presence and British policies shaped Indian society
- Understands the significance of the Treaties of Nanking (1842) and Shimonoseki (1895)
- Understands social conditions and change in Meiji Japan

35. Understands patterns of nationalism, state-building, and social reform in Europe 5-6and the Americas from 1830 to 1914

5-6
- Understands the emergence of nationalist movements in Italy and Germany
- Understand causes of large-scale population movements from rural areas to cities in continental Europe and how these movements affected the domestic and working lives of men and women
- Understands the impact of cultural achievements on 19th-century Europe and America
- Understands the political and social changes in 19th-century Latin America
- Understands aspects of education in 19th-century Europe
- Understands how major events in the United States affected the rest of the hemisphere

7-8
- Understands the ideas that influenced the nationalist movements
- Understands movements and ideas that contributed to social change in 19th-century North America and Europe
- Understands social change and the emergence of new social class culture in 19th-century Europe
- Understands influences on the government structure in Latin America and Mexico
- Understands expansion and nation-building in the United States and Canada in the 19th century

- Understands trends in immigration within and out of Europe in the 19th century
- Understands cultural trends in 19th-century Europe

9-12
- Understands the causes and results of the revolutions of 1848
- Understands the role of nationalism in conflicts within different nations
- Understands factors that led to social and political change in 19th-century Europe
- Understands the status of different groups in 19th-century Europe
- Understands the status of education in 19th-century Europe
- Understands the emergence of new social thought in the 19th century
- Understands how political and economic change influenced Latin American society in the 19th century
- Understands the chronology, major events, and outcomes of the Franco-Prussian War
- Understands the meaning of real politik and how Cavour and Bismarck practiced this philosophy
- Understands how different movements and ideas influenced society in the 19th century
- Knows the events and issues of the Dreyfus affair in France
- Understands sources that illustrate social conditions and cultural identity in 19th-century Europe

36. Understands patterns of global change in the era of Western military and economic domination from 1850 to 1914

5-6
- Understands the impact of new inventions and technological developments in various regions
- Understands the experiences of European migrants and immigrants in the 19th century
- Understands factors that contributed to European imperialist expansion between 1850 and 1914
- Understands political and economic changes in Japanese society in the 19th and 20th centuries
- Understands events that shaped African relations with other countries
- Understands major changes in the political geography of Africa between 1880 and 1914
- Understands trends in the population of Europe for the last three and a half centuries
- Knows the causes, course, and consequences of the Boxer Rebellion

7-8
- Understands major developments in science and the industrial economy
- Understands influences on European immigration and emigration between 1846 and 1932
- Understands justifications for extending imperial power into African and Asian countries
- Knows the causes and course of the Spanish-American War, and how this related to U.S. participation in Western imperial expansion
- Understands the extent of British rule in India, and British reaction to Indian nationalism
- Understands political and social elements of Chinese society in the late 19th and early 20th centuries
- Understands the role of trade in shaping political and social conditions in various regions
- Understands reasons for the changes in European population from the 17th to the 20th centuries
- Understands the geographic location of European interests in Asia in the late 19th century
- Understands the accomplishments and goals of specific African resistance movements

9-12
- Knows the factors that transformed the character of cities in various parts of the world
- Understands influences on and consequences of European immigration and settlement
- Understands the influence of European imperial expansion on African and Indian society
- Understands the effects of the Sino-Japanese War, the Russo-Japanese War, and the colonization of Korea on Japan's status as a world power, and how Japan justified its imperial expansion
- Knows where the British and French expanded into mainland Southeast Asia, how their colonial policies differed, and how Thailand avoided colonization
- Understands economic, social, and religious influences on African society
- Understands African resistance movements against the British
- Understands the debate on the westward movement in North America in the 19th century
- Understands the advantages and disadvantages of imperialism
- Knows the significance of major national and international rail lines in Africa and Eurasia constructed in the late 19th and early 20th centuries
- Understands the European intellectual justifications for imperialism
- Knows the causes and impact of the Indian Uprising of 1857
- Understands significant political events in 20th-century China
- Understands Western influence on Japanese society in the 19th century

37. Understands major global trends from 1750 to 1914

5-6   • Understands major shifts in world population and urbanization between 1750 and 1914
        • Understands the experiences of immigrants to North and South America in the 19th century

7-8   • Understands industrialization and its social impact in Great Britain, France, Germany, the United States, Russia, Japan, and other countries
        • Understands major patterns of long-distance migration of Europeans, Africans, and Asians
        • Understands major changes in world political boundaries during this era
        • Understands the causes of 19th-century reform movements or renewal in Buddhism, Christianity, Hinduism, Islam, and Judaism
        • Understands trends in world population between 1500 and 1900

9-12 • Understands the importance of ideas associated with republicanism, liberalism, socialism, and constitutionalism on 19th-century political life in different regions of the world
        • Understands patterns of social and cultural continuity in various societies from 1750 to 1914
        • Understands the process of educational reform in various Muslim regions during the 19th century

38. Understands reform, revolution, and social change in the world economy in the early century

5-6   • Understands factors that transformed American and European society in the early 20th century
        • Understands the consequences of the significant revolutions of the early 20th century
        • Understands why Dr. Sun Yatsen is an important figure in the history of modern China

7-8   • Understands the industrial power of Great Britain, France, Germany, Japan, and the United States in the early 20th century
        • Understands prominent features and ideas of liberalism, social reformism, conservatism, and socialism in the early 20th century
        • Understands events that led to revolutions in the early 20th century
        • Understands the consequences of changes inside Japan in the early 20th century

9-12 • Understands the diverse factors that contributed to the industrialization of various countries
        • Understands why European colonial territories and Latin American countries continued to maintain largely agricultural and mining economies in the early 20th century
        • Understands elements of the South African (Anglo-Boer) War
        • Understands the diverse events that led to and resulted from the Russian Revolution of 1905
        • Understands the reforms of Ottoman government advocated by the Young Turk movement
        • Understands the role of the peasantry in the Mexican Revolution
        • Understands events and ideas that led to China's revolutionary movements

39. Understands the causes and global consequences of World War I

5-6   • Understands the origins and significant features of World War I
        • Understands the immediate and long-term consequences of World War I
        • Understands the roles of significant individuals, and the events that led to the Russian Revolution
        • Understands the rise of Joseph Stalin, and his impact on the Soviet Union
        • Understands how the homefront contributed to World War I

7-8   • Understands events that contributed to the outbreak of World War I
        • Understands ways in which popular faith in science, technology, and material progress affected attitudes toward the possibility of war among European states
        • Understands the role of the U.S. and other countries in World War I
        • Understands the influence of Lenin and Stalin on the government, economy, and social conditions in Russia and the Soviet Union after the Revolution of 1917
        • Understands how different countries were aligned during World War I
        • Understands the role of Tsar Nicholas II and Rasputin prior to and during the Russian Revolution

9-12 • Understands arguments and theories regarding the causes of World War I
        • Understands the extent to which different sources supported the war effort
        • Understands Lenin's ideology and policies and their impact on Russia after the Revolution
        • Understands the impact of the Russian Revolution on other countries
        • Understands the role of Stalin in the emerging Soviet Union
        • Understands the Schlieffen Plan and whether it contributed to a military stalemate
        • Understands the strategies of the Allied and Central Powers at the beginning of the war, when these strategies changed, and how
        • Understands the human cost and social impact of World War I

40. Understands the search for peace and stability throughout the world in the 1920s and 1930s

5-6 • Understands treaties and other efforts to achieve peace and recovery from World War I
       • Understands how the settlements of World War I influenced different regions of the world
       • Understands the emergence of a new mass and popular culture between 1900 and 1940
       • Understands the economic and social impact of the Great Depression

7-8 • Understands the immediate and long-term political and social effects of World War I
       • Understands internal shifts in the political conditions of China and Japan in the 1920s and 1930s
       • Understands the goals and policies of European colonial rule in India, Africa, and Asia
       • Understands major discoveries in science and medicine in the first half of the 20th century
       • Understands influences on art and culture in Europe and around the world in the early 20th century
       • Understands how the Great Depression affected economies and systems of government globally
       • Understands the reflections of Depression-era hunger and poverty in the works of various artists

9-12 • Understands how the collapse of the German, Hapsburg, and Ottoman Empires and the creation of new states affected international relations in Europe and the Middle East
        • Understands how World War I influenced demographics and the international economy
        • Understands the shifts in the political conditions in nations around the world after World War I
        • Understands the impact of scientific and technological innovations on early 20th century society
        • Understands how the emergence of new art, literature, music, and scientific theories influenced society in the early 20th century
        • Understands the causes and consequences of the Great Depression
        • Understands how the treaties ending World War I and the League of Nations addressed different groups of people
        • Understands post-World War I shifts in borders in Europe and the Middle East
        • Understands elements of social and political change in China in the early 20th century
        • Understands the conditions of the Hussein-McMahon correspondence and the Sykes-Picot agreement, how they differed from the conditions of the treaties of Versailles and San Remo
        • Understands the origins and consequences of the U.S. Smoot-Hawley Tariff

41. Understands the causes and global consequences of World War II

5-6 • Understands the rise of fascism and Nazism in Europe and Japan
       • Understands influences on the outcome of World War II
       • Understands the human costs of World War II

7-8 • Understands events that led to the outbreak of World War II
       • Understands the positions of the major powers on fascist aggression, and the consequences of their failure to take forceful measures to stop this aggression
       • Understands the influence of Nazism on European society and Jewish culture
       • Understands the impact of World War II on civilian populations and soldiers

9-12 • Understands motives and consequences of the Soviet nonaggression pacts
        • Understands the Holocaust and its impact on Jewish culture and European society
        • Understands the overall effect of World War II on various facets of society
        • Understands the rise of Nazism and how it was received by society

- Understands the exceptional violence of the Spanish Civil War and understands how foreign intervention affected the outcome of this war
- Understands the argument that the severity of the Treaty of Versailles caused unavoidable revolt against the nations that imposed it
- Understands Japan's "greater East Asia co-prosperity" sphere and the support of this idea in European colonies in East Asia
- Understands the climax and moral implications of World War II

42. Understands major global trends from 1900 to the end of World War II

5-6
- Understands major shifts in world geopolitics between 1900 and 1945, and understands the growing role of the United States in international affairs
- Understands how scientific breakthroughs both benefitted and imperiled humankind

7-8
- Understands the nature and extent of Western power in the world in 1945 compared with 1900
- Understands the ideologies, policies, and governing methods of 20th century totalitarian regimes compared to those of contemporary democracies and absolutist states of earlier centuries
- Understands influences on movements for national self-rule or sovereignty in Africa and Asia
- Understands ways in which secular ideologies (e.g., nationalism, fascism, communism, materialism) challenged or were challenged by established religions and ethical systems
- Understands patterns of social and cultural continuity in various societies

9-12
- Understands how revolutionary movements in such countries as Mexico, Russia, and China either drew upon or rejected the ideals of 18th and 19th century revolutions
- Understands why mass consumer economies developed in some countries but not in others

43. Understands how post-World War II reconstruction occurred, new international power relations took shape, and colonial empires broke up

5-6
- Understands the shift in political and economic conditions after World War II
- Understands the development of the Cold War
- Understands political and social change in developing countries after World War II
- Understands the position of women in developing countries

7-8
- Understands the transformation of Western and Eastern Europe after World War II
- Understands post-war relations between the Soviet Union, Europe, and the United States
- Understands the rise of the Communist Party in China between 1936 and 1949
- Understands nationalist and independence movements in colonial countries after World War II
- Understands political conditions in Africa after World War II
- Understands important events in the struggle between Israelis and Palestinians since 1948

9-12
- Understands political shifts in Europe and Asia following World War II
- Understands the relations between the United States and the Soviet Union during the Cold War
- Understands reasons for the division of the Indian subcontinent
- Understands the impact of independence movements in various countries and whether they were successful
- Understands reasons for the shift in government in Africa and how Africans responded
- Understands factors that influenced political conditions in China after World War II
- Understands the strategic role of the Muslim countries during the Cold War
- Understands similarities between the stance of Buddhist priests against the Diem regime in Vietnam and the Muslim stance against the Kukarn regime in Indonesia
- Understands the significance of the Balfour Declaration, the goals of the Arab League and the Zionist Movement, and how the White Paper Reports affected inhabitants of Palestine

44. Understands the search for community, stability, and peace in an interdependent world

5-6
- Understands global influences on the environment
- Understands the impact of increasing economic interdependence in different regions of the world
- Understands efforts to improve political and social conditions around the world

- Understands how feminist movements and social conditions have affected the lives of women around the world, and the extent of women's progress toward social equality, economic opportunity, and political rights in various countries
- Understands scientific and technological trends of the second half of the 20th century
- Understands cultural trends of the second half of the 20th century

7-8
- Understands the causes and effects of population growth and urbanization
- Understands influences on economic development around the world
- Understands events that led to an easing of Cold War tensions from the 1970s to the early 1990s
- Understands instances of political conflict and terrorism in modern society
- Understands the definition of "fundamentalism," and the objectives of militant religious movements, as well as the factors that contribute to the growth of these movements
- Understands the emergence of a global culture
- Understands the importance or meaning of the natural environment for societies around the world
- Understands the role and difficulties of the present day migrant worker
- Understands the motivations, moral imperatives, and goals of specific separatist movements
- Understands the effects of modern communication on consumer tastes and demands

9-12
- Understands the influences on and impact of cultural trends in the second half of the 20th century
- Understands rates of economic development and the emergence of different economic systems
- Understands reasons for the great disparities between industrialized and developing nations
- Understands the oil crisis and its aftermath in the 1970s
- Understands the role of political ideology, religion, and ethnicity in shaping modern governments
- Understands the role of ethnicity, cultural identity, and religious beliefs in shaping economic and political conflicts across the globe
- Understands the impact of population pressure, poverty, and environmental degradation on the breakdown of state authority in various countries in the 1980s and 1990s
- Understands how trends in science have influenced society
- Understands influences on population growth, and efforts to control growth in modern society
- Understands the effectiveness of United Nations programs
- Understands common arguments of opposition groups in various countries around the world, common solutions they offer, and the position of these ideas with regard to Western economic and strategic interests
- Understands gender roles across the globe
- Understands how global political change has altered the world economy
- Understands how specific countries have implemented social and cultural changes
- Understands "liberation theology" and the conflicts that have surrounded this philosophy

45. Understands major global trends since Word War II

5-6
- Understands major patterns of international migration in the late 20th century compared to world population movements of the 19th century and the first half of the 20th
- Understands the advancement of human rights and democratic ideals during the 20th century

7-8
- Understands the changing configuration of political boundaries in the world since 1900 and connections between nationalist ideology and the proliferation of sovereign states
- Understands the origins and decline of the Cold War and its significance as a 20th-century event
- Understands the causes and consequences of the world's shift from bipolar to multipolar centers of economic, political, and military power

9-12
- Understands the usefulness of the concept of "postindustrial society" in comparing the late 20th century with the period from the industrial revolution to 1950
- Understands causes of economic imbalances and social inequalities among the world's peoples and efforts made to close these gaps
- Understands connections between globalizing trends in economy, technology, and culture and dynamic assertions of traditional cultural identity and distinctiveness

46. Understands long-term changes and recurring patterns in world history

5-6
- Understands why humans have built cities and how the nature of cities have changed over time
- Understands major patterns of long-distance trade from ancient times to the present and how trade has contributed to economic and cultural change in particular societies or civilizations
- Understands the importance of slavery and other forms of coerced labor in various societies
- Understands how ideals and institutions of freedom, equality, justice, and citizenship have changed over time and from one society to another
- Understands ways in which human action has contributed to changes in the environment

7-8
- Understands major changes in world population from paleolithic times to the present
- Understands the origins, development, and characteristics of capitalism
- Understands how nation-states differ from empires or other forms of political organization
- Understands political revolutionary movements of the past three centuries

9-12
- Understands the importance of the revolutions in tool-making, agriculture, and industrialization
- Understands the circumstances under which European countries came to exercise temporary military and economic dominance in the world in the late 19th and 20th centuries

Language Arts

1. Demonstrates competence in the general skills and strategies of the writing process

K-2
- Plans written work through discussion, drawing, and rehearsal
- Drafts and revises written work by rereading, rearranging text, and adding details
- Edits and publishes written work using a dictionary and incorporating visual aids
- Evaluates own and others' writing by asking questions and helping others to apply conventions
- Dictates or writes with a logical sequence of events
- Dictates or writes detailed descriptions of people, places, objects, or experiences
- Writes in response to literature
- Writes in a variety of formats

3-5
- Plans written work using graphic organizers, taking notes, and brainstorming
- Drafts and revises written work by developing central ideas and paragraphs
- Edits and publishes written work using appropriate page format
- Evaluates own and others' writing by identifying strengths and purposes for writing
- Writes compositions that show awareness of intended audience
- Writes compositions that convey an intended purpose
- Writes expository compositions that stay on topic and use a variety of details
- Writes narrative accounts that establish a context, plot, point of view, and conflict
- Writes autobiographical compositions that provide insight into why an incident is memorable
- Writes expressive compositions that use an authentic voice, narrative strategies, and imagery
- Writes in response to literature by making and supporting judgments about the text
- Writes personal letters

6-8
- Plans written work using outlines and writing models
- Drafts and revises written work by using an organizational scheme and making structural changes
- Edits for clarity and language usage and publishes written work using a word processor
- Evaluates own and others' writing by applying criteria generated by self and others
- Uses style and structure appropriate for specific audiences and purposes
- Writes expository compositions that organize and present information in a logical manner
- Writes narrative accounts that develop complex characters and use specific narrative actions
- Writes autobiographical compositions that reveal the writer's attitude towards the incident
- Writes biographical sketches that use a variety of strategies to illustrate the subject's character
- Writes persuasive compositions with a controlling idea and persuasive evidence
- Writes compositions that speculate on problems/solutions

- Writes in response to literature by summarizing a book or describing impressions of a text
- Writes business letters and letters of request and response

9-12
- Plans written work using structured overviews, speed writing, and diagrams
- Drafts and revises written work by rethinking content, organization, and style
- Edits using a checklist to guide proofreading and uses technology to publish written work
- Identifies strengths and weakness in own and others' writing
- Writes compositions that are focused for different audiences
- Writes compositions that fulfill different purposes
- Writes expository compositions that synthesize information from a variety of sources
- Writes fictional, biographical, autobiographical, and observational narrative compositions
- Writes persuasive compositions about problems/solutions and causes and effects
- Writes descriptive compositions
- Writes reflective compositions
- Writes in response to literature by suggesting an interpretation or focusing on the theme
- Writes personal and business correspondence, such as memos or job application letters

2. Demonstrates competence in the stylistic and rhetorical aspects of writing

K-2
- Uses general, frequently used words to convey basic ideas

3-5
- Uses descriptive language to describe familiar people, places, or objects
- Uses paragraph form in writing by indenting and including topic sentences
- Uses a variety of sentence structures

6-8
- Uses descriptive language to establish tone and mood
- Uses paragraph form in writing, including supporting and follow-up sentences
- Uses a variety of sentence structures to express expanded ideas
- Uses some explicit transitional devices

9-12
- Uses descriptive language to stimulate the imagination of the reader
- Uses paragraph form in writing, including clincher or closing sentences
- Uses a variety of sentence structures and lengths
- Uses a variety of transitional devices
- Uses technical terms and notations in writing
- Uses a variety of techniques to provide supporting detail
- Organizes ideas to achieve cohesion in writing
- Uses a variety of techniques to convey a personal style and voice

3. Uses grammatical and mechanical conventions in written compositions

K-2
- Forms letters in print and spaces words and sentences
- Uses complete sentences in written compositions
- Uses declarative and interrogative sentences in written compositions
- Uses nouns for simple objects, family members, and categories in written compositions
- Uses verbs for a variety of situations and as action words in written compositions
- Uses basic adjectives in written compositions
- Uses basic adverbs in written compositions
- Spells own first and last name and words from the appropriate grade-level list
- Capitalizes first and last names and the first word of a sentence
- Uses punctuation such as periods, question marks, and commas

3-5
- Writes in cursive
- Uses exclamatory and imperative sentences in written compositions
- Substitutes pronouns for nouns in written compositions
- Uses nouns, including plural, singular, regular, and irregular forms, in written compositions
- Uses verbs, including simple tenses and subject-verb agreement, in written compositions
- Uses indefinite, numerical, and predicate adjectives in written compositions

- Uses adverbs to make comparisons in written compositions
- Uses coordinating conjunctions to link ideas in written compositions
- Uses negatives in written compositions
- Spells words using initial consonant substitution and vowel combinations
- Capitalizes titles of people, proper nouns, and the heading, salutation, and closing of a letter
- Uses punctuation such as periods, commas, apostrophes, quotation marks, and colons

6-8
- Uses simple and compound sentences in written compositions
- Uses relative, demonstrative, and personal pronouns in written compositions
- Uses nouns, including possessives and irregular plurals, in written compositions
- Uses verbs, including linking and auxiliary verbs and verb phrases, in written compositions
- Uses pronominal, positive, comparative, and superlative adjectives in written compositions
- Chooses between forms of adverbs and adjectives for written compositions
- Uses prepositions and coordinating conjunctions in written compositions
- Uses interjections in written compositions
- Spells words using common prefixes and suffixes and rules for irregular structural changes
- Capitalizes titles, proper nouns, proper adjectives, nationalities, and brand names of products
- Uses punctuation such as exclamation marks, commas, quotation marks, colons, and hyphens
- Uses standard format in written compositions, including footnotes and italics

9-12
- Uses complex and compound-complex sentences in written compositions
- Uses reflexive, indefinite, interrogative, and compound personal pronouns
- Uses nouns, including collective, compound, noun phrases and clauses, in written compositions
- Uses verbs, including present, past, and future perfect tenses, in written compositions
- Uses adjectives, including adjective clauses and phrases, in written compositions
- Uses adverbs, including adverb clauses and phrases, in written compositions
- Uses correlative and subordinating conjunctions in written compositions
- Spells words from the appropriate grade-level list using a variety of strategies
- Capitalizes historical periods and events, geological eras, religious terms, and scientific terms
- Uses punctuation such as commas, quotation marks, colons, hyphens, semicolons, and dashes
- Uses commonly confused terms in written compositions
- Uses standard format in written compositions, including bold or underlined headings

4. Gathers and uses information for research purposes

K-2
- Generates questions about topics of personal interest
- Uses books to gather information

3-5
- Uses a variety of strategies to identify topics to investigate
- Uses encyclopedias to gather information for research topics
- Uses dictionaries to gather information for research topics
- Uses key words, indexes, cross-references, and letters on volumes to find information
- Uses multiple representations of information to find information for research topics
- Uses graphic organizers to gather and record information for research topics
- Compiles information into written reports or summaries

6-8
- Gathers data for research topics from interviews
- Uses the card catalog to locate books for research topics
- Uses a variety of indexes to gather information for research topics
- Uses a computer catalog to gather information for research topics
- Uses a variety of resource materials to gather information for research topics
- Determines the appropriateness of an information source for a research topic
- Organizes information and ideas from multiple sources in systematic ways
- Writes research papers that integrate a variety of information

9-12
- Uses government publications to gather information for research topics
- Uses microfiche to gather information for research topics
- Uses a variety of news sources to gather information for research topics
- Uses telephone information services in public libraries to gather information for research topics
- Synthesizes a variety of types of visual information for research topics
- Uses a variety of primary sources to gather information for research topics
- Considers the motives, credibility, and perspectives of the authors of primary sources
- Uses information in research reports based on the validity and reliability of the source
- Synthesizes information from multiple research studies to draw new conclusions
- Identifies and defends research questions and topics that may be important in the future
- Writes research papers that include a thesis statement
- Creates bibliographies for research topics

5. Demonstrates competence in the general skills and strategies of the reading process

K-2
- Understands that print conveys meaning
- Understands how print is organized and read
- Creates mental images from pictures and print
- Uses picture clues and captions to aid comprehension and to make predictions about content
- Decodes unknown words using sound/letter relationships and structural analysis
- Uses a picture dictionary to determine word meaning
- Uses self-correction strategies
- Reads aloud familiar stories, poems, and passages

3-5
- Previews texts
- Establishes a purpose for reading
- Represents concrete information as explicit mental pictures
- Makes, confirms, and revises simple predictions about what will be found in a text
- Decodes words using phonetic and structural analysis, syntactic structure, and semantic context
- Decodes unknown words using a variety of context clues
- Determines the meaning of unknown words using a glossary, dictionary, and thesaurus
- Monitors own reading strategies and makes modifications as needed
- Adjusts speed of reading to suit purpose and difficulty of the material
- Identifies the author's purpose

6-8
- Generates questions to be answered while reading
- Establishes and adjusts purposes for reading
- Represents abstract information as explicit mental pictures
- Uses a variety of strategies to define and extend understanding of word meaning
- Uses specific strategies to clear up confusing parts of a text
- Identifies specific devices an author uses to accomplish his or her purpose
- Reflects on what has been learned after reading and formulates responses to texts

9-12
- Determines figurative, idiomatic, and technical meanings of terms through context
- Extends general and specialized reading vocabulary
- Uses a range of automatic monitoring and self-correction methods
- Recognizes the effectiveness of writing techniques in accomplishing an author's purpose
- Understands influences on a reader's response to a text
- Represents key ideas and supporting details in outline or graph form
- Identifies philosophical assumptions and basic beliefs underlying an author's work

6 . Demonstrates competence in general skills and strategies for reading a variety of literary texts

K-2
- Applies reading skills and strategies to literary texts such as fairy tales and pictures books
- Identifies favorite books and stories
- Identifies setting, main characters, main events, and problems in stories
- Makes simple inferences regarding the order of events and possible outcomes

- Identifies the main ideas or theme of a story
- Relates stories to personal experiences

3-5
- Applies reading skills and strategies to a variety of literary texts, such as biographies and poems
- Knows the defining characteristics of literary forms and genres, such as biographies and poems
- Selects reading material based on personal criteria
- Understands the basic concept of plot
- Identifies differences among literary works in terms of settings, characters, and events
- Makes inferences regarding character traits and motives, and the consequences of their actions
- Understands simple dialogues and how they relate to a story
- Identifies recurring themes across literary works
- Makes connections between characters or events in a literary work and his or her own life.
- Shares responses to literature with peers

6-8
- Applies reading skills and strategies to literary texts, such as science fiction and tall tales
- Knows the characteristics of literary forms and genres, such as science fiction and tall tales
- Identifies specific questions of personal importance and seeks to answer them through literature
- Recognizes complex elements of plot
- Recognizes devices used to develop characters in literary texts
- Makes inferences and draws conclusions about story elements
- Understands complex, extended dialogues and how they relate to a story
- Recognizes the use of specific literary devices
- Understands the effects of the author's style on a literary text
- Identifies point of view in a literary text
- Makes connections between characters' motives and complex events and his or her own life
- Understands that people respond differently to literature

9-12
- Applies reading skills and strategies to literary texts, such as satires, parodies, and plays
- Knows the characteristics of literary forms and genres, such as satires, parodies, and plays
- Analyzes the effectiveness of complex elements of plot
- Understands simple and complex actions between main and subordinate characters in texts
- Recognizes archetypes and symbols across literary texts
- Makes connections among literary works based on theme
- Understands the effects of complex literary devices on the overall quality of a work
- Understands historical and cultural influences on literary works
- Makes abstract connections between his or her own life and literary texts
- Relates personal response to the text with that seemingly intended by the author

7. **Demonstrates competence in the general skills and strategies for reading a variety of informational texts**

K-2
- Applies reading skills and strategies to a variety of informational books
- Understands the main idea of simple expository information
- Summarizes information found in texts
- Relates new information to prior knowledge and experience

3-5
- Applies reading skills and strategies to informational texts such as letters, diaries, and magazines
- Knows the defining characteristics of informational texts such as letters, diaries, and magazines
- Uses text organizers to determine the main ideas and to locate information in a text
- Uses the various parts of a book to locate information
- Summarizes and paraphrases information in texts
- Uses prior knowledge and experience to understand and respond to new information
- Identifies the author's viewpoint in an informational text

6-8
- Applies reading skills and strategies to informational texts such as essays, editorials, and news
- Knows the defining characteristics of informational texts such as essays, editorials, and news
- Summarizes and paraphrases complex, explicit hierarchic structures in informational texts

- Identifies information-organizing strategies that are personally most useful
- Uses new information to adjust and extend personal knowledge base
- Identifies techniques used to convey viewpoint
- Seeks peer help to understand information
- Draws conclusions and makes inferences based on explicit and implicit information in texts
- Differentiates between fact and opinion in informational texts

9-12
- Applies reading skills and strategies to informational texts such as schedules and speeches
- Knows the defining characteristics of informational texts such as schedules and speeches
- Scans a passage to determine whether it contains relevant information
- Summarizes and paraphrases relationships among the concepts and details in informational texts
- Uses new information from texts to clarify or refine understanding of academic concepts
- Determines the effectiveness of techniques used to convey viewpoint
- Uses discussions with peers as a way of understanding information
- Understands the advantages and disadvantages of organizing text in different ways
- Evaluates the clarity and accuracy of information
- Supports inferences about information in texts by referring to text features

8. Demonstrates competence in speaking and listening as tools for learning

K-2
- Recognizes the characteristic sounds and rhythms of language
- Makes contributions in class and group discussions
- Asks and responds to questions
- Follows rules of conversation, such as taking turns and raising a hand to speak
- Uses different voice level, phrasing, and intonation for different situations
- Listens and responds to oral directions
- Listens to and recites familiar stories, poems, and rhymes with patterns
- Listens and responds to a variety of media
- Identifies differences between language used at home and language used in school

3-5
- Contributes to group discussions
- Asks questions in class
- Responds to questions and comments
- Listens to classmates and adults
- Has a clear main point when speaking to others
- Reads compositions to the class
- Makes eye contact while giving oral presentations
- Organizes ideas for oral presentations
- Listens to and identifies persuasive messages
- Identifies the use of nonverbal cues used in conversation
- Identifies specific ways in which language is used in real-life situations

6-8
- Plays a variety of roles in group discussions
- Asks questions to seek elaboration and clarification of ideas
- Listens in order to understand a speaker's topic, purpose, and perspective
- Conveys a clear main point when speaking to others and stays on the topic being discussed
- Presents simple prepared reports to the class
- Uses explicit techniques for presentations such as modulation of voice, eye contact, and posture
- Identifies strategies used by speakers in oral presentations
- Listens to and understands the impact of nonprint media on media consumers
- Identifies the ways in which language differs across a variety of social situations

9-12
- Evaluates own and others' effectiveness in group discussions and in formal presentations
- Asks questions as a way to broaden and enrich classroom discussions
- Adjusts message wording and delivery to particular audiences and for particular purposes
- Makes formal presentations to the class

- Uses a variety of explicit techniques for presentations and demonstrates poise and self-control
- Responds to questions and feedback about own presentations
- Makes informed judgments about nonprint media
- Compares form, meaning, and usefulness of different kinds of language
- Understands influences on language use

The Arts: Art Connections

1. Understands connections among the various art forms and other disciplines

K-4
- Knows how visual, aural, oral, and kinetic elements are used in the various art forms
- Knows how ideas and emotions are expressed in the various art forms
- Knows the similarities and differences in the meanings of common terms used in the arts
- Understands interrelationships between the arts and other subject matter

5-8
- Understands how characteristic materials of various arts are used to create distinct works of art
- Knows how works in various art forms share similar subject matter or cultural contexts
- Understands how characters, environments, and actions appear in the various art forms
- Knows how various concepts and principles are used in the arts and in other disciplines
- Knows the aesthetic impact of arts performances seen live
- Understands the functions and interactions between artists and audience members

9-12
- Knows ways in which various arts media can be integrated
- Understands how characteristics of the arts vary within a particular historical period or style
- Understands how elements, materials, technologies, processes, and organizational principles are used in the various art forms

The Arts: Dance

1. Identifies and demonstrates movement elements and skills in performing dance

K-4
- Uses basic nonlocomotor/axial movements
- Uses basic locomotor movements in different directions
- Creates shapes at different heights from the floor
- Defines and maintains personal space
- Uses movements in straight and curved pathways
- Moves to a rhythmic accompaniment and responds to changes in tempo
- Uses kinesthetic awareness, concentration, and focus in performing movement skills
- Knows basic actions and movement elements and how they communicate ideas

5-8
- Understands various movements and their underlying principles
- Knows basic dance steps, body positions, and spatial patterns for various dances
- Transfers a spatial pattern from the visual to the kinesthetic
- Transfers a rhythmic pattern from the aural to the kinesthetic
- Knows a range of dynamics/movement qualities
- Memorizes and reproduces movement sequences
- Knows appropriate vocabulary to describe action and movement elements in dance

9-12
- Uses appropriate body control in locomotor and nonlocomotor/axial movements
- Knows complex steps and patterns from various dance styles and traditions
- Understands various complex time elements
- Creates and performs combinations and variations in a broad dynamic range
- Uses projection in dance
- Memorizes and reproduces extended movement sequences and rhythmic patterns

2. Understands choreographic principles, processes, and structures

K-4
- Creates a sequence with a beginning, middle, and ending
- Improvises, creates, and performs dances based on personal ideas and other sources
- Knows how improvisation can be used to discover and invent movement
- Creates a dance phrase, repeats it, and varies it
- Uses basic partner skills

5-8
- Understands the principles of contrast and transition
- Understands the processes of reordering and chance
- Understands various choreographic structures and forms
- Uses partner skills such as creating shapes and taking or supporting weight

9-12
- Knows how improvisation is used to generate movement for choreography
- Understands a variety of traditional and contemporary structures and forms
- Identifies choreographic principles, processes, and structures used in dance

3. Understands dance as a way to create and communicate meaning

K-4
- Knows how dance is different from other forms of human movement
- Knows how dance may elicit a variety of interpretations and reactions

5-8
- Understands the difference between pantomiming and abstracting a gesture
- Understands how different accompaniment can affect the meaning of a dance
- Understands how lighting and costuming can contribute to the meaning of a dance
- Creates dance that communicates topics or ideas of personal significance

9-12
- Understands how movement choices can communicate abstract ideas and themes
- Understands how interpretation of dance can be influenced by personal experience

4. Applies critical and creative thinking skills in dance

K-4
- Knows how a variety of solutions can be used to solve a given movement problem
- Knows technical and artistic components of various forms of dance

5-8
- Knows appropriate audience response to dance performances
- Knows the critical elements that contribute to a dance in terms of space, time, force/energy
- Knows possible aesthetic criteria that could be used to evaluate dance

9-12
- Establishes and uses a set of aesthetic criteria to evaluate own work and work of others
- Formulates and answers one's own aesthetic questions

5. Understands dance in various cultures and historical periods

K-4
- Knows folk dances from various cultures
- Knows the cultural and/or historical context of various dances

5-8
- Knows similarities and differences among a variety of folk dances and classical dances
- Knows a variety of American folk, social, and theatrical dances
- Knows the role of dance in various cultures and time periods

9-12
- Knows similarities and differences among various forms of theatrical dances
- Knows traditions and techniques of classical dance forms
- Understands how dance and dancers are portrayed in contemporary media

6. Understands connections between dance and healthful living

K-4
- Knows how healthy practices enhance the ability to dance

5-8
- Knows strategies to prevent dance injuries
- Creates personal dance warmup techniques
- Creates goals to improve as a dancer

9-12 • Knows how lifestyle choices affect the dancer as a professional performer
     • Understands various contemporary and historical images of the body in dance

The Arts: Music

1. Sings, alone and with others, a varied repertoire of music

K-2 • Sings a variety of simple songs

3-5 • Sings on pitch and in rhythm, with appropriate timbre, diction, and posture
     • Sings expressively and with appropriate dynamics, phrasing, and interpretation
     • Blends vocal timbres, matches dynamic levels, and responds to cues of a conductor
     • Knows songs representing genres and styles from diverse cultures

6-8 • Sings accurately and appropriately music with moderate ranges and changes of tempo
     • Sings music written in two and three parts
     • Knows music that represents diverse genres and cultures

9-12 • Sings a varied repertoire of moderately difficult music with expression and technical accuracy
     • Sings music written in four parts, with and without accompaniment
     • Uses ensemble skills

2. Performs on instruments, alone and with others, a varied repertoire of music

K-2 • Echoes short rhythms and melodic patterns

3-5 • Performs on pitch, in rhythm, and with appropriate dynamics and timbre
     • Performs simple rhythmic, melodic, and chordal patterns accurately on a variety of instruments
     • Knows a varied repertoire of music representing diverse genres and styles
     • Performs in groups
     • Performs independent instrumental parts while others play contrasting parts

6-8 • Performs on an instrument accurately, independently, and appropriately
     • Performs with expression and accuracy music that has moderate ranges and changes of tempo
     • Performs music representing diverse genres and cultures
     • Plays by ear simple melodies and simple accompaniments

9-12 • Performs a varied repertoire of moderately difficult music with expression and accuracy
     • Uses ensemble skills when performing as part of a group

3. Improvises melodies, variations, and accompaniments

K-2 • Improvises "answers" in the same style to give rhythmic and melodic phrases

3-5 • Improvises simple rhythmic and melodic accompaniments
     • Improvises simple rhythmic variations and melodic embellishments
     • Improvises short songs and instrumental pieces using a variety of sound sources

6-8 • Improvises simple harmonic accompaniments
     • Improvises melodic embellishments and simple variations on given melodies
     • Improvises short melodies in a consistent style, meter, and tonality

9-12 • Improvises stylistically appropriate harmonizing parts
     • Improvises rhythmic and melodic variations on given melodies
     • Improvises original melodies in a consistent style, meter, and tonality

4. Composes and arranges music within specified guidelines

K-2 • Uses a variety of sound sources when composing

3-5
- Creates and arranges music to accompany readings or dramatizations
- Creates and arranges short songs and instrumental pieces within specified guidelines

6-8
- Knows how elements of music are used for various effects in compositions
- Composes short pieces within specified guidelines
- Arranges simple pieces for voices or instruments
- Uses a variety of sound sources and electronic media when composing and arranging

9-12
- Composes music in a variety of distinct styles
- Uses the elements of music for expressive effect
- Arranges pieces for voices or instruments that preserve the expressive effect of the music
- Composes and arranges music for voices and various instruments
- Understands the ranges and traditional uses of various sound sources

5. Reads and notates music

K-2
- Knows standard symbols used to notate meter, rhythm, pitch, and dynamics
- Uses a system to read simple pitch notation in the treble clef and major keys

3-5
- Reads notes and rests in simple meter signatures
- Knows symbols and traditional terms referring to dynamics, tempo, and articulation

6-8
- Reads sixteenth and dotted notes and rests in 6/8, 3/8 and 2/2 meter signatures
- Reads at sight simple melodies
- Knows standard symbols for pitch, rhythm, dynamics, tempo, articulation, and expression
- Uses standard notation to record musical ideas

9-12
- Reads an instrumental or vocal score of up to four staves
- Reads music that contains moderate technical demands and expanded ranges

6. Knows and applies appropriate criteria to music and music performances

K-2
- Knows personal preferences for specific musical works and styles
- Identifies simple music forms when presented aurally
- Responds to selected music characteristics or to specific music events

3-5
- Knows music of various styles representing diverse cultures
- Knows appropriate terminology used to explain music and music performances
- Identifies the sounds of a variety of instruments and voices

6-8
- Identifies specific music events when listening to music
- Understands how the elements of music are used in various genres and cultures
- Understands the basic principles of meter, rhythm, tonality, intervals, chords, and progressions
- Knows criteria that affect the quality and effectiveness of music performances and compositions

9-12
- Understands how elements of music are used in music from diverse genres and cultures
- Understands the technical vocabulary of music
- Understands a variety of compositional devices and techniques
- Knows specific criteria used to evaluate music performances, compositions, and arrangements

7. Understands the relationship between music and history and culture

K-2
- Knows characteristics that make certain music suitable for specific uses
- Knows appropriate audience behavior for the type of music performed

3-5
- Identifies music from various historical periods and cultures
- Knows how basic elements of music are used in music from various cultures
- Understands the roles of musicians in various settings and cultures

6-8   • Understands distinguishing characteristics of music genres and styles from various cultures
        • Understands characteristics that cause musical works to be considered exemplary
        • Understands functions of music, roles of musicians, and musical settings in various cultures

9-12 • Classifies unfamiliar aural examples of music
        • Knows sources of American music genres
        • Knows various roles that musicians perform

The Arts: Theatre

1. Demonstrates competence in writing scripts

K-4   • Selects characters, environments, and situations for simple dramatizations
        • Improvises dialogue to tell stories
        • Writes or records dialogue
        • Plans and records improvisations based on a variety of sources

5-8   • Creates characters, environments, and actions that create tension and suspense
        • Refines and records dialogue and action
        • Creates improvisations and scripted scenes based on a variety of sources

9-12 • Constructs imaginative scripts that convey story and meaning to an audience
        • Improvises, writes, and refines scripts based on a variety of sources

2. Uses acting skills

K-4   • Knows characters in dramatizations, their relationships, and their environments
        • Uses a variety of movement and vocal qualities for different characters
        • Assumes roles in a variety of dramatizations
        • Knows how to interact in improvisations

5-8   • Understands how elements of drama are used to discover and justify character motivation
        • Uses basic acting skills to develop characterizations
        • Invents character behaviors based on observations of people
        • Interacts as an invented character in improvised and scripted scenes

9-12 • Understands the physical, emotional, and social dimensions of characters from various texts
        • Knows various classical and contemporary acting techniques and methods
        • Develops and sustains characters in improvisations and productions

3. Designs and produces informal and formal productions

K-4   • Knows how visual elements and aural aspects are used to communicate locale and mood
        • Selects and organizes materials for scenery, properties, lighting, sound, costumes, and makeup
        • Creates environments for classroom dramatizations

5-8   • Understands the functions of production elements in creating an appropriate environment
        • Understands technical requirements for various improvised and scripted scenes
        • Uses visual elements, visual principles, and aural qualities to create environments
        • Creates elements of scenery, properties, lighting, sound, and costumes

9-12 • Understands the basic physical and chemical properties of the technical aspects of theatre
        • Understands production requirements for a variety of dramatic texts
        • Develops designs to convey environments that support the text
        • Creates functional scenery, properties, lighting, sound, costumes, and makeup
        • Realizes artistic interpretations for productions
        • Designs stage management, promotional, and business plans

4. Directs scenes and productions

K-4
- Knows various ways of staging classroom dramatizations
- Plans and prepares improvisations

5-8
- Plans visual and aural elements for various scenes
- Organizes rehearsals for various scenes

9-12
- Develops multiple interpretations and production choices for scripts and ideas
- Justifies interpretations and artistic choices
- Communicates directorial choices for improvised or scripted scenes
- Organizes and conducts rehearsals for a variety of productions

5. Understands how informal and formal theatre, film, television, and electronic media productions create and communicate meaning

K-4
- Understands the visual, aural, oral, and kinetic elements of dramatic performances
- Understands the wants and needs of characters
- Justifies personal preferences for dramatic performances
- Knows how alternative ideas can be used to enhance roles, environments, and situations
- Knows appropriate terminology used in analyzing dramatizations
- Identifies people, events, time, and place in classroom dramatizations

5-8
- Understands the effect of publicity, study guides, and programs on audience response
- Articulates the meanings constructed from various dramatic performances
- Understands the effectiveness of artistic choices found in dramatic performances
- Understands the effectiveness of collaborative contributions in developing scenes
- Applies research to script writing, acting, design, and directing choices

9-12
- Understands how social meanings communicated in productions relate to current issues
- Justifies personal aesthetic criteria for describing and evaluating dramatic texts and events
- Understands how the context of a production can enhance or hinder its effectiveness
- Knows how varying collaborative efforts and choices can affect productions
- Researches cultural, historical, and symbolic clues in dramatic texts
- Understands the validity of cultural, historical, and symbolic information used in productions

6. Understands the context in which theatre, film, television, and electronic media are performed today as well as in the past

K-4
- Compares similar characters and situations in dramas from and about various cultures
- Understands the various settings of dramas, theatre, film, television, and media productions
- Knows ways in which theatre reflects life

5-8
- Understands similarities and differences among archetypal characters and situations
- Understands the skills needed to pursue careers in theatre, film, television, and electronic media
- Understands the emotional and social impact of dramatic performances
- Knows ways in which theatre reflects a culture
- Knows how culture affects content and production values of dramatic performances
- Understands how social concepts apply in theatre

9-12
- Understands how similar themes are treated in drama from various cultures and periods
- Understands ways in which theatre can reveal universal concepts
- Understands similarities and differences among various representative theatre artists
- Knows cultural and historical influences on American theatre
- Understands ways in which experience can affect an artist's dramatic work

The Arts: Visual Arts

1. Understands and applies media, techniques, and processes related to the visual arts

K-4
- Knows the differences between art materials, techniques, and processes
- Knows how different materials, techniques, and processes can evoke different responses
- Knows how different media, techniques, and processes are used to communicate ideas
- Uses art materials and tools in a safe and responsible manner

5-8
- Understands what makes different media, techniques, and processes effective
- Knows characteristics and qualities of specific art media, techniques, and processes

9-12
- Applies media, techniques, and processes effectively
- Understands how ideas can be communicated through the use of media and techniques

2. Knows how to use the structures (e.g., sensory qualities, organizational principles, expressive features) and functions of art

K-4
- Knows the differences among visual characteristics and purposes of art
- Understands how different features and organizational principles cause different responses
- Uses visual structures and functions of art to communicate ideas

5-8
- Knows some of the effects of various visual structures and functions of art
- Understands what makes various organizational structures effective in communicating ideas
- Knows how structures and functions of art are used to improve communication of ideas

9-12
- Understands how the characteristics and structures of art are used to achieve various intentions
- Understands the effectiveness of various artworks in terms of structures and functions
- Knows how principles and functions can be used to solve specific visual arts problems

3. Knows a range of subject matter, symbols, and potential ideas in the visual arts

K-4
- Selects prospective ideas for works of arts
- Knows how subject matter, symbols, and ideas are used to communicate meaning

5-8
- Knows how visual, spatial, and temporal concepts work to communicate meaning
- Knows different subjects, themes, and symbols which convey intended meaning

9-12
- Understands how various values of artworks are tempered by culture and history
- Applies various subjects, symbols, and ideas in one's artworks

4. Understands the visual arts in relation to history and cultures

K-4
- Knows that the visual arts have both a history and a relationship to various cultures
- Identifies specific works of art as belonging to particular cultures, times, and places
- Knows how history, culture, and the visual arts can influence each other

5-8
- Understands similarities and differences among artworks from various eras and cultures
- Understands the historical and cultural contexts of a variety of art objects
- Understands how factors of time and place influence characteristics of a work of art

9-12
- Knows a variety of contexts regarding the characteristics and purposes of works of art
- Knows the function and meaning of specific art objects
- Understands relationships among works of art in terms of history, aesthetics, and culture

5. Understands the characteristics and merits of one's own artwork and the artwork of others

K-4
- Knows various purposes for creating works of visual art
- Knows how people's experiences can influence the development of specific artworks
- Understands that specific artworks can elicit different responses

5-8
- Distinguishes among multiple purposes for creating works of art
- Understands possible contemporary and historic meanings in specific artworks
- Understands how one's own artworks may elicit a variety of responses

9-12
- Identifies intentions of those creating artworks
- Understands some of the implications of intention and purpose in works of art
- Knows how specific works relate to historical and cultural contexts
- Understands how various interpretations can be used to evaluate works of visual art

Civics

1. Understands ideas about civic life, politics, and government

K-2
- Knows examples of actions based on individual initiative and actions directed by others
- Knows examples of authority and power without authority
- Knows some of the problems that might result from lack of effective authority

3-5
- Knows various people and groups who make, apply, interpret, and enforce rules and laws
- Knows the difference between power and authority
- Knows ways in which authority is used and ways in which power can be used without authority
- Knows possible consequences of the absence of government and rules and laws
- Knows the basic purposes of government in the United States
- Knows the major things governments do in one's school, community, state, and nation
- Knows how government makes it possible for people to work together to accomplish goals

6-8
- Distinguishes between private life and civic life
- Understands how politics enables people with differing ideas to reach binding agreements
- Knows institutions that have the authority to direct or control the behavior of its members
- Understands major ideas about why government is necessary
- Understands competing ideas about the purposes government should serve

9-12
- Understands how politics enables people to reach collective decisions and accomplish goals
- Knows formal institutions that have the authority to make and implement binding decisions
- Understands the nature of political authority
- Understands the sources of political authority and its functions
- Understands why politics is found wherever people gather as a group
- Understands major arguments for the necessity of politics and government
- Knows the primary purpose of various governments in the past and present
- Understands how the purposes served by a government affect individuals and society

2. Understands the essential characteristics of limited and unlimited governments

K-2
- Knows that people in positions of authority have limits on their authority

3-5
- Knows the basic conditions necessary to support a limited government
- Knows how laws can limit the power of people in government
- Knows the general characteristics of unlimited government
- Understands how limited government seeks to protect personal, political, and economic rights

6-8
- Knows some of the restraints placed on a limited government's power
- Understands the basic structure of authoritarian systems and totalitarian systems

9-12
- Understands what "civil society" is and how it provides opportunities for individuals to associate
- Understands how civil society allows for individuals or groups to influence government
- Understands how the relationships that make up civil society help maintain limited government
- Understands how constitutional democracies differ from authoritarian and totalitarian regimes
- Knows competing ideas about the relationships between economic and political freedoms
- Understands how political and economic freedoms serve to limit governmental power

3. **Understands the sources, purposes, and functions of law and the importance of the rule of law for the protection of individual rights and the common good**

K-2
- Knows that promoting justice is one of the fundamental purposes of law in American society
- Knows that justice means essentially the same thing as fairness
- Knows that distributive justice refers to problems of fairness arising over "who gets what"
- Knows that corrective justice deals with how to make things right when a wrong has occurred
- Knows that procedural justice refers to fair ways to gather information and make just decisions
- Knows that a good rule or law solves a specific problem, is fair, and "does not go too far"

3-5
- Knows common ways in which rules and laws can be used
- Knows the characteristics of an effective rule or law

6-8
- Understands the difference between the "rule of law" and the "rule of men"
- Understands how the rule of law can be used to restrict the actions of citizens and officials
- Understands the possible consequences of the absence of a rule of law

9-12
- Knows alternative ideas about the sources of law and different varieties of law
- Knows alternative ideas about the purposes and functions of law

4. **Understands the concept of a constitution, the various purposes that constitutions serve, and the conditions that contribute to the establishment and maintenance of constitutional government**

K-2
- Not appropriate for this level

3-5
- Not appropriate for this level

6-8
- Knows various uses of the term "constitution"
- Understands how a government with a constitution may still have unlimited power
- Knows examples of countries with constitutions that actually did limit the power of government
- Knows some basic uses of constitutions
- Knows how constitutions have been used to promote the interests of a particular group
- Knows how constitutions have been used to protect rights and promote the common good
- Knows the type of citizenry needed to establish and maintain constitutional government
- Knows the type of public servants needed to establish and maintain constitutional government

9-12
- Distinguishes between governments with a constitution and constitutional (limited) government
- Understands how constitutions set forth the structure of government
- Understands how constitutions may limit government's power
- Understands how constitutions have been disregarded or used to promote various interests
- Understands how constitutions can be vehicles for change and for resolving social issues
- Understands how constitutions may be used to preserve values of a political system or society
- Knows the social, economic, and political conditions that foster constitutional government
- Knows why some nations have and have not successfully established constitutional government
- Knows how citizens can insure the preservation and improvement of constitutional government

5. **Understands the major characteristics of systems of shared powers and of parliamentary systems**

K-2
- Not appropriate for this level

3-5
- Not appropriate for this level

6-8
- Understands the responsibilities of each branch of government in a system of shared powers
- Understands characteristics of systems of shared powers
- Understands characteristics of parliamentary systems
- Understands the purpose of the prime minster and cabinet in a Parliamentary system

9-12
- Understands the major characteristics of systems of shared powers
- Understands the major characteristics of parliamentary systems
- Understands the relative merits of systems of shared powers and parliamentary systems

6. Understands the advantages and disadvantages of federal, confederal, and unitary systems of government

K-2 • Not appropriate for this level

3-5 • Not appropriate for this level

6-8 • Knows the basic characteristics of a confederal system of government
• Knows the basic characteristics of a federal system of government
• Knows the basic characteristics of a unitary system of government

9-12 • Understands how power is distributed in confederal, federal, and unitary systems of government
• Knows the advantages and disadvantages of confederal, federal, and unitary systems

7. Understands alternative forms of representation and how they serve the purposes of constitutional government

K-2 • Not appropriate for this level

3-5 • Not appropriate for this level

6-8 • Not appropriate for this level

9-12 • Understands the major arguments for and against representative government
• Knows common bases upon which representation is or has been established
• Understands differing bases of electoral systems
• Understands differing theories of representation

8. Understands the central ideas of American constitutional government and how this form of government has shaped the character of American society

K-2 • Knows that America has had a historical commitment to the pursuit of justice

3-5 • Knows the fundamental values of American democracy
• Knows the fundamental principles of American democracy
• Knows how values and principles of American democracy are expressed in various documents
• Understands the focus on "the individual" in American society
• Understands the focus on the school, community, state, and nation in American society
• Understands the importance of equality of opportunity and equal protection of the law
• Understands the importance of respect for the law as a characteristic of American society
• Understands the importance of education as a characteristic of American society
• Understands the importance of work as a characteristic of American society

6-8 • Knows the essential ideas of American government that are expressed in the Declaration of Independence, the Constitution, and other writings
• Knows how provisions of the Constitution give government the power to fulfill its purposes
• Understands how the United States Constitution serves to limit the powers of government
• Understands how specific provisions of the Constitution limit the powers of government
• Knows opposing positions on issues involving constitutional protection of individual rights
• Understands important factors that have helped shape American society

9-12 • Knows major historical events that led to the creation of limited government in the United States
• Knows how the creation of American government was influenced by natural rights philosophy
• Knows ideas about republican government that influenced the development of the Constitution
• Understands the concept of popular sovereignty as a central idea of American government
• Understands the necessity for a written Constitution to set forth the organization of government
• Understands how the Constitution helps to insure a government that will not exceed its limits
• Understands how the design of the federal system works to limit governmental power
• Understands how the belief in limited government has influenced American society
• Knows ways in which Americans have sought to make the principles of the Constitution a reality
• Knows how the characteristics of American society compare with the those of other societies

9. Understands the importance of Americans sharing and supporting certain values, beliefs, and principles of American constitutional democracy

K-2 • No material specifically designated for this level

3-5 • Understands how Americans are united by the values, principles, and beliefs they share
• Understands how shared beliefs contribute to the continuation of American democracy
• Knows how documents in American history set forth shared values, principles, and beliefs
• Knows how various symbols are used to depict Americans' shared values, principies, and beliefs
• Knows how various holidays reflect the shared values, principles, and beliefs of Americans
• Knows how values of democracy can be promoted through respecting the rights of others
• Knows how the values of democracy can be fostered by helping to promote the common good
• Knows how the values of democracy can be promoted through participating in government

6-8 • Identifies fundamental values and principles that are expressed in various documents and individual and group actions that embody fundamental values and principles
• Understands how certain values are fundamental to American public life
• Understands popular sovereignty as opposed to state sovereignty
• Knows that constitutional government is a fundamental principle of American democracy

9-12 • Understands how the institutions of government reflect fundamental values and principles
• Understands the interdependence among certain values and principles (e.g., liberty and diversity)
• Understands the significance of fundamental values and principles for the individual and society

10. Understands the roles of voluntarism and organized groups in American social and political life

K-2 • No material specifically designated for this level

3-5 • Understands the importance of voluntarism as a characteristic of American society

6-8 • Knows factors that have influenced American voluntarism
• Knows services that are provided by charitable, religious, and civic groups in the community
• Knows volunteer opportunities that exist in one's own school and community

9-12 • Knows how the Puritan ethic encouraged American voluntarism
• Knows how groups have been involved in functions usually associated with government
• Knows the extent of voluntarism in American society compared to other countries
• Understands the relationship between voluntarism and Americans' ideas about limited government
• Understands issues regarding what responsibilities belong to the private sector, what responsibilities belong to the government, and how these responsibilities should be shared
• Knows the role of various organized groups in local, state, and national politics

11. Understands the role of diversity in American life and the importance of shared values, political beliefs, and civic beliefs in an increasingly diverse American society

K-2 • No material specifically designated for this level

3-5 • Understands the concept of diversity
• Knows some common forms of diversity in the United States
• Knows reasons why diversity is so prevalent in the United States
• Knows some of the benefits of diversity
• Knows some of the costs of diversity
• Knows conflicts that are caused by diversity
• Knows ways in which conflicts about diversity can be prevented
• Knows ways in which conflicts about diversity can be managed fairly when they occur

6-8 • Knows a variety of forms of diversity in American society
• Knows how diversity encourages cultural creativity
• Knows major conflicts in American society that have arisen from diversity
• Knows peaceful ways for resolving conflicts about diversity

- Knows how an American's identity stems from allegiance to shared political values
- Knows basic values and principles that Americans share
- Knows why it is important that Americans act on their shared political values and principles

9-12
- Knows how the diversity of American society has influenced American politics through time
- Knows different viewpoints regarding the role and value of diversity in American life
- Knows examples of conflicts relating to diversity and why they have or have not been resolved
- Knows why constitutional values must be adhered to when managing conflicts over diversity
- Knows beliefs that are common to American political culture
- Knows how shared values of American political culture are reflected in various documents

12. **Understands the relationships among liberalism, republicanism, and American constitutional democracy**

K-2
- Not appropriate for this level

3-5
- Not appropriate for this level

6-8
- Not appropriate for this level

9-12
- Understands that the central idea of liberalism is that the individual has rights that exist independently of government
- Knows the general history of liberalism
- Knows the difference between the use of the term "liberal" in referring to the American form of government and the use of the terms "liberal" and "conservative" in referring to political views
- Knows that in a democracy the people are the source of the government's authority
- Knows the difference between the use of the term "democratic" to refer to the American form of government and the use of the term to refer to the Democratic Party in the United States
- Knows how the ideas of liberalism and democracy are joined in the Declaration of Independence
- Understands that a "republic" is a state in which the citizenry as a whole is considered sovereign
- Knows the major ideas of republicanism
- Knows how ideas of classical republicanism are reflected in the United States Constitution
- Knows how the use of the term "republican" to refer to the American form of government differs from the use of the term to refer to the Republican Party in the United States
- Understands reasons why classical republicanism and liberalism are potentially in conflict
- Knows various viewpoints regarding the importance of civic virtue for American democracy

13. **Understands the character of American political and social conflict and factors that tend to prevent or lower its intensity**

K-2
- Not appropriate for this level

3-5
- Not appropriate for this level

6-8
- Knows conflicts that have arisen regarding fundamental values and principles
- Knows how disagreements regarding specific issues may arise between people
- Knows sources of political conflict that have arisen in the United States now and in the past
- Knows why political conflict in the United States has generally been less divisive than in many other nations
- Knows instances of divisive political conflict in the United States

9-12
- Understands issues that involve conflicts among fundamental values and principles
- Knows why people may agree on values or principles in the abstract but disagree when they are applied to specific issues
- Knows how the rights of organized labor and the role of government in regulating business have created political conflict
- Knows how the concept of a loyal opposition and recourse to the legal system to manage conflicts have helped to lessen the divisiveness of political conflict in the United States
- Knows how universal public education and the existence of a popular culture that crosses class boundaries have tended to reduce the intensity of political conflict

14. **Understands issues concerning the disparities between ideals and reality in American political and social life**

K-2   • Not appropriate for this level

3-5   • Not appropriate for this level

6-8   • Knows some important American ideals
          • Knows why political and social ideals are important, even if they cannot be fully achieved
          • Knows some of the discrepancies that have arisen between American ideals and the realities of political and social life in the United States
          • Knows efforts to reduce discrepancies between ideals and the reality of American public life
          • Knows how various actions can help to reduce discrepancies between reality and the ideals of American constitutional democracy

9-12   • Understands the importance of established ideals in political life
          • Knows discrepancies between American ideals and the realities of social and political life
          • Knows efforts to reduce discrepancies between ideals and reality in American public life

15. **Understands how the United States Constitution grants and distributes power and responsibilities to national and state government and how it seeks to prevent the abuse of power**

K-2   • No material specifically designated for this level

3-5   • Understands that the Constitution states that the fundamental purposes of American government are to protect individual rights and promote the common good
          • Knows that the Constitution describes how the government is organized, defines and limits the powers of government, and is the highest law in the land
          • Knows that the government was created by people who believed in the sovereignty of the public
          • Knows that Congress passes laws to protect individual rights and promote the common good
          • Knows that the executive branch carries out and enforces laws to protect individual rights and promote the common good
          • Knows that the judicial branch makes decisions concerning the law

6-8   • Understands the significance of the first three words of the Preamble to the Constitution
          • Understands how the legislative, executive, and judicial branches share power
          • Understands how the legislative branch can check the executive and judicial branches' powers
          • Understands how the executive branch can check the legislative and judicial branches' powers
          • Understands how the judicial branch can check the executive and legislative branches' powers
          • Knows the major parts of the federal system
          • Knows which powers are exercised by the state governments
          • Understands how citizens benefit from the national and state governments sharing power

9-12   • Understands how the overall design of the Constitution helps to prevent the abuse of power
          • Knows why the framers adopted a federal system in which power and responsibility are shared
          • Understands ways in which federalism is designed to protect rights to life, liberty, and property
          • Understands the importance of the Tenth Amendment
          • Understands the functions of the three branches and the independent regulatory agencies
          • Understands the extent to which each branch of the government reflects the people's sovereignty
          • Understands the overall design of the Constitution results in tensions among the three branches
          • Knows current issues concerning representation
          • Understands how and why beliefs about the purposes of the national government have changed

16. **Understands the major responsibilities of the national government for domestic and foreign policy, and understands how government is financed through taxation**

K-2   • Not appropriate for this level

3-5   • Not appropriate for this level

6-8
- Understands how and why domestic policies affect American citizens' lives, and knows historical and contemporary examples of important domestic policies
- Understands how and why foreign policies affect the lives of American citizens, and knows historical and contemporary examples of important foreign policies
- Understands why taxation is necessary to pay for government
- Knows major sources of revenue for the national government
- Knows major uses of tax revenues received by the national government

9-12
- Understands how specific foreign policies such as national security affect American citizens
- Understands arguments concerning the role of government in domestic and foreign policy
- Understands the tensions that results from citizens' desire for government services and benefits and their unwillingness to pay taxes for them
- Knows the history of taxation in the United States
- Understands the equity of various kinds of taxes

17. **Understands issues concerning the relationship between state and local governments and the national government and issues pertaining to representation at all three levels of government**

K-2
- No material specifically designated for this level

3-5
- Knows how to distinguish among national, state, and local governments
- Knows the major responsibilities of the legislative, executive, and judicial branches of his/her state government
- Knows major services provided by national, state, and local governments
- Knows how state and local government officials are chosen (i.e., by election or appointment)
- Knows how people can participate in their state and local government and why it is important
- Knows the names of his/her representatives at the national, state, and local levels
- Knows which levels of government he/she should contact to express his/her opinions or get help

6-8
- Understands that his/her state has a constitution because the United States is a federal system
- Knows the major purposes of his/her state constitution, and how it compares to the Constitution
- Understands why the United States Constitution cannot be violated by state governments
- Understands the process for changing their state constitution and cite examples of changes
- Knows the major responsibilities of his/her state and local governments
- Knows major sources of revenue for state and local governments
- Understands how he/she can contact his/her representatives and why it is important to do so

9-12
- Knows the limits the United States Constitution places on the powers of the states
- Understands that states have reserved powers and concurrent powers
- Understands how the relationship between state, local, and national government has changed
- Understands criteria for evaluating the argument that state and local governments provide significant opportunities for experimentation and innovation
- Understands criteria for evaluating the relationship between his/her state and local governments
- Understands how the policies of state and local governments provide citizens with ways to monitor and influence the actions of members of government and hold them accountable

18. **Understands the role and importance of law in the American constitutional system and issues regarding the judicial protection of individual rights**

K-2
- No material specifically designated for this level

3-5
- Knows that the judicial branch makes decisions concerning the law that aim to protect rights

6-8
- Understands the importance of the rule of law in establishing limits and protecting rights
- Knows historical and contemporary examples of the rule of law
- Knows principal varieties of law
- Understands criteria for evaluating the strengths and weaknesses of a rule or law
- Understands the process for drafting well constructed rules in his/her school or community

- Understands the basic concept of due process of law
- Understands the importance to individuals and to society of major due process protections
- Understands the importance of due process rights in administrative and legislative procedures
- Understands the merits of the adversary system and alternative means of conflict management
- Knows the basic principles of the juvenile system
- Understands current issues regarding judicial protection of the rights of individuals

9-12
- Understands how the rule of law makes possible a system of ordered liberty
- Knows historical and contemporary practices that illustrate the central place of the rule of law
- Knows events that illustrate the absence or breakdown of the rule of law
- Knows historical and contemporary illustrations of the idea of equal protection for all persons
- Understands how rights are protected by the trial and appellate levels of the judicial process
- Understands the effects of Americans relying on the legal system to solve problems
- Understands the importance of an independent judiciary in a constitutional democracy
- Knows historical instances in which judicial protections have not been extended to all persons
- Understands why due process rights are essential for protecting individual rights
- Knows how judicial review reflects the American idea of constitutional government

19. **Understands what is meant by "the public agenda," how it is set, and how it is influenced by public opinion and the media**

K-2
- Not appropriate for this level

3-5
- Not appropriate for this level

6-8
- Knows that the public agenda consists of those matters that occupy public attention
- Knows how the public agenda is shaped by leaders, interest groups, courts, and citizens
- Understands the importance of freedom of the press to informed participation in political life
- Knows how Congress, the president, the Supreme Court, and public officials use the media
- Understands how citizens can evaluate information and arguments received from various sources
- Understands the opportunities that the media provides for citizens to monitor their government

9-12
- Understands how political institutions and political parties shape the public agenda
- Understands why issues important to the nation do not become part of the public agenda
- Knows alternative views of the proper role of public opinion in a democracy
- Understands how public opinion is measured, used in public debate, and how it can be influenced
- Understands the influence that public opinion has on policy and the behavior of public officials
- Understands the extent to which the electronic media has replaced traditional forms of persuasion
- Knows criteria for evaluating various forms of political communication

20. **Understands the roles of political parties, campaigns, elections, and associations and groups in American politics**

K-2
- Not appropriate for this level

3-5
- Not appropriate for this level

6-8
- Understands the role of political parties
- Knows the various kinds of elections
- Understands the ways in which individuals can participate in political parties and elections
- Understands the historical and contemporary roles of associations and groups in politics
- Knows how and why Americans become members of political associations and groups

9-12
- Knows the origins and development of the two party system in the United States
- Understands how American political parties differ from ideological parties in other countries
- Knows the major characteristics of American political parties
- Understands why political parties are weaker today than they have been at times in the past
- Knows the characteristics of initiatives and referendums
- Understands the significance of campaigns and elections in the American political system

- Knows examples of groups performing functions otherwise performed by the government
- Understands the extent to which associations and groups enhance citizen participation

21. Understands the formation and implementation of public policy

K-2 • Not appropriate for this level

3-5 • Not appropriate for this level

6-8 • Understands what public policy is and knows examples at local, state, and national levels
- Knows how public policies are formed and implemented and how citizens can influence policies
- Understands reasons why agreement on certain issues of public policy may be difficult

9-12 • Knows a public policy issue well enough to identify the major groups interested in that issue
- Understands the processes by which a public policy concerning a issue is formed and carried out
- Knows the points at which citizens can influence the process of public policy formation
- Understands why conflicts about values makes agreement on certain issues difficult

22. Understands how the world is organized politically into nation-states, how nation-states interact with one another, and issues surrounding U.S. foreign policy

K-2 • No material specifically designated for this level

3-5 • Knows that a nation consists of its territory, people, laws, and government
- Knows that the United States is one nation and that it interacts with every other nation
- Knows the major ways nations interact with each other such as trade, diplomacy, and treaties
- Understands why it is important for nations to try to resolve problems peacefully

6-8 • Understands why the nation-state is the most powerful form of political organization
- Knows the most important means used by nation-states to interact with one another
- Knows reasons for the breakdown of order among nation-states
- Knows the powers the Constitution gives to the three branches of government in foreign affairs
- Knows various means used to attain the ends of United States foreign policy
- Knows current foreign policy issues and the means the United States is using to deal with them
- Knows the purposes and functions of major governmental international organizations (e.g., UN, NATO) and nongovernmental international organizations (e.g., International Red Cross)

9-12 • Understands the significance of principal foreign policies and events in the United States' relations with the world (e.g., Monroe Doctrine, World Wars I and II, NATO)
- Understands how and why the United States assumed the role of world leader after World War II
- Understands the positions that have characterized the United States' relations with the world
- Understands the tension between constitutional provisions and the requirements of foreign policy
- Understands the process by which United States foreign policy is made
- Understands how domestic politics may impose constraints or obligations on foreign policy
- Understands how national interest is used as a criterion for shaping American foreign policy
- Understands the influence of American constitutional values on American foreign policy
- Understands the current role of the United States in peacemaking and peacekeeping
- Understands the purposes and functions of major governmental international organizations
- Understands the role of the United States in creating and maintaining international organizations
- Knows important bilateral and multilateral agreements to which the United States is signatory

23. Understands the impact of significant political and nonpolitical developments on the United States and other nations

K-2 • Not appropriate for this level

3-5 • Not appropriate for this level

6-8 • Understands the impact that the American Revolution and the values and principles of American democracy has had on other nations

- Understands the influence that American ideas about rights have had on other nations
- Understands the impact that other nations' ideas about rights have had on the United States
- Understands the impact that political developments around the world have on the United States
- Understands the impact of major demographic trends on the United States
- Knows examples of environmental conditions that affect the United States' policies

9-12
- Understands the influence that American ideas about rights have had abroad and how other peoples' ideas about rights have influenced Americans
- Understands the effects that significant world political developments have on the United States
- Understands the effects that significant American political developments have on other nations
- Understands why transnational loyalties sometimes supersede allegiance to a nation-state
- Understands historical and contemporary responses of the American government to demographic and environmental changes that affect the United States
- Knows some of the principal economic, technological, and cultural effects the United States has had on the world
- Understands the principal effects that economic conditions, technological developments, and cultural developments in other nations have had on American society

24. Understands the meaning of citizenship in the United States, and knows the requirements for citizenship and naturalization

K-2
- No material specifically designated for this level

3-5
- Knows that a citizen has certain legally established rights and privileges
- Knows that citizens owe allegiance to the United States and in turn they receive services
- Knows the difference between a citizen and a non-citizen, and how people become citizens

6-8
- Understands that American citizenship is legally recognized full membership in a self-governing community that confers equal rights under the law and confers certain rights and privileges
- Knows that Americans are citizens of both their state and the United States
- Understands what constitutes citizenship by birth in the United States
- Understands the process by which noncitizens may become citizens
- Knows how naturalization in the United States compares with naturalization in other nations
- Knows the legally established criteria used for admission to citizenship in the United States

9-12
- Understands the process by which aliens may become citizens
- Understands how naturalization in America compares with naturalization in other countries
- Knows the criteria used for admission to citizenship in the United States

25. Understands issues regarding personal, political, and economic rights

K-2
- Knows that the right to privacy is a personal right guaranteed by the United States Constitution
- Knows that privacy refers to situations in which access to a certain thing is restricted
- Knows examples of privacy (e.g., writing a letter in private, telling someone a secret)

3-5
- Knows what constitutes personal rights and why they are important
- Knows what constitutes political rights and why they are important
- Knows what constitutes economic rights and why they are important
- Knows contemporary issues regarding rights

6-8
- Knows what constitutes personal rights and the major documentary sources of personal rights
- Understands the importance to individuals and society of various personal rights
- Knows what constitutes political rights and the major documentary sources of political rights
- Understands the importance to individuals and society of various political rights
- Knows important economic rights and statements of economic rights in the Constitution
- Understands the importance to individuals and society of various economic rights
- Understands basic contemporary issues involving personal, political, and economic rights

9-12 • Understands the importance to individuals and to society of various personal rights
• Understands contemporary issues that involve political rights
• Understands the argument that economic responsibilities follow from economic rights
• Understands contemporary issues that involve economic rights (e.g, taxation, zoning, patents)
• Knows major documentary sources of personal, political, and economic rights
• Understands how personal, political, and economic rights are secured

26. **Understands issues regarding the proper scope and limits of rights and the relationships among personal, political, and economic rights**

K-2 • Knows that the consequences of privacy can be both beneficial and costly
• Knows that there are conflicts over the scopes and limits of privacy

3-5 • Knows criteria necessary for analyzing and evaluating conflicts over privacy

6-8 • Understands what is meant by the "scope and limits" of a right
• Understands the argument that all rights have limits
• Understands different positions on a contemporary conflict between rights
• Understands different positions on a contemporary conflict between rights and other social values

9-12 • Knows how to distinguish among personal, political, and economic rights
• Understands different positions on a contemporary conflict between rights
• Knows examples of situations in which personal, political, or economic rights are in conflict
• Understands the argument that poverty serves to limit both political and economic rights
• Understands the argument that personal, political, and economic rights reinforce each other
• Understands the relationship between political rights and the economic right to acquire, use, transfer, and dispose of property
• Understands the relationship of political rights to economic rights

27. **Understands how certain character traits enhance citizens' ability to fulfill personal and civic responsibilities**

K-2 • Knows that a responsibility is a duty to do something or not to do something
• Knows examples of situations that involve responsibility and the sources of responsibility
• Knows some of the benefits of fulfilling responsibilities

3-5 • Knows the importance of personal responsibility, and knows examples of personal responsibility
• Understands why civic responsibility is important, and knows examples of civic responsibility
• Knows private character traits that contribute to the health of American democracy
• Knows public character traits that contribute to the health of American democracy

6-8 • Understands the importance for individuals and society of various personal responsibilities
• Understands contemporary issues that involve personal responsibilities
• Understands the importance for individuals and society of commonly held civic responsibilities
• Understands the meaning of civic responsibilities as distinguished from personal responsibilities
• Understands how citizens' responsibilities could require the subordination of their personal rights

9-12 • Understands the distinction between personal and civic responsibilities
• Understands how individuals and society benefit from the fulfillment of personal responsibilities
• Understands the importance of each citizen reaffirming basic constitutional principles
• Understands the importance for individuals and society of fulfilling civic responsibilities
• Understands when moral obligations require one to refuse to assume certain civic responsibilities
• Understands dispositions that lead citizens to become independent members of society
• Understands the importance of dispositions that foster respect for human dignity
• Understands the importance of dispositions that incline citizens toward public affairs

28. **Understands how participation in civic and political life can help citizens attain individual and public goals**

K-2   • No material specifically designated for this level

3-5   • Understands the importance of citizens monitoring their local, state, and national governments
   • Knows ways people can influence the decisions and actions of their government
   • Knows individuals or groups who monitor and influence the actions of their government

6-8   • Understands how participation in political life can help bring about personal and public goals
   • Understands the importance of both political and social participation
   • Understands how Americans can use a variety of means to monitor and influence the government
   • Knows examples of movements seeking to promote individual rights and the common good
   • Understands what civil disobedience is and how it differs from other forms of protest
   • Understands the importance of becoming knowledgeable about American democracy

9-12   • Understands how individual participation in the political process relates to the realization of the fundamental values of American constitutional democracy
   • Understands what distinguishes participation in political life from nonpolitical participation in civil society and private life, and understands the importance of both forms of participation
   • Knows the ways citizens can participate in the political process at local, state, and national levels
   • Knows historical and contemporary examples of citizen movements seeking to expand liberty, and/or to realize other values fundamental to American constitutional democracy
   • Understands the importance of voting as a form of political participation

29. **Understands the importance of political leadership, public service, and a knowledgeable citizenry in American constitutional democracy**

K-2   • Knows that a good leader puts the interests of the people ahead of personal interests
   • Knows the characteristics of a good leader

3-5   • Knows what political leaders do and why leadership is necessary in a democracy
   • Knows opportunities for leadership and public service
   • Understands the importance of individuals working cooperatively with their elected leaders
   • Knows the major duties, powers, privileges, and limitations of a position of leadership
   • Knows qualities leaders should have
   • Knows the criteria necessary for evaluating the strengths and weaknesses of candidates

6-8   • Understands why leadership is a vital necessity in a constitutional democracy
   • Knows personal qualities necessary for political leadership, such as a sense of ethics
   • Knows opportunities for leadership, and understands the importance of working with leaders
   • Understands the importance of public service in a constitutional democracy
   • Knows opportunities for public service in the student's own school, community, state, and nation
   • Understands the role of "the loyal opposition" in a constitutional democracy
   • Understands the argument that democracy requires the participation of a competent citizenry
   • Understands that citizens have the ability to reaffirm or change fundamental constitutional values

9-12   • Knows various ways students can exercise leadership in public affairs
   • Understands why a democracy requires the participation of an attentive and competent citizenry
   • Understands how awareness of the nature of American constitutional change gives citizens the ability to reaffirm or change fundamental constitutional values

Economics

1. **Understands that scarcity of productive resources requires choices that generate opportunity costs**

K-2   • Understands what goods and services are
   • Understands that people must make choices about using goods and services to satisfy wants
   • Understands what costs and benefits are

- Understands roles of consumers and producers
- Knows that natural resources are present without human intervention
- Knows what capital resources are
- Knows what human resources are
- Knows that choices about buying and consuming determine how resources will be used

3-5
- Knows what productive resources are
- Understands that goods and services are scarce
- Understands that federal, state, and local governments also have problems of scarcity
- Knows what an innovation is
- Knows what an entrepreneur does
- Understands the kinds of risks that entrepreneurs take
- Understands that an opportunity cost is what is given up when resources are used
- Understands that choices usually involve trade-offs
- Understands the concept of economic specialization
- Understands how labor productivity can be increased
- Understands how the quality of labor resources can be improved

6-8
- Understands that scarcity necessitates choice at both the personal and the societal levels
- Knows that economic decision making involves weighing costs and benefits of each choice
- Understands that the evaluation of choices and opportunity costs is subjective
- Knows ways that productivity can be measured
- Understands the relationship between labor productivity and standard of living

9-12
- Understands the concepts of marginal benefit and marginal cost
- Understands how optimal levels of production output can be determined
- Understands the effect of incentives that reward successful innovation and investments
- Understands trade-offs involved in investing in new physical or human capital
- Understands benefits, opportunity costs, and risks of measures to increase productivity

2. **Understands characteristics of different economic systems, economic institutions, and economic incentives**

K-2
- Not appropriate for this level

3-5
- Knows the influence of positive and negative incentives on people's choices and behavior
- Knows that the influence of an incentive can vary with the individual
- Understands that entrepreneurs and business firms take risks in the hope of earning profit
- Knows that households, as consumers, buy goods and services from business firms
- Knows that households sell productive resources to firms in order to earn income
- Understands advantages and disadvantages of various systems societies use to allocate resources

6-8
- Understands why employers are willing to pay wages and salaries to workers
- Knows how a command economic system works
- Knows how a market economic system works
- Understands that national economies may rely on both central planning and signals from markets
- Understands the types of specialized economic institutions found in market economies
- Understands that economic incentives are powerful forces affecting the way people behave
- Understands incentives and disincentives for entrepreneurs
- Understands the role of economic self-interest in a market economy
- Understands that many noneconomic factors influence economic behavior and decision making

9-12
- Understands that allocation methods can be evaluated by comparing costs and benefits
- Understands that economic institutions have different goals, rules, and constraints
- Understands how incorporation encourages investment
- Understands the importance of property rights, contract enforcement, standards for weights and measures, and liability rules
- Understands that people respond to incentives in order to obtain the highest possible return

3. Understands the concept of prices and the interaction of supply and demand in a market economy

K-2
- Knows that a price is the amount of money that people pay when they buy a good or service
- Knows that a market exists whenever buyers and sellers exchange goods and services

3-5
- Knows what the equilibrium price is
- Understands the effect of price on the quantity of a product that people buy
- Understands the effect of price on the willingness of businesses to sell a product
- Understands how money payments are transferred between households and businesses

6-8
- Knows what relative prices are and how they affect people's decisions
- Knows the basic economic questions: What goods and services will be produced? How will they be produced? Who will buy them?
- Understands that the price of a product influences and is influenced by prices of other products
- Understands the role of prices in the allocation of goods and services in a market economy
- Understands the "law of demand"
- Understands the effect of prices on producer costs, profits, decisions, and on quantity supplied

9-12
- Understands what causes changes in the demand for a product
- Understands what causes changes in the supply of a product
- Understands that changes in supply or demand cause relative prices to change
- Understands the causes of shortages or surpluses
- Understands the effects of shortages or surpluses
- Understands that price controls can create long-run allocation problems in the economy

4. Understands basic features of market structures and exchanges

K-2
- Understands the basic concept of an exchange (e.g., for money, for goods and services)
- Knows that money is a good that can be used to buy all other goods and services
- Understands that people expect to be better off after an exchange
- Knows that barter is trading for goods and services without using money

3-5
- Knows that competitive markets are those with many buyers and sellers
- Understands the advantages of money over barter as a means of exchange
- Understands that banks serve as intermediaries between savers and borrowers
- Understands that when people and nations specialize, they become more interdependent
- Understands the advantages of money for saving and for making comparisons of value
- Understands the advantages of active competition among sellers

6-8
- Understands various types of nonprice competition
- Understands how competition among buyers of a product results in higher prices for the product
- Understands the effects of laws and government regulations on competition
- Understands how money encourages people to specialize

9-12
- Knows how the basic money supply is usually measured
- Knows the effects of collusion among buyers or sellers
- Understands factors that influence the level of competition in an industry
- Understands the effect of entrepreneurs on competition, technological progress, and growth
- Understands that externalities are unintended side effects from a market exchange
- Understands what causes a natural monopoly
- Understands why natural monopolies are usually regulated
- Understands that when transaction costs decrease, more specialization and trading will occur

5. Understands unemployment, income, and income distribution in a market economy

K-2
- Not appropriate for this level

3-5
- Knows that unemployed people are those who are willing and able to work, but do not have jobs

6-8
- Knows the four basic categories of earned income: wages and salaries, rent, interest, and profit
- Understands factors that influence an individual's wages or salary
- Knows how the government defines "the labor force"
- Understands that the unemployment rate rises during a recession

9-12
- Understands factors that affect personal income
- Understands the concept of supply and demand in the labor market
- Understands how economists analyze the functional distribution of income
- Understands how economists analyze the personal distribution of income
- Understands that governments often redistribute income directly or indirectly
- Understands why the standard measure of the unemployment rate is flawed
- Understands factors that contribute to differing unemployment rates for various regions and groups
- Knows why full employment is not defined as 100 percent employment of the labor force
- Understands types of unemployment and different policies that may be required to reduce each

6. Understands the roles government plays in the United States economy

K-2
- Knows that some of the goods and services we use are provided by the government

3-5
- Knows that public goods and services are paid for through taxing and borrowing

6-8
- Knows ways that government helps markets to operate efficiently
- Understands why governments provide public goods and services

9-12
- Understands why policies sometimes have costs that outweigh their benefits for society
- Understands sources and uses of federal tax revenue
- Understands sources and uses of state and local government revenues
- Understands ways that the government can help correct or regulate production output
- Understands why governments provide an alternative method of supplying goods and services
- Understands why policies sometimes disperse costs widely and benefit relatively few people
- Understands why political leaders may not implement policies that entail immediate costs

7. Understands savings, investment, and interest rates

K-2
- Not appropriate for this level

3-5
- Understands that savings is the part of income not spent on taxes or consumption

6-8
- Understands that funds are channeled from savers to borrowers through banks

9-12
- Knows what an interest rate is and how interest rates are determined
- Knows the difference between the real interest rate and the nominal interest rate
- Understands the effects of interest rates on incentives for people to save and borrow
- Understands why real interest rates are normally positive
- Understands why riskier loans command higher interest rates than safer loans
- Understands how polices that raise and lower interest rates affect spending and investment
- Understands that expectations of increased inflation may lead to higher interest rates

8. Understands basic concepts of United States fiscal policy and monetary policy

K-2
- Not appropriate for this level

3-5
- Not appropriate for this level

6-8
- Not appropriate for this level

9-12
- Knows the tools and goals of fiscal policy
- Understands the concepts of balanced budget, budget deficit, and budget surplus
- Understands how the government finances a budget deficit
- Knows what the national debt is
- Understands the goals of monetary policy and the role of the Federal Reserve

- Understands how fiscal policies may be influenced by monetary policies and changes in spending
- Knows the major monetary policy tools that the Federal Reserve System uses
- Understands the relationship between the money supply and bank lending or repayment
- Understands effects of changes in the money supply and interest rates on economic growth

9. Understands how Gross Domestic Product and inflation and deflation provide indications of the state of the economy

K-2 • Not appropriate for this level

3-5 • Not appropriate for this level

6-8 • Knows what inflation is
- Knows what deflation is
- Understands that inflation reduces the value of money
- Knows what the Gross Domestic Product (GDP) refers to

9-12 • Knows that inflation is usually measured by the Consumer Price Index (CPI)
- Knows the difference between "nominal" GDP and "real" GDP
- Knows the factors upon which a country's GDP depends
- Understands factors that lead to economic growth (i.e., a sustained rise in GDP)
- Understands effects of economic growth on standard of living, employment, and profit
- Understands that inflation creates uncertainty because it affects different groups differently
- Understands factors that contribute to inflation
- Understands effects of government policies designed to reduce unemployment or inflation

10. Understands basic concepts about international economics

K-2 • Not appropriate for this level

3-5 • Knows that different currencies are used in different countries

6-8 • Knows that exports are goods and services produced in one nation but sold to buyers in another nation
- Knows that imports are goods or services bought from sellers in another nation
- Understands that international trade promotes greater specialization
- Knows what an exchange rate is and how exchange rates are determined
- Understands why foreign exchange markets are needed for international trade
- Understands why many nations restrict the free flow of goods and services
- Understands effects of increasing international interdependence
- Knows how real GDP per capita is used to compare economic development in different nations

9-12 • Understands factors that encourage international trade
- Understands the concepts of absolute advantage and comparative advantage
- Understands why comparative advantages change over time
- Understands how a change in exchange rates can affect the flow of trade between nations
- Knows that a nation pays for its imports with its exports
- Understands that foreign trade policies reflect economic and political interests and forces

Foreign Language

1. Uses the target language to engage in conversations, express feelings and emotions, and exchange opinions and information

K-4 • Knows how to express likes, dislikes, and simple preferences
- Uses basic vocabulary to describe assorted objects
- Knows how to give and follow simple instructions in the target language
- Knows how to exchange information with peers about preferences
- Knows how to use non-verbal language for clarification

- Knows how to exchange information about general events and transportation
- Uses appropriate vocabulary, gestures, and oral expressions for common or familiar interactions

5-8
- Uses verbal and written exchanges to gather and share personal data, information, and opinions
- Uses the target language to plan events and activities with others
- Uses vocabulary and cultural expressions to clarify messages
- Uses non-verbal and verbal cues to assist in communicating
- Uses appropriate vocabulary to give or follow directions
- Uses appropriate vocabulary to acquire goods and services
- Knows how to express preferences with peers who speak the language

9-12
- Knows how to adequately express one's point of view
- Uses appropriate vocabulary to exchange information about national and international topics
- Uses appropriate vocabulary to express personal reactions to literary texts
- Uses appropriate vocabulary to exchange opinions on contemporary or historical issues
- Uses rephrasing and circumlocution to communicate a message in the target language
- Uses adequate vocabulary and non-verbal skills to acquire goods and services
- Uses appropriate cultural responses in diverse exchanges
- Knows how to exchange information about current or past events and aspirations

2. Comprehends and interprets written and spoken language on diverse topics from diverse media

K-4
- Understands the basic ideas of oral messages and short conversations
- Understands the principal message in ability-appropriate, highly illustrated texts
- Understands the main ideas of ability-appropriate video or television programs
- Understands the main ideas and/or the principal characters in literary texts
- Understands brief written messages and personal notes on familiar topics
- Recognizes common phrase groupings and voice inflection
- Identifies people and objects based on descriptions

5-8
- Understands the main idea and themes from ability-appropriate spoken media
- Understands the content of ability-appropriate primary sources on familiar topics
- Understands spoken announcements and messages
- Recognizes and understands non-verbal and verbal cues
- Recognizes and understands various phrase groupings and structures in speech
- Uses known language to make guesses about the meaning of more complicated messages
- Understands the main ideas and details of ability-appropriate literature

9-12
- Understands various verbal presentations and forms of media
- Understands the main ideas and significant details of expository text forms
- Understands significant details of written literature
- Recognizes characteristic features of an author's style in target-language literature
- Understands culturally significant songs, folk tales, comedy, and anecdotes

3. Presents information, concepts, and ideas to an audience of listeners or readers on a variety of topics

K-4
- Presents simple oral reports or presentations
- Recites poetry, songs, proverbs, or short anecdotes or narratives
- Writes short, informal notes or messages that describe or provide information
- Presents information about family, school events, and celebrations

5-8
- Presents information in the target language on topics of shared personal interest
- Presents cultural and literary works in the target language
- Writes notes or short letters to peers in the target culture
- Summarizes the plot and provides brief descriptions of characters in literary texts
- Uses repetition, rephrasing, and gestures effectively in oral presentations

9-12 • Writes letters to peers in the target cultures
     • Summarizes orally or in writing the content of various expository texts
     • Presents cultural and literary works in the target language
     • Presents information orally or in writing on literary and cultural topics

4. **Demonstrates knowledge and understanding of traditional ideas and perspectives, institutions, professions, literary and artistic expressions, and other components of target culture**

K-4 • Knows various age-appropriate cultural activities practiced in the target culture
     • Knows simple patterns of behavior and interaction in various settings in the target culture
     • Knows and compares utilitarian forms of the culture
     • Knows some basic expressive forms of the target culture
     • Knows basic cultural beliefs and perspectives of people in the native and target cultures
     • Identifies professions that require proficiency in the target language

5-8 • Knows various age-appropriate cultural activities practiced in the target culture
     • Knows cultural traditions and celebrations that exist in the target culture
     • Knows and recognizes patterns of behavior in various settings in the target culture
     • Knows utilitarian forms of the target culture and their influences on the community
     • Knows and compares a variety of age-appropriate expressive forms of the culture
     • Knows how "local" opinions of the native culture compare with those from the target culture
     • Knows how various community members use the target language in their work

9-12 • Understands various patterns of behavior or interaction typical of one's age group
     • Knows age-appropriate utilitarian forms of the target culture and their significance
     • Understands age-appropriate expressive forms of the target culture and their significance
     • Understands contrasting ways information is reported in the target and native cultures
     • Understands contrasting ways issues are reflected in the target and native cultures
     • Understands how other cultures view the role of the native culture in the world arena
     • Identifies careers that require knowledge and proficiency in the target language

5. **Recognizes that different languages use different patterns to communicate and applies this knowledge to the native language**

K-4 • Knows words that have been borrowed from one language to another
     • Knows basic elements of the sound and writing systems of the target language
     • Understands that an idea may be expressed in multiple ways in the target language

5-8 • Understands how idiomatic expressions impact communication and reflect culture
     • Uses a variety of sources in the target language to obtain information
     • Uses various media from the target language and culture for entertainment

9-12 • Knows various linguistic elements of the target language
     • Understands that the ability to comprehend language surpasses the ability to produce language
     • Uses a dictionary or thesaurus written entirely in the target language

Geography

1. **Understands the characteristics and uses of maps, globes, and other geographic tools and technologies**

K-2 • Not appropriate at this level

3-5 • Knows the basic elements of maps and globes
     • Interprets topography using aerial photos and maps
     • Uses map grids to plot absolute location

6-8
- Knows the purposes and distinguishing characteristics of different map projections
- Uses thematic maps
- Understands concepts associated with Earth-Sun relations
- Knows the advantages and disadvantages of various geographic tools to illustrate a data set
- Knows the characteristics and uses of cartograms
- Knows how maps help find patterns of movement in space and time
- Knows the characteristics and purposes of geographic databases

9-12
- Understands the advantages and disadvantages of using maps from different sources
- Knows the characteristics and uses of geographic technologies
- Transforms primary data into maps, graphs, and charts

2. Knows the location of places, geographic features, and patterns of the environment

K-2
- Knows the location of school, home, neighborhood, community, state, and country

3-5
- Knows major physical and human features of places as they are represented on maps and globes
- Knows the location of major cities in North America
- Knows the approximate location of major continents, mountain ranges, and bodies of water

6-8
- Knows the location of physical and human features on maps and globes
- Knows how mental maps can reflect attitudes and perceptions of places
- Knows the relative location of, size of, and distances between places
- Knows the factors that influence spatial perception

9-12
- Knows the approximate locations of major political and economic cultures
- Knows the spatial dynamics of various contemporary and historical events
- Knows how mental maps influence human decisions about location, settlement, and public policy
- Knows common factors that affect mental maps

3. Understands the characteristics and uses of spatial organization of Earth's surface

K-2
- Identifies physical and human features in terms of the four spatial elements
- Knows the absolute and relative location of a community and places within it

3-5
- Knows patterns on the landscape produced by physical processes
- Understands the spatial organization of places
- Understands how transportation and communication technology has affected locations
- Knows different methods used to measure distance

6-8
- Understands distributions of physical and human occurrences with respect to spatial patterns
- Understands patterns of land use in urban, suburban, and rural areas
- Understands how places are connected
- Understands the patterns and processes of migration and diffusion

9-12
- Understands how concepts of spatial interaction account for patterns of movement in space
- Understands relationships in and between places
- Understands how specific characteristics affect peoples' perceptions and use of space
- Understands principles of location

4. Understands the physical and human characteristics of place

K-2
- Knows the physical and human characteristics of the local community
- Knows that places can be defined in terms of their predominant human and physical features

3-5
- Knows how the characteristics of places are shaped by physical and human processes

6-8
- Knows the human characteristics of places
- Knows the physical characteristics of places
- Knows how technology shapes human and physical characteristics of places
- Knows the causes and effects of changes in a place over time

9-12 • Knows how social, cultural, and economic processes shape the features of places
- Understands why places have specific physical and human characteristics in different parts of the world
- Knows the locational advantages and disadvantages of using places based on their characteristics

5. Understands the concept of regions

K-2 • Knows areas that can be classified as regions according to physical criteria

3-5 • Knows the characteristics of a variety of regions
- Understands how regions change over time and the consequences of these changes
- Knows how regions are similar and different in form and function

6-8 • Knows regions at various spatial scales
- Understands criteria that give a region identity
- Knows types of regions
- Knows factors that contribute to changing regional characteristics
- Understands the influences and effects of particular regional labels and images
- Understands ways regional systems are interconnected

9-12 • Understands how regional boundaries change
- Knows factors that contribute to the dynamic nature of regions
- Understands connections within and among the parts of a regional system
- Understands how changing conditions can result in the redefinition of a region
- Knows how the concept of a region can be used to simplify the complexity of Earth's space
- Understands the different ways in which regional systems are structured

6. Understands that culture and experience influence people's perceptions of places and regions

K-2 • Not appropriate at this level

3-5 • Understands ways in which people view and relate to places and regions differently

6-8 • Knows how places and regions serve as cultural symbols
- Knows how technology affects the ways in which culture groups perceive and use places
- Knows the ways in which culture influences the perceptions of places and regions

9-12 • Understands how places and regions unify or fragment society
- Understands how individuals view places and regions on the basis of a variety of personal factors
- Knows ways in which people's changing views of places and regions reflect cultural change

7. Knows the physical processes that shape patterns on Earth's surface

K-2 • Not appropriate at this level

3-5 • Knows the physical components of Earth's atmosphere, lithosphere, hydrosphere, and biosphere
- Understands how physical processes help to shape features and patterns on Earth's surface
- Knows how Earth's position relative to the Sun affects events and conditions on Earth

6-8 • Knows the major processes that shape patterns in the physical environment
- Knows the processes that produce renewable and nonrenewable resources
- Knows the consequences of a specific physical process operating on Earth's surface

9-12 • Understands the distribution of different types of climate
- Understands the effects of different physical cycles
- Understands how physical systems are dynamic and interactive
- Understands how physical processes affect different regions of the United States and world

8. Understands the characteristics of ecosystems on Earth's surface

K-2 • Not appropriate at this level

3-5
- Knows the components of ecosystems at a variety of scales
- Knows ways in which humans can change ecosystems
- Knows plants and animals associated with various vegetation and climate regions

6-8
- Understands the distribution of ecosystems from local to global scales
- Understands the functions and dynamics of ecosystems
- Understands ecosystems in terms of their characteristics and ability to withstand stress
- Knows changes that have occurred over time in ecosystems in the local region
- Knows the potential impact of human activities within a given ecosystem
- Understands the life cycle of a lake ecosystem from birth to death

9-12
- Understands how different relationships affect the distribution of ecosystems
- Knows ecosystems in terms of their biodiversity and productivity
- Knows the effects of biological magnification in ecosystems
- Knows the effects of both physical and human changes in ecosystems

9. Understands the nature, distribution, and migration of human populations on Earth's surface

K-2
- Not appropriate at this level

3-5
- Understands the characteristics of populations at a variety of scales
- Knows the spatial distribution of population
- Understands voluntary and involuntary migration
- Knows the causes and effects of human migration

6-8
- Understands demographic concepts and how they are used to describe population characteristics
- Knows the factors that influence patterns of rural-urban migration
- Knows the ways in which human movement and migration influence the character of a place

9-12
- Understands population issues
- Knows how improved transportation influences mobility, interdependence, and integration
- Knows how international migrations are shaped by push and pull factors
- Understands the impact of human migration on physical and human systems

10. Understands the nature and complexity of Earth's cultural mosaics

K-2
- Knows the basic components of culture

3-5
- Knows the similarities and differences in characteristics of culture
- Understands how different people living in the same region maintain different ways of life
- Understands how cultures differ in their use of similar environments and resources
- Understands cultural change

6-8
- Knows the distinctive cultural landscapes associated with migrant populations
- Knows ways in which communities reflect the cultural background of their inhabitants
- Understands the significance of patterns of cultural diffusion

9-12
- Knows how cultures influence the characteristics of regions
- Understands how human characteristics make specific regions of the world distinctive
- Understands the impact of political and economic alliances on the cohesiveness of world cultures
- Knows the role culture plays in incidents of cooperation and conflict in the present-day world
- Understands factors that contribute to cultural convergence or divergence

11. Understands the patterns and networks of economic interdependence on Earth's surface

K-2
- Knows the modes of transportation used to move people, products, and ideas from place to place

3-5
- Knows the factors that are important in the location of economic activities
- Knows economic activities that use natural resources in the local region, state, and nation
- Knows the impact of transportation and communication on trade and economic activities

- Knows the various ways in which people satisfy their basic needs and wants
- Knows how regions are linked economically and the impact of trade on peoples' livelihood

6-8
- Understands the spatial aspects of systems designed to deliver goods and services
- Understands issues related to the spatial distribution of economic activities
- Understands factors that influence the location of industries in the United States
- Understands the primary geographic causes for world trade
- Understands historic and contemporary economic trade networks
- Understands historic and contemporary systems of transportation and communication
- Knows primary, secondary, and tertiary activities in a geographic context

9-12
- Knows the spatial distribution of major economic systems
- Understands the historical movement patterns of people and goods
- Understands the relationships between settlement patterns, economic activities, and land values
- Understands the advantages and disadvantages of international economic patterns

12. Understands the patterns of human settlement and their causes

K-2
- Understands why people choose to settle in different places
- Knows the similarities and differences in housing and land use in urban and suburban areas

3-5
- Knows areas of dense human settlement and why they are densely populated
- Knows reasons for the population size and density of different regions
- Knows the settlement patterns that characterize the development of a community or state
- Knows the characteristics and locations of cities
- Knows similarities and differences among the world's culture hearths

6-8
- Knows the causes and consequences of urbanization
- Knows the similarities and differences in various settlement patterns of the world
- Knows ways in which shifts from a dispersed to a concentrated settlement form affect the landscape and society
- Knows the factors involved in the development of cities
- Knows the internal and spatial structures of cities

9-12
- Understands how the function of cities today differ from those of towns and villages and cities in earlier times
- Knows the shape of cities in the United States and factors that influence urban morphology
- Knows ways in which settlement characteristics of economically developed and developing nations compare
- Knows the impact of certain factors on the settlement patterns of an area
- Understands the physical and human impact of emerging urban forms in the present world

13. Understands the forces of cooperation and conflict that shape the divisions of Earth's surface

K-2
- Knows ways that people solve common problems by cooperating
- Knows examples of world conflict or cooperation

3-5
- Knows the functions of political units and how they differ on the basis of scale
- Knows how and why people divide Earth's surface into political and/or economic units
- Knows how and why people compete for control of Earth's surface

6-8
- Understands factors that contribute to cooperation or conflict
- Knows the social, political, and economic divisions on Earth's surface at the local, state, national, and international levels
- Understands the various factors involved in the development of nation-states
- Understands the reasons for multiple and overlapping spatial divisions in society
- Understands the factors that affect the cohesiveness and integration of countries
- Understands the symbolic importance of capital cities

9-12 • Understands how cooperation and/or conflict can lead to allocation of control of Earth's surface
 • Knows the causes of boundary conflicts and internal disputes between culture groups
 • Understands why the boundaries of congressional districts change in the United States
 • Understands the changes that occur in the organization of social, political, and economic entities on Earth's surface
 • Understands why some countries are land-locked
 • Understands how external forces can conflict with internal interests in a region

14. Understands how human actions modify the physical environment

K-2 • Knows ways in which people depend on the physical environment

3-5 • Knows the ways people alter the physical environment
 • Knows the ways in which the physical environment is stressed by human activities
 • Knows how human activities have increased the ability of the physical environment to support human life

6-8 • Understands the environmental consequences of people changing the physical environment
 • Understands how human changes in the physical environment in one place can cause changes in other places
 • Knows the ways people take aspects of the environment into account when deciding on locations for human activities
 • Understands how technology influences the human capacity to modify the environment
 • Understands the environmental consequences of major technological changes in history

9-12 • Understands how synergy, feedback loops, carrying capacity, and thresholds absorb the impacts of human activity
 • Understands the role of humans in decreasing the diversity of flora and fauna in a region
 • Understands the global impacts of human changes in the physical environment
 • Knows how people's changing attitudes toward the environment have led to landscape changes

15. Understands how physical systems affect human systems

K-2 • Not appropriate at this level

3-5 • Knows how humans adapt to variations in the physical environment
 • Knows how communities benefit from the physical environment
 • Knows the ways in which human activities are constrained by the physical environment
 • Knows natural hazards that occur in the physical environment

6-8 • Knows ways in which the physical environment affects the development of human systems
 • Knows how the physical environment affects life in different regions
 • Knows the ways in which the environment affects decisions regarding locations for human activities
 • Understands relationships between population density and environmental quality
 • Knows the effects of natural hazards on human systems in the United States and world

9-12 • Knows environmental changes that have reduced the capacity of the environment to support human activity
 • Knows how humans overcome "limits to growth" imposed by physical systems
 • Knows conditions and locations that place limits on plant growth and human settlement
 • Understands how people who live in naturally hazardous regions adapt to their environments
 • Knows factors that affect people's attitudes, perceptions, and responses toward natural hazards

16. Understands the changes that occur in the meaning, use, distribution, and importance of resources

K-2 • Knows the role that resources play in our daily lives

3-5 • Knows the characteristics, location, and use of renewable, flow, and nonrenewable resources
 • Knows how settlement patterns are influenced by the discovery and use of resources
 • Knows the relationships between economic activities and resources

- Knows the major transportation routes that link resources with customers and the transportation modes used
- Knows advantages and disadvantages of recycling and reusing different types of materials
- Knows the different ways in which resources are used and valued in different areas of the world

6-8
- Understands the reasons for conflicting viewpoints regarding how resources should be used
- Knows strategies for wise management and use of renewable, flow, and nonrenewable resources
- Knows world patterns of resource distribution and utilization
- Understands the consequences of the use of resources in the contemporary world
- Understands the role of technology in resource acquisition and use and its impact on the environment
- Understands how energy resources contribute to the development of human societies
- Understands how the development and use of alternative energy sources might impact societies

9-12
- Understands the relationships between resources and exploration, colonization, and settlement
- Understands programs and positions related to the use of resources on a local to global scale
- Understands the impact of policy decisions regarding the use of resources in regions of the world
- Knows issues related to the reuse and recycling of resources

17. Understands how geography is used to interpret the past

K-2
- Knows how areas of a community have changed over time

3-5
- Knows the factors that have contributed to changing land use in a community
- Knows how changes in peoples' perceptions of environments have affected human migration and settlement
- Knows the geographic factors that have influenced people and events in the past

6-8
- Knows how physical and human geographic factors have influenced major historic events
- Knows historic and current conflicts and competition regarding the use and allocation of resources
- Knows the ways in which the spatial organization of society changes over time
- Knows significant physical features that have influenced historic events

9-12
- Understands how the processes of spatial change have affected history
- Understands how people's perceptions of geographic features have led to changes in human societies
- Understands the impact of physical and human features on the evolution of historic events and movements

18. Understands global development and environmental issues

K-2
- Not appropriate at this level

3-5
- Knows the relationship between population growth and resource use
- Knows the ways in which resources can be managed and why it is important to do so
- Knows how differences in perception affect people's interpretations of the world
- Knows human-induced changes that are taking place in different regions

6-8
- Understands how the interaction between physical and human systems affects current conditions on Earth
- Understands the possible impact that present conditions and patterns might have on the future spatial organization of Earth
- Knows how the quality of environments in large cities can be improved
- Understands why different points of view exist regarding contemporary geographic issues

9-12
- Understands the concept of sustainable development and its effects in a variety of situations
- Understands why policies should be designed to guide the use and management of Earth's resources
- Understands contemporary issues in terms of Earth's physical and human systems

Health

1. Knows the availability and effective use of health services, products, and information

K-2 • Knows community health service providers and their roles

3-5 • Knows general characteristics of valid health information, products, and services
 • Knows various community agencies that provide health services
 • Knows a variety of consumer influences that affect decisions regarding health resources, products, and services

6-8 • Knows the costs and validity of common health products, services, and information
 • Knows how to locate and use community health information, products, and services
 • Knows ways to influence the consumer health service system
 • Knows community health consumer organizations and the advocacy services they provide
 • Knows situations that require professional health services

9-12 • Knows factors that influence personal selection of health care resources, products, and services
 • Knows how to determine whether various health information, products, and services are valid
 • Knows local, state, federal, and private agencies that protect and/or inform the consumer
 • Understands the cost and accessibility of a variety of health-care services
 • Knows situations that require professional health services

2. Knows environmental and external factors that affect individual and community health

K-2 • Knows sources and causes of pollution

3-5 • Knows how the physical environment can impact personal health
 • Knows how environmental problems are controlled
 • Knows how personal health can be influenced by society and science

6-8 • Knows factors within a community that influence the health of its members
 • Understands how various messages impact health practices
 • Knows efforts to contain an environmental crisis and prevent a recurrence
 • Understands how peer relationships affect health

9-12 • Knows how the health of individuals can be influenced by the community
 • Knows how individuals can improve or maintain community health
 • Understands how the environment influences the health of the community
 • Understands what influences the prevention and control of health problems
 • Knows how public health policies and government regulations impact health related issues
 • Understands how cultural diversity enriches and challenges health behaviors

3. Understands the relationship of family health to individual health

K-2 • Knows the roles of parents and the extended family in the health of children
 • Knows effective strategies to cope with change that may occur in families

3-5 • Knows how the family influences personal health
 • Knows characteristics needed to be a responsible friend and family member
 • Knows how health-related problems impact the whole family

6-8 • Knows strategies that improve or maintain family health
 • Understands the development of adolescent independence
 • Knows how communication techniques can improve family life

9-12 • Understands methods to facilitate the transition from child to adult
 • Knows the effects of teenage pregnancy on those involved and society
 • Understands the responsibilities inherent in dating, marriage, and parenthood

4. Knows how to maintain mental and emotional health

K-2 • Identifies and shares feelings in appropriate ways

3-5 • Knows the relationships between physical health and mental health
• Knows common sources of stress for children
• Knows about mood changes and the effects of strong feelings
• Knows behaviors that communicate care, consideration, and respect of self and others
• Understands responses to behavior
• Knows strategies for resisting negative peer pressure
• Knows how listening skills affect relationships

6-8 • Knows strategies to manage stress and feelings
• Knows characteristics and conditions associated with positive self-esteem
• Knows appropriate ways to build and maintain positive relationships
• Understands the difference between safe and risky or harmful behaviors in relationships
• Knows techniques for seeking help and support

9-12 • Knows skills used to communicate effectively
• Knows strategies for coping with and overcoming negative feelings
• Understands the role of denial on health, and ways to overcome denial

5. Knows essential concepts and practices concerning injury prevention and safety

K-2 • Knows basic safety practices
• Knows precautions that should be taken in special conditions
• Knows how to recognize emergencies and respond appropriately
• Knows ways to seek assistance if worried, abused, or threatened

3-5 • Knows safety rules and practices to be used in home, school, and community settings
• Knows methods used to recognize and avoid threatening situations
• Knows basic first aid procedures appropriate to common emergencies
• Knows the difference between positive and negative behaviors used in conflict situations
• Knows some non-violent strategies to resolve conflicts

6-8 • Knows injury prevention strategies for family health
• Knows strategies for managing a range of situations involving injury
• Knows potential signs of self- and other-directed violence
• Knows the various possible causes of and strategies to manage conflict among youth
• Knows how refusal and negotiation skills can be used to enhance health

9-12 • Knows injury prevention strategies for community health
• Knows possible causes of and prevention strategies for conflicts
• Knows strategies for solving interpersonal conflicts
• Knows how refusal, negotiation, and collaboration skills can be used to avoid harmful situations

6. Understands essential concepts about nutrition and diet

K-2 • Classifies foods and food combinations

3-5 • Knows the nutritional value of different foods
• Knows healthy eating practices
• Knows factors that influence food choices
• Knows the effects of different food-preparation methods and food-handling practices

6-8 • Understands how eating properly can help to reduce health risks
• Knows appropriate methods to maintain, lose, or gain weight
• Knows eating disorders that affect health adversely
• Knows the principles of food safety involved with food storage and preparation

9-12 • Understands how nutrient and energy needs vary
• Understands the reliability and validity of various sources of dietary information
• Understands the role of food additives and their relationship to health

7. Knows how to maintain and promote personal health

K-2 • Knows basic personal hygiene habits required to maintain health

3-5 • Understands the influence of different actions on a person's well-being
• Knows common health problems
• Knows behaviors that are safe, risky, or harmful
• Sets a personal health goal and makes progress toward its achievement
• Knows about making health-related decisions and setting health goals
• Knows the basic structure and functions of the human body systems

6-8 • Knows personal health strengths and risks
• Knows actions that can help to reduce health risks
• Knows strategies and skills that are used to attain personal health goals
• Understands how different factors influence personal health goals
• Knows how health is influenced by the interaction of body systems

9-12 • Knows how personal behaviors relate to health and well-being
• Understands the consequences of behaviors
• Understands how personal health needs change
• Understands the impact of personal behaviors on the body

8. Knows essential concepts about the prevention and control of disease

K-2 • Knows the signs and symptoms of common illnesses

3-5 • Knows ways in which a person can prevent or reduce the risk of disease and disability
• Knows the benefits of early detection and treatment of disease
• Knows ways to maintain a functional level of health in the presence of disease or disability

6-8 • Understands factors related to the cause or prevention of disease and other health problems
• Knows differences between various disease processes
• Understands personal rights and responsibilities involved in the treatment of disease

9-12 • Understands how the immune system functions
• Understands the importance of regular examinations in detecting and treating diseases early
• Understands the importance of prenatal and perinatal care
• Understands the social, economic, and political effects of disease

9. Understands aspects of substance use and abuse

K-2 • Knows how to distinguish between helpful and harmful substances

3-5 • Differentiates between the use and misuse of prescription and nonprescription drugs
• Knows influences that promote alcohol, tobacco, and other drug use
• Recognizes high-risk substance abuse situations that pose a threat to oneself or others
• Knows ways to avoid, recognize, and respond to negative social influences and pressure

6-8 • Knows conditions that may put people at higher risk for substance abuse problems
• Knows factors, signs, and symptoms involved in the development of a drug dependency
• Knows the short- and long-term consequences of the use of alcohol, tobacco, and other drugs
• Knows public policy approaches to substance abuse control and prevention
• Knows community resources that are available to assist people with substance problems

9-12 • Knows the effects associated with the use of drugs on reproduction and children
• Knows how substance abuse often plays a role in dangerous behavior and effects the community
• Understands that drug dependencies are treatable diseases/conditions

10. **Understands the fundamental concepts of growth and development**

K-2   • Understands individual differences
     • Knows the cycle of growth and development in humans

3-5   • Knows the changes that occur during puberty
     • Knows the rate of change during puberty varies and that characteristics of people vary

6-8   • Understands how the human body changes as people age
     • Knows the similarities and differences between male and female sexuality
     • Understands the processes of conception, prenatal development, and birth
     • Knows strategies for coping with concerns and stress related to adolescence

9-12 • Understands physical, mental, emotional, and social changes that occur throughout life
     • Understands factors that influence attitudes and behaviors regarding sexuality
     • Knows sound health practices in the prenatal period

Physical Education

1. **Uses a variety of basic and advanced movement forms**

K-2   • Uses a variety of basic locomotor movements
     • Uses a variety of basic non-locomotor skills
     • Uses a variety of basic object control skills
     • Uses simple combinations of fundamental movement skills
     • Uses control in weight-bearing activities on a variety of body parts
     • Uses control in balance activities on a variety of body parts
     • Uses control in travel activities on a variety of body parts
     • Uses smooth transitions between sequential motor skills
     • Uses locomotor skills in rhythmical patterns

3-5   • Uses mature form in object control skills
     • Uses basic sport-specific skills for a variety of physical activities
     • Uses mature form and appropriate sequence in selected modified games, sports, and dances
     • Uses mature form in balance activities on a variety of apparatuses
     • Uses beginning strategies for net and invasion games

6-8   • Uses intermediate sport-specific skills for individual, dual, and team sports
     • Uses intermediate sport-specific skills for dance and rhythmical activities
     • Uses intermediate sport-specific skills for outdoor activities

9-12 • Uses advanced sport-specific skills in selected physical activities
     • Uses skills in complex rather than modified versions of physical activities

2. **Uses movement concepts and principles in the development of motor skills**

K-2   • Understands a vocabulary of basic movement concepts
     • Understands terms that describe a variety of relationships with objects
     • Uses concepts of space awareness and movement control with a variety of basic skills
     • Understands the critical elements of a variety of basic movement patterns
     • Uses feedback to improve performance
     • Understands the importance of practice in learning skills

3-5   • Uses information from a variety of internal and external sources to improve performance
     • Understands principles of practice and conditioning that improve performance
     • Understands proper warm-up and cool-down techniques
     • Uses basic offensive and defensive strategies in unstructured game environments

6-8
- Understands principles of training and conditioning for specific physical activities
- Understands the critical elements of advanced movement skills
- Uses basic offensive and defensive strategies in sports
- Understands movement forms associated with highly skilled physical activities

9-12
- Understands biomechanical concepts that govern different types of movement
- Understands how sport psychology affects the performance of physical activities
- Understands the physiological principles governing fitness
- Uses offensive and defensive strategies and appropriate rules for sports

3. Understands the benefits and costs associated with participation in physical activity

K-2
- Understands the health benefits of physical activity

3-5
- Knows about opportunities for participation in physical activities
- Chooses physical activities based on a variety of factors
- Knows factors that inhibit physical activity
- Knows how to modify activities to be more health-enhancing
- Understands detrimental effects of physical activity
- Understands activities that provide personal challenge

6-8
- Understands long-term physiological benefits of regular physical activity
- Understands long-term psychological benefits of regular physical activity

9-12
- Understands factors that impact the ability to participate in physical activity
- Understands how various factors affect physical activity preferences and participation
- Understands the potentially dangerous consequences and outcomes of physical activity

4. Understands how to monitor and maintain a health-enhancing level of physical fitness

K-2
- Engages in basic activities that cause cardiorespiratory exertion
- Knows how to measure cardiorespiratory fitness
- Knows the physiological indicators of vigorous physical activity
- Engages in activities that develop muscular strength and endurance
- Engages in activities that require flexibility
- Knows how body composition influences physical fitness levels
- Knows similarities and differences in body height, weight, and shape

3-5
- Engages in activities that develop and maintain cardiorespiratory endurance
- Engages in activities that develop and maintain muscular strength
- Engages in activities that develop and maintain flexibility of the major joints
- Knows the effects of physical activity and nutrition on body composition
- Knows how to monitor intensity of exercise
- Meets health-related fitness standards for appropriate level
- Knows the characteristics of a healthy lifestyle
- Uses information from fitness assessments to improve selected fitness components
- Participates in moderate to vigorous physical activity in a variety of settings

6-8
- Engages in more advanced activities that develop and maintain cardiorespiratory endurance
- Engages in more advanced activities that develop and maintain muscular strength and endurance
- Engages in more advanced levels of activity that develop and maintain flexibility
- Understands the role of exercise and other factors in weight control and body composition
- Understands basic principles of training that improve physical fitness
- Meets health-related fitness standards for appropriate level
- Knows how to interpret the results of physical fitness assessments
- Knows how to differentiate the body's response to various exercise intensities

9-12
- Knows personal status of cardiorespiratory endurance
- Knows personal status of muscular strength and endurance
- Knows personal status of flexibility of the joints
- Knows personal status of body composition
- Meets health-related fitness standards for appropriate level of a physical fitness test
- Knows how to monitor and adjust activity levels
- Understands how to maintain an active lifestyle throughout life
- Designs a personal fitness program

5. Understands the social and personal responsibility associated with participation in physical activity

K-2
- Follows rules and procedures with little reinforcement
- Uses equipment and space safely and properly
- Understands the purpose of rules in games
- Understands the social contributions of physical activity
- Works cooperatively with another
- Understands the elements of socially acceptable conflict resolution in physical activities
- Understands the importance of playing, cooperating, and respecting others

3-5
- Knows how to develop rules, procedures, and etiquette that are safe and effective
- Works in a group to accomplish a set goal
- Understands the role of physical activities in learning more about others
- Understands the physical challenges faced by people with disabilities
- Understands the origins of different sports and how they have evolved

6-8
- Understands the importance of rules, procedures, and safe practice
- Understands proper attitudes toward both winning and losing
- Knows the difference between inclusive and exclusionary behaviors
- Understands physical activity as a vehicle for self-expression
- Understands that physical activity is a microcosm of modern culture and society

9-12
- Uses leadership and follower roles in accomplishing group goals in physical activities
- Works with others in a sport activity to achieve a common goal
- Understands how participation in physical activity fosters awareness of diversity
- Includes persons of diverse backgrounds and abilities in physical activity
- Understands the history and purpose of international competitions
- Understands the role of sport in a diverse world
- Understands the concept of "sportsmanship"

Technology

1. Knows the characteristics and uses of computer hardware and operating systems

K-2
- Identifies basic computer hardware
- Powers-up computer and starts a computer program
- Knows the alphanumeric keys and special keys
- Knows proper finger placement on the home row keys
- Handles diskettes and other computer equipment with care

3-5
- Knows the basic functions of hardware
- Uses proper fingering and posture while using the keyboard
- Knows potential hazards to computer media
- Knows basic facts about networked computers

6-8
- Knows the differing capacities and trade-offs for computer storage media
- Types with some facility, demonstrating some memorization of keys
- Connects via modem to other computer users
- Knows basic characteristics and functions of an operating system

9-12
- Knows of significant advances in computers and peripherals
- Uses a variety of input devices
- Knows limitations and trade-offs of various types of hardware
- Identifies malfunctions and problems in hardware
- Knows features and uses of current and emerging technology related to computing

2. Knows the characteristics and uses of computer software programs

K-2
- Types on a computer keyboard, using correct hand and body positions
- Knows basic distinctions among computer software programs
- Uses menu options and commands

3-5
- Uses word processor software
- Makes back-up copies of stored data
- Trouble-shoots simple problems in software
- Knows the common features and uses of data bases
- Uses data base software
- Knows how formats differ among software applications and hardware platforms

6-8
- Uses advanced features and utilities of word processors
- Knows the common features and uses of desktop publishing software
- Knows the common features and uses of spread sheets
- Uses a spread sheet
- Uses boolean searches on a data base

9-12
- Understands the uses of listservs, usenet newsreaders, and bulletin board systems
- Imports, exports, and merges data stored in different formats
- Imports and exports text, data, and graphics between software programs
- Identifies some advanced features of software products
- Uses desktop publishing software

3. Understands relationships among science, technology, society, and the individual

K-2
- Knows ways that technology is used at home and school
- Knows that new tools and ways of doing have positive or negative effects on people
- Understands that work created on a computer is the creator's property

3-5
- Knows that technologies often have costs as well as benefits
- Knows areas in which technology has improved human lives
- Knows that new inventions often lead to other new inventions and ways of doing things
- Understands the concept of software piracy

6-8
- Knows that scientific inquiry and technological design have similarities and differences
- Knows that science and technology cannot answer all questions or solve all problems
- Knows ways in which technology has influenced the course of history
- Knows that technology and science are reciprocal
- Knows ways in which technology and society influence one another
- Knows examples of copyright violations and computer fraud and possible penalties

9-12
- Knows that science and technology are pursued for different purposes
- Knows ways in which social and economic forces influence which technologies will be developed and used
- Knows that alternatives, risks, costs, and benefits must be considered when deciding on proposals to introduce new technologies or to curtail existing ones
- Knows that technological knowledge is often not made public
- Knows examples of advanced and emerging technologies and how they could impact society
- Observes common courtesies and acceptable use policies while telecomputing
- Knows human attributes needed to improve technology
- Identifies the role of technology in a variety of careers

4. Understands the nature of technological design

K-2
- Knows that objects can be natural or man-made
- Knows why tools are used
- Knows that people are always inventing new ways to solve problems and get work done

3-5
- Categorizes items into groups of natural objects and designed objects
- Identifies a simple problem that can be solved using technology
- Knows constraints that must be considered when designing a solution to a problem
- Implements proposed solutions
- Evaluates a product or design
- Knows that people have invented and used tools throughout history

6-8
- Identifies appropriate problems for technological design
- Designs a solution or product, taking into account needs and constraints
- Implements a proposed design
- Evaluates a technological design against the criteria established in the original purpose

9-12
- Proposes designs and chooses between alternative solutions
- Implements a proposed solution
- Evaluates a designed solution against criteria

5. Understands the nature and operation of systems

K-2
- Knows that most things are made of parts
- Knows the effects of putting parts together
- Understands how some elements or components of simple systems work together
- Creates and tests a simple linear system

3-5
- Knows that parts affect one another
- Knows that things made of parts sometimes may not work well
- Identifies the relationships between elements
- Assembles, disassembles, and tests systems

6-8
- Knows what systems are composed of
- Knows how different parts of a system can provide feedback for other parts of the system
- Identifies the elements, structure, sequence, operation, and control of systems
- Assembles and disassembles systems to manage, control, and improve their performance
- Knows that systems are usually linked to other systems and may contain or operate subsystems

9-12
- Knows that a system usually has properties that are different from those of its parts
- Knows that systems analysis facilitates many processes
- Knows how to define a system
- Knows how feedback is used in the operation of a system
- Knows that predicting the effects of change in a system is not always possible
- Knows that complex systems are subject to failure

Behavioral Studies

1. Understands that group and cultural influences contribute to human development, identity, and behavior

K-2
- Understands that people are alike and different in many ways
- Understands that there are different rules and patterns of behavior for different environments
- Understands that people often choose to do the same kinds of things that others do
- Understands that the groups to which a person belongs influence them

3-5
- Understands that people can learn about others in many different ways
- Understands that people sometimes imitate people or characters they see presented in the media

- Understands that people might feel uncomfortable around others who are different
- Understands that "acceptable" human behavior varies
- Understands that various factors contribute to the shaping of a person's identity
- Understands the way a person views an incident reflects personal beliefs

6-8
- Understands that each culture has distinctive patterns of behavior
- Understands that usually within any society there is agreement on "unacceptable" behavior
- Understands that punishments vary widely among, and even within, different societies
- Understands technology is important in spreading ideas, values, and behavior patterns
- Understands that various factors affect decisions that individuals make

9-12
- Understands that cultural beliefs strongly influence the values and behavior of the people
- Understands that punishment for "unacceptable" social behavior depends on various factors
- Understands that social distinctions are a part of every culture
- Understands that people often take differences to be signs of social class
- Understands that the difficulty of moving from one social class to another varies greatly
- Understands that heredity, culture, and personal experience interact in shaping human behavior
- Understands that various influences contribute to the shaping of a person's identity

2. Understands various meanings of social group, general implications of group membership, and different ways that groups function

K-2
- Knows that people are either born into or join groups
- Knows unique features of different groups to which she or he belongs
- Understands that different groups, societies, and cultures have some similar wants and needs
- Knows that people tend to live in groups in which individuals have different roles

3-5
- Understands people often like or dislike others based on whether they are part of certain groups
- Understands that individuals tend to support members of their own groups
- Understands that different groups have different expectations for how their members should act
- Understands that "rules" are sometimes written down and enforced, or understood from example
- Understands that members of a group sometimes do and say things they would not on their own
- Understands that different groups may have different ways of meeting similar wants and needs
- Knows expressions of culture
- Understands that "social group" has many meanings
- Understands that although rules usually remain the same, sometimes they change

6-8
- Understands that affiliation with a group can increase the power of members
- Understands that joining a group often has personal advantages
- Understands that group identity may create a feeling of superiority
- Understands that people sometimes react to all members of a group as though they were the same
- Understands that a variety of factors contribute to the ways in which groups respond
- Understands how various factors contribute to the development and transmission of culture
- Understands that there are similarities and differences within groups as well as among groups
- Understands that a large society may be made up of many groups

9-12
- Understands that a group may act as a whole, but individual members may hold varying beliefs
- Understands that organizations may serve purposes beyond those for which they officially exist
- Understands how the diverse elements of a culture function as an integrated whole
- Understands that groups have patterns for preserving and transmitting culture
- Understands that groups may have attributes that can help or hinder cross-cultural understanding

3. Understands that interactions among learning, inheritance, and physical development affect human behavior

K-2
- Knows that people use their senses to find out about their surroundings and themselves
- Understands that moving closer or further away from something changes the perception of it
- Understands that some of the things people do must be deliberately learned

- Understands that practice helps people to improve
- Knows that people can learn from each other in many ways

3-5
- Understands that human beings use past experiences to make judgments about new situations
- Understands that skills can be practiced until they become automatic
- Understands that people tend to repeat behaviors that feel good to avoid behaviors that feel bad
- Knows that learning is using what is already known to make sense out of new information
- Understands roles as learned behavior patterns in group situations
- Understands that as roles vary depending on expectations and changing conditions

6-8
- Understands that all behavior is affected by both inheritance and experience
- Knows that some species are limited to genetic behaviors, while others learn new behaviors
- Understands that the skill level a person can reach in an activity depends on a variety of factors
- Knows that human beings can detect a tremendous range of visual and olfactory stimuli
- Understands that generally, organisms can pay attention to only one input of information
- Understands learning often results from two things occurring at about the same time
- Understands that a vivid experience can connect two things permanently in people's minds
- Understands that language and tools enable human beings to learn

9-12
- Understands behavioral differences of individuals are the result of heredity and experience
- Understands instinctive behavior may not develop under abnormal conditions
- Understands various factors can affect how people interpret new perceptions or ideas
- Understands sometimes people ignore evidence that challenges their beliefs
- Understands that the context in which something is learned may limit how it can be used
- Knows that human thinking involves the interaction of ideas, and ideas about ideas
- Knows people can produce internal associations without getting information from their senses

4. **Understands conflict, cooperation, and interdependence among individuals, groups, and institutions**

K-2
- Knows that disagreements are common
- Understands that there are many ways of dealing with disagreements
- Understands that rules let people know what to expect

3-5
- Knows that communicating different points of view can help resolve a dispute
- Understands that resolving a conflict by force can lead to more problems
- Understands that one person's exercise of freedom may conflict with the freedom of others
- Understands that if a conflict cannot be settled by compromise, it could be decided by a vote
- Understands that beliefs and customs held by certain groups can help or hinder people
- Knows various forms that institutions take

6-8
- Understands possible social effects of being a member of a group
- Understands that most groups have formal or informal procedures for arbitrating disputes
- Understands how various institutions influence people, events, and elements of culture
- Understands how role, status, and social class may affect interactions
- Understands how tensions might arise between expressions of individuality social conformists

9-12
- Understands that conflict between people or groups may arise from competition
- Understands that social change, or the prospect of it, usually promotes conflict
- Understands circumstances that can make conflicts especially difficult to resolve
- Understands ways of responding to conflict may lead to compromise and also be inflammatory
- Understands that conflict within a group may be reduced by conflict between it and other groups
- Understands that intergroup conflict does not necessarily end when one group wins
- Understands the impacts social decisions have on the majority and minority of people
- Understands how social institutions develop and change over time
- Understands how changes in social and political institutions both reflect and affect individuals
- Understands that the decisions of one generation affect the next generation
- Understands that mass media, migrations, and conquest affect social change

Life Skills: Thinking and Reasoning

1. Understands and applies the basic principles of presenting an argument

K-2
- Understands that a person's ideas are more believable if that person can give good reasons for them
- Gives coherent answers when asked about personal beliefs and knowledge
- Asks "how do you know" in appropriate situations

3-5
- Uses facts from books, articles, and databases to support an argument
- Identifies basic informal fallacies, such as appeals to authority or vague references
- Understands that reasoning can be distorted by strong feelings
- Determines if arguments are supported by facts from books, articles, and databases
- Questions arguments that are based on the assertion that "everybody knows" or "I just know"
- Seeks reasons for believing things other than the assertion that "everybody agrees"
- Recognizes when a comparison is not fair because important characteristics are not the same

6-8
- Evaluates arguments that are based on quantitative data and mathematical concepts
- Questions claims that use vague references or refer to people speaking outside of their expertise
- Questions conclusions based on very small or biased samples, or samples with no central sample
- Distinguishes between information that is based on fact and information that is based on opinion
- Identifies and questions false analogies
- Questions arguments based on generalizations or stereotypes about groups of people
- Compares and contrasts the credibility of differing accounts of the same event

9-12
- Understands that people are selective about the information they use to try to prove a point
- Identifies techniques used to slant information in subtle ways
- Identifies the logic of arguments that are based on quantitative data
- Uses the critical assumptions behind a line of reasoning to judge the validity of an argument
- Understands that a convincing argument includes true statements and valid connections among them
- Uses tables, charts, and graphs to construct arguments
- Evaluates the overall effectiveness of complex arguments

2. Understands and applies basic principles of logic and reasoning

6-8
- Uses formal deductive connectors in the construction of deductive arguments
- Understands that some aspects of reasoning have very rigid rules but other aspects do not
- Understands that rules, good information, and logic can help figure out the truth about a situation
- Understands that reasoning by similarities can suggest ideas but cannot be used to prove things
- Understands that "if x is true, then y is true; but x isn't true, therefore y isn't true" is incorrect logic
- Understands that a single example can prove that something is false but not that something is true
- Understands that observations can be summarized to generally explain how something works
- Understands that people overgeneralize by making up rules on the basis of only a few observations
- Understands that personal values influence the types of conclusions people make
- Recognizes situations in which a variety of conclusions can be drawn from the same information

9-12
- Understands the differences between the formal and informal uses of logical connectors
- Analyzes the deductive validity of arguments based on implicit or explicit assumptions
- Understands formal and informal uses of the terms "sufficient" and "necessary"
- Understands the formal meaning of the logical quantifiers: "some," "none," and "all"
- Understands that formal logic is about connections between statements, not the truth of statements
- Knows that false conclusions can result from faulty logic applied to true statements or vice versa
- Understands that a reason may be sufficient but not necessary, or necessary but not sufficient
- Understands that logic can be used to test how well any general rule works
- Understands that it is easier to prove a general rule to be false than to prove a general rule to be true
- Understands that logic is not useful if the general rules involved do not always hold true
- Understands that people are likely to notice things that agree with the general rules that they believe
- Understands that complex logical arguments can be formulated from simpler logical arguments
- Identifies counter examples to conclusions that have been developed

3. Effectively uses mental processes that are based on identifying similarities and differences (compares, contrasts, classifies)

K-2
- Classifies objects by size, color, or other significant characteristics
- Identifies the similarities and differences between persons, places, things, and events
- Compares things in terms of number, shape, texture, size, weight, color, motion, sound, and behavior
- Recognizes simple patterns in the surrounding events and objects

3-5
- Understands that one way to make sense of something is to think how it is like something familiar
- Recognizes when comparisons might not be fair because some characteristics are not the same
- Compares people in terms of important ethnic, religious, and cultural characteristics
- Makes comparisons between countries in terms of concrete and abstract characteristics

6-8
- Uses a variety of criteria to compare consumer products
- Understands that an analogy not only contains some likenesses but also some differences
- Selects criteria or rules for category membership that are relevant and important
- Orders information and events chronologically or based on frequency of occurrence
- Orders information based on importance to a given criterion
- Articulates abstract relationships between existing categories of information
- Creates a table to compare specific abstract and concrete features of two items
- Compares similarities and differences of a variety of information sources for the same topic
- Identifies the abstract relationships that form the basis for analogies

9-12
- Uses a comparison table to compare multiple items on multiple abstract characteristics
- Compares abstract patterns of information from a variety of sources for the same topic
- Identifies abstract relationships between seemingly unrelated items
- Identifies the qualitative and quantitative traits that can be used to order and classify items

4. Understands and applies basic principles of hypothesis testing and scientific inquiry

K-2
- Asks "how do you know" when appropriate, and provides reasonable answers to the same question.
- Understands that changing one thing can cause changes in something else

3-5
- Keeps a notebook that describes observations made
- Attempts to verify the results of experiments done by others
- Distinguishes between actual observations and ideas or conclusions about what was observed
- Makes records of observations regarding time and place to formulate hypotheses
- Keeps systematic records of different types of weather information to formulate hypotheses

6-8
- Understands that there are a variety of ways that people can form hypotheses
- Verifies results of experiments
- Understands that there may be more than one valid way to interpret a set of findings
- Questions findings that do not specify whether the control group is similar to the experimental group
- Reformulates a new hypothesis for study after an old hypothesis has been eliminated
- Makes and validates conjectures about outcomes of alternatives or events regarding an experiment

9-12
- Critiques studies that present data, explanations, or conclusions as the only ones worth considering
- Tests hypotheses statistically
- Presents alternative explanations and conclusions to one's own experiments and those of others
- Critiques procedures, explanations, and conclusions in one's own experiments and those of others
- Gathers and analyzes field data using spatial sampling

5. Applies basic trouble-shooting and problem-solving techniques

K-2
- Identifies simple problems and possible solutions

3-5
- Identifies issues and problems in the school or community that one might help solve
- Studies problems in the community and how they were solved
- Analyzes the major goals and obstacles to those goals that have confronted people in the past

6-8
- Identifies alternative courses of action and predicts likely consequences of each
- Selects the most appropriate strategy or alternative for solving a problem
- Understands alternatives for resolving local problems and the consequences of each alternative

9-12
- Applies trouble-shooting strategies to complex real-world situations
- Understands that trouble-shooting almost anything may require many-step branching logic
- Trouble-shoots common mechanical and electrical systems and decides if expert advice is needed
- Isolates a problem component in a schematic diagram and traces it to the cause of the problem
- Engages in problem finding and framing for personal situations and situations in the community
- Represents a problem accurately in terms of resources, constraints, and objectives
- Provides summation of the effectiveness of problem-solving techniques
- Reframes problems when alternative solutions are exhausted
- Knows alternatives for solving historical problems, and why specific courses of action were taken
- Evaluates the feasibility of various solutions to problems; recommends and defends a solution

6. Applies decision-making techniques

K-2
- Makes and defends decisions about daily activities (e.g., what books to read)

3-5
- Studies decisions that were made in the community in terms of the alternatives that were considered
- Analyzes decisions made by people in the past in terms of alternatives that were considered

6-8
- Identifies situations in the community and in one's personal life in which a decision is required
- Secures factual information needed to evaluate alternatives
- Identifies values underlying considered alternatives and the criteria used to select among them
- Predicts the consequences of selecting each alternative
- Makes decisions based on the data obtained and the criteria identified
- When appropriate, takes action to implement a decision
- Makes effective decisions about consumer products based on a variety of important criteria
- Analyzes personal decisions in terms of the options that were considered
- Uses a grid or matrix to make or study decisions with a limited number of alternatives and criteria
- Selects appropriate locations for specific service industries within the community

9-12
- Understands how alternative decisions might have affected major historical events
- Analyzes decisions that can affect national or international policy and their consequences
- Uses a grid or matrix to make or study decisions with a large number of alternatives and criteria
- Uses a balance sheet to evaluate the costs and benefits of various alternatives within a decision
- Evaluates major factors that influence personal decisions

Life Skills: Working With Others

1. Contributes to the overall effort of a group

K-12
- Challenges practices in a group that are not working
- Demonstrates respect for others in the group
- Identifies and uses the strengths of others
- Takes initiative when needed
- Identifies and deals with causes of conflict in a group
- Helps the group establish goals
- Engages in active listening
- Takes the initiative in interacting with others
- Evaluates the overall progress of a group toward a goal
- Keeps requests simple
- Contributes to the development of a supportive climate in groups

2. **Uses conflict-resolution techniques**

K-12 • Communicates ideas in a manner that does not irritate others
• Resolves conflicts of interest
• Identifies goals and values important to opponents
• Understands the impact of criticism on psychological and emotional state, behavior, and beliefs
• Understands that being aggressive and/or passive is an ineffective response to criticism
• Understands that acknowledgement, agreement, and clarification are effective responses to criticism
• Determines the causes of conflicts
• Does not blame
• Identifies an explicit strategy to deal with conflict
• Determines the seriousness of conflicts
• Identifies mutually agreeable times for important conversations with opponents
• Identifies individual vs. group or organizational interests in conflicts
• Establishes guidelines and rules for negotiating
• Determines the mini-max position of those in a conflict

3. **Works well with diverse individuals and in diverse situations**

K-12 • Works well with the opposite gender
• Works well with different ethnic groups
• Works well with those of different religious orientations
• Works to satisfy needs of customers

4. **Displays effective interpersonal communication skills**

K-12 • Displays empathy with others
• Displays friendliness with others
• Displays politeness with others
• Seeks information nondefensively
• Provides feedback in a constructive manner
• Uses nonverbal communication such as eye contact, body position, voice tone effectively
• Does not react to speaker's inflammatory deliverance
• Identifies with speaker while maintaining objectivity
• Uses emotions appropriately in personal dialogues
• Makes use of confrontation when appropriate
• Makes eye contact when speaking
• Reacts to ideas rather than to the person presenting the ideas
• Adjusts tone and content of information to accommodate the likes of others
• Communicates in a clear manner during conversations
• Acknowledges the strengths of others

5. **Demonstrates leadership skills**

K-12 • Occasionally serves as a leader in groups
• Occasionally serves as a follower in groups
• Enlists others in working toward a shared vision
• Plans small wins
• Celebrates accomplishments
• Recognizes the contributions of others
• Passes on authority when appropriate

Life Skills: Self-Regulation

1. Sets and manages goals

K-12
- Sets explicit long-term goals
- Identifies and ranks relevant options in terms of accomplishing a goal
- Prepares and follows a schedule for carrying out options
- Understands personal wants versus needs
- Establishes personal milestones
- Identifies resources necessary to complete a goal
- Displays a sense of personal direction and purpose
- Maintains an awareness of proximity to goal
- Makes a cumulative evaluation of goal
- Understands the differences between various types of goals
- Sets routine goals for improving daily life
- Identifies explicit criteria for evaluating goals
- Makes contingency plans

2. Performs self-appraisal

K-12
- Distributes work according to perceived strengths
- Identifies personal styles
- Identifies personal strengths and weaknesses
- Utilizes techniques for overcoming weaknesses
- Identifies basic values
- Performs analysis of employability
- Understands preferred working environments
- Understands career goals
- Identifies a compensating strength for each weakness
- Develops an inventory of wants versus needs
- Determines explicit behaviors that are used and should be adopted to obtain wants and/or needs
- Identifies personal motivational patterns
- Keeps a log documenting personal improvement
- Summarizes personal educational background
- Summarizes personal work experience
- Identifies key accomplishments and successes in life
- Identifies peak experiences and significant life experiences
- Identifies desired future accomplishments
- Identifies preferred lifestyle

3. Considers risks

K-12
- Weighs risks in making decisions and solving problems
- Uses common knowledge to avoid hazard or injury
- Applies preventative measures prior to a task to minimize security or safety problems
- Selects an appropriate course of action in an emergency
- Identifies emergency and safety procedures before undertaking hazardous procedures
- Thinks clearly under stress

4. Demonstrates perseverance

K-12
- Demonstrates perseverance relative to personal goals
- Demonstrates a sense of purpose
- Maintains a high level of energy over a prolonged period of time when engaged in tasks
- Persists in the face of difficulty
- Concentrates mental and physical energies

5. Maintains a healthy self-concept

K-12 • Has basic belief in ability to succeed
       • Uses techniques to remind self of strengths
       • Uses techniques to offset the negative effects of mistakes
       • Avoids overreacting to criticism
       • Uses affirmations to improve sense of self
       • Analyzes self-statements for their positive and negative effects
       • Examines "shoulds" to determine their negative and positive effects
       • Revises "shoulds" to reflect the reality of personal needs
       • Understands that everyone makes mistakes
       • Understands that mistakes are a natural consequence of living and of limited resources
       • Takes criticism in a dispassionate manner
       • Analyzes criticisms to determine their accuracy and identifies useful lessons learned
       • Uses high self-esteem body language

6. Restrains impulsivity

K-12 • Keeps responses open as long as possible
       • Remains passive while assessing situation
       • Suspends judgment

Life Skills: Life Work

1. Makes effective use of basic tools

K-2 • Uses hammers, screwdrivers, clamps, rulers, scissors, and hard lenses; operates audio equipment
      • Assembles, describes, takes apart, and reassembles constructions
      • Uses a variety of materials to make something that can be used to perform a task.

3-5 • Chooses common materials for making simple mechanical constructions and controlling things
      • Measures and mixes dry and liquid materials in prescribed amounts, exercising reasonable safety

6-8 • Uses hand and power tools to work with a variety of materials
      • Inspects, disassembles, and reassembles simple mechanical devices and describes the various part

9-12 • Uses work space effectively
       • Understands the proper way to use new instruments
       • Uses power tools safely to shape, smooth, and join wood, plastic, and soft metal

2. Uses various information sources, including those of a technical nature, to accomplish specific tasks

9-12 • Interprets information from and detects inconsistencies in a data matrix
       • Follows basic linear paths in organizational charts
       • Identifies major sections in schematic diagrams
       • Uses the linear path of a flowchart to provide visual and textual directions to a procedure
       • Interprets symbols in a flowchart
       • Obtains factor specification information from various sources
       • Uses a table or chart to identify a malfunction in a mechanism
       • Interprets drawings for assembly or disassembly

3. Manages money effectively

9-12 • Prepares and follows a budget
       • Makes forecasts regarding future income and expenses
       • Uses sound buying principles for purchasing goods and services
       • Understands credit and uses it effectively

4. Pursues specific jobs

9-12
- Determines key contacts within a prospective employer's organization
- Determines specific procedures for applying for a specific job
- Identifies important benefits and procedures of prospective employers
- Identifies a prospective employer's products and services
- Identifies the procedures involved in applying for a job at a company's personnel office
- Fills out a job application
- Prepares letters of inquiry or application
- Identifies and engages in necessary steps to prepare for a job interview

5. Makes general preparation for entering the work force

9-12
- Understands basic market trends
- Determines the types of preparation and training needed for entry-level jobs
- Understands occupational apprenticeships and other training opportunities
- Understands available educational opportunities
- Understands availability of child care
- Understands significant life decisions and their effect on the present
- Analyzes a current job and its future possibilities
- Develops an employment profile
- Uses multiple resources to obtain information about prospective jobs
- Determines how private employment agencies operate on a fee basis to help people find jobs
- Prepares for common types of employment tests
- Applies for a social security card, work permit, license
- Prepares a resume summarizing experience, education, and job training
- Establishes an explicit career action plan
- Appraises prior work experience, career goals, personal character, job references, and aptitudes
- Understands the nature and function of worker's compensation and unemployment insurance
- Evaluates the chances of getting a job now and in the future in fields of work that are of interest
- Makes an accurate appraisal of available work options
- Makes an accurate appraisal of basic insurance needs

6. Makes effective use of basic life skills

9-12
- Uses a telephone effectively
- Uses public transportation effectively
- Understands the rules and regulations of the Internal Revenue Service
- Understands the availability of health care and child care services
- Understands the basic nature of contracts
- Understands the basic process of renting an apartment
- Understands basic banking services, including checking and savings accounts
- Understands the basic process of buying and maintaining a car
- Knows how to correctly enter information into basic forms

7. Displays reliability and a basic work ethic

9-12
- Completes tasks on time
- Chooses ethical courses of action
- Establishes an acceptable attendance record
- Uses appropriate language in work situations
- Maintains a sense of congeniality at work
- Maintains an effective work station
- Is attentive to requests and preferences of supervisors
- Requests clarification when needed
- Accurately identifies important goals and priorities of employer
- Practices appropriate hygiene and dress at work

- Carries out assigned tasks
- Does not bring personal problems into work
- Prepares, plans, and organizes job responsibilities
- Recognizes and respects authority
- Accepts guidance and constructive criticism
- Demonstrates loyalty to the organization

8. Operates effectively within organizations

9-12
- Understands the organization's basic goals and values
- Understands the extent to which organizational values are compatible with personal values
- Identifies how personal skills can be used to increase organizational effectiveness
- Uses strategies to make personal skills and abilities more visible to an organization

Time Audit Process

Academic Efficiency Index

The purpose of the Academic Efficiency Index (AEI) is to develop an estimate of the percentage of time students are engaged in academic work (in other words, an estimate of the efficiency with which time is used for instructional purposes). The term *academic work* is broadly defined to encompass any legitimate instructional area such as reading, mathematics, science, physical education, the arts, etc.

The process of arriving at an estimate of efficiency for a particular building can be seen by examining Figure C.1, which calls for a number of estimates of time, including the following:

Figure C.1

Estimate of Academic Efficiency

I.   Total school time

II. Noninstructional school time
     (such as lunch and homeroom)

III. Absenteeism

IV. Noninstructional class time
     (such as social activities and
     housekeeping tasks)

V.   Nonengaged time
     (the percentage of instructional
     time students aren't engaged in
     the work assigned to them)

VI. Academic Efficiency
     (the percentage of instructional
     time students are engaged in
     academic work)

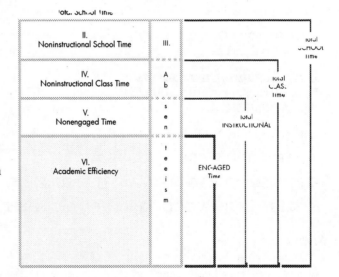

Keep in mind that the resulting figure is an estimate of academic efficiency. The intent is to compute an index that approximates the true situation in the same way that an economic index, such as the Gross National Product, estimates the health of the nation's productivity.

Note that although academic efficiency is a relatively reliable figure to use across a school, the data should not be used to compare schools or teachers. The few observations made here are not a reliable estimate of a particular teacher's use of time, nor are comparisons from one building to another appropriate. The purpose of the AEI is to provide schools with a sense of how they use time so that they might use it more efficiently in the future.

Academic Efficiency Index (AEI) Overview

Step 1

Complete lines 1–16 of the AEI WORKSHEET (Sections I, II, and III). Completing these lines involves consulting class schedules and records on absenteeism.

<u>Forms needed:</u> AEI WORKSHEET

Step 2

Review the forms and instructions for this step, which deal with estimating noninstructional class time and engagement rates. Determine which process you will use in your school.

Although there is only one process for estimating noninstructional class time, you'll notice there are two options for estimating engagement rate, Method A and Method B.

In Method A, the observer estimates student engagement while making observations about noninstructional class time.

In Method B, students self-report their level of engagement; the observer estimates only the noninstructional class time. There are a number of advantages to Method B:

1. It is less obtrusive; there is no third-party observer.

2. It gives teachers a tool to use from time to time to monitor their effectiveness in the classroom.

3. It is somewhat more reliable and valid, as long as students feel they are not being evaluated and will not be punished for reporting low levels of engagement.

<u>Forms and instructions needed:</u>
INSTRUCTIONS FOR ESTIMATING NONINSTRUCTIONAL CLASS TIME AND ENGAGEMENT RATE

OBSERVATION WORKSHEET - METHOD A

OBSERVATION WORKSHEET - METHOD B

ENGAGEMENT RATE SELF-REPORT WORKSHEET - METHOD B - (Grades 1–3)

ENGAGEMENT RATE SELF-REPORT WORKSHEET - METHOD B - (Grades 4–12)

Step 3

After selecting the process you will use (Method A or Method B), begin classroom observation of noninstructional class time and engagement time. Try to collect data from at least one-third to one-half of the teaching staff in your building.

<u>Forms and instructions needed if you are using Method A:</u>
INSTRUCTIONS FOR ESTIMATING NONINSTRUCTIONAL CLASS TIME AND ENGAGEMENT RATE

OBSERVATION WORKSHEET - METHOD A (one worksheet per classroom observed)

Academic Efficiency Index (AEI) Overview (continued)

<u>Forms and instructions needed if you are using Method B:</u>
INSTRUCTIONS FOR ESTIMATING NONINSTRUCTIONAL CLASS TIME AND ENGAGEMENT RATE

OBSERVATION WORKSHEET - METHOD B (one worksheet per classroom observed)

ENGAGEMENT RATE SELF-REPORT WORKSHEET - METHOD B - (one worksheet per student. Use Grades 1–3 Worksheet or Grades 4–12 Worksheet, as appropriate.)

Step 4

After all of the observations have been completed, transfer the information from the worksheets to the SUMMARY WORKSHEET and perform the calculations.

<u>Forms needed:</u>
SUMMARY WORKSHEET

completed OBSERVATION WORKSHEETS

If using Method B, student's ENGAGEMENT RATE SELF-REPORT WORKSHEETS

Step 5

Once you have completed Step 4, return to the AEI WORKSHEET and enter the information required on line 17–23 (section IV–V). Calculate the school's academic efficiency by completing the calculations on lines 24–28 (section VI).

<u>Forms needed:</u>
completed SUMMARY WORKSHEET

partially completed AEI WORKSHEET

Step 6

The last step is to create your school's ACADEMIC EFFICIENCY GRID (AEI). Follow the AEI GRID INSTRUCTIONS.

<u>Forms and instructions needed:</u>
AEI GRID INSTRUCTIONS

AEI GRID

completed AEI WORKSHEET

AEI Worksheet

School Name _____   School District _____

Date _____   Contact Person _____

I. **Enter the total school time as the number of minutes available in the school day.**

    A. Subtract the time students are supposed to be in school in the morning from the time they leave, using a 24-hour clock (e.g., a 3:30 p.m. dismissal is 15:30). Record this time in minutes.

                                        Line 1 _____

II. **Estimate the percentage of noninstructional school time and the percentage of class time.**

    B. Estimate the scheduled noninstructional school time (in minutes). (The following figures will be most reliable if a group of teachers is asked to discuss and agree on how much time is spent on each activity.)

        a. Lunch period   Line 2 _____

        b. Homeroom (secondary only)   Line 3 _____

        c. Breaks between classes (secondary only)   Line 4 _____

        d. Recess (elementary only)   Line 5 _____

        e. Announcements   Line 6 _____

        f. Other noninstructional activities*   Line 7 _____

        g. Total (Add Line 2 through Line 7)   Line 8 _____

    C. Calculate the percentage of the day scheduled for noninstructional school activities.

        (Line 8 _____ ÷ Line 1 _____) × 100   Line 9 _____ %

    D. Calculate the percentage of the school day scheduled for class time.

        (100 − Line 9 _____)   Line 10 _____ %

---

*In order to calculate Line 7 in Step II, add all of the minutes for noninstructional school activities throughout the year that do not occur daily, for example, fire drills, school pictures, immunizations, pep assemblies, and travel to and from field trips. If some activities do not include all students, use proportions. For example, if 10% of students are involved in a 60-minute activity, 10% of 60 minutes is 6 minutes.

Divide the total minutes per year by real student contact days. If 180 days are recorded, be sure to subtract early release days, in-service days, and conferences if you count those days as contact days; in other words, the divisor will probably be 176 or 177 real contact days instead of 180 days. The answer, number of minutes for noninstructional school "once in a while" activities, will give you the number of minutes lost per day to such activities.

AEI Worksheet (continued)

III. **Estimate the average amount of absenteeism per day.**

    E. Total number of students enrolled   Line 11 _____

    F. Average number of students absent per day   Line 12 _____

    G. Average number of partial absences per day**   Line 13 _____

    H. Total number of absences
       (Line 12 _____ + Line 13 _____)   Line 14 _____

    I. Percentage of students absent per day
       (Line 14 _____ ÷ Line 11 _____) × 100   Line 15 _____ %

    J. Percentage of students attending
       (100 − Line 15 _____)   Line 16 _____ %

IV. **Estimate the percentage of noninstructional class time and the percentage of instructional class time.**

    K. Average percentage of noninstructional class time (see Line 3 of Summary Worksheet under "Noninstructional Class Time" section)
                                                            Line 17 _____ %

    L. Percentage of the school day lost to noninstructional class time
       (Line 17 _____ × Line 10 _____) ÷ 100   Line 18 _____ %

    M. Percentage of the school day devoted to instruction
       (Line 10 _____ − Line 18 _____)   Line 19 _____ %

**If you want to be as precise as possible about absenteeism, consider such factors as tardiness and doctors' appointments. To consider such absenteeism, follow the directions below. Otherwise, record a zero on Line 13.

    a. Estimate the average number of students tardy each day.   _____

    b. Estimate the average length of time in minutes of each tardiness.   _____

    c. Estimate the average number of students absent for part of each
        day for other reasons (e.g., doctor's appointments, skipped classes).   _____

    d. Estimate the average length of time in minutes of each occasion
        of part-day absence (e.g., doctor's appointments, skipped classes).   _____

    e. Add lines *a* and *c*.   _____

    f. Add lines *b* and *d*.   _____

    g. Divide *f* by the quantity on Line 1 (total available time in school day).   _____

    h. This is the average number of partial absences per day.
        Multiply *g* by *e* and enter this number on Line 13.   _____

AEI Worksheet (continued)

V. **Estimate engagement rate and nonengagement rate.**

N. Average engagement rate (see Line 3 of Summary Worksheet under "Engagement Rate" section)

Line 20 _____ %

O. Percentage of school day in which students are engaged
(Line 20 _____ × Line 19 _____) ÷ 100

Line 21 _____ %

P. Percentage of time lost in class to inattentiveness
(100 − Line 20 _____)

Line 22 _____ %

Q. Percentage of school day lost to nonengagement
(Line 22 _____ × Line 19 _____) ÷ 100

Line 23 _____ %

VI. **Compute for academic efficiency.**

R. Efficiency loss due to noninstructional school time
(Line 9 _____ × Line 16 _____) ÷ 100

Line 24 _____ %

S. Efficiency loss due to absenteeism (Line 15 _____)

Line 25 _____ %

T. Efficiency loss due to noninstructional class time
(Line 18 _____ × Line 16 _____) ÷ 100

Line 26 _____ %

U. Efficiency loss due to student inattentiveness
(Line 23 _____ × Line 16 _____) ÷ 100

Line 27 _____ %

V. Academic efficiency
(Line 21 _____ × Line 16 _____) ÷ 100

Line 28 _____ %

These figures should add up to 100 if they are correct.

TOTAL _____

Instructions for Estimating Noninstructional Class Time and Engagement Rate

General Instructions for Observing Noninstructional Class Time

When making observations for noninstructional class time and student engagement, try to observe at least one-third of the teaching staff in the building. If your building has 20 or fewer staff members, observe one-half of the staff. Observations should be made across several time periods; balance them between morning and afternoon. If the observations are made in an elementary classroom, start midway through one subject, then continue across the transition and well into the second subject or period of instruction. (A great deal of time typically is lost during transitions.) In a secondary school, start the observations from the moment the bell rings to signal the start of class. If you enter midway through class (which is less desirable), stay until the final bell rings. We recommend that you observe a minimum of 20 minutes in each classroom.

During the observations you are looking for two types of activities: (1) those activities during which instruction and learning are taking place, and (2) those during which instruction and learning are not taking place.

When **Method A** is used to calculate student engagement, the observer estimates noninstructional class time at the same time that he or she estimates engagement rate.

When **Method B** is used, the observer calculates noninstructional time only. He or she works with the classroom teacher to arrange for students to self-report their engagement rates during the observation period.

Method A

Assume you are about to observe a class. Before observing the class, complete the information at the top of the form entitled OBSERVATION WORKSHEET - METHOD A, including the name of the school and the time the observation begins.

Now assume that the bell rings and you note that no instruction or learning is taking place because the teacher is taking roll. You immediately begin to time this noninstructional activity with your watch, and then record how long the roll-taking lasts on the worksheet in the section for Noninstructional Class Time (specifically, on the line marked "managing noncontent activities").

As soon as instruction/learning begins—that is, as soon as the teacher starts to lecture, asks students to start taking a test, etc.—shift your attention to the section (in the lower part of the worksheet) entitled Engagement Rate - Method A. Begin a series of visual sweeps of the entire classroom, watching each child for a few seconds to judge whether the child is engaged in the academic task assigned by the teacher. Use a "snapshot" technique to decide whether the student is focusing on his or her assigned task. Once you have decided about the engagement of a specific child, move on to the next child and then the next in some logical order (such as going up and down the rows of seats). If a child you have observed moves after your "snapshot" from being engaged to nonengaged or vice versa, ignore the change and keep going.

Instructions for Estimating Noninstructional Class Time and Engagement Rate (continued)

As you are making a sweep, keep mental count of the number of students who are engaged. Once you have made the sweep, record the number of students engaged and the total number of students observed in the appropriate boxes in the engagement rate table. (In most cases, the number of students observed will be the total number of students in the class. Occasionally, however, this number will vary because a student leaves or enters the room or because you are interrupted.) Each time you start a new sweep, move to the next set of boxes in the table and start your mental counter over at zero, both for the number of students engaged and for the total number of students observed.

When the student appears to be doing what was assigned, he or she is engaged in learning. If the student is sharpening a pencil and not doing math, the student is not engaged. If the student is staring out the window watching a squirrel, he or she is not engaged. If the student is looking in a book, apparently reading (and that is what was assigned), the student is engaged. You must make the judgment. Research shows that there is high reliability among raters using this process; that is, most observers, even if they are untrained, look at the same child and agree on the assessment. We recommend giving the student the benefit of the doubt if you can't decide.

Continue the sweeping process, taking about two to four minutes for a single sweep of a large class. You can easily do a half-dozen sweeps during a 10- to 15-minute period.

If the instructional process is stopped during the period you are monitoring, immediately record the number of students engaged (and the number of students observed), and begin timing the amount of time devoted to the interruption. The interruption could be caused by the teacher making an announcement, by the teacher stopping to reprimand a student who is misbehaving, or by someone from outside the classroom entering the room or making an announcement on the PA system. Record the length of the interruption—that is, the time taken for this noninstructional activity—in the Noninstructional Class Time section.

Once the interruption is over and the teacher continues instruction, turn your attention again to the Engagement Rate - Method A section of the worksheet. Start the sweep over, beginning at a new place in the classroom.

Continue to repeat the process described here each time instructional time is interrupted. Use cues as to the teacher's intentions or his or her behavior as the key to deciding when to measure noninstructional class time or to record engagement rates. If the teacher stops teaching to handle a discipline problem, to attend to a visitor, or to deal with any other management issue, shift to the Noninstructional Class Time section. If the teacher wants students to be learning—that is, if he or she is lecturing, having students take a test, or has asked them to do other seat work—observe engagement.

When a class observation is over, record the ending time at the top of the worksheet. Then, calculate the total observation time by subtracting the beginning time from the ending time. Enter the total time in Total Time of Observation (A).

Instructions for Estimating Noninstructional Class Time and Engagement Rate (continued)

Next, determine the total amount of noninstructional class time by adding the times recorded on the lines in numbers 1–6 in the Noninstructional Class Time section; record this number in Total Amount of Noninstructional Time (**B**), found in the middle of the worksheet.

Then, calculate the percentage of noninstructional class time by dividing **B** by **A** and multiplying by 100. Record this number on one of the lines under number 1 in the Noninstructional Class Time section on the SUMMARY WORKSHEET.

To calculate the engagement rate for the class, use the engagement rate table. Add the numbers in the row for "Number of students engaged" and record the total at **C**. Then add the numbers in the row for "Number of students observed" and record the total at **D**. Calculate the class's engagement rate by dividing **C** by **D** and then multiplying by 100. Enter it on one of the lines under number 1 in the "Engagement Rate" section on the SUMMARY WORKSHEET.

Method B

The difference between Method A and Method B is that in Method B, students self-report their engagement rates. The process for observing noninstructional class time is the same as in Method A.

There are two different versions of the ENGAGEMENT RATE SELF-REPORT WORKSHEET - METHOD B, one for grades 1–3 and one for grades 4–12. In each, students are asked to rate the extent to which they have been paying attention since the last time they were asked. Select the correct form and make copies, one for each student.

You will need the assistance of the classroom teacher to collect the student data. Arrange to have the teacher pass out copies of the student self-report forms at the beginning of the observation and discuss with students that, from time to time, the teacher will be asking them questions about how much they have been paying attention. It is important to emphasize that students aren't expected to be paying attention all of the time; stress that the information is anonymous, so they have more freedom to answer honestly. Let students know that their work will not be graded.

Prior to asking students to use the main section of the worksheet, give them an opportunity to practice by using the practice row on the worksheet.

Direct the teacher to stop at natural breaks in her instruction and to ask students to mark the degree to which they were paying attention on the self-report worksheet. Keep doing this until class has ended or until all time periods have been addressed (Time A, Time B, and so on).

Meanwhile, you can make observations about noninstructional class time in exactly the same manner explained in Method A, noting your observations on OBSERVATION WORKSHEET - METHOD B.

Instructions for Estimating Noninstructional Class Time and Engagement Rate (continued)

When the observation period if over, follow these instructions to calculate engagement rate for the class:

1. Make sure that all completed ENGAGEMENT RATE SELF-REPORT WORKSHEETS are carefully grouped by class.

2. Complete the lower section of each ENGAGEMENT RATE SELF-REPORT WORKSHEET. (This is a time-consuming process; you may want to enlist the help of volunteers [e.g., older students or other building staff besides teachers].)

3. Record the engagement rates for all the students in the class on a single piece of paper.

4. Total the engagement rates of all the students in the class and divide by the number of students to get the average class engagement rate.

5. Record each class engagement rate on one of the lines under number 1 in the Engagement Rate section on the SUMMARY WORKSHEET.

Observation Worksheet - Method A

School _____ Grade Level or Subject _____

Time observation began   _____

Time observation ended   _____

Total Time (in minutes) of Observation   (A) _____

Noninstructional Class Time

Directions: During those noninstructional activities listed below, record the amount of time (in minutes and seconds) spent on each activity.

1. Managing noncontent activities (e.g., taking roll, transitions, collecting/passing out materials, etc.)

    _____ _____ _____ _____ _____ _____

2. Socializing

    _____ _____ _____ _____ _____ _____

3. Disciplining (whole class interrupted)

    _____ _____ _____ _____ _____ _____

4. Outside interruptions

    _____ _____ _____ _____ _____ _____

5. Working with one or two students while others wait

    _____ _____ _____ _____ _____ _____

6. Other noninstructional activities

    _____ _____ _____ _____ _____ _____

Total Amount of Noninstructional Time (in minutes)   (B) _____

Percentage of noninstructional class time
$(B \div A) \times 100$ _____ %

Record this number on one of the lines under number 1 in the Noninstructional Class Time section on the SUMMARY WORKSHEET.

Engagement Rate - Method A

Directions: During instructional time, make systematic sweeps of the class during which you identify the number of students engaged and the number of students observed at the time of the sweeps.

	Sweeps											
	1	2	3	4	5	6	7	8	9	10	Totals	
Number of students engaged												(C)
Number of students observed												(D)

Class engagement rate
$(C \div D) \times 100$ _____ %

Enter this number on one of the lines under number 1 in the Engagement Rate section on the SUMMARY WORKSHEET.

Observation Worksheet - Method B

School _____ Grade Level or Subject _____

    Time observation began   _____

    Time observation ended   _____

    Total Time (in minutes) of Observation   (A) _____

Noninstructional Class Time

Directions: During those noninstructional activities listed below, record the amount of time (in minutes and seconds) spent on each activity.

   1.   Managing noncontent activities (e.g., taking roll, transitions, collecting/passing out materials, etc.)

     _____   _____   _____   _____   _____   _____

   2.   Socializing

     _____   _____   _____   _____   _____   _____

   3.   Disciplining (whole class interrupted)

     _____   _____   _____   _____   _____   _____

   4.   Outside interruptions

     _____   _____   _____   _____   _____   _____

   5.   Working with one or two students while others wait

     _____   _____   _____   _____   _____   _____

   6.   Other noninstructional activities

     _____   _____   _____   _____   _____   _____

Total Amount of Noninstructional Time (in minutes)   (B) _____

Percentage of noninstructional class time
$(B \div A) \times 100$ _____ %

Record this number on one of the lines under number 1 in the Noninstructional Class Time section on the SUMMARY WORKSHEET.

Engagement Rate Self-Report Worksheet - Method B
Grades 1–3

Teacher _____   Date _____

	No		Yes
Practice: Paying attention?	☹	😐	🙂
Time A: Paying attention?	☹	😐	🙂
Time B: Paying attention?	☹	😐	🙂
Time C: Paying attention?	☹	😐	🙂
Time D: Paying attention?	☹	😐	🙂
Time E: Paying attention?	☹	😐	🙂

STUDENTS: PLEASE DO NOT WRITE BELOW THIS LINE.

Total the number of circled faces in each column.   _____ _____ _____
(Do not count the circled faces in the practice row.)

Multiply each number by the number beneath it.   × 0   × .5   × 1

Enter the answers here.   _____ + _____ + _____

Add the three answers together.   _____

Divide by 5.   _____

The result is the student's **engagement rate**.
To convert to a percentage, multiply by 100.   _____ %

Engagement Rate Self-Report Worksheet - Method B
Grades 4–12

Date _____ School _____ Class _____

Check the box that most clearly represents how much you were paying attention.

Question: How much were you paying attention?

	Not at all		Somewhat		Totally
Practice	☐	☐	☐	☐	☐
Time A	☐	☐	☐	☐	☐
Time B	☐	☐	☐	☐	☐
Time C	☐	☐	☐	☐	☐
Time D	☐	☐	☐	☐	☐
Time E	☐	☐	☐	☐	☐
Time F	☐	☐	☐	☐	☐

STUDENTS: PLEASE DO NOT WRITE BELOW THIS LINE.

Count the number of checked responses in each column (with the exception of the practice response) and record below.

    ____   ____   ____   ____   ____

Multiply by: × 0   × .25   × .50   × .75   × 1.00

Answer   ____ + ____ + ____ + ____ + ____

Add multiplied answers together.   _____

Divide by 6.   _____

The result is the student's **engagement rate**.
To convert to percentage, multiply by 100.   _____ %

Summary Worksheet

Noninstructional Class Time

Directions:

1. List below the percentages of "noninstructional class time" gathered from the OBSERVATION WORKSHEET, Method A or Method B, for each classroom observed. Enter one observation on one line. Use as many lines as necessary.

   _____ _____ _____ _____ _____ _____

   _____ _____ _____ _____ _____ _____

   _____ _____ _____ _____ _____ _____

   _____ _____ _____ _____ _____ _____

2. Total the percentages in Item 1 and enter the total here: _____

3. Divide the total in Item 2 by the number of entries in Item 1. Record the answer here. Then enter the number on Line 17 in Item IV of the AEI WORKSHEET. _____

Engagement Rate

Directions:

1. On each line below, list the engagement rate gathered from each classroom observation or self-report. Use as many lines as necessary. If using Method A, enter the "class engagement rate" from the bottom of each OBSERVATION WORKSHEET. If using Method B, enter the average class engagement rates—one score for each class (see instructions for Method B).

   _____ _____ _____ _____ _____ _____

   _____ _____ _____ _____ _____ _____

   _____ _____ _____ _____ _____ _____

   _____ _____ _____ _____ _____ _____

2. Total the percentages in Item 1 and enter the total here: _____

3. Divide the total in Item 2 by the number of entries in Item 1. Record the answer here. Then enter the number on Line 20 in Item IV of the AEI WORKSHEET. _____

AEI Grid Instructions

Step 1: Use the blank Academic Efficiency Index Grid on page 287.

Step 2: Identify quantities in AEI.
- Fill in the quantities from the following lines on the AEI WORKSHEET:

  Line 16: _____ Line 10: _____ Line 19: _____ Line 21: _____

Step 3: Chart the portion of time lost to absenteeism.
- On the horizontal axis (bottom line) of the grid, find the point that corresponds with the quantity entered on Line 16.
- Draw a straight vertical line from this point to the top horizontal axis of the grid. This line, with the right edge of the grid, forms a long, narrow rectangle at the right of the grid.
- Place the title "Efficiency Loss Due to Absenteeism," or simply write "Absenteeism," in this space.

Step 4: Chart the noninstructional school time.
- On the left vertical axis (left edge) of the grid, find the point that corresponds to the quantity entered on Line 10.
- Draw a straight horizontal line to the edge of the long, narrow rectangle drawn in step 3. This line, with the top edge of the grid, forms a rectangle at the top of the grid.
- Place the title "Noninstructional School Time" in this space. If you want to place the arithmetic value in the space, do not use the amount on Line 10. It does not have the arithmetic value of the absenteeism removed. Use instead the numerical value from Line 24. It has the percentage of absenteeism factored out. Remember, the graph is a geometrical figure from which absenteeism has been removed. When reporting academic efficiency values, the percentage of time has been taken out mathematically. To avoid confusion, you may want to erase the column and rows of numbers used to draw the grid. They do not appear "correct" in relation to the figure you place inside the chart.

Step 5: Chart noninstructional class time.
- On the left vertical axis of the grid, find the point that corresponds to the quantity entered on Line 19.
- Draw a straight horizontal line to the edge of the rectangle drawn in step 3. This line, with the one drawn in step 4, forms another rectangle.
- Place the title "Noninstructional Class Time" in this space. If you want to represent the quantity of the space, enter the amount from line 26 here. Do not use the amount from Line 19 for the same reasons described earlier.

Step 6: Chart nonengaged time.
- On the left vertical axis of the grid, find a point that corresponds to the quantity in Line 21.
- Draw a straight horizontal line to the edge of the rectangle drawn in step 3. This line, with the one drawn in step 5, form another rectangle.
- Write the title "Nonengaged Time" here. Use the figure from Line 27 to quantify the space.

Step 7: Chart academic efficiency.
- In the remaining area of the grid, place the title "Academic Efficiency." The quantity of the space involved is shown on Line 28. Your final figure should resemble the one on page 271.

AEI Grid

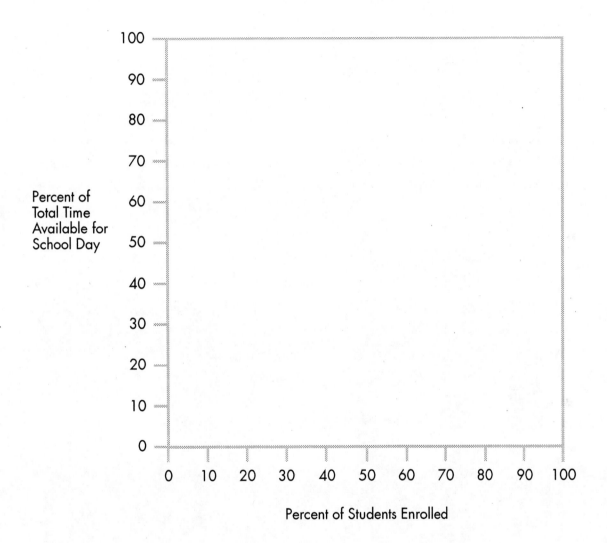

McREL Standards Survey Questionnaires

Questionnaire 1

Thank you for agreeing to participate in the educational standards opinion survey Gallup is conducting for the Mid-continent Regional Educational Laboratory (McREL). McREL is developing educational standards that will be used by schools nationwide. In this endeavor, they would like to know your opinions about what you think are appropriate levels of attainment in different subjects for high school graduates.

The survey you have received includes four subjects: World History, Health, Mathematics and Foreign Language. For each of these subjects, a number of levels of knowledge or attainment are proposed for high school graduates in our country. Your task will be to indicate if you think it is *definitely*, *probably*, *probably not* or *definitely not* a standard students should know or be able to do by the time they graduate from high school.

We urge you to fill out and return this IMPORTANT survey.

- Using the enclosed envelope, you will return the survey directly to The Gallup Organization for analysis and reporting.

- No individual responses will be reported and no attempt will be made to identify individual respondents.

- No one at McREL or any school will see any individual questionnaires.

- Your individual answers will be kept strictly confidential, so please freely express your opinions.

- Your responses should not be influenced by your own level of knowledge. They should be based on what you feel is appropriate for high school graduates today.

- You can give the same or different responses as you move from standard to standard.

Marking Instructions

- Use a blue or black ink pen only.
- Do not use ink that soaks through the paper.
- Make solid marks that fit in the response boxes.
- Make no stray marks on the survey.

RIGHT WAY   WRONG WAY

Please go to the next page to begin the survey

Subject I: World History

For each proposed standard please indicate with an ☒ in the box if you think it is *definitely*, *probably*, *probably not* or *definitely not* a level of knowledge that students today should have by the time they graduate from high school. Mark *don't know* only if you really are in doubt whether or not it is an appropriate level of attainment for high school graduates.

	Definitely	Probably	Probably Not	Definitely Not.	Don't Know
	▼	▼	▼	▼	▼
1. Understands physical, social, and cultural characteristics of the earliest human communities and the ways in which these communities were influenced by the environment.	☐	☐	☐	☐	☐
2. Understands methods used to study the earliest human communities.	☐	☐	☐	☐	☐
3. Understands characteristics of the earliest agricultural communities around the world and factors that contributed to their development, including environmental factors.	☐	☐	☐	☐	☐
4. Understands characteristics of civilizations in Mesopotamia, Egypt, and the Indus Valley. . .	☐	☐	☐	☐	☐
5. Understands how agricultural societies spread and new states emerged in ancient times	☐	☐	☐	☐	☐
6. Understands the political, social and cultural consequences of population movements and warfare in Europe and Asia in ancient times . .	☐	☐	☐	☐	☐
7. Understands characteristics of Judaism and events that led to the spread of Judaism.	☐	☐	☐	☐	☐
8. Understands the significance of the spread of iron technology in Sub-Saharan and West Africa.	☐	☐	☐	☐	☐
9. Understands how Greek civilization emerged and how interrelations developed among peoples of the eastern Mediterranean and Southwest Asia.	☐	☐	☐	☐	☐

	Definitely ▼	Probably ▼	Probably Not ▼	Definitely Not ▼	Don't Know ▼
10. Understands how major religious and large-scale empires arose in the Mediterranean basin, China and India	☐	☐	☐	☐	☐
11. Understands how early agrarian civilizations and cities arose in Middle and South America. .	☐	☐	☐	☐	☐
12. Understands the causes and consequences of the decline of the Roman and Han Empires and the rise of the Byzantine Empire	☐	☐	☐	☐	☐
13. Understands ways in which the spread of different religions influenced social and political conditions in various regions between the 4th and 8th centuries	☐	☐	☐	☐	☐
14. Understands characteristics of Gupta society in India between the 4th and 8th centuries . .	☐	☐	☐	☐	☐
15. Understands the causes and consequences of the development of Islamic civilization between the 7th and 10th centuries	☐	☐	☐	☐	☐
16. Understands the major developments in China and East Asia in the era of the Tang Dynasty from the 7th to the 10th century	☐	☐	☐	☐	☐
17. Understands the political, social, and cultural changes in Europe between the 6th and 11th century, including the effects of the development of feudalism.	☐	☐	☐	☐	☐
18. Understands the building of state societies in Africa, and the southward migrations of Bantu-speaking peoples	☐	☐	☐	☐	☐
19. Understands characteristics of Chinese, Japanese, and Cambodian societies and the Turkic Empires between the 10th and 13th centuries.	☐	☐	☐	☐	☐

	Definitely	Probably	Probably Not	Definitely Not	Don't Know
	▼	▼	▼	▼	▼

20. Understands social, political, economic, and intellectual developments in European society between the 11th and 14th centuries, including the role of feudalism and characteristics of city states such as Genoa, Venice, and Bruges. . . . . □ □ □ □ □

21. Understands the rise of the Mongol empire and its consequences for Asian and European peoples from 1200 to 1350 . . . . □ □ □ □ □

22. Understands the growth of states, towns, and trade in Sub-Saharan Africa between the 11th and 15th centuries . . . . □ □ □ □ □

23. Understands the characteristics of European society between 1300 and 1450, including the causes and consequences of the plague . . . □ □ □ □ □

24. Understands significant developments in Afro-Eurasia between 1300 and 1450, including the causes and consequences of the rise and decline of the Ottoman Empire. . . . . □ □ □ □ □

25. Understands characteristics of Caribbean, Middle American, North American, and South American societies between 1000 and 1500 . . □ □ □ □ □

26. Understands how the navigation of the oceans and the linking of all major regions of the world between 1450 and 1600 led to worldwide change. . . . . □ □ □ □ □

27. Understands the causes and consequences of the religious wars in Europe during the 16th and 17th centuries . . . . □ □ □ □ □

28. Understands the characteristics of the beliefs that emerged during the Renaissance, Reformation, and Enlightenment in Europe between the 15th and 18th centuries . . . . □ □ □ □ □

	Definitely ▼	Probably ▼	Probably Not ▼	Definitely Not ▼	Don't Know ▼

29. Understands how large territorial empires dominated much of Europe and Asia between the 16th and 18th centuries, including the Ming Dynasty and the Ottoman, Safavid, and Mughal Empires. . . . . ☐ ☐ ☐ ☐ ☐

30. Understands the economic, political and cultural relationships among peoples of Africa, Europe and the Americas between 1500 and 1750, including characteristics of European colonies and the characteristics of slavery in different regions of the world . . . . . ☐ ☐ ☐ ☐ ☐

31. Understands transformations in India and Asia in the era of European expansion from 1500 to 1800. . . . . ☐ ☐ ☐ ☐ ☐

32. Understands major global trends from 1450 to 1770, such as changes in boundaries, shifts in political power, and significant economic developments . . . . ☐ ☐ ☐ ☐ ☐

33. Understands the causes and consequences of the Latin American independence movements and the revolutions in France, the Americas, and Haiti in the late 18th and early 19th centuries. . . . . ☐ ☐ ☐ ☐ ☐

34. Understands the causes and consequences of the agricultural and industrial revolutions from 1700 to 1850. ☐ ☐ ☐ ☐ ☐

35. Understands how Eurasian societies were transformed in an era of global trade and the emergence of European power from 1750 to 1850, including Japan's political and social transformation in the 19th century and events that shaped the expansion and development of Russia in the 19th and early 20th century . . . ☐ ☐ ☐ ☐ ☐

36. Understands patterns of nationalism, state-building, and social reform in Europe and the Americas from 1830 up to World War I . . . . ☐ ☐ ☐ ☐ ☐

	Definitely ▼	Probably ▼	Probably Not ▼	Definitely Not ▼	Don't Know ▼
37. Understands patterns of global change in the era of Western military and economic domination from 1850 up to World War I, including characteristics of imperialism, the consequences of European immigration, and significant political events in 20th century China	□	□	□	□	□
38. Understands major global trends from 1750 up to World War I, including trends in world population and the consequences of reform movements in world religions	□	□	□	□	□
39. Understands global and economic trends in the high period of Western dominance.	□	□	□	□	□
40. Understands the causes and global consequences of World War I, including Lenin's and Stalin's policies and other significant developments in Russia in the early 20th century	□	□	□	□	□
41. Understands the search for peace and stability throughout the world in the 1920s and 1930s, including the causes of the Great Depression and the ways in which the emergence of new art, literature, music, and scientific theories influences society	□	□	□	□	□
42. Understands the causes and global consequences of World War II, including characteristics of Nazism, the impact of the Holocaust, and the significance of Japan's sphere of influence in East Asia	□	□	□	□	□
43. Understands how new international power relations took shape in the context of the Cold War and how colonial empires broke up.	□	□	□	□	□

	Definitely	Probably	Probably Not	Definitely Not	Don't Know
	▼	▼	▼	▼	▼

44. Understands the promises and paradoxes of the second half of the 20th century, including the influences on population growth, the characteristics of modern economic systems, and the effectiveness of the United Nations programs in improving health and welfare . . . . ☐ ☐ ☐ ☐ ☐

45. Understands major global trends since World War II, including economic, technological, and cultural trends . . . . ☐ ☐ ☐ ☐ ☐

46. Understands causes of economic imbalances and social inequalities among the world's peoples and efforts made to close these gaps . . ☐ ☐ ☐ ☐ ☐

47. Understands the importance of the revolutions in toolmaking, agriculture, and industrialization as major turning points in human history . . . . ☐ ☐ ☐ ☐ ☐

48. Understands the circumstances under which European countries came to exercise temporary military and economic dominance in the world in the late 19th and 20th centuries. . . . . ☐ ☐ ☐ ☐ ☐

Subject II: Health

For each proposed standard please indicate with an [X] in the box if you think it is *definitely*, *probably*, *probably not* or *definitely not* a level of knowledge that students today should have by the time they graduate from high school. Mark *don't know* only if you really are in doubt whether or not it is an appropriate level of attainment for high school graduates.

	Definitely ▼	Probably ▼	Probably Not ▼	Definitely Not ▼	Don't Know ▼
49. Knows the availability and effective use of health services, products, and information . . .	☐	☐	☐	☐	☐
50. Knows the environmental and other external factors that affect individual and community health, including the influence of research, medical advances, and public health policies on prevention and control of health problems	☐	☐	☐	☐	☐
51. Understands the relationship of family health to individual health, including the inherent responsibilities of dating, marriage, and parenthood	☐	☐	☐	☐	☐
52. Knows how to maintain mental and emotional health, including stress management and the importance of communication.	☐	☐	☐	☐	☐
53. Knows essential concepts and practices concerning injury prevention and safety	☐	☐	☐	☐	☐
54. Understands essential concepts about nutrition and diet.	☐	☐	☐	☐	☐
55. Knows how to maintain and promote personal health, and understands changes in personal health needs during the life cycle	☐	☐	☐	☐	☐
56. Knows essential concepts about the prevention and control of disease, including the importance of regular examinations for early detection and the treatment of disease	☐	☐	☐	☐	☐

	Definitely	Probably	Probably Not	Definitely Not	Don't Know
	▼	▼	▼	▼	▼
57. Understands aspects of substance use and abuse, including the influence of alcohol, tobacco, and other drugs on individuals and the community.	☐	☐	☐	☐	☐
58. Understands the fundamental concepts of growth and development, including physical, mental, emotional, and social changes that occur throughout life and how these changes differ among individuals.	☐	☐	☐	☐	☐
59. Understands the importance of sound health practices during the prenatal period	☐	☐	☐	☐	☐

Subject III: Mathematics

For each proposed standard please indicate with an $\boxed{X}$ in the box if you think it is *definitely*, *probably*, *probably not* or *definitely not* a level of knowledge that students today should have by the time they graduate from high school. Mark *don't know* only if you really are in doubt whether or not it is an appropriate level of attainment for high school graduates.

	Definitely ▼	Probably ▼	Probably Not ▼	Definitely Not ▼	Don't Know ▼
60. Ability to effectively use a variety of approaches when solving mathematical problems, including creating models and using logic and mathematical arguments	☐	☐	☐	☐	☐
61. Ability to work with relatively advanced number systems (such as the real number system and systems other than those in base-ten), including understanding roots, exponents, scientific notation and characteristics of and relationships between various number representations	☐	☐	☐	☐	☐
62. Ability to work with a variety of procedures when computing numbers, including arithmetic operations on real numbers, adding and subtracting algebraic expressions, counting procedures, and understanding properties of operations	☐	☐	☐	☐	☐
63. Ability to use various strategies to estimate quantities and measurements, to check reasonableness of computational results, and to find sources of error	☐	☐	☐	☐	☐
64. Ability to apply the principles of measurement (such as use of appropriate tools, units, and formulas), solve problems involving dimensions (for example, the perimeter, area, and volume of objects and figures), and solve time, rate and distance problems	☐	☐	☐	☐	☐

	Definitely ▼	Probably ▼	Probably Not ▼	Definitely Not ▼	Don't Know ▼
65. Ability to work with relatively advanced geometry concepts, such as characteristics and properties of figures, triangle and angle relationships and use of vectors.	☐	☐	☐	☐	☐
66. Ability to analyze data, using concepts such as mean, median, and standard deviation	☐	☐	☐	☐	☐
67. Ability to effectively present data in tables and graphs	☐	☐	☐	☐	☐
68. Ability to apply concepts of probability, including experimental, simulation, and theoretical methods	☐	☐	☐	☐	☐
69. Ability to work with relatively advanced algebraic concepts, such as use of variables, coordinates, expressions, and methods of solving equations, inequalities, and systems of equations	☐	☐	☐	☐	☐
70. Ability to work with properties of functions, including various representations and defining characteristics.	☐	☐	☐	☐	☐
71. Understanding of the nature and use of mathematics in science and other real-world applications	☐	☐	☐	☐	☐

Subject IV: Foreign Language

For each proposed standard please indicate with an $\boxed{\text{X}}$ in the box if you think it is *definitely*, *probably*, *probably not* or *definitely not* a level of knowledge that students today should have by the time they graduate from high school. Mark *don't know* only if you really are in doubt whether or not it is an appropriate level of attainment for high school graduates.

	Definitely	Probably	Probably Not	Definitely Not	Don't Know
72. Ability to verbally greet, give directions and express likes and dislikes in the foreign language.........................	☐	☐	☐	☐	☐
73. Ability to use the foreign language in conversations about family, cultural and current events........................	☐	☐	☐	☐	☐
74. Ability to identify the main ideas, details and themes from a wide number of media sources in the foreign culture, including literary texts, newspapers, television and the visual arts	☐	☐	☐	☐	☐
75. Ability to comprehend and interpret written and spoken language from a wide number of media sources in the foreign culture, including literary texts, newspapers, television and the visual arts	☐	☐	☐	☐	☐
76. Ability to present information, concepts and ideas in the foreign language to an audience of listeners	☐	☐	☐	☐	☐
77. Ability to make presentations in the foreign language under different types of situations, such as in plays or skits, video or audio tapes, reports and e-mail	☐	☐	☐	☐	☐
78. Knows simple patterns of behavior and interaction in the foreign culture, such as those that occur in school, the family and the community, and how these compare to one's own culture	☐	☐	☐	☐	☐

	Definitely	Probably	Probably Not	Definitely Not	Don't Know
	▼	▼	▼	▼	▼

79. Understands basic cultural beliefs and perspectives of the foreign culture, such as its religious and family values, and how these compare to one's own culture . . . . ☐ ☐ ☐ ☐ ☐

80. Demonstrates knowledge and understanding of the traditions of the foreign culture, as revealed in its songs, games, birthday celebrations, story telling, food, artwork and crafts . . . . ☐ ☐ ☐ ☐ ☐

81. Understands the basic nature of languages (sounds, grammar, context, borrowed words, formal and informal expressions, etc.) and how the foreign language differs from one's own language in terms of these functions . . . . ☐ ☐ ☐ ☐ ☐

Questionnaire 2

Thank you for agreeing to participate in the educational standards opinion survey Gallup is conducting for the Mid-continent Regional Educational Laboratory (McREL). McREL is developing educational standards that will be used by schools nationwide. In this endeavor, they would like to know your opinions about what you think are appropriate levels of attainment in different subjects for high school graduates.

The survey you have received includes five subjects: United States History, Physical Education, Science, Behavioral Studies and Technology. For each of these subjects, a number of levels of knowledge or attainment are proposed for high school graduates in our country. Your task will be to indicate if you think it is *definitely*, *probably*, *probably not* or *definitely not* a standard students should know or be able to do by the time they graduate from high school.

We urge you to fill out and return this IMPORTANT survey.

- Using the enclosed envelope, you will return the survey directly to The Gallup Organization for analysis and reporting.

- No individual responses will be reported and no attempt will be made to identify individual respondents.

- No one at McREL or any school will see any individual questionnaires.

- Your individual answers will be kept strictly confidential, so please freely express your opinions.

- Your responses should not be influenced by your own level of knowledge. They should be based on what you feel is appropriate for high school graduates today.

- You can give the same or different responses as you move from standard to standard.

Marking Instructions

- Use a blue or black ink pen only.
- Do not use ink that soaks through the paper.
- Make solid marks that fit in the response boxes.
- Make no stray marks on the survey.

RIGHT WAY   WRONG WAY

Please go to the next page to begin the survey

Subject I: United States History

For each proposed standard please indicate with an X in the box if you think it is *definitely*, *probably*, *probably not* or *definitely not* a level of knowledge that students today should have by the time they graduate from high school. Mark *don't know* only if you really are in doubt whether or not it is an appropriate level of attainment for high school graduates.

	Definitely ▼	Probably ▼	Probably Not ▼	Definitely Not ▼	Don't Know ▼
1. Understands the characteristics of societies in the Americas, western Europe, and West Africa, and interactions among these groups prior to European exploration of the Americas	☐	☐	☐	☐	☐
2. Understands the characteristics and consequences of European exploration, conquest and settlement in the Americas, including Columbus' voyages............	☐	☐	☐	☐	☐
3. Understands how early Europeans and Africans interacted with Native Americans in the Americas	☐	☐	☐	☐	☐
4. Understands how political, social, and religious institutions emerged in the North American colonies	☐	☐	☐	☐	☐
5. Understands how the values and institutions of European economic life took root in the colonies and how slavery reshaped European and African life in the Americas..........	☐	☐	☐	☐	☐
6. Understands the causes of the American Revolution, the ideas and interests involved in shaping the revolutionary movement, and reasons for the American victory..........	☐	☐	☐	☐	☐
7. Understands the impact of the American Revolution on the politics, economy, and society of the times	☐	☐	☐	☐	☐

	Definitely ▼	Probably ▼	Probably Not ▼	Definitely Not ▼	Don't Know ▼
8. Understands the institutions and practices of government created during the revolution and how these elements were revised between 1787 and 1815 to create the foundation of the American political system	☐	☐	☐	☐	☐
9. Understands characteristics of the United States' territorial expansion between 1801 and 1861, including federal policy toward Native Americans	☐	☐	☐	☐	☐
10. Understands foreign policy and related events of the 19th century, including the Monroe Doctrine, Manifest Destiny, the War of 1812, and the Mexican-American War	☐	☐	☐	☐	☐
11. Understands how the Industrial Revolution, increasing immigration, the rapid expansion of slavery, and the westward movement changed American lives and led to regional tensions	☐	☐	☐	☐	☐
12. Understands significant characteristics of American politics in the first half of the 19th century, including Jacksonian Democracy. . . .	☐	☐	☐	☐	☐
13. Understands events that led to the sectional conflict between the North and the South (Missouri Compromise and the Compromise of 1850), and the viewpoints of those favoring and opposing slavery during this time	☐	☐	☐	☐	☐
14. Understands the characteristics of slavery in the period before the Civil War, and the growing abolitionist movement opposing it.	☐	☐	☐	☐	☐
15. Understands cultural, religious, and social reform movements during the period before the Civil War, including Transcendentalism, the Second Great Awakening, the rise of Utopian communities, and the rights and contributions of women	☐	☐	☐	☐	☐

	Definitely	Probably	Probably Not	Definitely Not	Don't Know
	▼	▼	▼	▼	▼
16. Understands the causes of the Civil War	☐	☐	☐	☐	☐
17. Understands the course and character of the Civil War, including its military, political, and social effects on society	☐	☐	☐	☐	☐
18. Understands important civil and military leaders and their actions during the Civil War period, including Abraham Lincoln and the Emancipation Proclamation, the leadership of Jefferson Davis, and the campaigns of Ulysses S. Grant and William T. Sherman	☐	☐	☐	☐	☐
19. Understands the social, political, and economic factors that characterized the Reconstruction period after the Civil War and the impact of that period on society, including the significance of President Andrew Johnson's impeachment, and the addition of the 14th and 15th amendments to the U.S. constitution	☐	☐	☐	☐	☐
20. Understands how the rise of big business, heavy industry, and mechanized farming transformed American society............	☐	☐	☐	☐	☐
21. Understands massive immigration after 1870 and how new social patterns, conflicts, and ideas of national unity developed amid growing cultural diversity	☐	☐	☐	☐	☐
22. Understands the nature of work (factory work, child labor, etc.), the labor movements, and the characteristics of political parties and elections of the late 19th century	☐	☐	☐	☐	☐
23. Understands the federal Indian policy and the political and cultural characteristics of Native American life in the late 19th century	☐	☐	☐	☐	☐
24. Understands factors that contributed to U.S. expansionist foreign policy in the late 19th century, including economic interests, nationalism, and racial beliefs............	☐	☐	☐	☐	☐

	Definitely ▼	Probably ▼	Probably Not ▼	Definitely Not ▼	Don't Know ▼
25. Understands how progressives and others addressed problems of industrial capitalism, urbanization, and political corruption in the early 20th century	☐	☐	☐	☐	☐
26. Understands efforts to achieve women's right to vote in the early 20th century	☐	☐	☐	☐	☐
27. Understands the changing role of the United States in world affairs through World War I	☐	☐	☐	☐	☐
28. Understands how the United States changed between the post-World War I years and the eve of the Great Depression, including social and cultural development—such as the impact of the radio, print media, and the movies—and economic and political developments, such as the rise of a consumer culture and the impact of women's voting rights	☐	☐	☐	☐	☐
29. Understands the causes of the Great Depression and how it affected American society	☐	☐	☐	☐	☐
30. Understands how the New Deal addressed the Great Depression, transformed the role of the federal government, and initiated the welfare state	☐	☐	☐	☐	☐
31. Understands the causes, origins, and course of World War II, the character of the war at home and abroad, and how it reshaped the U.S. role in world affairs.	☐	☐	☐	☐	☐
32. Understands the economic boom and social, religious, and cultural changes of post-World War II America, including those initiated by the Cold War	☐	☐	☐	☐	☐
33. Understands the domestic policies of the post-World War II period, including those of the Truman, Eisenhower, Kennedy, and Johnson presidencies	☐	☐	☐	☐	☐

	Definitely ▼	Probably ▼	Probably Not ▼	Definitely Not ▼	Don't Know ▼
34. Understands the Cold War and the Korean and Vietnam conflicts in domestic and international politics	☐	☐	☐	☐	☐
35. Understands the struggle for racial and gender equality and for the extension of civil liberties, including the Warren Court decisions and the civil rights movement	☐	☐	☐	☐	☐
36. Understands developments in foreign and domestic policies from the Nixon through the Clinton presidencies	☐	☐	☐	☐	☐
37. Understands the major social and economic developments in contemporary America—including the women's movement, changing immigration and internal migrations, the changing workplace and the influence of the media on American culture	☐	☐	☐	☐	☐

Subject II: Physical Education

For each proposed standard please indicate with an ☒ in the box if you think it is *definitely*, *probably*, *probably not* or *definitely not* a level of knowledge that students today should have by the time they graduate from high school. Mark *don't know* only if you really are in doubt whether or not it is an appropriate level of attainment for high school graduates.

	Definitely ▼	Probably ▼	Probably Not ▼	Definitely Not ▼	Don't Know ▼
38. Has and demonstrates use of advanced skills for selected sports or other physical activities, such as dance and outdoor activities	☐	☐	☐	☐	☐
39. Knows the rules and strategies for the selected sports or other physical activities	☐	☐	☐	☐	☐
40. Understands the concepts and principles associated with the development of motor skills.	☐	☐	☐	☐	☐
41. Understands the concepts and principles governing fitness maintenance and improvement, such as the overload principle.	☐	☐	☐	☐	☐
42. Understands how "sport" psychology affects the performance of physical activities, including the effect of anxiety on performance.	☐	☐	☐	☐	☐
43. Understands factors that impact the ability to participate in a physical activity (for example, cost, availability of facilities, and equipment required) and those that affect preferences, such as age, gender, race, and social status . . .	☐	☐	☐	☐	☐
44. Understands the potentially dangerous consequences and outcomes from participation in physical activity, such as physical injury and potential conflicts with others	☐	☐	☐	☐	☐
45. Understands how to monitor and maintain a health-enhancing level of physical fitness	☐	☐	☐	☐	☐

	Definitely ▼	Probably ▼	Probably Not ▼	Definitely Not ▼	Don't Know ▼
46. Knows the status of one's own heart and respiratory endurance, flexibility of joints, and muscular strength.	☐	☐	☐	☐	☐
47. Meets health-related fitness standards appropriate for one's level of physical capability	☐	☐	☐	☐	☐
48. Understands the social and personal responsibilities associated with participation in sports and other physical activities, such as working with others to achieve common goals, and the awareness of cultural, ethnic, gender, and physical diversity. . . . . : . . .	☐	☐	☐	☐	☐

Subject III: Science

For each proposed standard please indicate with an [X] in the box if you think it is *definitely*, *probably*, *probably not* or *definitely not* a level of knowledge that students today should have by the time they graduate from high school. Mark *don't know* only if you really are in doubt whether or not it is an appropriate level of attainment for high school graduates.

	Definitely	Probably	Probably Not	Definitely Not	Don't Know
49. Understands basic features of the Earth, including its composition and atmosphere and the causes of weather, climate, and seasons . . .	☐	☐	☐	☐	☐
50. Understands basic Earth processes, including the causes and effects of rock and geological cycles and movements of Earth's underlying plates	☐	☐	☐	☐	☐
51. Understands how fossils and sedimentary rock layers reveal evidence of past life and environments on Earth	☐	☐	☐	☐	☐
52. Understands essential ideas about the composition and structure of the universe and the Earth's place in it, including characteristics and motions of objects in the Solar System and in the universe	☐	☐	☐	☐	☐
53. Understands the diversity and unity that characterize life, and knows classification systems used to group organisms	☐	☐	☐	☐	☐
54. Understands the genetic basis for the transfer of biological characteristics from one generation to the next, including the passing of hereditary traits through sexual and asexual reproduction and the characteristics and functions of DNA, genes, and chromosomes . .	☐	☐	☐	☐	☐
55. Knows the general structure and functions of cells in organisms	☐	☐	☐	☐	☐

	Definitely	Probably	Probably Not	Definitely Not	Don't Know
	▼	▼	▼	▼	▼

56. Understands how species depend on one another and on the environment for survival . . . . □ □ □ □ □

57. Understands the cycling of matter and the flow of energy through the living environment, including photosynthesis and respiration and food chains and webs . . . . □ □ □ □ □

58. Understands the basic concepts of the evolution of species. . . . . □ □ □ □ □

59. Understands basic concepts about the structure and properties of matter, including the make-up of atoms, molecules, elements, and compounds; the states of matter; the conservation of mass; and the factors and processes involved in chemical reactions . . . . . □ □ □ □ □

60. Understands the characteristics, sources, and transformations of different energy types, such as heat, light, sound, electrical, and nuclear energy . . . . □ □ □ □ □

61. Understands different types of motion, including electromagnetic motion and sound waves, and the principles that explain them, including effects of balanced and unbalanced forces . . . . □ □ □ □ □

62. Knows the kinds of forces that exist between objects and within atoms, including the characteristics and effects of magnetic, electric, electromagnetic, and gravitational forces . . . . □ □ □ □ □

63. Understands that scientific knowledge involves an ongoing process of testing, revising and occasionally discarding theories and that it is built on logical arguments, solid evidence, and skepticism . . . . □ □ □ □ □

	Definitely	Probably	Probably Not	Definitely Not	Don't Know
	▼	▼	▼	▼	▼

64. Knows that scientific inquiry involves identifying and clarifying the questions, methods, controls, and variables in scientific experiments, and that the results of scientific inquiry emerge from different types of investigations and public communication among scientists. . . . .   ☐   ☐   ☐   ☐   ☐

65. Understands that people of all ages, abilities, and backgrounds participate in the enterprise of science and that it is made up of a variety of disciplines that require the hard work of individuals and teams. . . . .   ☐   ☐   ☐   ☐   ☐

Subject IV: Behavioral Studies

For each proposed standard please indicate with an $\boxed{X}$ in the box if you think it is *definitely*, *probably*, *probably not* or *definitely not* a level of knowledge that students today should have by the time they graduate from high school. Mark *don't know* only if you really are in doubt whether or not it is an appropriate level of attainment for high school graduates.

	Definitely	Probably	Probably Not	Definitely Not	Don't Know
66. Understands that heredity, group, and cultural influences contribute to human development, identity, and behavior.	☐	☐	☐	☐	☐
67. Understands that social distinctions are a part of every culture and that they can take many different forms, such as social class based on parentage or wealth	☐	☐	☐	☐	☐
68. Understands that while a group may act, hold beliefs, and/or present itself as a cohesive whole, individual members may hold widely varying beliefs, so the behavior of a group may not be predictable from an understanding of each of its members	☐	☐	☐	☐	☐
69. Understands how the diverse elements that contribute to the development and transmission of culture (language, literature, the arts, traditions, beliefs, values, and behavior patterns) function as an integrated whole	☐	☐	☐	☐	☐
70. Understands that social groups may have patterns of behavior, values, beliefs, and attitudes that can help or hinder cross-cultural understanding	☐	☐	☐	☐	☐
71. Understands that differences in behavior of individuals arise from the interaction of heredity and experience and that even instinctive behavior may not develop well if a person is exposed to abnormal conditions.	☐	☐	☐	☐	☐

	Definitely	Probably	Probably Not	Definitely Not	Don't Know
72. Understands the basic factors that influence how human beings interpret new ideas and evaluate different types of evidence, including that people might ignore evidence that challenges their beliefs and accept evidence that supports them....................	☐	☐	☐	☐	☐
73. Understands the basic characteristics of human thinking and learning, including that the context in which something is learned may limit how that knowledge is used......	☐	☐	☐	☐	☐
74. Understands the basic social, economic, and political factors that contribute to conflicts in society; the challenges associated with these conflicts; and ways to respond to and reduce them...............................	☐	☐	☐	☐	☐
75. Understands the basic characteristics and influences of different social, political, and religious institutions in our society and how they change over time	☐	☐	☐	☐	☐
76. Understands how mass media, migrations, and conquest affect social change by exposing one culture to another, and that extensive borrowing among cultures has led to the virtual disappearance of some cultures but only modest change in others............	☐	☐	☐	☐	☐

Subject V: Technology

For each proposed standard please indicate with an ⟦X⟧ in the box if you think it is *definitely*, *probably*, *probably not* or *definitely not* a level of knowledge that students today should have by the time they graduate from high school. Mark *don't know* only if you really are in doubt whether or not it is an appropriate level of attainment for high school graduates.

	Definitely ▼	Probably ▼	Probably Not ▼	Definitely Not ▼	Don't Know ▼
77. Knows the characteristics and uses of computer hardware and operating systems, and knows how to connect to other computers and computer networks	☐	☐	☐	☐	☐
78. Knows the characteristics and uses of computer software programs, including the common features and uses of word processing, database, and spreadsheet programs	☐	☐	☐	☐	☐
79. Understands individual and social issues related to the use and development of technology, including the influences of science, technology, and society upon one another.	☐	☐	☐	☐	☐
80. Understands the nature of technological designs and is able to identify a problem, choose from among alternative solutions, implement a solution and evaluate the solution based on costs, benefits, risks, constraints, and trade-offs.	☐	☐	☐	☐	☐
81. Understands the nature and operation of systems, including how systems are monitored and controlled through the use of feedback	☐	☐	☐	☐	☐

Questionnaire 3

Thank you for agreeing to participate in the educational standards opinion survey Gallup is conducting for the Mid-continent Regional Educational Laboratory (McREL). McREL is developing educational standards that will be used by schools nationwide. In this endeavor, they would like to know your opinions about what you think are appropriate levels of attainment in different subjects for high school graduates.

The survey you have received includes four subjects: Civics, Language Arts, Life Skills, Economics. For each of these subjects, a number of levels of knowledge or attainment are proposed for high school graduates in our country. Your task will be to indicate if you think it is *definitely*, *probably*, *probably not* or *definitely not* a standard students should know or be able to do by the time they graduate from high school.

We urge you to fill out and return this IMPORTANT survey.

- Using the enclosed envelope, you will return the survey directly to The Gallup Organization for analysis and reporting.

- No individual responses will be reported and no attempt will be made to identify individual respondents.

- No one at McREL or any school will see any individual questionnaires.

- Your individual answers will be kept strictly confidential, so please freely express your opinions.

- Your responses should not be influenced by your own level of knowledge. They should be based on what you feel is appropriate for high school graduates today.

- You can give the same or different responses as you move from standard to standard.

Marking Instructions

- Use a blue or black ink pen only.
- Do not use ink that soaks through the paper.
- Make solid marks that fit in the response boxes.
- Make no stray marks on the survey.

RIGHT WAY   WRONG WAY

Please go to the next page to begin the survey

Subject I: Civics

For each proposed standard please indicate with an $\boxed{X}$ in the box if you think it is *definitely*, *probably*, *probably not* or *definitely not* a level of knowledge that students today should have by the time they graduate from high school. Mark *don't know* only if you really are in doubt whether or not it is an appropriate level of attainment for high school graduates.

	Definitely	Probably	Probably Not	Definitely Not	Don't Know
1. Understands ideas about civic life, politics, and government, including ideas about how individuals, government, and society are interrelated.	☐	☐	☐	☐	☐
2. Understands various forms of government and the relationships of limited and unlimited government to political and economic freedoms.	☐	☐	☐	☐	☐
3. Understands the sources, purposes, and functions of law	☐	☐	☐	☐	☐
4. Understands the concept of a constitution, the various purposes that constitutions serve, and the conditions that contribute to the establishment and maintenance of constitutional government	☐	☐	☐	☐	☐
5. Understands the major characteristics of systems of shared powers and of parliamentary systems, including the respective responsibilities of the legislative, executive, and judicial branches	☐	☐	☐	☐	☐
6. Understands characteristics of confederal systems of government, such as the Confederate States of America; federal systems of government, such as the United States; and unitary systems of government, such as the state governments of the United States.	☐	☐	☐	☐	☐

	Definitely	Probably	Probably Not	Definitely Not	Don't Know
7. Understands the characteristics and theories of various forms of representation, including arguments for and against representative government as distinguished from direct popular rule	☐	☐	☐	☐	☐
8. Understands the central ideas of American constitutional government and how this form of government has shaped the character of American society	☐	☐	☐	☐	☐
9. Understands the significance of fundamental values and principles of American constitutional democracy for the individual and society, including values and principles such as equality, sovereignty, and checks and balances	☐	☐	☐	☐	☐
10. Understands the characteristics of voluntarism in American society and the relationship between American voluntarism and Americans' ideas about limited government . .	☐	☐	☐	☐	☐
11. Understands the role of diversity in American life and the importance of shared values, political beliefs, and civic beliefs in an increasingly diverse American society.	☐	☐	☐	☐	☐
12. Understands the relationships among liberalism, republicanism, and American constitutional democracy	☐	☐	☐	☐	☐
13. Understands the character of American political and social conflict and factors that tend to prevent or lower its intensity	☐	☐	☐	☐	☐
14. Understands issues concerning and the reasons for the discrepancies between American ideals and the realities of American social and political life and examples of historical and contemporary efforts to reduce these discrepancies.	☐	☐	☐	☐	☐

	Definitely ▼	Probably ▼	Probably Not ▼	Definitely Not ▼	Don't Know ▼
15. Understands the reasons the framers of the U.S. Constitution adopted a federal system in which power and responsibility are divided and shared between a national government and state governments	☐	☐	☐	☐	☐
16. Understands the ways in which United States federalism is designed to protect individual rights to life, liberty, and property, including the extent to which the three branches of government (legislative, executive, and judicial) reflect the people's sovereignty	☐	☐	☐	☐	☐
17. Understands the major responsibilities of the national government for domestic and foreign policy, and understands how government is financed through taxation.	☐	☐	☐	☐	☐
18. Understands issues concerning the relationships among local, state, and national governments, including the kinds of powers reserved to the states under the Tenth Amendment.	☐	☐	☐	☐	☐
19. Understands how the rule of law and due process rights serve to protect individual rights and promote the common good	☐	☐	☐	☐	☐
20. Understands the importance of an independent judiciary in a constitutional democracy	☐	☐	☐	☐	☐
21. Understands the effects of Americans relying on the legal system to solve social, economic, and political problems rather than using other means, such as private negotiations, mediation, and participation in the political process	☐	☐	☐	☐	☐
22. Understands what is meant by "the public agenda," how it is set, and how it is influenced by public opinion and the media.	☐	☐	☐	☐	☐

	Definitely ▼	Probably ▼	Probably Not ▼	Definitely Not ▼	Don't Know ▼
23. Understands the origins, development, and characteristics of the two-party system in the United States	☐	☐	☐	☐	☐
24. Understands the roles of political parties, campaigns, elections, and associations and groups in American politics	☐	☐	☐	☐	☐
25. Understands the process by which public policy concerning a local, state, or national issue is formed and carried out	☐	☐	☐	☐	☐
26. Understands how the world is organized politically into nation-states, how nation-states interact with one another, and the related issues surrounding U.S. foreign policy	☐	☐	☐	☐	☐
27. Understands the major foreign policy positions that have characterized the United States' relations with the world, including its current leadership role in the world	☐	☐	☐	☐	☐
28. Understands the purposes and functions of major governmental international organizations (such as NATO) and major non-governmental organizations (such as the Roman Catholic Church and multinational corporations)	☐	☐	☐	☐	☐
29. Understands the impact of significant political and nonpolitical developments on the United States and other nations, including the influence that American ideas about rights have had abroad and how other peoples' ideas about rights have influenced Americans	☐	☐	☐	☐	☐
30. Understands the meaning of citizenship in the United States, and knows the requirements for citizenship and naturalization	☐	☐	☐	☐	☐
31. Understand the relationships among personal, political, and economic rights, and how these different rights can both reinforce and conflict with one another	☐	☐	☐	☐	☐

	Definitely	Probably	Probably Not	Definitely Not	Don't Know
	▼	▼	▼	▼	▼
32. Understands how certain character traits enhance citizens' ability to fulfill personal and civic responsibilities..................	☐	☐	☐	☐	☐
33. Understands the importance of political leadership, public service, and a knowledgeable citizenry in American constitutional democracy, including how participation in civic and political life can help citizens attain individual and public goals...............................	☐	☐	☐	☐	☐

Subject II: Language Arts

For each proposed standard please indicate with an $\boxed{X}$ in the box if you think it is *definitely*, *probably*, *probably not* or *definitely not* a level of knowledge that students today should have by the time they graduate from high school. Mark *don't know* only if you really are in doubt whether or not it is an appropriate level of attainment for high school graduates.

	Definitely	Probably	Probably Not	Definitely Not	Don't Know
34. Demonstrates competence in the general skills and strategies of the writing process, including the ability to draft, revise, edit, and proofread written work	☐	☐	☐	☐	☐
35. Writes different kinds of compositions (such as descriptive, persuasive, and analytical compositions) for a variety of audiences and purposes	☐	☐	☐	☐	☐
36. Demonstrates competence in the stylistic and rhetorical aspects of writing, including using vocabulary and details to support ideas and a variety of structural elements, such as paragraphs and different sentence types, lengths, and transitions	☐	☐	☐	☐	☐
37. Writes with a command of the grammatical and mechanical conventions of composition, including correct spelling, capitalization, punctuation, parts of speech, language terms, and appropriate format	☐	☐	☐	☐	☐
38. Effectively gathers and uses information for research purposes, including identifying important research questions and topics, using a variety of information sources, summarizing information, and creating bibliographies.	☐	☐	☐	☐	☐

	Definitely	Probably	Probably Not	Definitely Not	Don't Know
	▼	▼	▼	▼	▼

39. Demonstrates competence in the general skills and strategies of the reading process, including understanding influences on a reader's response to a text, using context to understand its meaning and the ability to analyze key ideas and events that may have influenced a text. . . . . ☐ ☐ ☐ ☐ ☐

40. Demonstrates competence in general skills and strategies for reading literature, such as identifying and analyzing literary elements of text (plot, literary devices, dialogue, action, and character), relating literary elements to his/her own life, and making connections among literary works . . . . ☐ ☐ ☐ ☐ ☐

41. Demonstrates competence in the general skills and strategies for reading information, such as scanning informational texts for relevant information, identifying how the material is organized and using indexes, appendixes, glossaries, and table of contents . . . . ☐ ☐ ☐ ☐ ☐

42. Demonstrates competence in applying the reading process to different types of literary texts, such as fiction, biographies, autobiographies, science fiction, poems, satires, parodies and plays. . . . . ☐ ☐ ☐ ☐ ☐

43. Demonstrates competence in applying the reading process to specific types of informational texts, such as essays, textbooks, historical documents, editorials, news stories, letters, and diaries . . . . ☐ ☐ ☐ ☐ ☐

44. Demonstrates competence in speaking and listening as tools for learning, including participating in group discussions, making effective formal presentations, and making informed judgements about nonprint media . . . . ☐ ☐ ☐ ☐ ☐

45. Demonstrates an understanding of the history of the English language . . . . ☐ ☐ ☐ ☐ ☐

	Definitely ▼	Probably ▼	Probably Not ▼	Definitely Not ▼	Don't Know ▼
46. Demonstrates an understanding of the social, political, and geographic influences on language use.........................	☐	☐	☐	☐	☐
47. Demonstrates an ability to compare different forms of the English language, such as the way it is used in a public speech compared to the way it is spoken at home or in other informal settings	☐	☐	☐	☐	☐
48. Demonstrates a familiarity with selected literary works of enduring quality, including knowing the characteristics of classic literary works and awareness of a variety of American, British and world classic literature and authors...............................	☐	☐	☐	☐	☐

Subject III: Life Skills

For each proposed standard please indicate with an $\boxed{X}$ in the box if you think it is *definitely*, *probably*, *probably not* or *definitely not* a level of knowledge that students today should have by the time they graduate from high school. Mark *don't know* only if you really are in doubt whether or not it is an appropriate level of attainment for high school graduates.

	Definitely ▼	Probably ▼	Probably Not ▼	Definitely Not ▼	Don't Know ▼
49. Understands and applies the basic principles of presenting an argument, including identifying the logic and validity of arguments, the techniques used to slant information, and the differences between fact and opinion	☐	☐	☐	☐	☐
50. Understands and applies basic principles of logic and reasoning, including understanding the formal and informal meanings of logical connectors, quantifiers, and terms; how logic is used to create and test rules, form arguments, and reach conclusions; and how to form alternative conclusions	☐	☐	☐	☐	☐
51. Effectively uses mental processes to compare, contrast, and classify persons, places, things, and events	☐	☐	☐	☐	☐
52. Understands and applies basic principles of hypothesis testing and scientific inquiry, including gathering and analyzing data, analyzing the validity of explanations and conclusions presented in studies, verifying the results of experiments, and presenting alternative explanations and conclusions to experiments	☐	☐	☐	☐	☐
53. Applies basic trouble-shooting and problem-solving techniques in real-world situations by identifying the problem, representing it accurately, evaluating various solutions and recommending and defending the selected solution	☐	☐	☐	☐	☐

	Definitely	Probably	Probably Not	Definitely Not	Don't Know
	▼	▼	▼	▼	▼

54. Applies decision-making techniques, such as using appropriate criteria, considering alternatives, and using a balance sheet or a decision-making grid or matrix to select the most appropriate alternative . . . .

	☐	☐	☐	☐	☐

55. Demonstrates the ability to contribute to the overall effort of a group through respecting other members of the group, contributing to a supportive climate in the group, engaging in active listening, identifying and using the strengths of others, taking initiative when needed, helping establish and evaluate progress toward group goals, challenging practices that aren't working, and identifying and dealing with causes of conflict in the group . . . .

	☐	☐	☐	☐	☐

56. Understands causes of conflict and conflict-resolution techniques, including the use of negotiation skills and effective responses to criticism. . . . .

	☐	☐	☐	☐	☐

57. Demonstrates the ability to work well in diverse situations and with diverse individuals, including persons who are of the opposite gender or from a different ethnic group or religious orientation. . . . .

	☐	☐	☐	☐	☐

58. Displays effective interpersonal communication skills, that is, interacts verbally and non-verbally in a clear, appropriate, and effective manner and considers the views and feelings of others when communicating. . . . .

	☐	☐	☐	☐	☐

59. Demonstrates leadership skills, that is, serves as a leader and follower in groups, passes on authority when appropriate, works with others toward planned goals and celebrates accomplishments . . . .

	☐	☐	☐	☐	☐

	Definitely	Probably	Probably Not	Definitely Not	Don't Know
	▼	▼	▼	▼	▼

60. Sets and manages goals, including carrying out the necessary steps to achieve them and making contingency plans . . . .   ☐   ☐   ☐   ☐   ☐

61. Performs self-appraisal, including identifying 1) personal attributes, experiences, accomplishments and goals; 2) career preferences and goals; and 3) acceptable wants and needs and ways in which they can be obtained . . . .   ☐   ☐   ☐   ☐   ☐

62. Demonstrates the ability to consider the risks involved in situations and seek preventive measures to avoid hazard or injury . . . .   ☐   ☐   ☐   ☐   ☐

63. Demonstrates a sense of purpose and perseverance relative to personal goals and in the face of difficulty . . . .   ☐   ☐   ☐   ☐   ☐

64. Uses techniques to maintain or improve self-image and self-esteem and keeps mistakes and criticism in perspective. . . . .   ☐   ☐   ☐   ☐   ☐

65. Controls impulsive behavior by suspending judgment and keeping responses open while assessing a situation . . . .   ☐   ☐   ☐   ☐   ☐

66. Makes effective use of basic tools by using work space effectively, working with various tools and materials to construct objects, and following instructions when using new instruments . . . .   ☐   ☐   ☐   ☐   ☐

67. Demonstrates the ability to manage money effectively, including preparing and following a budget, making forecasts regarding future income and expenses, using sound buying principles for purchases, and using credit sensibly . . . .   ☐   ☐   ☐   ☐   ☐

	Definitely	Probably	Probably Not	Definitely Not	Don't Know
	▼	▼	▼	▼	▼

68. Knows strategies for pursuing and finding a job, including determining procedures for applying for a specific job, obtaining information about the products and procedures of a prospective employer, preparing letters of inquiry or job applications, and preparing for job interviews . . . . ☐ ☐ ☐ ☐ ☐

69. Knows how to make general preparations for entering the work force, including evaluating educational opportunities and analyzing the job market, preparing a resumé, applying for necessary permits and licenses, preparing for common employment tests, knowing what factors to consider when choosing a job, and developing an explicit career action plan . . . . ☐ ☐ ☐ ☐ ☐

70. Demonstrates the ability to handle basic adult living situations, such as renting an apartment, conducting banking services, buying and maintaining a car, using health and child care services, understanding the basic nature of contracts, using a telephone and public transportation effectively, and dealing with the rules and regulations of the Internal Revenue Service . . . . ☐ ☐ ☐ ☐ ☐

71. Displays reliability and a basic work ethic, that is, completes work effectively and in a way that is acceptable to supervisors, behaves appropriately and shows loyalty and respect to authority figures and the organization, and develops plans and strategies that make personal skills more useful to an organization . . . . ☐ ☐ ☐ ☐ ☐

72. Demonstrates competence in using different information sources, including charts, diagrams, drawings, and tables. . . . . ☐ ☐ ☐ ☐ ☐

Subject IV: Economics

For each proposed standard please indicate with an $\boxed{X}$ in the box if you think it is *definitely*, *probably*, *probably not* or *definitely not* a level of knowledge that students today should have by the time they graduate from high school. Mark *don't know* only if you really are in doubt whether or not it is an appropriate level of attainment for high school graduates.

	Definitely ▼	Probably ▼	Probably Not ▼	Definitely Not ▼	Don't Know ▼
73. Understands the different types of economic resources (natural, human, and capital) and how each operates in terms of the principle of scarcity, which determines their allocation . . .	☐	☐	☐	☐	☐
74. Understands that the alternative uses of the same resource, known as opportunity cost, is the cost that occurs when a limited resource is applied to its best use.	☐	☐	☐	☐	☐
75. Understands the differences between barter and money exchange, and the advantages of money over barter.	☐	☐	☐	☐	☐
76. Understands the different types of economic systems (market and command) and how each of these systems produces, distributes, and allocates resources.	☐	☐	☐	☐	☐
77. Understands the role of economic institutions in a market system, such as corporations, labor unions, banks, and the stock market . . .	☐	☐	☐	☐	☐
78. Understands the concept of prices and the interaction of supply and demand in a market economy.	☐	☐	☐	☐	☐
79. Understands the characteristics of competition in a market system, including how it is affected by monopolies, collusion, and government regulation and why there are market failures and corrections.	☐	☐	☐	☐	☐

	Definitely ▼	Probably ▼	Probably Not ▼	Definitely Not ▼	Don't Know ▼
80. Understands the concepts of unemployment and unemployment rate, and the types and causes of unemployment as they relate to the labor force in a market economy.	☐	☐	☐	☐	☐
81. Understands income distribution in a market economy, including types of income (for example, wages and salaries, rent, interest, and profit) and factors that affect them, such as taxation, transfer payments, training programs, level of education, supply and demand for labor, and technology.	☐	☐	☐	☐	☐
82. Understands the role government plays in the United States economy, such as providing public goods and services, protecting property, and providing standards and a stable currency	☐	☐	☐	☐	☐
83. Understands the different types of taxation (federal, state, local) and the services provided by each (e.g., national defense from federal revenues, education from state and local revenues)	☐	☐	☐	☐	☐
84. Understands the difference between fiscal and monetary policy in the United States and the basic relationships between the money supply, interest rates, spending and economic growth, as well as the general ways the government responds to budget deficits and the basic role the Federal Reserve System plays in monetary policy.	☐	☐	☐	☐	☐
85. Understands the definition of Gross Domestic Product and the main factors that influence its growth or decline	☐	☐	☐	☐	☐
86. Understands the definitions of inflation and deflation, their general causes and effects, and the main policies the government uses to combat inflation.	☐	☐	☐	☐	☐

	Definitely	Probably	Probably Not	Definitely Not	Don't Know
	▼	▼	▼	▼	▼

87. Understands the basic concepts about international economics, including the characteristics of international trade, currency exchange rates and markets, barriers to trade, and the costs and benefits of trade policies . . . | ☐ | ☐ | ☐ | ☐ | ☐ |

88. Understands the role of interest rates in a market economy and their effect on savings and investment. . . . . | ☐ | ☐ | ☐ | ☐ | ☐ |

89. Understands the concept of entrepreneurship and the role of entrepreneurs in a market economy. . . . . | ☐ | ☐ | ☐ | ☐ | ☐ |

Questionnaire 4

Thank you for agreeing to participate in the educational standards opinion survey Gallup is conducting for the Mid-continent Regional Educational Laboratory (McREL). McREL is developing educational standards that will be used by schools nationwide. In this endeavor, they would like to know your opinions about what you think are appropriate levels of attainment in different subjects for high school graduates.

The survey you have received includes three subjects: Geography, The Arts, and Historical Understanding. For each of these subjects, a number of levels of knowledge or attainment are proposed for high school graduates in our country. Your task will be to indicate if you think it is *definitely*, *probably*, *probably not* or *definitely not* a standard students should know or be able to do by the time they graduate from high school.

We urge you to fill out and return this IMPORTANT survey.

- Using the enclosed envelope, you will return the survey directly to The Gallup Organization for analysis and reporting.

- No individual responses will be reported and no attempt will be made to identify individual respondents.

- No one at McREL or any school will see any individual questionnaires.

- Your individual answers will be kept strictly confidential, so please freely express your opinions.

- Your responses should not be influenced by your own level of knowledge. They should be based on what you feel is appropriate for high school graduates today.

- You can give the same or different responses as you move from standard to standard.

Marking Instructions

- Use a blue or black ink pen only.
- Do not use ink that soaks through the paper.
- Make solid marks that fit in the response boxes.
- Make no stray marks on the survey.

RIGHT WAY   WRONG WAY

Please go to the next page to begin the survey

Subject I: Geography

For each proposed standard please indicate with an ⟨X⟩ in the box if you think it is *definitely*, *probably*, *probably not* or *definitely not* a level of knowledge that students today should have by the time they graduate from high school. Mark *don't know* only if you really are in doubt whether or not it is an appropriate level of attainment for high school graduates.

	Definitely ▼	Probably ▼	Probably Not ▼	Definitely Not ▼	Don't Know ▼
1. Understands the characteristics and uses of maps, globes, and other geographic tools and technologies, including the advantages and disadvantages of using different types of maps.	☐	☐	☐	☐	☐
2. Knows the approximate location of different countries, major urban centers, and main geographic features in the world.	☐	☐	☐	☐	☐
3. Knows the approximate geographic boundaries of major contemporary and historical events, such as the boundaries of the recent Soviet Union and the spread of the bubonic plague in the 14th century	☐	☐	☐	☐	☐
4. Knows the ways in which "mental maps" influence human decisions about location, settlement, and public policy, such as locating houses in areas with scenic views and decisions to migrate based on television programs and movies or newspaper and magazine advertisements	☐	☐	☐	☐	☐
5. Understands how various factors in physical space, such as the distance between two places and the type of routes connecting them, account for patterns of movement in space, such as trade routes, migration patterns, and the number of people traveling to a given work location	☐	☐	☐	☐	☐

	Definitely ▼	Probably ▼	Probably Not ▼	Definitely Not ▼	Don't Know ▼
6. Understands how characteristics such as age, sex, employment, and income level affect the way people perceive and use space, such as the greater use of public transit by lower-income workers and the greater distances traveled on vacations by higher-income people.........	☐	☐	☐	☐	☐
7. Knows how social, cultural, and economic factors—such as the values people hold, population growth, urbanization, and technological development—shape the features and appearance of places around the world......................	☐	☐	☐	☐	☐
8. Knows the locational advantages and disadvantages of using places for different activities based on their physical characteristics, such as flood plain, forest, tundra, earthquake zone, river crossing, and coastal flood zone....................	☐	☐	☐	☐	☐
9. Understands the social, environmental, economic, and political factors that change regional boundaries, such as wars and shifts in population, and the factors that contribute to the dynamic nature of regions, such as new technology and capital investment.........	☐	☐	☐	☐	☐
10. Understands ways in which the concept of a region can be used to simplify the complexity of the Earth's space, such as arranging areas into sections to help understand particular topics or problems....................	☐	☐	☐	☐	☐
11. Knows different ways in which regional systems are structured, such as hub-and-spoke airline operations and postal service zip codes............................	☐	☐	☐	☐	☐
12. Understands why places and regions are important to individual human identity and as symbols for unifying or fragmenting society, such as Jerusalem as a holy city for Muslims, Christians, and Jews...........	☐	☐	☐	☐	☐

	Definitely ▼	Probably ▼	Probably Not ▼	Definitely Not ▼	Don't Know ▼
13. Knows ways in which peoples' changing views of places and regions reflect cultural change, such as rural settings becoming attractive as recreation areas to people living in densely populated cities and old mining ghost towns becoming tourist centers	☐	☐	☐	☐	☐
14. Knows the dynamics of the key components of the Earth's physical systems, such as the atmosphere, ocean circulation, and landforms, and how they interact and affect different regions of the world	☐	☐	☐	☐	☐
15. Knows how the Earth-Sun relationship creates the cycles of the seasons	☐	☐	☐	☐	☐
16. Understands how relationships between soil, climate, and plant and animal life affect the distribution of ecosystems, such as the effects of solar energy and water supply on the nature of plant communities	☐	☐	☐	☐	☐
17. Knows about the productivity and biodiversity of ecosystems and their potential value as sources of oxygen, food, and raw materials to all living things	☐	☐	☐	☐	☐
18. Knows the effects of both physical and human changes in ecosystems, such as how acid rain resulting from air pollution affects water bodies and forests and how the depletion of the atmosphere's ozone layer through the use of chemicals may affect the health of humans	☐	☐	☐	☐	☐
19. Knows global population issues and government policies concerning them, such as ongoing policies around the world to limit population growth	☐	☐	☐	☐	☐
20. Understands that international migrations are shaped by push and pull factors, such as political and economic conditions, religious values, and family ties	☐	☐	☐	☐	☐

	Definitely	Probably	Probably Not	Definitely Not	Don't Know
	▼	▼	▼	▼	▼

21. Understands the impact of human migrations on physical and human conditions, such as the social and environmental impact of the Dust Bowl, the environmental impact of European settlement, and the impact of migration to suburbs on transportation and housing in present American society . . . . ☐ ☐ ☐ ☐ ☐

22. Understands how human characteristics make specific regions of the world distinctive, such as the effects of early Spanish settlement in the southwestern United States and the impact of Buddhism on cultures in Southeast Asia . . . . ☐ ☐ ☐ ☐ ☐

23. Understands that the historical movement patterns of people and goods are related to economic activity, such as the patterns of trade routes in the era of sailing ships . . . . . . ☐ ☐ ☐ ☐ ☐

24. Understands the relationship between settlement patterns, economic activity, and land values, such as the effect that the location of particular types of industries and companies have on the value of the land . . . . ☐ ☐ ☐ ☐ ☐

25. Understands the distribution of different types of economies around the world, such as Singapore's market economy and North Korea's command economy, and their relative merits in terms of the social welfare and productivity of workers . . . . ☐ ☐ ☐ ☐ ☐

26. Understands the advantages and disadvantages of international economic patterns, such as how land values in an area may change due to the investment of foreign capital and the consequences of an international debt crisis . . . . ☐ ☐ ☐ ☐ ☐

27. Understands ways in which cities today differ from towns and cities in earlier times, including greater diversity and availability of products and services today . . . . ☐ ☐ ☐ ☐ ☐

	Definitely	Probably	Probably Not	Definitely Not	Don't Know
	▼	▼	▼	▼	▼
28. Understands the physical and human impact of emerging urban forms in the present day world, such as the rise of the megalopolis, edge cities, and the increasing number of ethnic enclaves in urban areas.............	☐	☐	☐	☐	☐
29. Knows the similarities and differences between settlement characteristics in developed and developing nations, such as how cities expand, their transportation patterns, and the types of services offered....	☐	☐	☐	☐	☐
30. Knows how cooperation and conflict among humans can affect the shape of political, social, and economic boundaries, such as those of countries, planning commissions, and school districts........................	☐	☐	☐	☐	☐
31. Understands the causes of boundary conflicts and internal disputes between cultural groups, such as those causing the friction between the Spanish majority and the Basque minority in Spain, and the civil war between the Hutus and Tutsis in Rwanda.................	☐	☐	☐	☐	☐
32. Understands how external forces can conflict economically and politically with internal interests in a region, such as the consequences of the French colonization of Indo-China in the 19th century and the friction between Hindus and Moslems in the Indian subcontinent.........................	☐	☐	☐	☐	☐
33. Understands how the concepts of synergy, feedback loops, carrying capacity, and thresholds relate to the limitations of the physical environment to absorb the impacts of human activity, such as levee construction on a flood plain and logging in an old-growth forest	☐	☐	☐	☐	☐

	Definitely	Probably	Probably Not	Definitely Not	Don't Know
	▼	▼	▼	▼	▼

34. Understands the role of human beings in decreasing the plant and animal life in a region, including when acid rain falls on rivers and forests and when toxic materials are dumped in oceans. ☐ ☐ ☐ ☐ ☐

35. Understands the ways in which human-induced changes in the physical environment in one place can cause changes in other places, such as the effects of a factory's airborne emissions on air quality in communities located downwind . . . . ☐ ☐ ☐ ☐ ☐

36. Understands how humans use technology and culture to overcome the "limits to growth" imposed by the physical environment. . . . . . . ☐ ☐ ☐ ☐ ☐

37. Understands how people who live in naturally hazardous regions adapt to the environment, such as erecting sea walls to protect coastal areas subject to severe storms and constructing earthquake-resistant housing in areas subject to earthquakes . . . . ☐ ☐ ☐ ☐ ☐

38. Understands programs and positions related to the use of resources locally and globally, such as community regulations for water usage during drought periods and different points of view regarding uses of the world's rain forests . . . . ☐ ☐ ☐ ☐ ☐

39. Knows issues related to the use and recycling of resources, such as those involved with the recycling of waste and the storing of toxic materials. . . . . ☐ ☐ ☐ ☐ ☐

40. Understands how geography is used to interpret the past, such as how changes in transportation affected the American West and the impact of resources and markets on the industrialization of England . . . . ☐ ☐ ☐ ☐ ☐

	Definitely ▼	Probably ▼	Probably Not ▼	Definitely Not ▼	Don't Know ▼
41. Understands why policies designed to guide the use and management of the Earth's resources should reflect multiple points of view, such as the views of both developed and developing countries.	☐	☐	☐	☐	☐
42. Understands the concept of sustainable development and its effects in a variety of situations, such as overcutting and subsequent destruction of the rain forests in Indonesia because of demand for lumber in foreign markets	☐	☐	☐	☐	☐
43. Knows common factors that affect mental maps, such as how differences in culture, life experiences, age, and gender influence people's housing preferences or their view of public life	☐	☐	☐	☐	☐
44. Understands the principles of location, such as the merits in retailing of locating in malls rather than in dispersed locations and the advantages of building factories where the geographic and economic factors (terrain, labor and transportation costs, etc.) are optimal.	☐	☐	☐	☐	☐
45. Understands how site, climatic and tectonic processes, settlement and migration patterns, and situation components have an influence on physical and cultural characteristics in different parts of the world.	☐	☐	☐	☐	☐
46. Understands the distribution of different types of climate (such as marine climate or continental climate) that are produced by processes such as air-mass circulation, temperature, and moisture	☐	☐	☐	☐	☐
47. Knows how cultures influence the characteristics of a region, such as its traditions, social institutions, and level of technological achievement	☐	☐	☐	☐	☐

Subject II: The Arts

For each proposed standard please indicate with an $\boxed{\text{X}}$ in the box if you think it is *definitely*, *probably*, *probably not* or *definitely not* a level of knowledge that students today should have by the time they graduate from high school. Mark *don't know* only if you really are in doubt whether or not it is an appropriate level of attainment for high school graduates.

	Definitely	Probably	Probably Not	Definitely Not	Don't Know
48. Understands connections among various art forms and other subjects.	☐	☐	☐	☐	☐
49. Identifies and demonstrates movement elements and skills in performing dance.	☐	☐	☐	☐	☐
50. Understands the principles behind dance arrangements	☐	☐	☐	☐	☐
51. Understands dance as a way to create and communicate meaning	☐	☐	☐	☐	☐
52. Applies critical and creative thinking skills in dance	☐	☐	☐	☐	☐
53. Understands dance in various cultures and historical periods	☐	☐	☐	☐	☐
54. Understands connections between dance and healthful living.	☐	☐	☐	☐	☐
55. Is able to sing, alone and with others, different types of music	☐	☐	☐	☐	☐
56. Performs on instruments, alone and with others, different types of music.	☐	☐	☐	☐	☐
57. Improvises musical melodies, variations, and accompaniments.	☐	☐	☐	☐	☐
58. Composes and arranges music within specified guidelines.	☐	☐	☐	☐	☐
59. Reads music that contains moderate technical demands, expanded ranges, and varied interpretations	☐	☐	☐	☐	☐

	Definitely	Probably	Probably Not	Definitely Not	Don't Know
60. Knows and applies appropriate criteria to music and music performances, such as technical musical terms and what affects the quality of musical performances	☐	☐	☐	☐	☐
61. Understands the relationships among music and history and culture.	☐	☐	☐	☐	☐
62. Demonstrates competence in writing scripts.	☐	☐	☐	☐	☐
63. Develops and uses acting skills.	☐	☐	☐	☐	☐
64. Designs and produces informal and formal theater productions.	☐	☐	☐	☐	☐
65. Directs acting scenes and organizes and conducts rehearsals for informal or formal theater productions.	☐	☐	☐	☐	☐
66. Understands how informal and formal theater, film, television, and electronic media productions create and communicate meaning.	☐	☐	☐	☐	☐
67. Understands the context in which theater, film, television, and electronic media are performed today as well as in the past	☐	☐	☐	☐	☐
68. Applies media, techniques and processes in visual arts (drawing, painting, etc.) with sufficient skill, confidence, and sensitivity that one's intentions are carried out in the artwork.	☐	☐	☐	☐	☐
69. Understands how the characteristics and structures of visual art are used to accomplish commercial, personal, community, and other artistic intentions	☐	☐	☐	☐	☐
70. Knows a range of subject matter, symbols, and potential ideas in the visual arts.	☐	☐	☐	☐	☐

	Definitely ▼	Probably ▼	Probably Not ▼	Definitely Not ▼	Don't Know ▼
71. Understands the visual arts in relation to history and cultures	☐	☐	☐	☐	☐
72. Understands the characteristics and merits of one's own artwork and the artwork of others	☐	☐	☐	☐	☐

Subject III: Historical Understanding

For each proposed standard please indicate with an ⊠ in the box if you think it is *definitely*, *probably*, *probably not* or *definitely not* a level of knowledge that students today should have by the time they graduate from high school. Mark *don't know* only if you really are in doubt whether or not it is an appropriate level of attainment for high school graduates.

	Definitely ▼	Probably ▼	Probably Not ▼	Definitely Not ▼	Don't Know ▼
73. Knows how to identify the time structure and connections disclosed in historical narratives	☐	☐	☐	☐	☐
74. Understands alternative systems of recording time—such as European, Egyptian, Indian, Mayan, Muslim, and Jewish—and the astronomical systems on which they are based, including solar, lunar, and semilunar	☐	☐	☐	☐	☐
75. Understands historical continuity and change related to a particular development or theme, such as the themes underlying the Industrial Revolution or the evolution of democracy in the U.S.	☐	☐	☐	☐	☐
76. Understands the organizing principles that are used when defining major historical periods	☐	☐	☐	☐	☐
77. Analyzes the values held by major figures who have influenced history and the role their values played in influencing history	☐	☐	☐	☐	☐
78. Analyzes the influences specific ideas and beliefs had on a period of history and understands how events might have been different in the absence of those ideas and beliefs.	☐	☐	☐	☐	☐
79. Analyzes the effects that specific "chance events" had on history and understands how things might have been different in the absence of those events	☐	☐	☐	☐	☐

	Definitely ▼	Probably ▼	Probably Not ▼	Definitely Not ▼	Don't Know ▼
80. Analyzes the effects specific decisions had on history and understands how things might have been different in the absence of those decisions.	☐	☐	☐	☐	☐
81. Understands that the consequences of human intentions are influenced by the available means for carrying them out.	☐	☐	☐	☐	☐
82. Understands that change and continuity (that is, non-change) are equally probable and likely	☐	☐	☐	☐	☐
83. Knows how to avoid seizing upon particular lessons of history as cures for present ills	☐	☐	☐	☐	☐
84. Understands that the irrational, such as the assassination of John F. Kennedy or Archduke Ferdinand, and the accidental, such as the discovery of America by Christopher Columbus, have affected past events.	☐	☐	☐	☐	☐
85. Analyzes how specific historical events would be interpreted differently based on newly uncovered records and information.	☐	☐	☐	☐	☐
86. Understands how the past affects our private lives and society in general.	☐	☐	☐	☐	☐
87. Knows how to perceive past events within the context of the culture and meaning of things at the time	☐	☐	☐	☐	☐
88. Evaluates the validity and credibility of different historical interpretations	☐	☐	☐	☐	☐
89. Uses historical maps to understand the relationships between historical events and geography.	☐	☐	☐	☐	☐
90. Knows how to evaluate the credibility and authenticity of historical sources.	☐	☐	☐	☐	☐

Content Vocabulary

Introduction: Constructing the Lists

The lists of terms and phrases that can be found in the accompanying tables are organized into 14 major subject areas. Terms and phrases within each subject area are then organized by grade-level spans. These subject areas and grade-level spans[16] parallel those found in McREL's standards database, *Content Knowledge: A Compendium of Standards and Benchmarks for K–12 Education* (2nd ed.) (Kendall & Marzano, 1997), widely recognized as the most valid and comprehensive synthesis to date of the nationally recognized documents in each of the subject areas.

In developing this list, we analyzed the information in each standard and in each benchmark to extract the key vocabulary terms and phrases. Specifically, each benchmark was analyzed to determine the principle concept or concepts it addressed. Once the concept was identified, analysts next determined whether the word or phrase that identified the concept had already been identified in the course of the analysis across all standards in all subject areas. If it was determined that the same concept or phrase had been identified previously, and thus that the term would be a duplicate entry, acceptance or deletion was determined on two criteria: If the term identified had already appeared at an earlier grade level, then the term was not added; if the subject-area context for the term did not impart any unique characteristics to the concept, it was not added. If the term was a duplicate but the subject area provided a unique context for the term, then the term was added and marked with an asterisk (*).

The exception to this convention is the broad subject area of The Arts, because of the unique nature of the components of this area. For this section only, we varied the process described above in that we did not delete a term or phrase if it was included in an earlier Arts standard. For example, the reader will note that the term *tempo* appears in Dance, Music, and Theatre. If we had strictly followed the process described above, the term would have been deleted from both Music and Theatre since the Dance standards appear first (due only to alphabetizing). It was our opinion that following

---

[16]The grade-level spans typically used are K–2, 3–5, 6–8, and 9–12; however, some variations exist due to differences in the way subject matter was organized in the national standards documents in different content areas.

such a convention would result in the deletion of key terms and phrases from Music, Theatre, and the Visual Arts, simply because Dance appears first in an alphabetized list. Terms and phrases that are listed more than once within The Arts are marked with the symbol †.

Benchmarks in all subject areas were analyzed for ancillary, or supporting material, such as examples (what we refer to as "e.g.'s," facts or concepts typically included as parenthetical material in the *Compendium*). For the subject area of Geography, we took an additional step relative to examples. If examples appeared to represent a fairly large universe of items, they were included on the list but marked to indicate their status as example terms, rather than central concepts. For example, the entry *Gateway Arch in St. Louis* (Standard 6, Grades 6–8) is marked because it represents a large, but finite class of similar items, some of which also are included on the list (e.g., *Golden Gate Bridge in San Francisco, Opera House in Sydney, Australia, Tower Bridge in London*), that exemplify the entry *cultural symbols*. Such terms were included on the list based on the presumption that they represent the most commonly known or most significant examples of the class they are intended to represent, and also because they serve to give the user a sense of the set of terms or concepts they represent. Although some terms and phrases found in other subject areas also could be viewed as examples rather than as concepts, we determined that this distinction was much clearer in Geography.

Finally, readers will note that the Language Arts section includes an appendix of literary works. The material identified on this list was specifically mentioned in the nationally recognized documents for Language Arts.

1. Problem Solving

LEVEL 1: Grades K-2
- modeling problems
- numerical problem
- problem solving
- solve*
- table (data)
- whole number

LEVEL 2: Grades 3-5
- counter example*
- diagram*
- invalid argument
- logic*
- method*
- process of elimination
- reasoning*
- solution*
- strategy*
- trial and error
- valid argument
- verify*

LEVEL 3: Grades 6-8
- deductive reasoning
- graphical
- inductive reasoning
- pictorial
- symbol*

LEVEL 4: Grades 9-12
- generalization*
- mathematical notation
- mathematical proof
- relationship
- theorem

2. Concept of Numbers

LEVEL 1: Grades K-2
- cardinal numbers
- counting
- number line
- ordinal numbers
- set
- unit

LEVEL 2: Grades 3-5
- decimal
- equivalent
- even numbers
- fraction

- mixed numbers
- odd numbers
- percent
- place value
- relative magnitude
- three-dimensional
- two-dimensional

LEVEL 3: Grades 6-8
- composite numbers
- divisibility
- exponent
- integer
- multiple
- negative (integers)
- positive (integers)
- prime numbers
- proportion
- ratio
- rational numbers
- Roman numerals
- root (square root, cube root)
- scientific notation
- square numbers
- subset

LEVEL 4: Grades 9-12
- absolute value
- binary multiplication
- discrete mathematics
- finite graph
- irrational numbers
- logarithm
- matrices
- natural numbers
- real numbers
- remainder
- sequence*

3. Computation

LEVEL 1: Grades K-2
- addition
- estimation
- inverse relationship
- subtraction

LEVEL 2: Grades 3-5
- addends
- computation
- division
- factor
- multiplication

- operation
- product
- rounding
- sum

LEVEL 3: Grades 6-8
- algorithm
- associative property
- commutative property
- computational methods
- distributive property
- identity property
- order of operations
- rate
- root-extraction
- squares and cubes

LEVEL 4: Grades 9-12
- Fibonacci sequence
- permutations and combinations
- power (exponentiation)
- radical expression
- reciprocal
- recurrence relation
- simplify

4. Measurement

LEVEL 1: Grades K-2
- distance
- height*
- length*
- measure*
- nonstandard unit
- standard unit
- temperature*
- time*
- weight*

LEVEL 2: Grades 3-5
- angle
- area
- capacity*
- circumference
- mass*
- measurement tool
- metric unit
- perimeter
- protractor
- ruler*
- volume*

*Word or phrase appears more than once.

LEVEL 3: Grades 6-8
- cubic unit
- degree of accuracy
- formula*
- grid*
- indirect measurement
- parallelogram
- precision
- significant digit
- square unit

LEVEL 4: Grades 9-12
- absolute error
- acceleration
- relative error
- surface area*
- velocity*

5. Geometry

LEVEL 1: Grades K-2
- above
- behind
- below
- between
- corner
- geometric shape
- inside
- outside
- side

LEVEL 2: Grades 3-5
- acute angle
- congruence
- cube
- dimensionality
- intersecting
- motion geometry
- obtuse angle
- parallel
- perpendicular
- polygon
- right angle
- similarity
- sphere
- symmetry

LEVEL 3: Grades 6-8
- angle bisector
- compass*
- dilation
- geometric construction
- line segment
- perpendicular bisector
- planar cross section
- Pythagorean Theorem
- rotation
- scale drawing
- straightedge
- tessellation
- translation

LEVEL 4: Grades 9-12
- arc
- chord
- cosine
- force*
- interior angle
- midpoint
- ordered pair
- polar coordinates
- proof
- scalar multiplication
- sine
- tangent
- transversal
- trigonometry
- vector
- vector addition
- velocity*

6. Statistics and Data Analysis

LEVEL 1: Grades K-2
- graph*

LEVEL 2: Grades 3-5
- bar graph
- cluster
- data*
- extreme
- gap*
- line graph
- pie chart
- sample
- spread

LEVEL 3: Grades 6-8
- bias*
- box-and-whisker plot
- central tendency
- circle graph
- conjectures*
- distribution (data)
- frequency*
- hypothesis*
- mean
- median
- mode
- outlier
- random sample
- range
- sampling error
- scatter plot
- statistic*
- stem-and-leaf plot

LEVEL 4: Grades 9-12
- central limit theorem
- confidence interval
- correlation
- quartile deviation
- randomness
- regression line
- sampling distribution
- standard deviation
- two-way table
- variability

7. Probability

LEVEL 1: Grades K-2
- prediction*

LEVEL 2: Grades 3-5
- certainty
- chance
- likely
- sample space
- uncertainty
- unlikely

LEVEL 3: Grades 6-8
- area model
- counting procedure
- experiment*
- experimental probability
- odds
- probability*
- simulation*

*Word or phrase appears more than once.

- theoretical probability
- tree diagram

LEVEL 4: Grades 9-12
- compound event
- conditional probability
- dependent event
- discrete probability distribution
- independent event
- normal curve
- random variable

8. Functions and Algebra

LEVEL 1: Grades K-2
- pattern*
- set of numbers

LEVEL 2: Grades 3-5
- equation
- horizontal axis (X-axis)
- linear pattern
- number sentence
- open sentence
- rectangular coordinate system
- repeating pattern
- variable
- vertical axis (Y-axis)

LEVEL 3: Grades 6-8
- expression*
- function
- inequality
- linear equation
- slope
- slope-intercept form
- substitution
- Venn diagram

LEVEL 4: Grades 9-12
- direct variation
- domain
- inverse variation
- polynomial equation
- sigma notation
- sinusoidal function

9. Nature and Uses of Mathematics

LEVEL 1: Grades K-2
- no new vocabulary

LEVEL 2: Grades 3-5
- no new vocabulary

LEVEL 3: Grades 6-8
- abstract idea
- mathematician

LEVEL 4: Grades 9-12
- natural science
- technology*

*Word or phrase appears more than once.

1. Features of the Earth

LEVEL 1: Grades K-2

- atmosphere*
- daily patterns
- Earth*
- form*
- gas
- ice
- liquid
- rain
- rock
- season
- short- and long-term change
- snow
- soil
- solid
- temperature*
- water*
- weather*
- weather patterns

LEVEL 2: Grades 3-5

- axis*
- cloud
- condensation
- evaporation
- fog
- fresh water
- ocean
- precipitation*
- process
- rotation*
- states (of matter)
- substance
- water droplet
- wind*

LEVEL 3: Grades 6-8

- air mass
- body (astronomical)
- circulation (of air, water)
- climate*
- climatic patterns
- component*
- composition*
- Earth's core
- Earth's layers
- emit
- energy*
- geological shift
- glacier
- hydrosphere*
- impact*

- intensity*
- lithosphere*
- mantle
- meteor
- ocean currents
- percolation
- phenomena
- plant growth
- pressure*
- principle*
- reflection*
- retention
- revolution*
- solar system
- solvent
- surface
- surface run-off
- system
- tilt
- water cycle

LEVEL 4: Grades 9-12

- decay
- density*
- energy source
- energy transfer
- external energy
- formation
- gravitational energy
- intensity*
- internal energy
- land mass
- radioactive isotope
- unequal heating
- vapor

2. Earth Processes

LEVEL 1: Grades K-2

- boulder
- pebble
- sand
- shape*
- size*

LEVEL 2: Grades 3-5

- bedrock
- breakage (of rocks)
- capacity*
- deposition*
- Earth features
- earthquake
- erosion*
- evidence*

- landslide
- mineral
- organism
- product
- rapid process
- sediment
- slow process
- texture*
- volcanic eruptions
- wave
- weathered rock
- weathering

LEVEL 3: Grades 6-8

- asteroid
- bacteria
- breaking (of layers)
- comet
- compact
- constructive forces
- crustal deformation
- debris
- destructive forces
- Earth's age
- Earth's crust
- fertility
- folding (of layers)
- fungi*
- igneous
- land form
- lithospheric plates
- metamorphic
- natural forces
- new rock
- plate motions
- plate tectonics
- recrystallize
- resistance*
- rock cycle
- sedimentary
- successive layers
- uplifting (of layers)

LEVEL 4: Grades 9-12

- carbon cycle*
- colliding plates
- convection current
- correlate
- crustal plates
- decay rate (of radioactive isotopes)
- evolution
- geochemical cycle
- geologic time scale
- internal heat

*Word or phrase appears more than once.

- modern atmosphere
- molten rock
- mountain building
- nitrogen cycle*
- one-celled organisms
- photosynthesizing organisms
- reformation
- rock sequences
- sea floor spreading
- sedimentation

3. Composition and Structure of the Universe and Earth's Place in It

LEVEL 1: Grades K-2
- brightness
- day*
- directions (cardinal)
- disperse
- month*
- Moon
- night
- sky
- stars
- Sun*

LEVEL 2: Grades 3-5
- astronomical
- constellation
- magnify
- orbit
- pattern*
- planet
- stellar distance
- telescope

LEVEL 3: Grades 6-8
- billion
- day cycle
- disk shaped
- Earth as a unique planet
- eclipse
- elliptical
- galaxy
- incomprehensible
- meteoroid
- movement patterns
- particle rings
- phases of the Moon
- satellite
- surface features

- tide
- universe
- year cycle

LEVEL 4: Grades 9-12
- accelerator
- "big bang" theory
- black hole
- blue giant
- chaotic
- Doppler shift
- electromagnetic wave
- expand
- expanding universe
- light elements
- nebular cloud
- neutron star
- nuclear fusion
- origin of the universe
- planet formation
- radio telescope
- red giant
- red shift
- scientific evidence
- simulate
- space probe
- star destruction
- star dust
- star formation
- star systems
- white dwarf
- x-ray telescope

4. Diversity and Unity that Characterize Life

LEVEL 1: Grades K-2
- animal features
- environment*
- plant features

LEVEL 2: Grades 3-5
- birth*
- death
- edible plant
- grouping
- growth and development
- life cycle*
- living thing
- nonedible plant
- reproduction

LEVEL 3: Grades 6-8
- chemical process
- classify*
- common ancestry
- consumer*
- decomposer
- ecosystem*
- external features (of organisms)
- fertile
- internal features (of organisms)
- internal structure
- invertebrate
- mate
- offspring
- producer*
- sexual reproduction
- species
- taxonomic group
- unicellular organism
- unity among organisms
- vertebrate

LEVEL 4: Grades 9-12
- degree of kinship
- DNA
- DNA sequence
- evolutionary relationship
- hierarchy
- shared derived characteristics
- subgroups*

5. Biological Characteristics

LEVEL 1: Grades K-2
- animal
- individual*
- plant
- resemble

LEVEL 2: Grades 3-5
- characteristics*
- inherit
- interaction

LEVEL 3: Grades 6-8
- asexual reproduction
- continuation (of species)
- disadvantageous characteristics
- dominant traits
- egg
- genes
- genetic diversity
- genetic variation

*Word or phrase appears more than once.

- hereditary information
- hereditary traits
- recessive traits
- sperm
- traits

LEVEL 4: Grades 9-12
- chemical properties
- chromosome
- chromosome pairs
- encode
- generation*
- heritable characteristics
- mutation
- polymer
- recombination
- replicate
- representative
- sex cells
- structural properties
- subunits of DNA (A, G, C, T)
- template

6. Structure and Function of Cells

LEVEL 1: Grades K-2
- air
- food*
- light*
- nutrients
- shelter

LEVEL 2: Grades 3-5
- function
- growth
- structure*
- survival

LEVEL 3: Grades 6-8
- cell division
- cell growth
- circulatory system
- complementary
- digestion
- digestive system
- disease*
- energy conversion
- excretion
- excretory system
- immune system*
- infection
- intrinsic failure
- movement*
- multicellular

- muscular system
- nervous system
- organ
- organ system
- reproductive system
- respiration
- respiratory system
- single celled
- tissue

LEVEL 4: Grades 9-12
- amino acids
- cell extensions
- cell membrane
- cell nucleus
- cell organelles
- cell regulation
- cell wall
- chain molecules
- chloroplast
- cytoplasm
- differentiation
- embryo
- enzyme
- excitatory molecules
- Golgi apparatus
- inhibitory molecules
- mitochondrion
- nerve
- progeny
- protein
- protein synthesis
- selective expression
- sequence (of chain molecules)
- transport
- vacuole
- waste disposal

7. Survival of Species

LEVEL 1: Grades K-2
- life
- support*

LEVEL 2: Grades 3-5
- behavior*
- behavior patterns*
- beneficial change
- detrimental change
- environmental factors
- external cue
- internal cue

LEVEL 3: Grades 6-8
- abiotic
- behavioral response
- environmental stimuli
- homeostasis
- host
- internal stimuli
- parasite
- population*
- predation
- predator
- prey
- symbiotic relationships

LEVEL 4: Grades 9-12
- depletion (of resources)
- direct harvesting
- equilibrium
- fluctuate
- human consumption
- human population growth
- interdependencies
- interrelationships
- irreversible damage
- pollution*

8. Matter and Energy in the Living Environment

LEVEL 1: Grades K-2
- resources*

LEVEL 2: Grades 3-5
- essential
- food chain*
- food web*

LEVEL 3: Grades 6-8
- conservation of matter
- oxidation
- photosynthesis
- recycle

LEVEL 4: Grades 9-12
- carbon
- carbon dioxide
- chemical elements
- chemical and physical organization
- complexity*
- disorganized state
- nitrogen
- organic compound
- sustain
- transform

*Word or phrase appears more than once.

9. Evolution

LEVEL 1: Grades K-2
- dinosaur
- fossil
- giant tree fern
- horsetail tree
- mammoth
- trilobite

LEVEL 2: Grades 3-5
- no new vocabulary

LEVEL 3: Grades 6-8
- appearance
- biological adaptation
- biological evolution
- diversification
- diversity (of species)*
- extinction
- fossil record
- geologic evidence
- physiology
- survival of the fittest

LEVEL 4: Grades 9-12
- advantageous characteristics
- anatomical characteristics
- biochemical characteristics
- capabilities
- chance
- common descent
- complex organism
- finite resources
- genetic variability
- microorganism
- natural selection
- neutral characteristics
- origin of life
- patterns of relationship
- theory of evolution

10. Structure and Properties of Matter

LEVEL 1: Grades K-2
- cooling
- dissolve
- freeze
- heating
- material
- metal*
- mix*
- properties
- weight*

LEVEL 2: Grades 3-5
- changing state
- conductivity
- density*
- graduated cylinder
- magnetism
- magnification
- mass*
- solubility
- volume*

LEVEL 3: Grades 6-8
- atom
- chemical change
- chemical reaction
- chromatography
- compound
- concentration*
- constant
- crystal
- element
- exposure
- filtering
- highly reactive metals
- highly reactive nonmetals
- less-reactive metals
- matter
- mixture
- motion of atoms (in solids, liquids, and gas)
- nonreactive gases
- particle
- physical change
- random motion
- reaction
- reaction rate
- rusting
- screening
- surface area*

LEVEL 4: Grades 9-12
- acid/base reaction
- actual mass vs. relative mass
- arrangement of atoms
- atomic mass
- atomic number
- Avogadro's hypothesis
- catalyst
- chemical bonding
- complete mole concept
- crystalline solid
- electric force
- electron
- electron configuration
- femtosecond
- greenhouse gases
- hadron
- ion
- isotope
- large molecule
- molar volume
- molecular structure
- negatively charged atom
- neutron
- nucleus of an atom
- oils
- oxidation/reduction reaction
- ozone
- periodic table
- positively charged atom
- proton
- quark
- radical reaction
- sharing electrons
- spontaneous nuclear reaction
- structure of an atom
- synthetic polymer
- transferring electrons

11. Energy Types, Sources, and Conversions

LEVEL 1: Grades K-2
- electrical circuit
- electricity*
- heat
- light*
- magnetic effect

LEVEL 2: Grades 3-5
- battery
- byproduct
- complete loop
- conduction (of heat)
- convert
- electric current
- energy form
- generator
- mechanical and electrical machines
- wire

LEVEL 3: Grades 6-8
- arrangement of atoms
- attraction (between charges)
- chemical energy
- conservation of energy
- convection

*Word or phrase appears more than once.

- disorderly motion
- elastically distorted shapes
- electrical energy
- heat energy
- infrared radiation
- mechanical energy
- mechanical motion
- molecule
- nuclear reaction
- radiation
- repulsion (between charges)
- Sun's energy
- ultraviolet radiation
- visible light
- wavelength

LEVEL 4: Grades 9-12
- atomic interactions
- endothermic reaction
- energy contained by a field
- entropy
- exothermic reaction
- fission
- fusion
- kinetic energy
- molecular motion
- potential energy

12. Principles of Motion

LEVEL 1: Grades K-2
- circular motion
- motion*
- relative position
- sound*
- straight line motion
- vibrating object
- vibration
- zigzag motion

LEVEL 2: Grades 3-5
- absorb (light)
- change direction and speed
- effect of a force
- force*
- frequency*
- measuring position over time
- pitch*
- reflect (light)
- refract (light)
- strength of a force*

LEVEL 3: Grades 6-8
- absence of force
- balanced force
- constant speed
- direction (of motion)*
- electromagnetic radiation
- friction
- graphing motion
- magnitude
- position (of an object)
- scattering (of light)
- transmission (of light)
- unbalanced force
- wavelength
- wave-like disturbance

LEVEL 4: Grades 9-12
- accelerated charged object
- changes in wavelength
- decelerated charged object
- Doppler effect
- electromagnetic spectrum
- F = ma
- gamma ray
- interaction of waves with matter
- inversely proportional
- laws of motion
- light waves
- microwave
- net force
- radio wave
- relative motion
- seismic waves
- sound waves
- speed of light
- theory of special relativity
- water waves
- x-ray

13. Kinds of Forces

LEVEL 1: Grades K-2
- magnet

LEVEL 2: Grades 3-5
- attract
- electrically charged material
- gravity
- repel

LEVEL 3: Grades 6-8
- gravitational force
- magnetic force

LEVEL 4: Grades 9-12
- atomic bomb*
- electric motor
- electrically neutral
- electromagnetic force
- hydrogen bomb
- insulator
- like charges repel
- negative charge
- nuclear force
- opposite charges attract
- positive charge
- proportional
- semiconductor
- strength of a force*
- superconductor

14. Scientific Knowledge

LEVEL 1: Grades K-2
- duplicate
- results*
- scientific investigation

LEVEL 2: Grades 3-5
- replicable results

LEVEL 3: Grades 6-8
- accepted results
- acknowledge
- conflicting interpretations
- consistent results
- core idea
- experiment*
- experimental confirmation
- interpretation*
- observational confirmation
- open communication
- process of science
- questioning
- response to criticism
- scientific idea
- tentative
- theory
- yield consistent results

LEVEL 4: Grades 9-12
- criteria*
- discarded theories
- empirical standards
- modifications (of scientific knowledge)
- openness to criticism

*Word or phrase appears more than once.

- prediction*
- public knowledge
- reporting methods and procedures
- revise theories
- rules of evidence
- scientific advancement
- skepticism*
- test theories
- validity*

15. Scientific Inquiry

LEVEL 1: Grades K-2
- balance*
- experiment*
- gather information
- learning
- magnifier
- observation
- ruler*
- thermometer
- tool*

LEVEL 2: Grades 3-5
- calculator*
- conduct experiments
- conduct investigations
- controlled experiment
- data collection
- differing interpretations
- equipment*
- extend the senses
- make results public
- microscope
- naturalistic observation
- review others' work
- scientific data
- scientific explanation
- scientific knowledge
- scientist*
- systematic observations

LEVEL 3: Grades 6-8
- alternative explanations
- analyze scientific data
- bias*
- computer hardware
- computer software
- critique explanations and procedures
- displacement
- establish relationships
- evaluate*
- examine evidence
- experimental procedures

- faulty reasoning
- formulate questions
- gather scientific data
- hypothesis*
- interpret data
- logical argument*
- logical reasoning
- mathematical model
- propose alternative explanations
- provide causes for effects
- relevant evidence
- scientific models
- scientific principles
- scientific theories
- synthesize evidence
- the scientific method
- theoretical model

LEVEL 4: Grades 9-12
- conceptual knowledge
- conceptual principles
- conditions (of an investigation)
- controls
- critical response
- design of investigation
- focus (of data)
- formula*
- historical body of scientific knowledge
- measuring instruments
- method*
- natural occurrence
- natural world
- scientific argument
- scientific communication
- test conclusions
- test predictions
- testable hypothesis
- variables

16. Scientific Enterprise

LEVEL 1: Grades K-2
- science
- share findings
- teamwork

LEVEL 2: Grades 3-5
- engineer*
- events in nature
- objects in nature
- ongoing process
- scientific contributions

- scientific inquiry*
- scientist*
- technology*

LEVEL 3: Grades 6-8
- accepted ideas
- common knowledge*
- engineering
- ethics
- fields of science
- funding for research
- habits of mind
- insight
- intellectual honesty
- motivation*
- openness to new ideas
- potential subject
- reasoning*
- research institute
- research priorities
- right to refuse to participate
- risk*
- science and society
- scientific innovators
- scientific research
- scientific settings
- skepticism*
- skill
- social priorities
- societal challenge
- tolerance of ambiguity

LEVEL 4: Grades 9-12
- biochemistry
- censorship
- discipline (of study)
- diverse cultures
- ethical traditions
- field studies
- geophysics
- levels of complexity
- peer review
- social enterprise
- truthful reporting

*Word or phrase appears more than once.

1. Chronological Relationships and Patterns

LEVEL 1: Grades K-2

- beginning*
- calendar time
- change and continuity
- day*
- end
- family history*
- historical stories
- historical time
- long ago*
- middle*
- month *
- myth*
- narrative*
- picture time line
- time*
- today
- tomorrow
- weeks
- yesterday

LEVEL 2: Grades 3-5

- century
- data*
- decade
- era*
- event*
- future
- historical development*
- local history
- past
- present*
- sequence of events
- state history *
- time line*
- years

LEVEL 3: Grades 6-8

- A.D. (Anno Domini)
- autobiography*
- B.C. (Before Christ)
- B.C.E. (Before the Common Era)
- biography*
- C.E. (Common Era)
- historical narrative
- literary narrative
- multiple tier time line
- periodize
- temporal structure

LEVEL 4: Grades 9-12

- alternative systems for recording time
- astronomical systems
- Egyptian time
- fixed points for measuring time
- historical periodization
- Indian time
- Jewish time
- lunar year
- Mayan time
- Muslim time
- semilunar calendar
- solar year*

2. Historical Perspective

LEVEL 1: Grades K-4

- no benchmarks

LEVEL 2: Grades 5-6

- author's interpretation*
- "chance events"
- historical fiction*
- norms and values
- predict*

LEVEL 3: Grades 7-8

- artifacts*
- bias*
- eyewitness account
- hearsay
- historical account
- motive*
- primary source*
- secondary source*

LEVEL 4: Grades 9-12

- accidental
- authenticity
- credibility*
- historical empathy
- historical interpretations
- historical map
- human intentions
- irrational
- lessons of history
- presentism
- validity*

*Word or phrase appears more than once.

1. Family Life

LEVEL 1: Grades K-2

- beliefs *
- celebrations
- community*
- community celebrations
- cultural heritage
- cultural traditions
- family history*
- family life
- generations*
- home*
- long ago*
- mementos
- oral traditions
- personal family heritage
- present*
- recent past
- religious observances
- roles*
- schooling experiences
- stories
- style of homes*
- technology*
- transportation
- values*

LEVEL 2: Grades 3-4

- daily life
- ethnic traditions
- farm family
- food production
- ideals
- national holidays
- national traditions
- proverbs*
- rural settings
- urban settings
- visual arts and crafts

2. Local Communities

LEVEL 1: Grades K-2

- architecture
- colonial community
- contribution*
- eastern Canada
- Far West
- goods and services*
- Hawaiian culture
- historical figures
- landscape

- Native American culture
- Old Northwest
- pioneer
- Plymouth
- Post Vincennes
- prairies
- recreation*
- San Antonio
- Southwest
- St. Augustine
- Williamsburg*

LEVEL 2: Grades 3-4

- Astoria
- Cherokee
- Chinese community in San Francisco
- economic activities*
- ethnically diverse
- founding
- free African-American communities
- historical development*
- Hopi*
- Inuit*
- Iroquois*
- Italian community in New York
- land use*
- local community
- local resources
- mining towns
- New Orleans
- Nez Perce
- perspective*
- rituals
- Sacramento
- significant events
- Sioux
- trading settlements
- urban communities

3. State/Regional History

LEVEL 1: Grades K-2

- adapt (environment)
- archaeological evidence
- early explorers
- ethnic groups
- legend*
- monuments
- motto
- myth*
- origins
- racial groups

- region*
- settlers
- slogans
- state history*
- states
- statues
- symbols*

LEVEL 2: Grades 3-4

- chronological order
- cities
- counties
- countries of origin
- environmental problems*
- first inhabitants
- geographic reasons
- geography
- population*
- rivers*
- statehood
- successive groups

4. Democratic Values

LEVEL 1: Grades K-2

- Abraham Lincoln
- American symbols
- Angel Island
- Benjamin Franklin*
- Cesar Chavez
- Clara Barton
- eagle
- Eleanor Roosevelt*
- Elizabeth Blackwell
- Ellis Island
- England
- English colonists
- equality
- fairness
- "father of our country"
- fire department
- Fourth of July*
- fraternal organizations
- Frederick Douglass*
- fundamental values
- George Washington*
- houses of worship
- human rights*
- independence
- Jackie Robinson
- Jonas Salk
- liberties
- Liberty Bell

*Word or phrase appears more than once.

- Lincoln Memorial
- Martin Luther King, Jr.*
- Martin Luther King, Jr. Day*
- Mary McLeod Bethune
- Memorial Day*
- Mt. Rushmore
- national flag
- police department
- principles of American democracy
- protection of individual rights
- responsibility for the common good
- revolutionary leaders
- Rosa Parks
- Sojourner Truth*
- Statue of Liberty*
- Susan B. Anthony
- Thomas Jefferson*
- veteran's memorials
- White House

LEVEL 2: Grades 3-4

- Betty Zane
- Bill of Rights*
- Booker T. Washington
- courage
- Declaration of Independence*
- delegate
- Emancipation Proclamation*
- equal protection of the law*
- equality of opportunity*
- freedom of expression*
- freedom of speech and religion
- Harriet Tubman*
- homeless
- James Armistead
- justice*
- Labor Day*
- Lee Iacocca
- limited government*
- low-income areas
- majority rule*
- Mayflower Compact*
- minority rights*
- moral responsibility
- national symbols
- patriotic
- persistence*
- Pledge of Allegiance*
- Presidents' Day*
- protest
- respect for others
- right to life, liberty, and the pursuit

- of happiness
- rights of the individual
- sayings
- Thanksgiving*
- truth*
- U.S. Constitution*
- Veterans Day*
- volunteering
- voting rights
- W.E.B. DuBois

5. Immigration and Migration

LEVEL 1: Grades K-2

- "on the trail"

LEVEL 2: Grades 3-4

- Black Hawk's War*
- Cherokee Trail of Tears
- Dust Bowl*
- European colonization and expansion
- forced relocation
- freed African-Americans
- immigrant groups
- immigration screening
- Indian removal
- Mexican migrant workers
- migrate
- ports of entry
- Puerto Rican migrant workers
- Spanish colonization of the Southwest
- Tecumseh

6. Regional Folklore

LEVEL 1: Grades K-2

- Brer Rabbit
- cultural history
- Davey Crockett*
- Joe Magarac
- John Henry
- Paul Bunyan
- Pecos Bill
- regional folk heroes

LEVEL 2: Grades 3-4

- American Indian Chiefs
- Billy the Kid
- cowboys
- Daniel Boone
- frontiersmen

- Geronimo
- Jedediah Smith
- mountain men
- outlaws

7. Africa, Americas, Asia, and Europe

LEVEL 1: Grades K-2

- art forms
- celebrations in England
- celebrations in Germany
- celebrations in Scandinavia
- ceremonies
- Chinese New Year
- Christmas
- Cinco de Mayo
- dance
- harvest festival
- Japanese tea ceremony
- journeys of Christopher Columbus
- journals of Marco Polo
- masks
- paintings*
- sculptures
- spring festival

LEVEL 2: Grades 3-4

- ancient Greece
- Bantu migrations of Africa
- Bering land bridge*
- bridges and aqueducts of ancient Rome
- Columbian Exchange*
- Cubans
- Eastern Hemisphere
- Egyptian pyramids
- era*
- Eric the Red
- European explorers
- Ferdinand Magellan
- Haitians
- Hanging Gardens of Babylon
- historians
- industry*
- Jacques Cartier
- matrilineal families in Africa
- medieval European city
- medieval families
- Rome
- Taj Mahal in India
- Tenochtitlan*
- Timbuktu

*Word or phrase appears more than once.

- trade
- urban centers
- Vasco de Gama*
- Vietnamese boat people
- Western Hemisphere
- written records
- Zheng He*

8. The Impact of Major Discoveries and Inventions

LEVEL 1: Grades K-2

- airplanes
- Alexander Graham Bell
- alphabets
- automobiles
- chariot*
- domesticated animals
- Erie Canal
- Galileo
- George Washington Carver
- hieroglyphics
- hot air balloons
- hunters and gatherers
- inventors
- Louis Pasteur
- Marie Curie
- marine transportation
- modern space advancements
- motorized vehicles
- nonmotorized vehicles
- pictograph
- pony express
- printing techniques
- railroads*
- satellite transmission
- scientists*
- smoke signals
- "talking drums" of Africa
- telegraph*
- telephone*

LEVEL 2: Grades 3-4

- aircraft
- aircraft carriers
- Amelia Earhart
- ancient times

- Arab dhow
- astronomical discoveries*
- basic tools
- bathyscaphs
- Braille alphabet
- British Isles
- camel caravans
- Chinese sailing vessels*
- computer*
- cuneiform
- currachs
- dugout Phoenician ships
- East Asia
- Henry Ford
- highways
- Inca*
- interstate highway system
- invention of paper*
- John Glenn
- marine vessels
- Mayan calendar
- Middle Ages
- mummification
- Muslim
- Native American canoes
- natural resource*
- Norse long ships
- Peru
- Portuguese caravel
- radio*
- railroad transportation
- rocketry
- Roman system of roads
- Sally Ride
- Southwest Asia*
- square riggers
- steam engine*
- submarines
- technological developments
- technological inventions
- television
- trade routes
- travel
- water*
- wheel*
- wind*
- workers

*Word or phrase appears more than once.

1. Americas, Western Europe, and Western Africa after 1450

LEVEL 2: Grades 5-6

- Age of Exploration
- Bering land bridge*
- Cayuga
- family organization
- hunter-gatherer*
- Iroquois*
- land use*
- linguistic diversity*
- Mohawk
- Oneida
- Onondaga
- political authority*
- pre-Columbus
- property
- property holding
- Pueblo*
- religion
- Seneca
- urban dwellers

LEVEL 3: Grades 7-8

- Catholic Church
- dissent
- European Crusades*
- European overseas exploration
- Iberia*
- institutions of capitalism
- Islam*
- Mississippian mound-building society
- religious reformers
- Western Europe

LEVEL 4: Grades 9-12

- Algonkian
- Benin*
- cross-cultural contacts
- development of urban centers
- emerging capitalist economy
- European coastal trading
- expansion of commerce
- Hopi*
- John White
- Mali
- Native American origin stories
- rise of centralized states
- Songhai
- spirit of individualism
- Theodore deBry

- trans-Saharan slave trade
- Zuni culture

2. Early European Exploration and Colonization

LEVEL 2: Grades 5-6

- American Southwest
- Aztec
- Cabeza de Vaca
- conquest of Spanish America
- Dutch explorers
- English explorers
- Francisco Vasquez de Coronado
- French explorers
- Inca*
- Spanish explorers

LEVEL 3: Grades 7-8

- Aztec empire*
- Columbian Exchange*
- Incan empire
- 1492
- price revolution
- rise of global trade

LEVEL 4: Grades 9-12

- accession of Elizabeth I
- African slave trade
- "Black Legend"
- Caribbean slaves
- enclosure movement
- encomienda system*
- European urban proletariat
- Francisco Pizarro
- Hernando Cortés
- Indian laborers
- Protestant propaganda
- Spanish conquest
- sugar trade

3. European Exploration of the Americas

LEVEL 2: Grades 5-6

- Chesapeake colonies
- European immigrants
- indentured servant
- lower South colonies
- Mid-Atlantic colonies
- New England colonies
- slave importation

LEVEL 3: Grades 7-8

- French and Indian War
- fur trade
- Seven Years War*

LEVEL 4: Grades 9-12

- chattel slavery
- Dutch West Indies
- European wars for control
- Germans
- Peace of Paris
- Puritans*
- Quakers
- Scots-Irish

4. Political, Religious, and Social Institutions in Colonial America

LEVEL 2: Grades 5-6

- Benjamin Franklin*
- Boston
- colonial self-government
- electricity*
- Enlightenment*
- French Quebec
- King James I
- Mayflower Compact*
- New York
- Philadelphia
- Puritanism
- Santa Fe
- Williamsburg*

LEVEL 3: Grades 7-8

- Anne Hutchison
- Bacon's rebellion
- Benjamin Franklin's *Autobiography*
- English Bill of Rights (1689)*
- English civil war*
- English Common Law
- Glorious Revolution
- individualism
- Magna Carta (1215)*
- participatory government
- Paxton Boys Massacre
- religious dissenters
- religious freedom
- separation of church and state
- thirteen virtues

LEVEL 4: Grades 9-12

- Carolina Regulators
- covenant community

*Word or phrase appears more than once.

- Great Awakening
- Leisler's Rebellion
- private property
- property rights*
- public education
- Roger Williams

5. Slavery and Economic Development in the Americas

LEVEL 2: Grades 5-6
- family farmer
- New England merchants
- plantation farmer
- the middle passage
- yeoman farmer

LEVEL 3: Grades 7-8
- African slavery
- Atlantic economy
- chattel racial slavery
- mercantilism*
- mother country*
- Navigation Acts
- resistance to slavery

LEVEL 4: Grades 9-12
- African cultural heritage
- South Carolina
- triangular trade*
- West Indian colonies

6. Causes of the American Revolution

LEVEL 2: Grades 5-6
- American democracy
- Declaration of Independence*
- George Washington*
- John Adams
- John Hancock
- July 4, 1776
- Lexington and Concord
- Richard Henry Lee
- Samuel Adams
- taxation without representation
- Thomas Jefferson*
- Treaty of Paris (1763)

LEVEL 3: Grades 7-8
- imperial policy
- "shot heard round the world"

LEVEL 4: Grades 9-12
- Battle of Saratoga
- French Declaration of the Rights of Man and Citizen*
- hoarding and profiteering
- inalienable rights to freedom
- John Locke
- King's Mountain
- Loyalists
- Patriots
- pro-slavery Americans
- Two Treatises on Government
- wartime inflation

7. Impact of the American Revolution

LEVEL 2: Grades 5-6
- abolitionists
- Articles of Confederation (1781)*
- Shay's Rebellion
- thirteen colonies

LEVEL 3: Grades 7-8
- Continental Congress
- Northwest Ordinance of 1787*

LEVEL 4: Grades 9-12
- 18th-century republicanism
- foreign trade
- internal trade
- judicial independence
- representation*
- separation of powers*
- service to the common good

8. Institutions Created as a Result of the Revolution

LEVEL 2: Grades 5-6
- abolition*
- Alexander Hamilton
- Bill of Rights*
- checks and balances*
- Connecticut Compromise
- Constitutional Convention
- New Jersey Plan
- U.S. Constitution*
- Virginia Plan
- Whiskey Rebellion

LEVEL 3: Grades 7-8
- Anti-Federalist
- Democratic-Republican Party
- election of 1800
- Federalist Party
- First Congress
- French Revolution*
- James Madison
- Jay's Treaty
- John Marshall
- Judiciary Act of 1789
- *Marbury v. Madison* (1803)*
- "midnight judges"
- U.S. Supreme Court
- western farmers

LEVEL 4: Grades 9-12
- Alien and Sedition Acts
- Constitution of 1787
- *Dartmouth College v. Woodward* (1819)
- distribution of power*
- Federalist
- *Gibbons v. Ogden* (1824)
- *McCulloch v. Maryland* (1819)

9. Territorial Expansion, 1801-1861

LEVEL 2: Grades 5-6
- Cherokee removal
- Chickasaw removal
- Choctaw removal
- Creek removal
- Davey Crockett*
- James Monroe
- Jim Bowie
- Louisiana Territory
- Manifest Destiny
- Mexican-American War
- Monroe Doctrine*
- Napoleon Bonaparte*
- Sam Houston
- Seminole removal
- Texas War for Independence (1836)
- the Alamo
- Trail of Tears
- Treaty of Guadalupe Hidalgo (1848)
- War of 1812

LEVEL 3: Grades 7-8
- Black Hawk War
- Britain*
- Lewis and Clark expedition

*Word or phrase appears more than once.

- Louisiana Purchase
- removal policies
- Russia

LEVEL 4: Grades 9-12
- assimilation
- isolation
- James K. Polk
- Lone Star Republic
- Northwest Territory
- Texas Revolution (1836-1845)

10. Impact of Industrial Revolution, Westward Expansion, and the Expansion of Slavery

LEVEL 2: Grades 5-6
- active resistance to slavery
- "American Museum"
- antebellum period
- canal system
- cotton gin
- escaped slaves
- factory system
- frontier
- immigration
- Know-Nothing party
- minstrel shows
- Mormon
- nativist movement
- New England mill town
- passive resistance to slavery
- plantation owners
- P.T. Barnum
- railroad system
- spinning jenny
- steam locomotive
- telegraph*
- Underground Railroad
- urbanization*
- western migration
- western territories

LEVEL 3: Grades 7-8
- child labor
- Church of Latter Day Saints
- enslaved
- free black communities
- Haitian revolution*
- industrialization*
- labor movement

- national bank
- plantation system*
- protective tariffs
- racial hostility
- slave holders
- trans-Mississippi region

LEVEL 4: Grades 9-12
- African-American communities
- Andrew Jackson
- Bank Recharter Bill of 1832
- capitalistic institutions
- economic depression of 1819
- economic depression of 1837
- economic depression of 1857
- freed slaves
- industrial revolution*
- market revolution
- Mormon migration to the West
- Old Hickory
- Second Great Awakening
- slave revolts

11. Political Democracy After 1800

LEVEL 2: Grades 5-6
- "common man"
- disenfranchisement
- Missouri Compromise of 1820
- "spoils system"
- suffrage*
- universal white male suffrage

LEVEL 3: Grades 7-8
- bank recharter
- Compromise of 1850
- Democrats
- electoral qualifications
- nullification
- sectionalism
- states' rights
- tariff policy
- Whig party

LEVEL 4: Grades 9-12
- anti-slavery advocates
- National Democratic party
- National Republican party
- proslavery

12. Antebellum Reform Movements

LEVEL 2: Grades 5-6
- reform movements
- religious revival
- women's rights

LEVEL 3: Grades 7-8
- "Declaration of Sentiments" of 1848
- Seneca Falls Convention
- temperance
- women's suffrage

LEVEL 4: Grades 9-12
- evangelical movement
- evangelical Protestants
- gender roles*
- legal rights
- southern women
- Transcendentalism
- Utopian

13. Causes of the Civil War

LEVEL 2: Grades 5-6
- agricultural economy
- Civil War
- industrial North

LEVEL 3: Grades 7-8
- Dred Scott decision
- free labor system
- James Buchanan
- Northern "free labor" ideology
- secession

LEVEL 4: Grades 9-12
- American party system
- Kansas-Nebraska Act
- Wilmot Proviso

14. Course of the Civil War and its Effects on the American People

LEVEL 2: Grades 5-6
- Antietam
- Battle of Bull Run
- Chattanooga
- Confederacy
- Emancipation Proclamation*
- Fort Sumter

*Word or phrase appears more than once.

- Fredericksburg
- General Robert E. Lee
- Manassas
- Shiloh
- Union
- Vicksburg

LEVEL 3: Grades 7-8
- African-American Union soldiers
- conscription
- divided loyalties

LEVEL 4: Grades 9-12
- "Five Civilized Tribes"
- General Ulysses S. Grant
- Gettysburg Address*
- "hammering campaigns"
- Jefferson Davis
- New York City draft riots of July 1863
- Union Army
- William T. Sherman
- writ of habeas corpus

15. Reconstruction

LEVEL 2: Grades 5-6
- Andrew Johnson
- "Black Reconstruction"
- Fifteenth Amendment
- Fourteenth Amendment*
- Freedmen's Bureau
- political cartoon*
- Reconstruction
- Thirteenth Amendment

LEVEL 3: Grades 7-8
- Compromise of 1877
- Congressional authority
- impeachment*
- Reconstruction Amendments
- Tenure of Office Act

LEVEL 4: Grades 9-12
- amnesty
- citizenship
- corruption
- "due process"
- "equal protection of the laws"
- pardon
- Radical Republicans
- redeemers

16. Transformation of American Society

LEVEL 2: Grades 5-6
- farming
- frontier
- Great Plains
- mining*
- ranching

LEVEL 3: Grades 7-8
- American Dream
- American Northeast
- American South
- American West
- conservation movement
- environmentalism
- extractive mining
- farm organizations
- gridiron pattern
- philanthropists
- rapid industrialization
- rapid urbanization
- urban political machine

LEVEL 4: Grades 9-12
- crop lien system
- demographic*
- environmental damage
- federal Indian policy
- federal land policy
- federal water policy
- racial roles
- redistribution of wealth
- staple crop production
- strip mining*
- urban bosses
- western buffalo herds

17. Immigration After 1870

LEVEL 2: Grades 5-6
- American culture
- anti-Chinese movement
- Asian Americans
- Hispanic Americans
- Jim Crow laws
- leisure activities
- lynching
- popular culture

LEVEL 3: Grades 7-8
- Catholic immigrants
- discrimination*
- Jewish immigrants
- regional artists and writers
- Social Darwinism*

LEVEL 4: Grades 9-12
- American ideals
- American values
- equal rights and opportunities
- mainstream America
- parochial school
- public education
- public policy*
- public school
- racial inequality
- Victorianism
- voluntary organizations

18. American Labor Movement

LEVEL 2: Grades 5-6
- coal mine strikes
- 1896 election
- labor conflict
- Mother Mary Jones
- political cartoon*
- Thomas Nast

LEVEL 3: Grades 7-8
- business regulations
- civil service reform
- monetary policy*
- political reform
- Populism
- Populist party
- Socialist party
- tariffs*

LEVEL 4: Grades 9-12
- big business
- "Cross of Gold" speech
- depression of 1873-1879
- depression of 1893-1897
- election of 1896
- "full dinner pail"
- Greenback Labor party
- labor conflicts of 1894
- male-dominated jobs
- Mark Hanna
- Omaha Platform of 1892
- radicalism
- trade unions

*Word or phrase appears more than once.

- William Jennings Bryan
- William McKinley
- workforce

19. Post-Civil War Indian Policy and Foreign Policy

LEVEL 2: Grades 5-6
- Native American land holdings
- reservations
- "second great removal"
- Spanish-American War*

LEVEL 3: Grades 7-8
- Cuba
- Dawes Severalty Act of 1887
- Filipino insurrection
- missionaries*
- Philippine annexation
- tribal identity

LEVEL 4: Grades 9-12
- Emilio Aguinaldo
- geopolitics
- nationalism*
- 19th-century artists
- Protestant missionary zeal
- racial ideology

20. The Progressive Movement

LEVEL 2: Grades 5-6
- Eighteenth Amendment
- moral reform
- Progressive Era
- Progressive idea of democracy
- Progressive movement
- settlement houses
- Seventeenth Amendment
- Sixteenth Amendment*
- social reform*
- Theodore Roosevelt
- William H. Taft
- Woodrow Wilson

LEVEL 3: Grades 7-8
- "Americanization"
- Charles Evans Hughes
- election of 1912
- Hiram Johnson
- Industrial Workers of the World
- New Freedom

- New Nationalism
- Progressivism
- Robert La Follette

LEVEL 4: Grades 9-12
- Carrie Chapman Catt
- International Ladies Garment Workers Union
- NAACP*
- National Women's Suffrage Association
- new nativism
- Nineteenth Amendment

21. U.S. Foreign Policy through World War I

LEVEL 2: Grades 5-6
- Allied Powers
- Allied victory
- American Expeditionary Force
- Central Powers*
- League of Nations*
- neutrality
- 1914
- Open Door Policy
- Panama Canal
- Versailles Treaty
- Woodrow Wilson's Fourteen Points*
- World War I*

LEVEL 3: Grades 7-8
- big stick diplomacy
- chemical warfare
- dollar diplomacy
- economic mobilization
- "Gentleman's Agreement"
- industrial research
- military mobilization
- Russian Revolution of 1917*
- system of alliances

LEVEL 4: Grades 9-12
- civil liberties
- "Great Migration"
- Mexican Revolution*
- moral diplomacy
- neutral nations
- Panama Revolution of 1903
- propaganda campaigns
- Roosevelt Corollary
- spirit of disillusionment

22. Changes in U.S. Culture Between World War I and Depression

LEVEL 2: Grades 5-6
- amusement parks
- assembly lines
- electrification
- elevators
- "Golden Door"
- Harlem Renaissance
- household appliances
- leisure time
- mass culture*
- media*
- national parks
- nativism
- 1920s
- professional sports*
- prohibition
- rapid transit
- steel construction
- suburbs

LEVEL 3: Grades 7-8
- Calvin Coolidge
- Equal Rights Amendment
- Garvey Movement
- Herbert Hoover
- Ku Klux Klan*
- labor policies
- "Lost Generation"
- mass advertising
- modern corporation
- Scopes trial
- social realists
- spheres of influence
- Warren G. Harding

LEVEL 4: Grades 9-12
- civic center
- consumer culture
- jazz*
- "New Klan"
- new paternalism
- "New Woman"
- "Red Scare"
- Sacco and Vanzetti trial
- secondary education
- Victorian values

*Word or phrase appears more than once.

23. Causes of Great Depression

LEVEL 2: Grades 5-6
- Dust Bowl*
- Great Depression*
- stock market crash of 1929
- tenants

LEVEL 3: Grades 7-8
- ethnic minorities
- racial minorities
- white sharecroppers

LEVEL 4: Grades 9-12
- no new vocabulary

24. New Deal

LEVEL 2: Grades 5-6
- "court packing" proposal
- Franklin D. Roosevelt
- New Deal

LEVEL 3: Grades 7-8
- Dr. Francis Townsend
- Eleanor Roosevelt*
- Roosevelt coalition
- Senator Huey Long
- "Share the Wealth" program
- Tennessee Valley
- Townsend Plan
- Works Progress Administration
- WPA projects

LEVEL 4: Grades 9-12
- Agricultural Adjustment Act
- American Federation of Labor
- CIO (Committee for Industrial Organization)
- civil rights*
- Civil Works Administration
- Civilian Conservation Corps
- EPIC
- Federal Emergency Relief Administration
- "fireside chats"
- Indian Reorganization Act of 1934
- John Collier
- National Industrial Recovery Act
- National Recovery Administration
- nonunion workers
- Public Works Administration
- Rural Electrification Administration

- Second New Deal
- Tennessee Valley Authority Act

25. Causes and Course of World War II

LEVEL 2: Grades 5-6
- Axis Powers
- December 7, 1941
- European theater
- General Douglas MacArthur
- internment of Japanese Americans
- national aggression
- North Africa
- Pacific theater
- Pearl Harbor
- World War II

LEVEL 3: Grades 7-8
- Adolf Hitler
- atomic bomb*
- "Battle for Britain"
- communism
- fascism*
- final solution
- genocide
- Harry S. Truman
- Holocaust
- Jewish refugees
- national socialism
- Nazi
- Nazi-Soviet Non-Aggression Pact of 1939*
- Normandy Invasion
- United Nations*

LEVEL 4: Grades 9-12
- Communist Party
- D-Day
- East Asian Co-Prosperity Sphere
- Four Freedoms Speech
- Good Neighbor Policy
- November 10 proposal
- rationing
- relocation centers
- V-E Day
- war bonds
- War Powers Act of March 1942

26. Post-War Society

LEVEL 2: Grades 5-6
- G.I. Bill*
- sustained economic growth
- U.S. space program

LEVEL 3: Grades 7-8
- demobilization
- middle class
- professional sectors
- reconversion
- white collar

LEVEL 4: Grades 9-12
- affluence
- baby boom generation
- Cold War*
- "crabgrass frontier"
- gap*
- income gap
- poverty
- suburbanization*

27. Cold War, Vietnam, and Korea

LEVEL 2: Grades 5-6
- Eastern Europe
- "flawed peace"
- Israel*
- U.S. foreign policy
- Vietnam War

LEVEL 3: Grades 7-8
- Chinese Revolution
- containment policy
- Dwight D. Eisenhower
- dynamic conservatism
- Eisenhower Doctrine
- John F. Kennedy
- Korean War*
- Lyndon B. Johnson
- Marshall Plan*
- Paris Peace Accord of 1973
- Richard Nixon
- Soviet Union*
- Truman Doctrine

LEVEL 4: Grades 9-12
- anti-colonial movements
- "atomic diplomacy"
- Bay of Pigs
- British mandate over Palestine
- Cuban missile crisis*
- Grand Alliance
- "self-determination"

*Word or phrase appears more than once.

28. Post-War Domestic Policy

LEVEL 2: Grades 5-6
- Camelot images
- Jacqueline Kennedy
- "New Frontier"

LEVEL 3: Grades 7-8
- desegregation
- Fair Deal
- Great Society
- Kennedy assassination
- loyalty programs
- McCarthyism
- "Modern Republicanism"
- 1960 presidential campaign
- second environmental movement
- Senator Joseph McCarthy

LEVEL 4: Grades 9-12
- anti-communist movements
- Civil Rights Act of 1964
- liberalism*
- War on Poverty

29. Civil Rights Movement

LEVEL 2: Grades 5-6
- *Brown v. Board of Education* (1954)*
- "civil disobedience"
- freedom of religion*
- "freedom rides"
- Martin Luther King, Jr.*
- Martin Luther King's "I Have a Dream" speech*
- National Organization for Women
- "nonviolent resistance"
- Warren Court
- women's movement

LEVEL 3: Grades 7-8
- Black Power
- counter-feminist organizations
- *de facto* segregation
- *de jure* segregation
- *Engel v. Vitale* (1962)
- Little Rock, 1957
- Malcolm X
- modern feminism
- segregation

LEVEL 4: Grades 9-12
- Asian Civil Rights Movement
- due process rights*
- farm labor movement
- La Raza Unida
- Native American Civil Rights Movement
- "one man, one vote"
- *Plessy v. Ferguson* (1896)
- *Roe v. Wade* (1973)
- Title VII

30. Foreign and Domestic Policy, Nixon through Clinton

LEVEL 2: Grades 5-6
- George Bush
- Gerald Ford
- Jimmy Carter
- "law and order"
- "New Federalism"
- "Reagan Revolution"
- Ronald Reagan
- "Silent Majority"
- Watergate

LEVEL 3: Grades 7-8
- arms limitations
- Bill Clinton
- Camp David Accords
- "closed shop"
- detente
- "featherbedding"
- Iranian hostage crisis
- "open shop"
- People's Republic of China
- "right to work"
- supply-side economics

LEVEL 4: Grades 9-12
- Desert Storm
- energy crisis
- "evil empire"
- human rights*
- "imperial presidency"
- inflation*
- Iran-Contra affair
- Kuwait
- national debt*
- Persian Gulf
- recession*
- "southern strategy"

31. Contemporary Economic, Social, and Cultural Issues

LEVEL 2: Grades 5-6
- computer revolution
- entertainment
- interest groups
- religious diversity
- spectator sports

LEVEL 3: Grades 7-8
- Christian evangelical movement
- desegregation of schools
- disabled
- labor force*
- mainstream culture and society
- racial and ethnic minorities
- "Rust belt"
- service industries*
- "Sun belt"

LEVEL 4: Grades 9-12
- abortion
- bilingual education
- career choices
- demographic and residential mobility
- Gay Liberation Movement
- gay rights
- global trade and competition
- income disparities
- migration patterns
- multiculturalism
- new technology
- religious evangelism
- rights of the disabled
- stagnation of wages
- traditional American family
- TV shows
- women in the clergy

*Word or phrase appears more than once.

1. Earliest Human Communities

LEVEL 2: Grades 5-6
- Africa
- Americas
- anthropological discoveries
- Cro-Magnon
- Eurasia
- hominid evolution
- hunter-gatherer*
- Neanderthal

LEVEL 3: Grades 7-8
- *Australopithecines*
- *Homo erectus*
- Ice Age
- *Homo sapiens sapiens*

LEVEL 4: Grades 9-12
- burials
- carvings
- Mesolithic
- nonhominid
- nonverbal evidence
- primate

2. Agricultural Societies

LEVEL 2: Grades 5-6
- agrarian communities
- agricultural communities
- fishing communities
- tropical agriculture

LEVEL 3: Grades 7-8
- food plant domestication
- human social development
- world-wide settlement patterns

LEVEL 4: Grades 9-12
- animal domestication
- female deity worship
- Neolithic revolution
- sedentary agriculture
- subsistence methods

3. Mesopotamia, Egypt, and the Indus Valley

LEVEL 2: Grades 5-6
- Egypt
- Indus Valley
- Mesopotamia*
- Nile Valley*
- Nubia
- Southwest Asian civilization
- Tigris-Euphrates Valley

LEVEL 3: Grades 7-8
- Epic of Gilgamesh
- Great Plague
- Greco-Roman antiquity
- Italian Humanism
- Samarkand
- Timur the Lame [Tamerlane]
- Zheng He maritime expeditions

LEVEL 4: Grades 9-12
- Babylon
- biblical account of Genesis
- Black Death
- Boccaccio
- centralized monarchies
- code of Hammurabi
- cremation of Strasbourg Jews
- "Great Schism"
- Hongwu emperor
- Indus trade network
- Jewish scapegoating
- Joan of Arc
- pogroms in the Holy Roman Empire
- pre-Yuan Empires

4. Agrarian Societies and New States in the Third and Second Millennia BCE

LEVEL 2: Grades 5-6
- ancestor worship
- bronze tool-making technology
- Chinese civilization
- Huang He [Yellow River] civilization
- Mediterranean basin
- megalithic stone buildings
- Pharaoh
- Shang Dynasty
- Stonehenge

LEVEL 3: Grades 7-8
- bow and arrow
- Crete
- gender roles*
- Minoan civilization
- plow
- pottery*
- urban societies

LEVEL 4: Grades 9-12
- Aegean Basin
- Minoan trade
- sail
- social hierarchy
- weaving
- wheel*

5. Eurasia in the Second Millennium BCE

LEVEL 2: Grades 5-6
- Central Asian steppes
- chariot*
- kinship-based pastoral society
- Mycenaean Greek society
- siege of Troy

LEVEL 3: Grades 7-8
- Anatolia
- Aryan culture
- Hittite people
- Indo-Aryan-speaking peoples
- Indo-European language*
- Indo-Gangetic plain
- Indus cities
- Iranian Plateau
- Middle Kingdom
- Mycenaean-speaking peoples
- New Kingdom*
- Old Kingdom
- Queen Hatshepsut
- Ramses II
- Thutmose III
- Trojan war
- Vedas
- Vedic gods

*Word or phrase appears more than once.

LEVEL 4: Grades 9-12
- Akenaton [Amenhotep IV]
- Atonism
- Iliad
- Mahabarata
- monotheism
- Odyssey
- Ramayana*
- Sumerians
- Vedic hymns

6. Eurasia and Africa, 4000 to 1000 BCE

LEVEL 2: Grades 5-6
- no new vocabulary

LEVEL 3: Grades 7-8
- Neolithic agricultural societies

LEVEL 4: Grades 9-12
- aristocratic power
- state authority
- taxation systems

7. Technological Innovation and Cultural Change, 1000 to 600 BCE

LEVEL 2: Grades 5-6
- Aegean region
- Babylonian Captivity
- Carthage
- cavalry warfare
- Greek city-states
- Hebrew Scriptures
- Jewish monotheism
- Judaism
- Kushite society
- New Kingdom*
- nomadic societies
- pastoral nomadism
- Phoenicia
- polytheism
- Southwest Asia*

LEVEL 3: Grades 7-8
- Assyrian Empire
- Babylonian Empire
- iron-making technology
- kingdom of Askum
- Meroitic period

- Northern Africa
- Scythian society

LEVEL 4: Grades 9-12
- Jewish diaspora
- West Africa

8. Aegean Civilization, the Eastern Mediterranean, and Southwest Asia, 600 to 200 BCE

LEVEL 2: Grades 5-6
- Alexander of Macedon
- Athenian democracy
- Classical Greek art and architecture
- Cyrus I
- Greek myths
- Persian Empire
- Persian Wars
- Socrates
- Spartan military aristocracy

LEVEL 3: Grades 7-8
- Athenian society
- Cleisthenes
- creation myths of Babylon
- creation myths of Egypt
- creation myths of Greece
- creation myths of Sumer
- Darius the Great
- Hellenistic period
- Solon

LEVEL 4: Grades 9-12
- Herodotus
- Plato's *Republic*
- Rabbinic Judaism
- Zoroastrianism

9. Empires in the Mediterranean Basin, China, and India, 500 BCE to 300 CE

LEVEL 2: Grades 5-6
- Apostle Paul
- Ashoka
- Augustus*
- Buddhism*
- Cicero
- Cincinnatus

- Confucianism
- Confucius
- Constantine
- Daoism
- Italian peninsula
- Jesus of Nazareth
- Julius Caesar
- Nero
- New Testament
- Pompeii
- Qin emperor Shi Huangdi
- Roman Empire
- Roman Republic
- Rome
- Scipio Africanus
- silk roads
- Tiberius Gracchus

LEVEL 3: Grades 7-8
- Brahmanism
- Chandragupta
- Gangetic states
- Han Empire
- Hebrew Torah
- "Mandate of Heaven"
- Mauryan Empire
- nirvana
- Quin Empire
- Shang Empire
- Upanishad
- Zhou Dynasty

LEVEL 4: Grades 9-12
- Greek language
- Latin language
- Ramayana*
- Roman Constitution

10. Agrarian Civilizations in Mesoamerica

LEVEL 2: Grades 5-6
- Olmec civilization
- Mesoamerica

LEVEL 3: Grades 7-8
- no new vocabulary

LEVEL 4: Grades 9-12
- Mayan civilization
- Zapotec civilization

*Word or phrase appears more than once.

11. Global Trends, 1000 BCE to 300 CE

LEVEL 2: Grades 5-6
- Afro-Eurasia
- coerced labor
- cultural integration
- slavery

LEVEL 3: Grades 7-8
- belief systems*
- classical civilizations
- communications networks
- economic integration
- legal codes
- merchant communities
- military power
- state bureaucracy
- state power
- trade networks
- tributary systems of production
- written languages

LEVEL 4: Grades 9-12
- interregional contacts

12. Imperial Crises, 300 to 700 CE

LEVEL 2: Grades 5-6
- Brahma
- caste system
- dharma
- Gupta era
- Hinduism
- karma
- reincarnation
- ritual sacrifice

LEVEL 3: Grades 7-8
- Ammianus
- Indonesian archipelago
- Malayo-Polynesia
- missionary activity
- monastic life
- nomadic invasions
- universal salvation

LEVEL 4: Grades 9-12
- Chandragupta II
- Germanic peoples
- Hun invasions
- Indian concept of ideal kingship

13. Islamic Civilization, 700 to 1000 CE

LEVEL 2: Grades 5-6
- Abbasid era
- Arabian peninsula
- Baghdad
- Byzantium
- daily Islamic prayer [Salat]
- Hajj
- invention of paper*
- Islam*
- Islamic law
- Muhammad
- Muslim culture
- Qur'an
- Ramadan
- Sunnah

LEVEL 3: Grades 7-8
- Bulgar invaders
- Iberia*
- Sassanids
- Syria

LEVEL 4: Grades 9-12
- Arab Caliphate
- Arabia
- Balkans
- Battle of Tours of 733
- Constantinople
- Greek Orthodox Christianity
- Latin Christianity
- Russian Chronicle
- Sassanid Persian Empires
- Slavic world
- Sunni and Shi'ite factions
- Ukraine
- Umyyad Dynasty
- Vladimir of Kiev

14. Tang Dynasty, 600 to 900 CE

LEVEL 2: Grades 5-6
- court of Heian
- Great Canal of China
- imperial Japanese society
- Korea
- monsoon winds*
- Straits of Malacca
- Tang Dynasty

LEVEL 3: Grades 7-8
- China's colonization of Vietnam
- Shinto

LEVEL 4: Grades 9-12
- Chinese writing system

15. Europe, 500 to 1000 CE

LEVEL 2: Grades 5-6
- Black Sea
- Britain*
- Charlemagne
- Christianizing of Western and Central Europe
- Ireland
- King Alfred of England ["Alfred the Great"]
- monks
- Norse Explorations
- Norse invasions
- Norse migrations
- nuns

LEVEL 3: Grades 7-8
- Carolingian Empire
- Clothilde
- Clovis
- convent
- Greenland
- Medieval Europe
- monastery
- Newfoundland
- Rules of St. Benedict
- Saxon peoples
- secular leaders

LEVEL 4: Grades 9-12
- Anglo-Saxon Boniface
- Charlemagne's empire
- counts
- dukes
- Frankish Empire
- hereditary, autonomous power
- Latin Catholic and Byzantine churches
- missionaries*
- "Romanization of Europe"
- Viking longboat

*Word or phrase appears more than once.

16. Africa and Oceania

LEVEL 2: Grades 5-6
- New Zealand
- Oceania
- Pacific Islands
- tropical Africa

LEVEL 3: Grades 7-8
- Ghana empire
- griot "keeper of tales"
- Niger River
- state-building

LEVEL 4: Grades 9-12
- Bantu-speaking peoples
- Jenne-jeno
- Kumbi-Saleh

17. Mesoamerica, Andean South America in the First Millenium CE

LEVEL 2: Grades 5-6
- Andean South America
- Mayan monumental architecture
- Mayan pyramids
- Moche civilization
- Teotihuacan civilization

LEVEL 3: Grades 7-8
- Andean societies
- kinship groups
- Mayan city-states
- Oaxaca
- regulated family and community life

LEVEL 4: Grades 9-12
- Mayan deities
- Mayan world view

18. Global Trends, 300 to 1000 CE

LEVEL 2: Grades 5-6
- Buddhism
- Christianity
- Hinduism
- Islam

LEVEL 3: Grades 7-8
- Muslim civilization
- Sub-Saharan Africa*

LEVEL 4: Grades 9-12
- no benchmarks

19. Cultural Exchange in Asian and Islamic Societies, 10th-13th Centuries

LEVEL 2: Grades 5-6
- Ashikaga periods
- Indian Ocean*
- Japanese feudal society
- Mongol invasions
- Song Dynasty

LEVEL 3: Grades 7-8
- Angkor
- Cairo*
- Champa
- neo-Confucianism
- Turkestan
- Turkic migration

LEVEL 4: Grades 9-12
- Angkor Wat
- Cambodia
- Christian Crusades
- Damascus
- North African Islamic reform movements
- samurai
- Sicily
- Sufism
- Vietnamese independence from China

20. European Society and Culture, 1000 to 1300 CE

LEVEL 2: Grades 5-6
- Battle of Hastings
- chivalry
- courtly love
- European Crusades*
- feudalism
- manorialism
- medieval English legal and constitutional practice
- medieval universities
- serfdom
- William the Conqueror

LEVEL 3: Grades 7-8
- Early Middle Ages
- feudal lords
- High Middle Ages
- Norman conquest
- Reconquest of Spain
- representative institutions
- Roman Catholic Church
- secular states
- Spanish Muslim society

LEVEL 4: Grades 9-12
- anti-Semitism
- Aristotle
- English Parliament*
- French Estates-General
- Genoa
- Italian city-state
- knights
- Magna Carta (1215)*
- Plato
- Venice

21. Mongol Empire

LEVEL 2: Grades 5-6
- Chinggis Khan
- Mongol Empire

LEVEL 3: Grades 7-8
- Batu
- "Golden Horde"
- Mongol conquests

LEVEL 4: Grades 9-12
- Marco Polo
- "Pax Mongolica"

22. Sub-Saharan Africa, 11th-15th Centuries

LEVEL 2: Grades 5-6
- Benin*
- Ile-Ife
- Mali Empire
- Solomon
- Songhay Empire
- trans-Saharan caravan trade

*Word or phrase appears more than once.

LEVEL 3: Grades 7-8
- Bantu state of Great Zimbabwe
- Christian Ethiopian kingdom
- Coptic Christians
- Zagwe Dynasty

LEVEL 4: Grades 9-12
- Ethiopian rock churches
- Swahili

23. Afro-Eurasia, 1300 to 1450

LEVEL 2: Grades 5-6
- capture of Constantinople in 1453
- Hundred Years War
- Ottoman Empire
- plague

LEVEL 3: Grades 7-8
- no new vocabulary

LEVEL 4: Grades 9-12
- no new vocabulary

24. Civilizations and States in the Americas, 1000 to 1500

LEVEL 2: Grades 5-6
- Aztec Empire*
- Aztec "Foundation of Heaven"
- Incan society
- Tenochtitlan*

LEVEL 3: Grades 7-8
- Anasazi
- Machu Picchu
- North American mound-building peoples
- North American plains
- Pueblo*
- Southwestern deserts
- Toltecs
- tropical forests of the Yucatan

LEVEL 4: Grades 9-12
- Cuzco
- mound centers in the Mississippi valley

25. Global Trends, 1000 to 1500 CE

LEVEL 2: Grades 5-6
- long-distance trade routes in the "Southern Seas"

LEVEL 3: Grades 7-8
- no new vocabulary

LEVEL 4: Grades 9-12
- no new vocabulary

26. Global Transformation, 1450 to 1600

LEVEL 2: Grades 5-6
- Arab sailing vessels
- astrolabe
- Bartholomew de las Casas
- Chinese sailing vessels*
- compass*
- Cortés's journey into Mexico
- European overseas voyages
- interregional trading system
- King Affonso II of the Kongo
- naval warfare
- Portuguese maritime expansion
- quadrant
- Spanish and Portuguese innovations in shipbuilding
- Spanish exploration
- voyages of Columbus

LEVEL 3: Grades 7-8
- commercial crops
- commercial expedition
- "conquest, exchange, and discovery"
- disease microorganisms
- domestic crops
- exploratory expeditions
- flora and fauna exchange
- indigenous populations of the Americas
- international seaborne trade
- pathogens*
- Pizarro
- Siamese

LEVEL 4: Grades 9-12
- cassava
- colonial government
- *encomienda* system*

- expulsion of Jews and Muslims from Spain
- New World
- "noble savage"
- plantation system*
- Red Sea

27. European Transformation, 1450 to 1750

LEVEL 2: Grades 5-6
- Age of Enlightenment
- astronomical discoveries*
- Copernicus
- Diderot
- Diderot's encyclopedia
- English civil war*
- English Revolution of 1688
- fortification
- gunpowder
- Newton
- Reformation
- Renaissance
- Scientific Revolution

LEVEL 3: Grades 7-8
- absolutist monarchs
- "agrarian revolution"
- Alps
- Catherine the Great
- Dutch Republic
- Elizabeth I
- Francis Bacon
- Greek rationalism
- Humanist ideals
- Italian renaissance
- medieval theology
- modern nationalism
- Muslim science
- new global knowledge
- Peter the Great
- printing press technology
- Renaissance humanism
- René Descartes
- Roman republicanism
- Spanish silver trade
- St. Petersburg
- trial of Galileo
- "window on the West"
- world trade*

*Word or phrase appears more than once.

LEVEL 4: Grades 9-12
- academies
- Caucasus
- Cavaliers
- Chinese humanist philosophy
- Descartes' *Discourse on Method*
- Duchy of Moscow
- Dutch merchant classes
- English merchant classes
- "Enlightened Despot"
- Frederick the Great
- French salons
- Galileo's ideas about the solar system
- Joseph II
- Louis XIV
- Machiavelli
- popular publishing
- Roundheads
- Russian expansion (16th-18th centuries)
- Siberia
- *The Prince* by Machiavelli
- universalism

28. Eurasian Empires, 16th to 18th Centuries

LEVEL 2: Grades 5-6
- celestial empire
- imperial absolutism
- Ming Dynasty
- Mughal conquest of India
- Mughal Empires
- Safavid Golden Age
- Shah Abbas I
- Sulieman the Magnificent
- Turkic Safavids
- Turkic warrior class
- Vasco da Gama*
- Zheng He*

LEVEL 3: Grades 7-8
- Akbar
- China as the "Middle Kingdom"
- East India Company

LEVEL 4: Grades 9-12
- Austria

29. Africa, Europe, and America, 1500 to 1750

LEVEL 2: Grades 5-6
- Atlantic basin
- Brazil
- British North America
- Caribbean
- colonies
- crops from the colonies
- mercantilism*
- "middle passage"
- mother country*
- Netherlands
- polygynous marriage
- Seven Years War*
- slave life on plantations
- trans-Atlantic African slave trade
- world economy

LEVEL 3: Grades 7-8
- American Indian nations
- Ashanti
- colonies in Massachusetts
- colonies in Peru
- colonies in the Great Lakes region
- colony of Barbados
- Kongo

LEVEL 4: Grades 9-12
- aboriginal populations
- African kingdom of Palmares
- colonial slave rebellions
- converting non-Europeans
- early modern societies
- *hacienda* labor system
- Spanish viceroyalties of Peru and Mexico

30. Transformations in Asian Societies in the Era of European Expansion

LEVEL 2: Grades 5-6
- Chinese and Japanese brush paintings
- conversion
- Indonesia
- Tokugawa shogunate

LEVEL 3: Grades 7-8
- brush painting
- Gangzhou [Canton]
- "Hermit Kingdom" [Korea]
- Manchu Empire

LEVEL 4: Grades 9-12
- Bhati movement
- Emperor Aurazngzeb
- Joseph Francois Dupleix's theory of "divide and rule"
- Kangzi emperors
- Maratha
- Qianlong emperors
- Sikh*

31. Global Trends, 1450 to 1770

LEVEL 2: Grades 5-6
- lateen sails

LEVEL 3: Grades 7-8
- capitalistic enterprise
- class relations
- commercialization
- race relations

LEVEL 4: Grades 9-12
- Puritans*
- Western European capitalism

32. Political Revolutions, 18th and 19th Centuries

LEVEL 2: Grades 5-6
- American Revolution
- French Revolution*
- Latin American independence movements
- "Liberty, Equality, Fraternity"
- Napoleon Bonaparte*

LEVEL 3: Grades 7-8
- Agustin de Iturbide in the Creole-dominated revolt of 1821
- bourgeoisie
- clergy
- constitutional monarchy
- democratic despotism
- Estates-General
- Father Miguel Hidalgo
- French Declaration of the Rights of Man and Citizen*

*Word or phrase appears more than once.

- Mexican Revolution*
- Napoleon's invasion of Iberia
- Napoleon's invasion of Portugal
- Napoleonic empire
- nobility
- Old Regime France
- peasantry
- *sans culottes*

LEVEL 4: Grades 9-12

- Catholic Clergy
- "Code Napoleon"
- Haitian revolution*
- mestizo
- Monroe Doctrine*
- mulatto
- New Granada
- Olympe de Gouge's "Declaration of the Rights of Women and the Female Citizen"
- Protestant Clergy

33. Agricultural and Industrial Revolutions, 1700 to 1850

LEVEL 2: Grades 5-6

- abolition movement
- Edmund Cartwright
- Frederick Douglass*
- industrial revolution*
- industrialism
- industrialization*
- James Hargreaves
- James Watt
- John Kay
- textile industry

LEVEL 3: Grades 7-8

- contract labor migration
- crop rotation
- Harriet Tubman*
- labor union*
- revolution ideology
- seed drill
- social reform*
- Sojourner Truth*
- stock breeding
- three-piece iron
- world manufacturing production

LEVEL 4: Grades 9-12

- Adam Smith
- Adam Smith's "pin" story
- British West Indies
- free enterprise
- principle of the "Invisible Hand"
- profit motive
- *The Wealth of Nations*

34. Eurasian Transformation, 1750 to 1870

LEVEL 2: Grades 5-6

- Commodore Matthew Perry
- "father of modern Egypt" [Muhammad Ali of Egypt]
- French invasion of Egypt in 1798
- janissary
- Meiji Restoration
- opium trade in China
- Russian expansion (18th-19th centuries)

LEVEL 3: Grades 7-8

- Boxer Rebellion
- Opium War
- reform programs of Selim III and Mahmud II

LEVEL 4: Grades 9-12

- Charter Oath of 1868
- Czar Nicholas I
- czarist reform movements of the 1820s
- Decembrist uprising
- Meiji slogans
- Pan-Slavism
- Polish rebellion
- process of Russification
- Taiping Rebellion
- Trans-Siberian railroad

35. Nationalism, State Building, and Social Reform in Europe and the Americas, 1830-1914

LEVEL 2: Grades 5-6

- Garibaldi
- German nationalist movements
- Italian nationalist movements
- Redshirts

LEVEL 3: Grades 7-8

- Bismarck's "Blood and Iron" speech
- caudillo ruler
- "high culture"
- Karl Marx
- Romanticism
- unifications of Italy and Germany
- women's suffrage

LEVEL 4: Grades 9-12

- Austro-Hungarian Empire
- Cavour
- Chartist movement
- Dreyfus affair
- Franco-Prussian War
- Greek independence movement
- Impressionism
- Marx and Engel's *Communist Manifesto*
- Mary Wollstonecraft's Vindication of the Rights of Women
- Realism
- realpolitik
- revolutions of 1848

36. Global Change in the Era of Western Domination, 1850 to 1914

LEVEL 2: Grades 5-6

- Afrikaners
- European imperialist expansion
- European migrants and immigrants
- Zulu empire

LEVEL 3: Grades 7-8

- African resistance movements
- Cecil Rhodes' "scramble for Africa"
- Darwin

*Word or phrase appears more than once.

- Indian Uprising of 1857
- Maxwell
- Pasteur
- Spanish-American War*
- Suez Canal
- Tippu Tip
- Zanzibar
- Zulus

LEVEL 4: Grades 9-12
- China's 1911 republican revolution
- colonization of Korea
- French notion of mission civilisatrice
- German concept of Kultur
- Japanese imperial expansion
- Mahdi uprising
- revolutions in Sudan
- Rudyard Kipling's *White Man's Burden*
- Russo-Japanese War
- scientific racism
- Sino-Japanese War
- Social Darwinism*
- Sun Yatsen

37. Global Trends, 1750 to 1914

LEVEL 2: Grades 5-6
- Bombay
- Buenos Aires
- Cairo*
- London
- San Francisco
- Tokyo

LEVEL 3: Grades 7-8
- 19th-century reform movements

LEVEL 4: Grades 9-12
- al-Afghani
- constitutionalism
- expanding Western hegemony
- socialism

38. Reform, Revolution, and Social Change in the Early 20th Century

LEVEL 2: Grades 5-6
- Mexican Revolution*

LEVEL 3: Grades 7-8
- Alfred Krupp
- Emmeline Pankhurst
- New Culture movement
- Russian "Bloody Sunday" in 1905
- social reformism
- welfare state

LEVEL 4: Grades 9-12
- October Manifesto
- South African (Anglo-Boer) War
- Young Turk movement

39. Causes and Consequences of World War I

LEVEL 2: Grades 5-6
- Central Powers*
- collectivization
- first Five Year Plan
- Stalin
- Lenin
- Rasputin
- Russian Revolution of 1917*
- Soviet Union*
- theaters of conflict
- trench warfare
- Tsar Nicholas II
- World War I*

LEVEL 3: Grades 7-8
- Great Powers in Europe
- kulaks
- militarism
- Stalin's purges
- the Great War
- "total war"

LEVEL 4: Grades 9-12
- Bolsheviks
- Lenin's promise of "land, bread, peace"
- Red Russians
- Stalinist totalitarianism

- war propaganda
- White Russians

40. Search for Peace and Stability, 1920s and 1930s

LEVEL 2: Grades 5-6
- Great Depression*
- Matisse
- League of Nations*
- mass popular culture*
- Middle East
- Pablo Picasso
- Pan-Arabism
- Treaty of Versailles (1919)

LEVEL 3: Grades 7-8
- Chinese Communist Party
- Conference of Versailles
- Curie
- Dorothea Lange
- Einstein
- Freud
- Kuomintang Party
- reparation payments
- U.S. isolationist policies
- Woodrow Wilson's Fourteen Points*

LEVEL 4: Grades 9-12
- Cubism
- Dadaism
- Hemingway
- Expressionism
- Freud's psychoanalytic method
- Hapsburg Empire
- jazz*
- Mao Zedong
- pre-World War I "spheres of influence"
- "racial equality clause" in the preamble to the Covenant of the League of Nations
- Socialist Realism
- Surrealism
- theories of the unconscious

*Word or phrase appears more than once.

41. Causes and Consequences of World War II

LEVEL 2: Grades 5-6
- Churchill
- fascism*
- Franco
- Hitler
- Mussolini
- Nazi "war against the Jews"
- Nazism
- Roosevelt
- Spanish Civil War

LEVEL 3: Grades 7-8
- fascist aggression
- Jewish resistance movements

LEVEL 4: Grades 9-12
- George Orwell
- Japan's "greater East Asia co-prosperity" sphere
- *Mein Kampf*
- Munich Agreement in 1938
- Nazi party platform
- Nazi-Soviet Non-Aggression Pact of 1939*
- Soviet nonaggression pacts

42. Global Trends, 1900 Through the End of World War II

LEVEL 2: Grades 5-6
- regimes
- United Nations*
- world geopolitics

LEVEL 3: Grades 7-8
- liberal democratic ideals
- materialism
- 20th-century totalitarian

LEVEL 4: Grades 9-12
- mass consumer economies

43. Power Relations and the Breakup of Colonial Empires

LEVEL 2: Grades 5-6
- Cold War*
- Cuban missile crisis*

- Hungarian revolt
- Indonesian civil war
- Israel*
- Korean War*
- Polish worker's protest
- Soviet invasion of Czechoslovakia (1968)
- Suez crisis (1956)

LEVEL 3: Grades 7-8
- Cultural Revolution
- division of Germany and Berlin
- European Economic Community
- Ghandi's call for nonviolent action
- Great Leap Forward
- Marshall Plan*
- Mohandas Ghandi
- North Atlantic Treaty Organization
- Warsaw Pact

LEVEL 4: Grades 9-12
- Arab League
- Diem regime
- German Federal Republic
- Guatemala
- Jiang Jieshi
- Kashmir
- White Paper Reports
- Zionist Movement

44. Search for Community, Peace, and Stability in an Interdependent World

LEVEL 2: Grades 5-6
- conquest of smallpox
- "consumer societies"
- development of antibiotics
- global market economy
- global natural environment
- Pacific Rim economy
- Singapore
- South Korea
- U.N. Declaration of Human Rights

LEVEL 3: Grades 7-8
- "fundamentalism"
- Helsinki Accords*
- mass consumption of resources
- militant religious movements
- neo-colonialism
- Reagan-Gorbachev "summit diplomacy"

- reformist economic policies in post-Mao China
- Soviet invasion of Afghanistan (1979)
- Tiannamen Square protest (1989)

LEVEL 4: Grades 9-12
- Abstract Expressionism
- black markets
- Existentialism
- Geneva Accords
- jihad
- "liberation theology"
- oil crisis of 1970s
- "one-child" policy in China
- 1994 Cairo Conference on World Population
- Pop Art
- United Nations programs

45. Global Trends Since World War II

LEVEL 2: Grades 5-6
- international migration*
- political boundaries

LEVEL 3: Grades 7-8
- bipolar centers of power multipolar centers of power

LEVEL 4: Grades 9-12
- "postindustrial society"

46. Long-Term Changes and Recurring Patterns in World History

LEVEL 2: Grades 5-6
- long-distance trade

LEVEL 3: Grades 7-8
- emergence of capitalism
- major disease pandemics

LEVEL 4: Grades 9-12
- no new vocabulary

*Word or phrase appears more than once.

1. Writing Process

LEVEL 1: Grades K-2

- beginning*
- capitalization
- conventions
- describe
- details
- dictionary*
- draft
- edit*
- ending
- evaluate*
- experience*
- focus*
- format*
- grammar
- ideas*
- illustration
- letter*
- mechanics
- middle*
- observations*
- picture book
- place*
- plan*
- poem*
- prewriting
- proofread
- publish
- punctuation
- record reactions
- record*
- rehearse*
- resources*
- response*
- revise
- sequence*
- spelling
- story

LEVEL 2: Grades 3-5

- address
- audience
- autobiography
- brainstorm
- central idea
- character*
- closing
- composition
- conflict*
- context*

- dialogue*
- example*
- explain
- expressive
- facts*
- feedback*
- graph*
- graphic organizer
- greeting
- idea cluster
- imagery
- indentation
- margin
- narrative*
- notes*
- organization*
- page format
- personal letters*
- plot
- point of view*
- presentation
- purpose*
- references*
- reflection*
- relevant*
- sensory details
- setting*
- story maps
- structure*
- suspense*
- tension*
- title
- topic
- voice
- webs
- word choice

LEVEL 3: Grades 6-8

- anecdote
- background knowledge
- business letter
- citation
- counterargument
- critical standards
- entertain
- evidence*
- expression*
- figurative language
- gesture*
- impression
- inconsistency*
- influence

- inform
- journal
- letter of request and response
- log*
- movement*
- outline
- peer response
- persona
- persuade
- private audience
- problem/solution*
- public audience
- scheme
- self-assessment*
- slang
- sources*
- structural
- style*
- subject
- syntactical
- transitions

LEVEL 4: Grades 9-12

- ambiguity
- articulate
- business correspondence
- checklist
- complexity*
- depth
- diagram*
- formality
- interior monologue
- interpretation*
- job application*
- linguistic structure
- memo
- nuance
- overview
- pace
- perspective*
- position
- readability
- reasoning*
- redraft
- refine
- reflect
- resumé*
- rhetorical device
- speed writing
- synthesize
- thesis

*Word or phrase appears more than once.

2. Stylistic and Rhetorical Aspects of Writing

LEVEL 1: Grades K-2
- words

LEVEL 2: Grades 3-5
- indent
- paragraph*
- sentence structure
- topic sentence

LEVEL 3: Grades 6-8
- follow-up sentence
- mood*
- sequential
- supporting sentence

LEVEL 4: Grades 9-12
- clincher sentence
- closing sentence
- cohesion*
- notations
- phrase
- progression
- restatement
- technical terms
- terms

3. Grammar and Mechanics

LEVEL 1: Grades K-2
- action word
- adjective
- adverb
- comma
- declarative sentence
- interrogative sentence
- letter (alphabet)
- noun
- period
- print*
- question mark
- sentence
- space
- verb

LEVEL 2: Grades 3-5
- abbreviation
- action verb
- apostrophe
- colon
- common noun
- consonant
- contraction
- coordinating conjunction
- cursive
- direct quotation
- double negative
- exclamatory sentence
- heading
- imperative sentence
- indefinite adjective
- initials
- irregular plural
- negatives
- numerical adjective
- past/present verb tense
- plural noun
- possessive noun
- predicate adjective
- pronoun
- proper noun
- quotation marks
- regular plural
- salutation
- simple tense
- singular noun
- subject noun
- subject-verb agreement
- vowel

LEVEL 3: Grades 6-8
- auxiliary verb
- comparative adjective
- compound sentence
- demonstrative pronoun
- exclamation mark
- footnotes
- hyphen
- interjection
- irregular structural change
- italics
- linking verb
- object pronoun
- personal pronoun
- positive adjective
- possessive pronoun
- preposition
- prepositional phrase
- pronominal adjective
- proper adjective
- relative pronoun
- simple sentence
- subject pronoun
- superlative adjective
- verb phrase

LEVEL 4: Grades 9-12
- adjective clause
- adjective phrase
- adverb clause
- adverb phrase
- collective noun
- complex sentence
- compound adjective
- compound noun
- compound personal pronoun
- compound verb
- compound-complex sentence
- conjunctive adverb
- contrasting expressions
- correlative conjunction
- dash
- divided quotations
- future perfect tense
- indefinite pronoun
- independent clause
- interrogative pronoun
- modifier
- nonrestrictive clause
- noun clause
- noun phrase
- past perfect tense
- present perfect tense
- progressive verb form
- reflexive pronoun
- semicolon
- subordinating conjunction

4. Research

LEVEL 1: Grades K-2
- books
- charts*
- information
- pictures
- research
- table of contents

LEVEL 2: Grades 3-5
- compile
- cross-reference
- encyclopedia*
- idea web

*Word or phrase appears more than once.

- index
- investigate
- key word
- list
- report*
- summary
- volume*

LEVEL 3: Grades 6-8

- almanac
- atlas
- card catalog
- component*
- computer catalog
- data*
- graphic representation*
- integrate
- interview
- Reader's Guide to Periodical Literature
- systematic*
- time line*

LEVEL 4: Grades 9-12

- American Psychological Association
- artifacts*
- bibliography
- credibility*
- defend*
- government publication
- microfiche
- Modern Language Association
- primary source*
- reliability
- secondary source*
- style sheet format
- telephone information service
- thesis statement
- validity*
- visual information

5. Reading Process

LEVEL 1: Grades K-2

- author*
- back cover
- cue*
- decode
- flow
- front cover
- meaning
- mental image
- meter

- miscue
- passage
- phonetic analysis
- picture caption
- picture clue
- picture dictionary
- prediction*
- prefix
- print*
- read
- reread
- rhythm*
- root word
- self-correct
- structural analysis
- suffix
- syllable
- title page

LEVEL 2: Grades 3-5

- author's purpose
- confirm
- context clue
- glossary
- modification
- monitor*
- preview
- read ahead
- reading strategy
- semantic context
- skim
- syntactic structure
- text
- text format
- textual clue
- thesaurus*

LEVEL 3: Grades 6-8

- abstract information
- analogy*
- concept
- derivation
- device*
- generalization *
- idiom
- interpret*
- literary form
- metaphor
- persuasive technique*
- simile
- word origin

LEVEL 4: Grades 9-12

- acronym
- code
- philosophical assumptions
- subvocalizing

6. Literary Texts

LEVEL 1: Grades K-2

- fable
- fairy tale
- fiction
- folktale
- inference
- legend*
- literary passage
- main character
- main events
- main idea
- myth*
- nonfiction
- order of events
- outcome*
- poem*
- predictable book
- problem*
- theme*

LEVEL 2: Grades 3-5

- action*
- biography*
- characteristics*
- connections*
- consequences*
- criteria*
- fantasy
- genre*
- historical fiction*
- motive*
- qualities*
- recommendation
- recurring theme

LEVEL 3: Grades 6-8

- cause-and-effect relationship
- character development
- character traits
- digressive time
- first person
- flashback
- foreshadowing
- progressive time

*Word or phrase appears more than once.

- resolution
- science fiction
- stereotype
- subordinate character
- supernatural tale
- tall tale
- third person

LEVEL 4: Grades 9-12
- allusion
- American literature
- archetype
- ancient literature
- Bible
- British literature
- culture*
- diction*
- external conflict
- internal conflict
- irony
- literary device
- parody
- play
- satire
- symbol
- symbolism
- time frame
- universal theme
- world literature

7. Informational Texts
LEVEL 1: Grades K-2
- expository
- prior knowledge
- retell
- summarize*

LEVEL 2: Grades 3-5
- appendix
- biographical sketch
- diary*
- graphic features
- magazine
- paraphrase
- procedures*
- summary sentence
- text organizers
- textbook
- viewpoint

LEVEL 3: Grades 6-8
- editorial
- essay
- explicit*
- hierarchic structures
- implicit*
- language structure
- periodicals*
- primary source historical document
- techniques*

LEVEL 4: Grades 9-12
- reorganize
- scan
- text features
- text structure

8. Speaking and Listening
LEVEL 1: Grades K-2
- audiotapes*
- contribution*
- discussion*
- intonation*
- language*
- media*
- oral directions
- pattern*
- phrasing
- raising hands
- rhymes
- rules of conversation
- staying on topic
- taking turns
- videotape*
- voice level

LEVEL 2: Grades 3-5
- commands
- content*
- conversation*
- eye contact*
- interrupt
- main point
- memory aids
- nonverbal cues
- notes*
- oral presentation
- peer pressure
- persuasive messages

LEVEL 3: Grades 6-8
- active listener
- advertising
- clarification*
- discussion leader
- elaboration
- enunciation
- facilitator
- inflection
- media consumer
- modulation
- non-print media
- nonverbal messages
- persuasive technique*
- physical gestures
- posture*
- role
- tempo*

LEVEL 4: Grades 9-12
- arguments
- delivery
- formal presentation*
- image
- informed judgement
- message wording
- poise
- political belief
- self-control*
- social power*
- statistic*
- visual aids

*Word or phrase appears more than once.

LEVEL I: Primary

Fairy Tales
- Andersen, Hans Christian "Cinderella"
- "Chicken Little"
- "Goldilocks and the Three Bears"
- "Jack and the Beanstalk"
- "The Little Red Hen"
- "The Three Billy Goats Gruff"
- "The Ugly Duckling"

Folktales and Legends
- "Anansi"
- Hogrogian, Nonny "One Fine Day"
- Steptoe, John "Mufaro's Beautiful Daughters: An African Tale"

Fables and Myth
- Aesop's fables "Tortoise and Hare"

Novels
- Dickens, Charles *A Christmas Carol*
- Potter, Beatrix *Peter Rabbit*
- Yashima, Mitsu and Taro *Momo's Kitten*

Poetry
- Blake, William "Spring"
- Giovanni, Nikki "Because"
- Longfellow, Henry Wadsworth "Paul Revere's Ride"

LEVEL II: Upper Elementary

Mythology from Around the World
- Classical Greek Mythology
- D'Aulaire, Ingri, and Edgar P. D'Aulaire *D'Aulaires' Book of Greek Myths*

Adaptations from the Classics
- "Pollyanna"
- "Rip Van Winkle"
- "The Adventures of Tom Sawyer"

Folktales
- Blair, Walter *Tall Tale America*
- Louie, Ai-Lang *Yeh Shen: A Cinderella Story from China*
- Luenn, Nancy *The Dragon Kite*

Unabridged Fiction
- Bryan, Ashley *Beat the Story Drum, Pum-Pum*
- Cleary, Beverly *Ramona and Her Father*
- Dahl, Roald *James and the Giant Peach*
- Grahame, Kenneth *Wind in the Willows*
- Greene, Bette *Philip Hall Likes Me, I Reckon Maybe*
- Hahn, Jae, Hyun *Seven Korean Sisters*
- Hamilton, Virginia *Zeely*
- L'Engle, Madeleine *A Wrinkle in Time*
- Lord, Bette B. *In the Year of the Boar and Jackie Robinson*
- Speare, Elizabeth G. *The Sign of the Beaver*
- Sperry, Armstrong *Call It Courage*
- Van Allsburg, Chris *Jumanji*

- Williams, Vera B. *A Chair for My Mother*
- White, E. B. *Charlotte's Web*

Poetry
- Angelou, Maya "Life Doesn't Frighten Me"
- Blake, William "The Tiger"
- Dickinson, Emily "A Bird Came Down the Walk"
- Greenfield, Eloise "Things"
- Hughes, Langston "Dreams"
- Hughes, Langston "I, Too"
- Hughes, Langston *The Dream Keeper*
- Longfellow, Henry Wadsworth "The Arrow and the Song"
- Millay, Edna St. Vincent "Afternoon on a Hill"
- Silverstein, Shel "Clarence"
- Whitman, Walt "I Hear America Singing"
- Whitman, Walt "O Captain! My Captain!"
- Wilbur, Richard "Some Opposites"

Nonfiction - Information
- Aliki *Corn is Maize: The Gift of the Indians and The Story of Johnny Appleseed*
- Baylor, Byrd *The Way to Start a Day*
- Meyers, Susan *Pearson, a Harbor Seal Pup*

Nonfiction - Biography
- Fritz, Jean *And Then What Happened, Paul Revere?* and *What's the Big Idea, Ben Franklin?* and *Where Was Patrick Henry on the 29th of May?*

LEVEL III: Middle School

Greek and Roman Mythology
- Aphrodite/Venus
- Apollo/Mars

Classic American Literature
- Alcott, Louisa May *Little Women*
- Cooper, James Fennimore *The Last of the Mohicans*
- London, Jack *Call of the Wild*
- Twain, Mark *The Adventures of Tom Sawyer, The Adventures of Huckleberry Finn, A Connecticut Yankee in King Arthur's Court*
- Steinbeck, John *Of Mice and Men*
- Hemingway, Ernest *The Old Man and the Sea*
- Wilder, Thornton *Our Town*

Classic British Literature
- Stevenson, Robert Louis *Dr. Jeckyl and Mr. Hyde*
- Swift, Jonathan *Gulliver's Travels*
- Orwell, George *Animal Farm*
- Defoe, Daniel *Robinson Crusoe*
- Dickens, Charles *Great Expectations*
- Eliot, George *Silas Marner*
- Wilde, Oscar *The Canterville Ghost*
- Bronte, Charlotte *Jane Eyre*
- Bronte, Emily *Wuthering Heights*
- Shakespeare, William *The Taming of the Shrew, Romeo and Juliet, Julius Caesar, A Midsummer Night's Dream*

*Word or phrase appears more than once.

Classic World Literature
- Frank, Anne *The Diary of a Young Girl*
- Verne, Jules *Twenty Thousand Leagues Under the Sea*

Adapted/Retold and Exerpted Literature
- Angelou, Maya *I Know Why the Caged Bird Sings*
- *Romeo and Juliet*

Modern/Contemporary Fiction
- Armstrong, William H. *Sounder*
- Bradbury, Ray *Fahrenheit 451*
- Bradbury, Ray *All Summer in a Day*
- Cormier, Robert *I Am the Cheese*
- George, Jean Craighead *Julie of the Wolves*
- Gibson, William *The Miracle Worker*
- Golding, William *Lord of the Flies*
- Hamilton, Virginia *The House of Dies Drear*
- Hansberry, Lorraine *A Raisin in the Sun*
- Hinton, S. E. *The Outsiders*
- Knowles, John *A Separate Peace*
- Lawrence, Jerome and Robert Lee *Inherit the Wind*
- Lee, Harper *To Kill a Mockingbird*
- L'Engle, Madeleine *A Wrinkle in Time*
- Lewis, C. S. *The Lion, the Witch and the Wardrobe*
- O'Dell, Scott *Island of the Blue Dolphins*
- Paulsen, Gary *The River*
- Rawls, Wilson *Where the Red Fern Grows*
- Rose, Reginald *Twelve Angry Men*
- Saint-Exupery, Antoine de *The Little Prince*
- Schaeffer, Jack *Shane*
- Speare, Elizabeth *The Witch of Blackbird Pond*
- Taylor, Mildred D. *Roll of Thunder, Hear My Cry*
- Thurber, James *"The Secret Life of Walter Mitty"*
- Tolkien, J. R. R. *The Hobbit*
- White, T.H. *The Once and Future King*
- Yep, Laurence *Dragonwings*
- Yep, Laurence *Child of the Owl*
- Zindel, Paul *The Pigman*

Poetry and Poets
- Angelou, Maya "Caged Bird," "Woman Work"
- Dickinson, Emily "I Like to See It Lap the Miles"
- Frost, Robert "Stopping by the Woods on a Snowy Evening," "The Road Not Taken"
- Hughes, Langston *Don't You Turn Back*
- Longfellow, Henry Wadsworth "A Psalm of Life," "Song of Hiawatha"
- Poe, Edgar Allan "Annabel Lee," "The Raven"
- Shakespeare, William "All the World's a Stage" from *As You Like It*
- Williams, William Carlos "This Is Just to Say"

Nonfiction - Information
- Kennedy, John. F. Inaugural Address

Nonfiction - Biography
- McGovern, Ann *The Secret Soldier: The Story of Deborah Sampson*
- Reiss, Johanna *The Upstairs Room*

LEVEL IV: *High School*

CLASSIC AMERICAN LITERATURE
Poetry
- Dickinson, Emily
- Whitman, Walt *Leaves of Grass*

Fiction
- Cather, Willa *My Antonia*
- Chopin, Kate *The Awakening*
- Crane, Stephen *Red Badge of Courage*
- Harte, Bret "Outcasts of Poker Flat"
- Hawthorne, Nathanial *The Scarlet Letter*, "Young Goodman Brown"
- Irving, Washington "The Devil and Tom Walker"
- James, Henry *Portrait of a Lady*
- Lewis, Sinclair *Babbitt*
- London, Jack *Call of the Wild*
- Melville, Herman "Benito Cereno," "Billy Budd," *Moby Dick*
- Norris, Frank *McTeague*
- Poe, Edgar Allan "Fall of the House of Usher"
- Stowe, Harriet Beecher *Uncle Tom's Cabin*
- Twain, Mark *Huckleberry Finn*
- Wharton, Edith *Ethan Frome*

Nonfiction
- *Declaration of Independence*
- Franklin, Ben *Poor Richard's Almanack*
- Thoreau, Henry David *Walden*

MODERN/CONTEMPORARY AMERICAN LITERATURE
Poetry
- cummings, e. e.
- Frost, Robert "The Road Not Taken"
- Hughes, Langston

Fiction
- Anaya, Rudolfo A. *Bless Me, Ultima*
- Baldwin, James *Go Tell It on the Mountain*
- Bradbury, Ray *Fahrenheit 451* and *The Martian Chronicles*
- Cisneros, Sandra *The House on Mango Street*
- Clark, Walter Van Tilburg *Ox-bow Incident*
- Cormier, Robert *After the First Death, I Am the Cheese, The Chocolate War*
- Dos Passos, John
- Ellison, Ralph *Invisible Man*
- Faulkner, William *The Light in August, The Bear*
- Fitzgerald, F. Scott *The Great Gatsby*
- Gaines, Ernest J. *The Autobiography of Miss Jane Pittman*

*Word or phrase appears more than once.

- Gibson, William *The Miracle Worker*
- Hemingway, Ernest *A Farewell to Arms, For Whom the Bell Tolls, The Sun Also Rises, The Old Man and the Sea*
- Heller, Joseph *Catch 22*
- Hinton, S. E. *The Outsiders*
- Hurston, Zora Neale *Their Eyes Were Watching God*
- Kincaid, Jamaica *Annie John*
- Knowles, John *A Separate Peace*
- Lee, Harper *To Kill a Mockingbird*
- McCullers, Carson *The Heart is a Lonely Hunter, The Ballad of the Sad Cafe: The Novels and Stories of Carson McCullers*
- Momaday, N. Scott *House Made of Dawn*
- Morrison, Toni *Beloved, Song of Solomon, Sula, The Bluest Eye*
- Peck, Robert Newton *A Day No Pigs Would Die*
- Plath, Sylvia *The Bell Jar*
- Potok, Chaim *The Chosen*
- Salinger, J. D. *Catcher in the Rye*
- Steinbeck, John *The Grapes of Wrath, Of Mice and Men*
- Walker, Alice *The Color Purple*
- Welty, Eudora
- Wright, Richard *Native Son and Black Boy*
- Zindel, Paul *The Pigman*

Drama

- Albee, Edward *American Dream, Zoo Story, Who's Afraid of Virginia Woolf*
- Fugard, Athol *Master Harold and the Boys*
- Gibson, William *The Miracle Worker*
- Hansberry, Lorraine *A Raisin in the Sun*
- Lawrence, Jerome and Robert E. Lee *Inherit the Wind, The Night Thoreau Spent in Jail*
- McCullers, Carson *The Member of the Wedding*
- Miller, Arthur *Death of a Salesman, The Crucible*
- O'Neill, Eugene *Anna Christie, The Emperor Jones, The Hairy Ape, The Iceman Cometh, Long Day's Journey into Night*
- Wilder, Thornton *Our Town*
- Williams, Tennessee *A Streetcar Named Desire, The Glass Menagerie, Cat on a Hot Tin Roof*

Nonfiction
- Angelou, Maya *I Know Why the Caged Bird Sings*

British Literature
Poetry
- Auden, W. H. *Collected Poems*
- Browning, Robert *Robert Browning's Poetry: Authoritative Texts, Criticism*
- Burns, Robert *The Poetical Works of Burns*
- Byron, George Gordon "Don Juan"
- Chaucer, Geoffrey *Canterbury Tales*
- Coleridge, Samuel Taylor *The Rime of the Ancient Mariner*
- Donne, John *The Complete Works of John Donne*

- Eliot, T. S "The Hollow Men," "The Love Song of J. Alfred Prufrock," *The Waste Land*
- Hardy, Thomas *The Complete Poems of Thomas Hardy*
- Hopkins, Gerard Manley *The Complete Poems of Gerard Manley Hopkins*
- Keats, John "Ode on a Grecian Urn"
- Milton, John *Paradise Lost*
- Shakespeare, William *Sonnets*
- Shelley, Percy Bysshe *The Poetical Works of Shelley*
- Tennyson, Alfred "Charge of the Light Brigade"
- Thomas, Dylan *The Poems of Dylan Thomas*
- Wordsworth, William *The Poetical Works of Wordsworth*
- Yeats, William Butler "The Second Coming"

Fiction
- Austen, Jane *Pride and Prejudice*
- Bronte, Charlotte *Jane Eyre*
- Bronte, Emily *Wuthering Heights*
- Bunyan, John *Pilgrim's Progress*
- Carroll, Lewis *Alice in Wonderland*
- Christie, Agatha
- Clarke, Arthur C. *Childhood's End*
- Conrad, Joseph *The Heart of Darkness, Lord Jim*
- Dickens, Charles, *Oliver Twist, A Tale of Two Cities, Great Expectations, Hard Times*
- Doyle, Sir Arthur Conan *Hound of the Baskervilles*
- Eliot, George *The Mill on the Floss* and *Silas Marner*
- Fielding, Henry *Tom Jones*
- Forster, E.M. *Passage to India*
- Golding, William *Lord of the Flies*
- Greene, Graham *The Power and the Glory*
- Hardy, Thomas *Return of the Native, Tess of the D'Urbervilles, The Mayor of Casterbridge*
- Huxley, Aldous *Brave New World*
- Joyce, James *Ulysses, A Portrait of the Artist as a Young Man*
- Lawrence, D.H. "The Rocking Horse Winner" and *Sons and Lovers*
- Orwell, George *1984* and *Animal Farm*
- Shelley, Mary *Frankenstein*
- Stevenson, Robert Louis *The Strange Case of Dr. Jekyll and Mr. Hyde, The Black Arrow, Kidnapped*
- Swift, Jonathan *Gulliver's Travels,* "A Modest Proposal"
- Tolkien, J.R.R. *The Hobbit*
- Trollope, Anthony *Barchester Towers*
- White, T. H. *The Once and Future King*
- Wilde, Oscar *The Picture of Dorian Gray*
- Woolf, Virginia

Drama
- Marlowe, Christopher *Doctor Faustus*
- Shakespeare, William *Romeo and Juliet, Hamlet, Julius Caesar, Macbeth, Antony and Cleopatra, The Tempest, Othello, King Lear, Merchant of Venice, The Taming of the Shrew, Twelfth Night, A Midsummer Night's Dream*

*Word or phrase appears more than once.

- Shaw, George Bernard *Androcles and the Lion, Arms and the Man, Caesar and Cleopatra, Major Barbara, Pygmalian, Saint Joan*
- Sheridan, Richard B. *The Rivals* and *The School for Scandal*
- Thomas, Dylan *Under Milkwood: A Play for Voices*
- Wilde, Oscar *The Importance of Being Earnest*

WORLD LITERATURE

- Achebe, Chinua *Things Fall Apart*
- Anouilh, Jean *Antigone*
- Azuela, Mariano *The Underdogs*
- Balzac, Honore de *Old Goriot*
- Beckett, Samuel *Waiting for Godot, Beowulf*
- Brecht, Bertold *Mother Courage and Her Children*
- Camus, Albert *The Stranger, The Plague*
- Cervantes *Don Quixote*
- Chekhov, Anton *The Cherry Orchard*
- Dante *The Divine Comedy*
- Dostoevsky, F. *The Brothers Karamazov, Crime and Punishment, The Idiot*
- Flaubert, Gustave *Madame Bovary*
- Garcia Lorca, Federico *Blood Wedding*
- Garcia Marquez, Gabriel *Love in the Time of Cholera*
- Giraudoux, Jean *The Madwoman of Chaillot*
- Goethe, Johann Wolfgang von *Faust*
- Hesse, Hermann *Siddhartha, Beneath the Wheel*
- Hugo, Victor *The Hunchback of Notre Dame, Les Miserables*
- Ibsen, Henrik *A Doll's House, An Enemy of the People, Hedda Gabler, The Master Builder, The Wild Duck*
- Kafka, Franz *Metamorphosis*
- Kawabata, Yasunari *Snow Country*
- Mishima, Yukio *The Sound of Waves*
- Paton, Alan *Cry, the Beloved Country*
- Remarque, Erich Maria *All Quiet on the Western Front*
- Rostand, Edmond *Cyrano de Bergerac*
- Saint-Exupery, Antoine de *The Little Prince*
- Sartre, Jean-Paul *No Exit*
- Solzhenitsyn, Alexander *One Day in the Life of Ivan Denisovich*
- Tolstoy, A. *Anna Karenina, The Death of Ivan Ilyich, War and Peace*
- Turgenev, Ivan *Fathers and Sons*
- Verne, Jules *Around the World in Eighty Days, 20,000 Leagues under the Sea*
- Voltaire *Candide*
- Zola, Emile

CLASSICAL/ANCIENT LITERATURE

- Aeschylus *Oresteian Trilogy*
- Aristophanes *Lysistrata*
- Euripedes *Medea*
- Homer *The Iliad* and *The Odyssey*
- Ovid *Metamorphoses*
- Plato *The Republic, The Last Days of Socrates [Euthyphro, The Apology, Crito, Phaedo]*
- Sophocles *Antigone, Oedipus at Colonus, Oedipus Rex*
- Virgil *Aeneid*

THE BIBLE AS LITERATURE

- David and Goliath
- Jesus betrayed for 30 pieces of silver
- Job
- Samson and Delilah
- Sodom and Gomorrah
- The story of Creation in Genesis

*Word or phrase appears more than once.

1. Connections among Art Forms and Other Disciplines

LEVEL 2: *Grades K-4*

- art form
- aural
- contrast*
- form*
- kinetic
- line
- oral
- pattern*
- visual*

LEVEL 3: *Grades 5-8*

- action*
- aesthetic
- audience interaction
- balance*†
- character*
- cultural context
- environment*
- historical period
- movement*
- shape
- stimulus
- style*†
- subject [of an art work]

LEVEL 4: *Grades 9-12*

- artistic processes
- art media
- organizational principles
- theme*

*Word or phrase appears more than once.

†Word or phrase appears more than once in The Arts.

1. Movement Elements and Skills

LEVEL 2: Grades K-4

- accompaniment
- angle
- axial movement
- bend
- concentration*
- curve
- dancer
- diagonal
- focus*
- gallop
- hop
- leap
- level
- locomotor movement*†
- movement element
- personal space
- rhythm*†
- skip
- slide
- space
- stretch
- swing
- tempo*†
- twist

LEVEL 3: Grades 5-8

- articulation of movement
- balance†
- ballet
- body alignment
- body position*
- collapse
- combination*
- dab
- direction*
- dynamic
- elevation
- fall
- float
- Ghanaian dance
- glide
- initiation of movement
- landing*
- Middle Eastern dance
- modern dance
- movement sequence
- movement theme
- punch
- recovery

- spatial patterns*
- square dance
- step
- sustained
- vibratory
- weight shift

LEVEL 4: Grades 9-12

- agility
- choreography
- coordination
- dance tradition
- flexibility*
- line of gravity
- meter†
- musicality
- projection
- rhythmic acuity
- time element

2. Choreographic Principles, Processes, and Structures

LEVEL 2: Grades K-4

- copying
- dance phrase
- following
- force/energy
- improvisation
- leading
- mirroring
- movement problem
- sequence*

LEVEL 3: Grades 5-8

- AB form†
- ABA form†
- call and response†
- canon
- chance (in a dance movement or phrase)
- complementary shape
- contrasting shape
- narrative*
- reordering
- supporting weight
- taking weight
- transition

LEVEL 4: Grades 9-12

- palindrome
- rondo
- round†
- theme and variation

3. Communicate Meaning

LEVEL 2: Grades K-4

- interpretation*

LEVEL 3: Grades 5-8

- abstracted gesture
- costuming†
- lighting†
- pantomime

LEVEL 4: Grades 9-12

- no new vocabulary

4. Creative and Critical Thinking

LEVEL 2: Grades K-4

- body shape
- pathway

LEVEL 3: Grades 5-8

- aesthetic criteria†

LEVEL 4: Grades 9-12

- no new vocabulary

5. Dance in Various Cultures and Time Periods

LEVEL 2: Grades K-4

- folk dance
- setting*

LEVEL 3: Grades 5-8

- classical dance
- jazz dance
- social dance
- tap dance
- theatrical dance

LEVEL 4: Grades 9-12

- Balinese dance

6. Dance and Health

LEVEL 2: Grades K-4

- nutrition*
- healthy practices

LEVEL 3: Grades 5-8

- injury-prevention strategies*
- warm-up techniques*

LEVEL 4: Grades 9-12

- body image

*Word or phrase appears more than once.
†Word or phrase appears more than once in The Arts.

1. Singing

LEVEL 1: Grades K-2
- ostinato
- partner song
- round†

LEVEL 2: Grades 3-5
- alto
- bass
- conductor*
- cue*
- diction*
- Dixieland music
- lullaby
- march
- musical part
- musical phrase
- patriotic song
- pitch*
- posture*
- soprano
- tempo*†
- tenor
- timbre
- work song

LEVEL 3: Grades 6-8
- a capella
- barbershop music
- breath control
- chorus
- expression*
- harmony
- intonation*
- madrigal
- music in two and three parts
- scale
- sonata
- syncopation

LEVEL 4: Grades 9-12
- ensemble skill
- rhythmic unity

2. Performing on Instruments

LEVEL 1: Grades K-2
- melody

LEVEL 2: Grades 3-5
- chord
- electronic instrument
- fretted instrument
- harmonic progression
- keyboard instrument
- percussion instrument
- style*†

LEVEL 3: Grades 6-8
- acoustic instrument
- string instrument
- technical accuracy
- wind instrument

LEVEL 4: Grades 9-12
- consonance
- contour
- dissonance
- musical articulation
- point of climax
- register
- rubato
- tone*†

3. Improvisation

LEVEL 1: Grades K-2
- improvise

LEVEL 2: Grades 3-5
- embellishment
- MIDI (Musical Instrument Digital Interface)
- musical piece

LEVEL 3: Grades 6-8
- blues music
- classical music
- duple meter
- folk music
- gospel music
- jazz music
- opera
- oratorio
- pentatonic tonality
- pop music
- rock music
- symphonic
- triple meter

LEVEL 4: Grades 9-12
- hymn
- minor key
- tonality

4. Composition and Arrangement

LEVEL 1: Grades K-2
- compose

LEVEL 2: Grades 3-5
- arrangement

LEVEL 3: Grades 6-8
- balance†
- musical element
- range
- release
- tension*

LEVEL 4: Grades 9-12
- composition*
- musical form
- texture*

5. Reading and Notating Music

LEVEL 1: Grades K-2
- key
- key signature
- major key
- meter†
- rhythm*†
- symbols for dynamics (e.g., p, f, <, and >)
- symbols for notes (e.g., for dotted note, eighth note, half note, quarter note, whole note)
- time signature (e.g., 2/4, 3/4, 4/4)
- treble clef

LEVEL 2: Grades 3-5
- accelerando
- accent
- crescendo
- diminuendo
- flat
- forte
- legato
- marcato
- measure*
- piano
- presto
- repeat
- rest
- ritard
- sharp

*Word or phrase appears more than once.
†Word or phrase appears more than once in The Arts.

- staccato
- symbols for articulation (e.g., for accents, legato, marcato, staccato)
- tie

LEVEL 3: Grades 6-8
- allegro
- andante
- bass clef
- coda
- fine
- symbols for notes (e.g., for sixteenth note)
- time signature (e.g., 2/2/ [alla breve], 3/8, 6/8)

LEVEL 4: Grades 9-12
- musical staff

6. Applying Criteria to Performances

LEVEL 1: Grades K-2
- AB form†
- ABA form†
- call and response†

LEVEL 2: Grades 3-5
- no new vocabulary

LEVEL 3: Grades 6-8
- music event

LEVEL 4: Grades 9-12
- expressive device
- imitation
- inversion
- motive*
- retrograde

7. Music, History and Culture

LEVEL 1: Grades K-2
- no new vocabulary

LEVEL 2: Grades 3-5
- genre*†

LEVEL 3: Grades 6-8
- no new vocabulary

LEVEL 4: Grades 9-12
- Broadway musical
- swing music

*Word or phrase appears more than once.
†Word or phrase appears more than once in The Arts.

1. Writing Scripts

LEVEL 2: Grades K-4
- character*
- dialogue*
- dramatization*

LEVEL 3: Grades 5-8
- scene
- script
- suspense*

LEVEL 4: Grades 9-12
- no new vocabulary

2. Acting Skills

LEVEL 2: Grades K-4
- locomotor movement*†
- nonlocomotor movement
- role
- social pretend play
- tempo*†
- tone*†
- vocal pitch

LEVEL 3: Grades 5-8
- body alignment
- breath control
- diction
- improvise
- sensory recall

LEVEL 4: Grades 9-12
- acting techniques (classical and contemporary)
- ensemble
- genre*†

3. Design and Production

LEVEL 2: Grades K-4
- color*
- costuming†
- lighting†
- locale
- makeup
- mood*
- prop
- scenery
- set
- sound*
- visual and aural elements

LEVEL 3: Grades 5-8
- emphasis

- repetition*
- set design
- visual principles

LEVEL 4: Grades 9-12
- physical and chemical properties of media

4. Direction

LEVEL 2: Grades K-4
- stage
- staging

LEVEL 3: Grades 5-8
- rehearse*

LEVEL 4: Grades 9-12
- artistic choice
- constructed meaning
- director

5. Creating and Communicating Meaning

LEVEL 2: Grades K-4
- intent
- structure
- oral and kinetic elements

LEVEL 3: Grades 5-8
- actor
- collaboration
- playwright
- publicity
- program
- study guide

LEVEL 4: Grades 9-12
- aesthetic criteria†

6. Cultural and Temporal Context of Performances

LEVEL 2: Grades K-4
- no new vocabulary

LEVEL 3: Grades 5-8
- archetype*
- archetypal characters (superhero, trickster, villain, warrior)

LEVEL 4: Grades 9-12
- no new vocabulary

*Word or phrase appears more than once.
†Word or phrase appears more than once in The Arts.

1. Media, Techniques, and Processes

LEVEL 2: Grades K-4

- art material
- art media
- art process
- art technique
- brush
- canvas
- casting
- clay
- color value
- color variation
- construction
- film
- oil paint
- overlapping
- paint
- sculpture
- shading
- size variation
- tools
- videotape*
- watercolor
- wood*

LEVEL 3: Grades 5-8

- camera
- easel
- kiln
- knife
- lathe
- press

LEVEL 4: Grades 9-12

- no new vocabulary

2. Structures and Functions

LEVEL 2: Grades K-4

- art element
- artistic function
- cold color
- complementary color
- depth
- dimension
- perspective*
- visual structure
- texture
- warm color

LEVEL 3: Grades 5-8

- definition
- hue
- intensity*
- motion
- placement

LEVEL 4: Grades 9-12

- artistic intention
- discrimination of impressions
- halftone
- highlight
- negative space
- positive space
- shadow edge

3. Subject Matter, Symbols, and Potential Ideas

LEVEL 2: Grades K-4

- symbol*

LEVEL 3: Grades 5-8

- context*
- spatial concept
- temporal concept
- visual concept

LEVEL 4: Grades 9-12

- functional value

4. Historical and Cultural Significance of Visual Arts

LEVEL 2: Grades K-4

- no new vocabulary

LEVEL 3: Grades 5-8

- cultural context*
- historical context

LEVEL 4: Grades 9-12

- aesthetics

5. Merits of Artwork

LEVEL 2: Grades K-4

- artist
- artistic purpose

LEVEL 3: Grades 5-8

- art history

LEVEL 4: Grades 9-12

- art criticism

*Word or phrase appears more than once.
†Word or phrase appears more than once in The Arts.

1. Civic Life, Politics, and Government

LEVEL 1: Grades K-2
- authority*
- power without authority

LEVEL 2: Grades 3-5
- absence of government
- absence of rules of laws
- city council
- common good
- community*
- consent of the governed
- courts
- governor
- laws*
- nation
- national government*
- politics
- power
- rights of individuals
- rules*
- state
- tribal government

LEVEL 3: Grades 6-8
- binding agreements
- character of citizens
- civic life
- Congress
- economic security
- institutions
- law enforcement*
- liberty
- national security
- private life
- religious beliefs*
- school board
- state legislature
- voting

LEVEL 4: Grades 9-12
- democratic legislature
- monarchy
- political authority*
- relationship between government and individual
- relationship between government and society
- tribal council

2. Limited and Unlimited Government

LEVEL 1: Grades K-2
- limited authority

LEVEL 2: Grades 3-5
- economic rights*
- limited governmen*
- personal rights*
- political discrimination
- political rights*
- religious discrimination*
- unlimited government

LEVEL 3: Grades 6-8
- authoritarian system
- constitutional government
- totalitarian system

LEVEL 4: Grades 9-12
- civil society
- economic freedoms
- political freedoms

3. Sources, Purpose, and Functions of Law

LEVEL 1: Grades K-2
- corrective justice
- distributive justice
- good rules or laws
- justice*
- procedural justice

LEVEL 2: Grades 3-5
- effective rules and laws
- uses of rules and laws

LEVEL 3: Grades 6-8
- rule of law
- rule of men

LEVEL 4: Grades 9-12
- common law
- divine law
- international law
- legislatures
- natural law
- sources of law
- sovereigns
- statute law
- Supreme Being

4. Constitutional Government

LEVEL 1: Grades K-2
- no benchmarks

LEVEL 2: Grades 3-5
- no benchmarks

LEVEL 3: Grades 6-8
- constitution
- public servants
- uses of constitutions

LEVEL 4: Grades 9-12
- Fourteenth Amendment*
- Japanese Constitution

5. Systems of Shared Powers

LEVEL 1: Grades K-2
- no benchmarks

LEVEL 2: Grades 3-5
- no benchmarks

LEVEL 3: Grades 6-8
- cabinet
- English Parliament*
- parliamentary systems
- president's Cabinet
- prime minister
- system of shared powers
- vote of no confidence

LEVEL 4: Grades 9-12
- Israeli Parliament
- limiting power

6. Federal, Confederal, and Unitary Systems

LEVEL 1: Grades K-2
- no benchmarks

LEVEL 2: Grades 3-5
- no benchmarks

LEVEL 3: Grades 6-8
- central government
- confederal system of government
- Confederate States of America
- distribution of power*

*Word or phrase appears more than once.

- federal system of government
- national government*
- state government
- unitary system of government
- United States under the Articles of Confederation

LEVEL 4: Grades 9-12
- abuse of power
- popular will

7. Forms of Representation

LEVEL 1: Grades K-2
- no benchmarks

LEVEL 2: Grades 3-5
- no benchmarks

LEVEL 3: Grades 6-8
- no benchmarks

LEVEL 4: Grades 9-12
- constituency
- direct popular rule
- electoral systems
- obligations of representatives
- proportional systems
- representation based on age, sex, or property
- representation based on citizenship, social class, or caste
- representation based on geographic areas
- representation based on religion, race, and ethnicity
- representative government
- theories of government

8. American Constitutional Government

LEVEL 1: Grades K-2
- pursuit of justice

LEVEL 2: Grades 3-5
- Bill of Rights (1791)*
- Declaration of Independence (1776)*
- diversity*
- equal access to public facilities
- equal opportunity in education

- equal opportunity in employment
- equal opportunity in housing
- equal protection of the law*
- equality of opportunity*
- exercising power through representatives
- exercising power through voting
- freedom to express opinions and persuade others
- fundamental principles of American democracy
- fundamental values of American democracy
- importance of education
- importance of respect for the law
- importance of work
- patriotism
- Preamble to the United States Constitution
- public or common good
- right to liberty
- right to life*
- right to participate in political life
- right to property
- right to the pursuit of happiness
- sovereignty of the people
- truth*

LEVEL 3: Grades 6-8
- Articles I, II, and III of the Constitution
- checks and balances*
- constitutional protection of individual rights
- cruel and unusual punishment
- death penalty
- delegated or enumerated powers
- due process of law
- equal protection of the law*
- ex post facto
- freedom of assembly
- freedom of press
- freedom of religion*
- freedom of speech
- general welfare provision of the Constitution
- habeas corpus*
- hate speech
- limits on speech
- necessary and proper clause of the Constitution

- right to counsel*
- search and seizure
- separation of church and state
- separation of powers*
- sharing of powers
- social equality
- trial by jury
- universal public education
- warrantless searches

LEVEL 4: Grades 9-12
- Articles of Confederation (1781)*
- English Bill of Rights (1689)*
- Magna Carta (1215)*
- natural rights philosophy
- republican government

9. American Values and Principles

LEVEL 1: Grades K-2
- no benchmarks

LEVEL 2: Grades 3-5
- Columbus Day
- *E Pluribus Unum*
- flag
- Fourth of July*
- great seal
- importance of shared beliefs, values, and principles
- Labor Day*
- Martin Luther King, Jr. Day*
- Memorial Day*
- national anthem
- oaths of office
- Pledge of Allegiance
- Presidents' Day*
- Statue of Justice
- Statue of Liberty*
- Thanksgiving*
- Uncle Sam
- Veterans Day*

LEVEL 3: Grades 6-8
- civilian control of the military
- civil rights movement
- difference between citizens and subjects
- Martin Luther King's "I Have a Dream" speech*
- openness and free inquiry

*Word or phrase appears more than once.

- popular sovereignty
- shared powers
- state sovereignty
- suffrage
- The Federalist

LEVEL 4: Grades 9-12
- no new vocabulary

10. Organized Roles of Voluntarism and Organized Groups

LEVEL 1: Grades K-2
- no benchmarks

LEVEL 2: Grades 3-5
- voluntarism

LEVEL 3: Grades 6-8
- charitable groups
- civic groups
- religious charity groups

LEVEL 4: Grades 9-12
- professional organizations
- Puritan ethic
- service groups
- unions
- voluntary associations

11. Diversity in American Life

LEVEL 1: Grades K-2
- no benchmarks

LEVEL 2: Grades 3-5
- benefits of diversity
- conflicts about diversity
- costs of diversity
- discrimination based on age
- discrimination based on beliefs
- discrimination based on disability
- ethnic discrimination
- gender discrimination
- racial discrimination
- religious discrimination*

LEVEL 3: Grades 6-8
- Catholic/Protestant conflicts in the nineteenth century
- conflict about civil rights of minorities and women

- conflict about the rights of Native Americans
- ethnic conflict in urban settings
- Gettysburg Address*
- linguistic diversity*
- North/South conflict
- regional diversity
- socioeconomic diversity

LEVEL 4: Grades 9-12
- Martin Luther King, Jr.'s "Letter from the Birmingham Jail"

12. Liberalism, Republicanism, and American Constitutional Democracy

LEVEL 1: Grades K-2
- no benchmarks

LEVEL 2: Grades 3-5
- no benchmarks

LEVEL 3: Grades 6-8
- no benchmarks

LEVEL 4: Grades 9-12
- civic virtue
- conservative
- Democratic Party
- Enlightenment*
- liberal
- liberalism*
- Protestant Reformation
- republic
- Republican Party
- republicanism
- "self-evident Truths"

13. Political and Social Conflict In America

LEVEL 1: Grades K-2
- no benchmarks

LEVEL 2: Grades 3-5
- no benchmarks

LEVEL 3: Grades 6-8
- affirmative action

- majority rule*
- minority rights*

LEVEL 4: Grades 9-12
- right to life*

14. Ideals vs. Reality in American Life

LEVEL 1: Grades K-2
- no benchmarks

LEVEL 2: Grades 3-5
- no benchmarks

LEVEL 3: Grades 6-8
- abolition
- civil rights*
- environmental protection movements
- public life
- suffrage*

LEVEL 4: Grades 9-12
- Head Start
- union movements

15. Distribution of Power

LEVEL 1: Grades K-2
- no benchmarks

LEVEL 2: Grades 3-5
- clean air laws
- executive branch
- judicial branch
- legislative branch
- freedom of expression*
- freedom of religion*
- pure food and drug laws*
- U.S. Constitution*

LEVEL 3: Grades 6-8
- American tribal governments
- coining money
- Constitutional amendments
- District of Columbia
- federal judiciary
- impeachment*
- interstate commerce
- power to borrow money
- power to regulate voting
- power to tax

*Word or phrase appears more than once.

- veto power
- Virgin Islands
- "We the People . . ."

LEVEL 4: Grades 9-12
- advice and consent
- Federal Communications Commission
- Federal Reserve System*
- Food and Drug Administration
- framers of the Constitution
- geographical and group representation
- independent regulatory agencies
- judicial review
- legislative districting
- Supreme Court
- Tenth Amendment
- term limitations
- the power of impeachment
- the power of the purse

16. Domestic and Foreign Policy

LEVEL 1: Grades K-2
- no benchmarks

LEVEL 2: Grades 3-5
- no benchmarks

LEVEL 3: Grades 6-8
- Aid to Families with Dependent Children
- arms control
- Article I, Sections 7 and 8
- civil rights laws
- domestic policy
- Environmental Protection Act
- federal debt
- foreign policy
- government revenues, taxes, and tariffs
- immigration acts
- Marshall Plan*
- Medicaid
- Medicare
- minimum wage laws
- Monroe Doctrine*
- Pure Food and Drug Act
- Sixteenth Amendment*
- Social Security*

LEVEL 4: Grades 9-12
- equity of taxes
- foreign aid

17. Relationships Among Local, State, and National Governments

LEVEL 1: Grades K-2
- no benchmarks

LEVEL 2: Grades 3-5
- government officials
- local government
- mayor
- national government*
- president
- state government

LEVEL 3: Grades 6-8
- state constitution
- state sales tax

LEVEL 4: Grades 9-12
- chartering local governments
- chartering regional governments
- concurrent powers
- conduct of elections
- fair and public notice of government meetings
- Fourteenth Amendment*
- legislating taxation
- licensing
- protecting the environment
- public trials
- regulating trade and industry
- reserved powers

18. Law and Individual Rights

LEVEL 1: Grades K-2
- no benchmarks

LEVEL 2: Grades 3-5
- right to a fair trial
- right to practice one's religious beliefs
- right to vote

LEVEL 3: Grades 6-8
- adversary system
- arbitration
- *Brown v. Board of Education* (1954)*
- conflict management
- due process protections
- fair notice of a hearing
- habeas corpus*
- impartial tribunal
- judicial protection
- juvenile system
- litigation
- *Marbury v. Madison* (1803)*
- mediation
- negotiation*
- presumption of innocence
- protection against double jeopardy
- right against self-incrimination
- right of appeal
- right to counsel*
- speedy and public trials
- the right to adequate notice
- the right to counsel
- trail by jury
- *U.S. v. Nixon* (1974)

LEVEL 4: Grades 9-12
- Americans with Disabilities Act
- business corruption
- civil law
- congressional compliance
- constitutional law
- constitutional limitations
- criminal law
- due process rights*
- equal opportunity legislation
- government corruption
- independent judiciary
- Ku Klux Klan*
- perjury
- police corruption
- power of judicial
- system of ordered liberty
- urban riots
- vigilantism

*Word or phrase appears more than once.

19. Public Agenda

LEVEL 1: Grades K-2
- no benchmarks

LEVEL 2: Grades 3-5
- no benchmarks

LEVEL 3: Grades 6-8
- freedom of press
- public agenda

LEVEL 4: Grades 9-12
- campaign advertisements
- Chief Joseph's "I Shall Fight No More Forever"
- Lincoln's "House Divided" Speech
- political cartoon*
- public opinion
- Sojourner Truth's "Ain't I a Woman?"

20. Elections

LEVEL 1: Grades K-2
- no benchmarks

LEVEL 2: Grades 3-5
- no benchmarks

LEVEL 3: Grades 6-8
- AFL-CIO
- civil rights groups
- Common Cause
- congressional election
- general election
- Greenpeace
- labor union*
- League of Women Voters
- local election
- NAACP*
- National Education Association
- political parties
- presidential election
- primary election
- recall election
- religious organizations
- state election
- suffragists

LEVEL 4: Grades 9-12
- initiatives
- referendums
- third parties
- two-party system

21. Public Policy

LEVEL 1: Grades K-2
- no benchmarks

LEVEL 2: Grades 3-5
- no benchmarks

LEVEL 3: Grades 6-8
- capital punishment
- environmental protection*
- gun control

LEVEL 4: Grades 9-12
- no new vocabulary

22. Nation States and Foreign Policy

LEVEL 1: Grades K-2
- no benchmarks

LEVEL 2: Grades 3-5
- cultural contacts
- diplomacy
- military force
- treaties and agreements

LEVEL 3: Grades 6-8
- Amnesty International
- covert action
- economic incentives
- economic sanctions
- governmental international organizations
- humanitarian aid
- International Red Cross
- military intervention
- nation-state*
- NATO
- nongovernmental international organizations
- OAS
- threat of military force
- World Council of Churches
- World Court

LEVEL 4: Grades 9-12
- Antarctic Treaty
- GATT
- Helsinki Accords*
- International Monetary Fund
- Most Favored Nation Agreements
- NAFTA*

- Organization of American States
- power to declare war
- UNICEF
- World Bank

23. Significant Political and Nonpolitical Developments

LEVEL 1: Grades K-2
- no benchmarks

LEVEL 2: Grades 3-5
- no benchmarks

LEVEL 3: Grades 6-8
- democracy movements
- economic rights*
- natural rights
- social rights
- United Nations Charter
- Universal Declaration of Human Rights

LEVEL 4: Grades 9-12
- European Union

24. U.S. Citizenship

LEVEL 1: Grades K-2
- no benchmarks

LEVEL 2: Grades 3-5
- alien
- jury duty
- naturalization
- non-citizen
- public office

LEVEL 3: Grades 6-8
- no new vocabulary

LEVEL 4: Grades 9-12
- no new vocabulary

*Word or phrase appears more than once.

25. Personal, Political, and Economic Rights

LEVEL 1: Grades K-2
- personal rights
- right to privacy

LEVEL 2: Grades 3-5
- equal pay for equal work
- economic rights
- welfare
- right to associate with whomever one chooses
- right to choose one's work
- right to criticize the government
- right to join political parties
- right to own property
- right to speak freely
- political rights
- school prayer
- right to seek and hold political office

LEVEL 3: Grades 6-8
- freedom of conscience
- freedom to marry whom one chooses
- freedom to have children
- freedom to live where one chooses
- freedom of movement
- freedom to travel freely
- freedom of expression
- freedom to emigrate
- right to enter into lawful contracts
- right to establish a business
- right to join professional associations
- right to own a business
- right to patent and copyright
- requirement of just compensation

LEVEL 4: Grades 9-12
- Northwest Ordinance
- eminent domain
- vigilant citizenry

26. Scope and Limits of Rights

LEVEL 1: Grades K-2
- no new vocabulary

LEVEL 2: Grades 3-5
- no new vocabulary

LEVEL 3: Grades 6-8
- clear and present danger rule
- compelling government interest test
- libel
- "scope and limits" of a right
- slander

LEVEL 4: Grades 9-12
- urban decay

27. Personal and Civic Responsibilities

LEVEL 1: Grades K-2
- responsibility*

LEVEL 2: Grades 3-5
- civic mindedness
- civic responsibility
- civility
- compassion
- compromise*
- critical mindedness
- honesty
- negotiation*
- open mindedness
- persistence*
- personal responsibility
- respect for the law
- respect for the rights of others
- self-discipline
- self-governance

LEVEL 3: Grades 6-8
- accepting responsibility for one's actions
- adhering to moral principles
- considering the rights and interests of others
- informed (about public issues)
- monitoring governmental agencies
- monitoring political leaders
- performing public service
- serving in the armed forces
- supporting one's family
- taking care of one's self

LEVEL 4: Grades 9-12
- chauvinism
- jingoism

28. Civic and Political Participation

LEVEL 1: Grades K-2
- no benchmarks

LEVEL 2: Grades 3-5
- Chamber of Commerce
- civilian review boards
- media
- taxpayer associations
- peaceful demonstrations
- petitions
- P.T.A.

LEVEL 3: Grades 6-8
- civil disobedience

LEVEL 4: Grades 9-12
- community organizing
- political life
- picketing

29. Political Leadership and Public Service

LEVEL 1: Grades K-2
- leader*

LEVEL 2: Grades 3-5
- candidate
- leadership*
- public service

LEVEL 3: Grades 6-8
- loyal opposition
- political leadership
- public affairs

LEVEL 4: Grades 9-12
- no new vocabulary

*Word or phrase appears more than once.

1. Resources and Opportunity Costs

LEVEL 1: Grades K-2
- benefit
- capital resource
- choice
- consumer*
- cost*
- goods*
- human capital
- human resource
- labor
- natural resource*
- needs and wants*
- physical capital
- producer*
- resource
- services*

LEVEL 2: Grades 3-5
- capital
- division of labor
- entrepreneur
- innovation
- invention*
- investment
- opportunity cost
- productive resource
- productivity
- risk*
- scarcity
- specialization*
- technology*
- trade-off*

LEVEL 3: Grades 6-8
- output*
- standard of living*

LEVEL 4: Grades 9-12
- marginal benefit
- marginal cost
- optimal level

2. Economic Systems, Institutions, and Incentives

LEVEL 1: Grades K-2
- no benchmarks

LEVEL 2: Grades 3-5
- allocation
- business*
- distribution
- firm
- household
- incentive
- income*
- penalty
- profit
- revenue
- reward

LEVEL 3: Grades 6-8
- banking system*
- collective bargaining
- command economic system
- cooperative
- corporation
- economic institution*
- economic self-interest
- fringe benefit
- labor union*
- market economic system
- nonprofit organization
- partnership
- salary*
- tax exemption
- wage
- work rule

LEVEL 4: Grades 9-12
- constraint*
- contract enforcement
- incorporation
- investor
- liability rules
- property rights*
- return [on investment]
- shareholder
- standard measures
- standard weights
- stockholder

3. Supply and Demand in a Market Economy

LEVEL 1: Grades K-2
- market
- price

LEVEL 2: Grades 3-5
- equilibrium price
- market clearing price
- tax

LEVEL 3: Grades 6-8
- relative price
- substitute product

LEVEL 4: Grades 9-12
- ceiling
- complementary product
- demand
- demand curve
- floor
- input*
- price control
- shortage
- supply
- supply curve
- surplus

4. Market Structures and Exchanges

LEVEL 1: Grades K-2
- barter
- exchange
- money

LEVEL 2: Grades 3-5
- borrower
- competition*
- currency
- customer service
- interdependence*
- product quality
- purchasing power
- saver
- self-sufficiency

LEVEL 3: Grades 6-8
- special interest group

*Word or phrase appears more than once.

LEVEL 4: Grades 9-12
- anti-trust
- collusion
- externality
- money supply
- monopoly
- natural monopoly
- public service commission
- tariffs*
- transaction cost

5. Unemployment and Income in a Market Economy

LEVEL 1: Grades K-2
- no benchmarks

LEVEL 2: Grades 3-5
- unemployment

LEVEL 3: Grades 6-8
- interest*
- labor force*
- labor market
- recession
- rent
- unemployment rate

LEVEL 4: Grades 9-12
- cyclical unemployment
- discrimination*
- frictional unemployment
- full-time employment
- functional distribution of income
- labor force immobility
- part-time employment
- personal distribution of income
- seasonal unemployment
- structural unemployment
- transfer payment

6. Role of Government in the U.S. Economy

LEVEL 1: Grades K-2
- government

LEVEL 2: Grades 3-5
- public goods
- public services*

LEVEL 3: Grades 6-8
- nonexclusion
- shared consumption
- standard currency

LEVEL 4: Grades 9-12
- federal revenue
- income tax
- local government revenue
- national debt*
- payroll tax
- property tax
- sales tax
- Social Security*
- state revenue
- subsidy
- trade barrier

7. Savings, Investment, and Interest Rates

LEVEL 1: Grades K-2
- no benchmarks

LEVEL 2: Grades 3-5
- savings

LEVEL 3: Grades 6-8
- fund

LEVEL 4: Grades 9-12
- default
- inflation*
- interest rate
- loan repayment
- nominal interest rate
- real interest rate

8. Fiscal and Monetary Policy

LEVEL 1: Grades K-2
- no benchmarks

LEVEL 2: Grades 3-5
- no benchmarks

LEVEL 3: Grades 6-8
- no benchmarks

LEVEL 4: Grades 9-12
- balanced budget
- budget deficit
- budget surplus

- circulation of money
- discount rate
- expenditure
- Federal Reserve System*
- fiscal policy
- government security
- monetary policy*
- reserve requirement

9. GDP, Inflation, and Deflation

LEVEL 1: Grades K-2
- no benchmarks

LEVEL 2: Grades 3-5
- no benchmarks

LEVEL 3: Grades 6-8
- deflation
- economic indicator
- Gross Domestic Product
- total market value

LEVEL 4: Grades 9-12
- Consumer Price Index
- fixed income
- nominal GDP
- real GDP

10. International Economics

LEVEL 1: Grades K-2
- no benchmarks

LEVEL 2: Grades 3-5
- no new vocabulary

LEVEL 3: Grades 6-8
- barrier to trade
- exchange rate
- export*
- foreign exchange market
- import
- international trade
- per capita GDP
- quota

LEVEL 4: Grades 9-12
- absolute advantage
- comparative advantage*
- flow of trade

*Word or phrase appears more than once.

1. Conversations

LEVEL 2: Grades K-4

Vocabulary in the target language for...

- expressing likes and dislikes
- describing everyday objects
- giving and following simple instructions
- exchanging information and preferences
- exchanging information about general events
- greetings, introductions, leave takings, and other common interactions

Gestures in the target language for...

- greetings, introductions, leave takings, and other common interactions

LEVEL 3: Grades 5-8

Vocabulary in the target language for...

- gathering and sharing information and opinions
- planning events
- seeking clarification
- giving and following directions
- purchasing goods and services
- expressing preferences

Gestures in the target culture for...

- greetings, introductions, leave takings, and other common interactions

Nonverbal and verbal cues in the target language

LEVEL 4: Grades 9-12

Vocabulary in the target language for...

- discussing current and past events
- discussing literary texts
- making inquiries about available services
- engaging in everyday conversations with members of the target culture

Circumlocution and rephrasing in the target language

2. Comprehending

LEVEL 2: Grades K-4

- native language
- phrase groupings
- voice inflection

LEVEL 3: Grades 5-8

- informed guesses
- phrase structures

LEVEL 4: Grades 9-12

- no new vocabulary

3. Writing and Speaking

LEVEL 2: Grades K-4

- no new vocabulary

LEVEL 3: Grades 5-8

- no new vocabulary

LEVEL 4: Grades 9-12

- no new vocabulary

4. Cultural Knowledge and Understanding

LEVEL 2: Grades K-4

Terms in the target culture regarding...

- age-appropriate cultural activities
- age-appropriate patterns of behavior and interaction
- common cultural toys, dress, dwellings, and food
- age-appropriate artwork and other expressive forms of the culture
- basic cultural beliefs

LEVEL 3: Grades 5-8

Terms in the target culture regarding...

- age-appropriate cultural activities
- traditions and celebrations

- age-appropriate patterns of behavior and interaction
- educational institutions and means of transportation

- age-appropriate artwork and other expressive forms of the culture
- beliefs about native culture

LEVEL 4: Grades 9-12

Terms in the target culture regarding...

- age-appropriate cultural activities
- age-appropriate patterns of behavior and interaction
- age-appropriate artwork and other expressive forms of the culture
- social, economic, and political institutions and laws
- role of native culture in the world arena
- ways in which reporting of events differ around the world
- professions that require knowledge of the target language and culture

5. Language Patterns

LEVEL 2: Grades K-4

- word borrowings
- sound systems
- writing systems

LEVEL 3: Grades 5-8

- idiomatic expressions
- word equivalencies

LEVEL 4: Grades 9-12

- tense in the target language

*Word or phrase appears more than once.

1. Tools and Technologies

LEVEL 1: Grades K-2
- no benchmarks

LEVEL 2: Grades 3-5
- absolute location
- aerial photographs
- letter/number system
- cardinal directions*
- intermediate directions
- legend*
- map grid
- maps
- meridians
- principal parallels
- projection
- scale
- title*▼
- topography

LEVEL 3: Grades 6-8
- axis*
- cartogram
- census data
- disease patterns▼
- distortion
- Earth-Sun relations
- economic features▼
- energy consumption cycles▼
- flat-map projection
- geographic databases
- land-use data
- language-use patterns▼
- latitude
- longitude
- major parallels
- mapping hurricane tracks
- population patterns▼
- revolution*
- rotation*
- seasons
- thematic maps
- vegetation

LEVEL 4: Grades 9-12
- geographic information systems [GIS]
- maps developed by different sources/points of view
- primary data
- satellite-produced imagery▼

2. Locations of Places, Features, Patterns

LEVEL 1: Grades K-2
- location of community
- location of country
- location of home
- location of neighborhood
- location of school
- location of state

LEVEL 2: Grades 3-5
- major bodies of water
- continents
- fast food restaurants▼
- fire stations▼
- globe
- historic sites▼
- human features
- lakes▼
- landforms▼
- major mountain ranges
- major cities in North America
- physical features
- recreation areas▼
- rivers*
- shopping areas▼
- wetlands▼

LEVEL 3: Grades 6-8
- climate regions
- culture hearth
- Huang Ho▼
- mental maps
- Mesopotamia*▼
- Nile Valley*▼
- major ocean currents
- major urban centers in the United States
- relative location
- spatial perception
- wind patterns
- Yucatan Peninsula▼

LEVEL 4: Grades 9-12
- AIDS▼
- Americentric mental map
- bubonic plague▼
- Chernobyl nuclear accident▼
- contagious diseases
- economic cultures
- Eurocentric mental map
- political cultures
- public policy*
- settlement
- Sinocentric
- spatial dynamics

3. Spatial Organization

LEVEL 1: Grades K-2
- area
- community parks▼
- line
- local landmarks▼
- local stores▼
- point*
- region*
- volume*

LEVEL 2: Grades 3-5
- Appalachian Mountains▼
- changing technology
- drainage basin▼
- kilometers
- leeward▼
- measuring distance
- perception*
- physical processes
- ridge-and-valley pattern
- river system
- windward▼

LEVEL 3: Grades 6-8
- global migration patterns
- imported resources▼
- interdependence*
- land use*
- language*
- manufactured goods▼
- patterns of diffusion
- patterns of land use
- rural
- suburban
- urban

*Word or phrase appears more than once.

▼Readers should note that this term or phrase was offered as an example of a given class of words and, thus, should not be taken as required or exhaustive.

LEVEL 4: Grades 9-12
- commodity flows▼
- complementarity
- distance decay▼
- employment levels
- intervening opportunity▼
- law of retail gravitation▼
- principles of location
- public transit
- threshold population▼

4. Physical and Human Characteristics of Place

LEVEL 1: Grades K-2
- airports▼
- creeks▼
- hospitals▼
- human characteristics of the local community
- physical characteristics of the local community
- sports stadiums▼

LEVEL 2: Grades 3-5
- population distribution

LEVEL 3: Grades 6-8
- clearing of forests▼
- cultural characteristics of places
- forest cover▼
- population characteristics
- satellite dishes▼
- soils▼
- temperature fluctuations▼
- urban growth▼
- water distribution▼
- wildlife▼

LEVEL 4: Grades 9-12
- agricultural revolution▼
- belief systems*▼
- coastal flood zone▼
- industrial revolution*▼
- social, cultural, economic processes
- tundra▼
- urbanization*

5. Regions

LEVEL 1: Grades K-2
- economic regions
- landform regions
- language regions
- political regions
- population regions
- soil regions
- vegetation regions
- water basins

LEVEL 2: Grades 3-5
- ethnic composition▼

LEVEL 3: Grades 6-8
- Amsterdam▼
- Bible Belt▼
- Capitol Hill▼
- circuit-court district▼
- cultural ties▼
- developed regions
- fanshed of a sports team▼
- formal regions
- functional regions
- Great American Desert▼
- hemisphere
- less-developed regions
- marketing areas▼
- media image▼
- migration
- perceptual regions
- regional labels
- regional systems
- Riviera▼
- Rust belt*▼
- school district▼
- spatial scales
- Sun belt*▼
- the South▼
- Twin Peaks of San Francisco▼
- watersheds▼

LEVEL 4: Grades 9-12
- capital investment▼
- Caribbean Basin's transition▼
- climate shifts
- county, state, and national levels of political parties
- defense alliance▼
- economic alliance

- environmental degradation▼
- hub and spoke▼
- market patterns▼
- municipalities
- postal service zip codes▼
- power blocs▼
- precinct
- seismic activity
- Social Security numbers▼
- tourism

6. Perceptions of Places and Regions

LEVEL 1: Grades K-2
- no benchmarks

LEVEL 2: Grades 3-5
- perception of place

LEVEL 3: Grades 6-8
- arid lands
- cultural symbols
- Everglades▼
- Gateway Arch in St. Louis▼
- Golden Gate Bridge in San Francisco▼
- Inuit people*▼
- irrigation▼
- Opera House in Sydney, Australia▼
- perceptions of value and beauty
- Tower Bridge in London▼
- tradition

LEVEL 4: Grades 9-12
- gambling centers▼
- Jerusalem as a holy city▼
- mining ghost towns▼
- perceptions of distance
- sense of rootedness▼
- sense of belonging▼

7. Physical Processes

LEVEL 1: Grades K-2
- no benchmarks

LEVEL 2: Grades 3-5
- atmosphere*
- biomes
- biosphere
- deposition*

*Word or phrase appears more than once.

▼Readers should note that this term or phrase was offered as an example of a given class of words and, thus, should not be taken as required or exhaustive.

- erosion*
- hill▼
- hydrosphere*
- lithosphere*
- mud slides▼
- oceans▼
- plains▼
- plateau▼
- Sun*
- weather*▼

LEVEL 3: Grades 6-8
- coastal ecosystem
- earthquake zone▼
- erosional agents
- fossil fuels
- hurricane▼
- hydroelectric power▼
- ocean circulation system▼
- soil fertility▼
- tectonic plates▼
- volcanic activity▼

LEVEL 4: Grades 9-12
- air-mass circulation
- continental climate
- deposition of sediment
- desertification▼
- dust storm▼
- flash floods▼
- marine climate▼
- ocean circulation▼
- precipitation*▼
- soil degradation
- world atmospheric circulation▼

8. Ecosystems

LEVEL 1: Grades K-2
- no benchmarks

LEVEL 2: Grades 3-5
- coastal zones
- ecosystem*
- food chain*
- food web*
- fungi*▼
- grasses▼
- grassland areas
- marine vegetation

- midlatitude forest
- tropical rain forest

LEVEL 3: Grades 6-8
- air pollution▼
- atmospheric warming▼
- carbon cycle*
- cycling of energy▼
- eutrophication
- feeding levels▼
- flood plain
- flora and fauna
- flow of energy▼
- lake ecosystem
- life cycle*
- nitrogen cycle*
- oxygen cycle

LEVEL 4: Grades 9-12
- biodiversity
- biological magnification
- contaminants▼
- raw materials

9. Population

LEVEL 1: Grades K-2
- no benchmarks

LEVEL 2: Grades 3-5
- age distribution▼
- infant mortality▼
- international migration*
- involuntary migration
- life expectancy▼
- population density
- voluntary migration

LEVEL 3: Grades 6-8
- crude birth rate
- crude death rate
- demographic*
- doubling time
- population growth rates
- rural-urban migration
- urban commuting▼

LEVEL 4: Grades 9-12
- global air routes▼
- infrastructure
- interstate highway system▼
- population gains

- population losses
- push and pull factors
- regional integration
- regional interdependence
- socioeconomic conditions
- suburban development▼
- transportation system

10. Cultural Mosaics

LEVEL 1: Grades K-2
- beliefs*
- customs*
- economic activities*
- education systems
- forms of shelter
- language as a part of culture
- social organization

LEVEL 2: Grades 3-5
- clothing styles
- Europeans▼
- food preferences
- Hindus▼
- Muslims▼
- Native Americans▼

- Riyadh, Saudi Arabia▼
- Sikh*▼

LEVEL 3: Grades 6-8
- Chinatown▼
- cultural diffusion
- Little Italy▼
- terraced rice fields▼
- satellite television dishes▼

LEVEL 4: Grades 9-12
- Buddhism*▼
- Central Europe▼
- cultural convergence
- cultural divergence
- ethnic elitism
- ethnic ties
- Kurds▼
- linguistic ties
- NAFTA*▼
- post-reunification Germany
- Southeast Asia▼
- sub-Saharan Africa*▼

*Word or phrase appears more than once.

▼Readers should note that this term or phrase was offered as an example of a given class of words and, thus, should not be taken as required or exhaustive.

11. Economic Interdependence

LEVEL 1: Grades K-2

- modes of transportation

LEVEL 2: Grades 3-5

- agriculture▼
- communication system
- developed country
- developing country
- fishing▼
- forestry▼
- global market▼
- goods and services*
- major transportation routes
- mining*▼
- national market▼
- natural resource*
- needs and wants*
- Pacific Rim nations▼
- products*
- refrigerated trucking▼
- regional market▼
- rural regions
- Southwest Asia*▼
- specialization*
- urban region

LEVEL 3: Grades 6-8

- comparative advantage*
- crop failures▼
- exports
- facsimile transmission services
- factors of production
- imports
- labor strikes▼
- migrant workers
- primary economic activities
- satellite-based communications systems
- secondary economic activities
- spatial patterns*
- tertiary economic activities
- trade advantage▼
- trading patterns
- triangular trade*▼
- war▼
- world trade*

LEVEL 4: Grades 9-12

- command economy
- foreign capital▼
- hinterlands▼
- international debt crisis▼
- land values▼
- market economy
- monoculture▼
- spatial distribution
- traditional economy
- zoning regulations*▼

12. Settlement Patterns

LEVEL 1: Grades K-2

- housing
- transportation facilities

LEVEL 2: Grades 3-5

- boomtowns▼
- decentralization
- fertile soil▼
- ghost towns▼
- river transportation▼
- single-industry towns▼
- suburbanization*

LEVEL 3: Grades 6-8

- agricultural settlement patterns
- agricultural surplus
- concentric zone model
- geographic factors for location
- governmental centers▼
- industrial development
- planned cities▼
- plantations▼
- port cities▼
- sector model of cities
- subsistence farming
- truck-farming communities▼
- urban settlement patterns

LEVEL 4: Grades 9-12

- edge cities▼
- ethnic enclaves▼
- light-rail systems▼
- megalopolis▼
- metropolitan corridors▼
- public safety

- urban morphology
- ex-urban areas▼
- zoning regulations*

13. Cooperation and Conflict

LEVEL 1: Grades K-2

- community house-building projects
- neighborhood crime-watch
- refugee problems
- trade pacts

LEVEL 2: Grades 3-5

- census district
- cooperative relationships
- economic inequalities
- economic unit
- law enforcement*▼
- law making▼
- political control
- political units
- powers of taxation▼
- precinct
- provinces
- provision of services▼
- school attendance zone▼
- township▼

LEVEL 3: Grades 6-8

- boundary disputes
- Canberra▼
- capital cities
- control of strategic locations
- cultural differences*
- domination
- economic competition
- economic divisions
- economic groupings▼
- nationalism*
- nation-state*
- political alliances▼
- political divisions
- postal zones▼
- scarce resources
- self-rule▼
- social divisions
- telephone area codes▼
- The Hague▼
- the World Court▼

*Word or phrase appears more than once.

▼Readers should note that this term or phrase was offered as an example of a given class of words and, thus, should not be taken as required or exhaustive.

- transnational corporations▼
- voting wards▼
- world religions▼

LEVEL 4: Grades 9-12
- Basque minority/Spanish majority▼
- British Empire▼
- Carolingian Empire▼
- congressional districts
- free-trade zones
- French colonization of Indochina▼
- Han Dynasty▼
- Hutus and Tutsis in Rwanda▼
- imperial powers
- internal disputes
- internal interests
- land-locked countries
- North Korea/South Korea▼
- Roman Empire▼
- regional school districts▼
- statutory requirements▼
- The Pampas in Argentina▼

14. Humans' Effect on the Physical Environment

LEVEL 1: Grades K-2
- clean air▼
- food*▼
- mineral resources▼
- water*▼

LEVEL 2: Grades 3-5
- dry-land farming techniques▼
- flood-control projects▼
- reforestation▼
- water pollution▼

LEVEL 3: Grades 6-8
- acid rain▼
- airborne emissions▼
- chemical fertilizers and pesticides▼
- dams▼
- deforestation▼
- downstream▼
- downwind▼
- groundwater quality▼
- hybridization of crops▼
- levees▼

- nuclear power plants▼
- nuclear-waste storage▼
- ozone depletion*▼
- pesticides▼
- soil acidification▼
- soil salinization▼
- steam power*▼
- steel-tipped plows

LEVEL 4: Grades 9-12
- arid areas▼
- carrying capacity
- feedback loops
- habitat destruction▼
- historic preservation▼
- logging
- overfishing▼
- runoff▼
- synergy
- threshold*
- toxic dump▼
- wilderness areas

15. Physical Systems' Effect on Human Systems

LEVEL 1: Grades K-2
- no benchmarks

LEVEL 2: Grades 3-5
- earthquakes▼
- historic area
- industrial center▼
- mines▼
- natural hazard
- port▼
- recreational activities
- tornadoes▼
- tourist center▼
- wind storms▼

LEVEL 3: Grades 6-8
- coastline settlements▼
- early American industrial development▼
- earthquake preparedness
- erosional processes▼
- evacuation routes
- flood-prone areas

- hurricane shelters
- hurricane-prone areas
- landform relief▼
- resource distribution
- storm processes▼
- tidal processes▼
- tundra environment
- water-generated power▼

LEVEL 4: Grades 9-12
- depleted rainforests of central Africa▼
- drought-plagued Sahel▼
- earthquake-resistant construction techniques
- Great Plains Dust Bowl▼
- human adaptation
- limits on plant growth
- "limits to growth"
- physical systems
- Ring of Fire▼
- sea walls▼
- Siberia's resources▼
- sub-Arctic environment▼

16. Importance of Resources

LEVEL 1: Grades K-2
- resources to generate electricity
- resources to produce automobiles, clothing, food, medicine

LEVEL 2: Grades 3-5
- 19th-century Colorado mining towns▼
- barges▼
- coal▼
- fall line
- flow resources
- fossil fuels▼
- iron ore▼
- major industrial districts
- minerals▼
- nonrenewable resources
- pipelines▼
- railroads*▼
- recycling
- renewable resources
- reusing

*Word or phrase appears more than once.

▼Readers should note that this term or phrase was offered as an example of a given class of words and, thus, should not be taken as required or exhaustive.

- running water▼
- ships▼
- timber▼

LEVEL 3: Grades 6-8

- accessibility to resources
- agricultural soils
- air quality
- alternative energy sources
- buffalo in western United States▼
- competition for resources
- diamonds▼
- earth-moving machinery ▼
- electric cars▼
- energy resources
- gold▼
- Iraqi invasion of Kuwait in 1991▼
- Japanese occupation of Manchuria of the 1930s▼
- manufacturing practices
- molybdenum▼
- old-growth forest
- petroleum▼
- rate of resource consumption
- resource utilization
- satellite-imagery technology▼
- semiarid areas▼
- silver▼
- solar energy▼
- standard of living*
- strip mining*
- thermal energy▼
- timber cutting
- urban public transportation
- water quality
- water-rationing
- wind energy▼
- wise management

LEVEL 4: Grades 9-12

- California resources
- colonization
- drought
- economy of Nauru▼
- exploration
- hazardous waste (movement, handling, processing, and storage)
- Malaysian rain forests▼
- manufacturers
- mercantilism*

- petroleum consumption
- phosphate reserves
- overcutting pine forests of Nova Scotia▼
- recyclable material
- relocation strategies of industries
- resource management
- toxic waste handling, movement, processing, and storage
- water usage regulations

17. Geography and the Past

LEVEL 1: Grades K-2

- animal population
- plant population
- style of homes*

LEVEL 2: Grades 3-5

- history of oil discovery
- Indian Ocean*▼
- land-use regulations
- monsoon winds*
- Muslim trading vessels
- population shifts
- road development
- street development
- trade routes
- trade winds

LEVEL 3: Grades 6-8

- artesian wells of the Great Plains
- Brenner Pass▼
- Burma Pass▼
- Cumberland Gap▼
- Delaware River▼
- hydrologic features
- Khyber Pass▼
- land-survey systems
- major springs
- major water crossings
- major water gaps
- migrants▼
- mountain passes
- Ogallala Aquifer▼
- prevailing ocean currents▼
- prevailing wind currents▼
- Tacoma Strait▼
- triangle trade▼

LEVEL 4: Grades 9-12

- center-pivot irrigation
- cultural conflict
- decolonization
- human control over nature
- large-scale agriculture
- migration counterstreams
- migration streams
- national transportation systems
- regions of contact
- social integration
- spatial change
- spread of bubonic plague▼
- world economic development patterns

18. Global Issues

LEVEL 1: Grades K-2

- no benchmarks

LEVEL 2: Grades 3-5

- human-induced changes
- soil conservation practices

LEVEL 3: Grades 6-8

- bicycle lanes▼
- conservationist▼
- developing nation▼
- forester▼
- gender-based divisions of labor▼
- greenways▼
- national forest▼
- nuclear power▼
- patterns of consumption
- patterns of production
- pedestrian walkways▼
- solar power▼
- transportation corridors

LEVEL 4: Grades 9-12

- foreign markets
- Great Barrier Reef▼
- natural disaster
- population decline
- processes of desertification
- processes of land degradation
- rain forests in Indonesia▼
- rutile sands of Australia▼
- sustainable development
- world temperature increase

*Word or phrase appears more than once.

▼Readers should note that this term or phrase was offered as an example of a given class of words and, thus, should not be taken as required or exhaustive.

1. Health Sciences, Products, and Information

LEVEL 1: Grades K-2

- dentists
- dietitians
- health
- nurses
- paramedics
- physicians
- sanitarians

LEVEL 2: Grades 3-5

- health-care workers
- HMOs
- mental health clinics
- pressure*
- public health clinics
- substance abuse treatment centers

LEVEL 3: Grades 6-8

- American Heart Association
- American Lung Association
- assertive consumerism
- community health
- community health consumer organizations
- consumer health service system
- Diabetes Association
- professional health services

LEVEL 4: Grades 9-12

- alcohol- or drug-related problems
- depression
- EPA
- FDA
- health insurance
- neglect and child abuse
- OSHA
- prenatal and perinatal care
- prevention
- prosecutor's office
- rehabilitation
- treatment

2. Environmental and External Factors

LEVEL 1: Grades K-2

- pollution

LEVEL 2: Grades 3-5

- personal health
- physical environment

LEVEL 3: Grades 6-8

- cultural beliefs
- discrimination
- environmental crisis
- health fads
- health practices
- nuclear leaks
- oil spills
- ozone depletion
- peer relationships
- prejudice
- risk-taking behaviors
- socioeconomic considerations
- solid waste contamination

LEVEL 4: Grades 9-12

- child care centers
- cultural diversity
- DSS regulations
- food banks
- food production controls
- food supply
- government regulations
- health-related issues
- household waste disposal controls
- licensing laws
- nuclear waste disposal
- public health policies and laws
- quality
- Right to Know laws
- safe food handling

3. Family and Individual Health

LEVEL 1: Grades K-2

- birth*
- divorce
- extended family
- marriage
- pregnancy
- religious beliefs*

- relocation
- unemployment*
- values*

LEVEL 2: Grades 3-5

- physical health
- psychological health
- responsibility*
- social health

LEVEL 3: Grades 6-8

- behavior*
- communication techniques
- feelings of others

LEVEL 4: Grades 9-12

- dating relationships
- parenthood
- teenage pregnancy

4. Mental Health

LEVEL 1: Grades K-2

- no new vocabulary

LEVEL 2: Grades 3-5

- disabilities
- handicapping conditions
- listening skills
- mental health*
- mood*
- stress*

LEVEL 3: Grades 6-8

- interpersonal communication
- positive relationships
- self-esteem*
- stress management

LEVEL 4: Grades 9-12

- coping strategies
- denial
- emotional health*
- rejection
- social isolation

5. Safety

LEVEL 1: Grades K-2

- abuse
- bruises
- cut*
- emergency*
- emotional abuse

---

*Word or phrase appears more than once.

- fire fighters
- fire safety
- first-degree burns
- medical personnel
- physical abuse
- police officers
- precautions*
- recreation safety
- safety practices
- scratches
- sexual abuse
- simple injuries
- strangers
- traffic safety
- water safety

LEVEL 2: Grades 3-5
- bleeding
- breathing problems
- choking
- first aid
- helmet
- minor burns
- nonviolent conflict resolution
- poisonings
- precautions*
- protective equipment
- safety rules
- seat belt
- shock
- sunscreen

LEVEL 3: Grades 6-8
- abdominal thrust procedure [Heimlich maneuver]
- cardiopulmonary resuscitation [CPR]
- emergency plan
- injury prevention strategies
- negotiation skills
- other-directed violence
- refusal skills
- safety hazards
- self-directed violence

LEVEL 4: Grades 9-12
- collaboration skills
- conflict prevention strategies
- interpersonal conflicts
- neighborhood safety
- safe driving skills

6. Nutrition and Diet
LEVEL 1: Grades K-2
- food combinations
- food groups

LEVEL 2: Grades 3-5
- activity level
- food choices
- food handling
- food preparation
- healthy eating practices
- nutritional value

LEVEL 3: Grades 6-8
- anemia
- anorexia
- bulimia
- cancer
- cooking temperatures
- dental health
- eating disorders
- food storage
- hand washing
- heart disease
- malnutrition
- osteoporosis
- overeating
- refrigeration
- storage temperatures

LEVEL 4: Grades 9-12
- diet aids
- dietary supplements
- energy needs
- fad diets
- food additives
- food labels
- gender*
- life cycle*
- nutrient needs

7. Maintaining Health
LEVEL 1: Grades K-2
- ears
- eyes
- gums
- hair
- hygiene*
- nails
- nose
- skin
- teeth

LEVEL 2: Grades 3-5
- disease*
- exercise*
- human body systems
- personal health goal
- recreation*
- well-being

LEVEL 3: Grades 6-8
- health screenings
- personal health assessment
- personal health risks
- personal health strengths
- self-examinations

LEVEL 4: Grades 9-12
- long-term consequences
- nutrition plan
- physical fitness
- short-term consequences

8. Disease Prevention
LEVEL 1: Grades K-2
- congestion
- coughs
- fever
- illnesses
- rashes
- symptoms
- wheezing

LEVEL 2: Grades 3-5
- early detection and treatment
- immunizations
- over-the-counter medicines
- prescription medicines

LEVEL 3: Grades 6-8
- chronic disease
- communicable disease
- degenerative disease processes
- family history*
- lifestyle*
- pathogens*
- risk factors

LEVEL 4: Grades 9-12
- immune system*
- perinatal
- prenatal

*Word or phrase appears more than once.

9. Substance Abuse

LEVEL 1: Grades K-2
- harmful substances

LEVEL 2: Grades 3-5
- alcohol
- drug use
- drunk and drugged driving
- nonprescription drugs
- peer and adult modeling
- self-control*
- social influences
- social pressure
- substance abuse*
- tobacco

LEVEL 3: Grades 6-8
- apathy
- cirrhosis
- domestic violence
- drug dependency
- drug-seeking behavior
- emphysema
- frustration tolerance
- genetic inheritability
- low self-esteem
- lung cancer
- paranoia
- public policy*
- tolerance level
- warning labels

LEVEL 4: Grades 9-12
- date rape
- needle sharing
- sexual activity

10. Growth and Development

LEVEL 1: Grades K-2
- growth cycle
- infancy
- old age

LEVEL 2: Grades 3-5
- acne
- puberty
- sexual maturation
- voice change

LEVEL 3: Grades 6-8
- adolescence
- conception
- male and female sexuality
- prenatal development

LEVEL 4: Grades 9-12
- fetus
- middle age
- young adulthood

*Word or phrase appears more than once.

1. Basic and Advanced Movement Forms

LEVEL 1: Grades K-2
- ball
- basketball
- bending (fitness)
- body control
- catch
- foot dribble
- galloping
- glove
- hand dribble
- headstands
- hopping
- jumping
- kick and strike
- landing*
- lifting
- locomotor movement*
- motor skill
- nonlocomotor skills
- object control skills
- rhythmical skills
- running
- skipping
- sliding
- softball
- stretching
- take-offs
- turning
- twisting
- underhand and overhand throw
- weight-bearing activities

LEVEL 2: Grades 3-6
- balance board
- basketball pass
- batting
- fielding (sports)
- large apparatus
- net and invasion games
- opponent*
- pass
- punt
- racket sport
- shooting
- sideline soccer
- skates
- soccer dribble
- sports

- stealing the ball
- striking pattern

LEVEL 3: Grades 7-8
- individual, dual, and team sports
- outdoor activities

LEVEL 4: Grades 9-12
- aquatics
- participants
- strategies

2. Movement Concepts and Principles

LEVEL 1: Grades K-2
- feedback*
- follow through
- peer/coach review
- personal space
- practice*
- ready position
- space awareness

LEVEL 2: Grades 3-6
- cool down
- defensive strategies
- external sources
- internal sources
- offensive strategies
- self-assessment*
- student journal
- warm up*

LEVEL 3: Grades 7-8
- advanced movement skills
- freestyle swimming
- racing start
- serve the ball
- spike the ball
- team sport
- training conditioning
- volleyball

LEVEL 4: Grades 9-12
- biomechanical concepts
- fitness
- gymnastic skills
- law of specificity
- overload principle
- sport psychology

3. Costs and Benefits

LEVEL 1: Grades K-2
- health benefits
- physical activity
- physical endurance

LEVEL 2: Grades 3-6
- adventure
- clubs
- competitive activities
- health-enhancing
- intramural sports
- muscle soreness
- over-training
- overuse injuries
- recreational leagues
- risk taking
- substance abuse*
- temporary tiredness

LEVEL 3: Grades 7-8
- body composition
- cardiovascular strength
- emotional health*
- flexibility*
- mental health*
- muscular strength
- physiological benefits
- psychological benefits
- self-image
- stress reduction

LEVEL 4: Grades 9-12
- equipment*
- facilities
- physical injury

4. Maintaining Physical Fitness

LEVEL 1: Grades K-2
- body shape
- breathing rate
- cardiorespiratory exertion
- climbing
- exercise*
- fat body mass
- hanging
- heart rate
- heartbeat
- height*
- joint

*Word or phrase appears more than once.

- lean body mass
- perspiration
- physiological indicators
- pulse rate
- range of motion
- weight*

LEVEL 2: Grades 3-6
- aerobic capacity
- arm-shoulder stretches
- curl-ups
- fitness standards
- isometric strength activities
- jump rope
- lifestyle*
- nutrition*
- perceived exertion
- physical fitness tests
- pull-ups
- push-ups
- recovery rate
- trunk twists

LEVEL 3: Grades 7-8
- calisthenics
- cardiorespiratory endurance
- fitness goals
- heart rate recovery
- heart rate reserve
- resistance*
- resting heart rate
- threshold*
- weight training

LEVEL 4: Grades 9-12
- cardiovascular efficiency
- personal status
- respiratory efficiency

5. Social and Personal Responsibility

LEVEL 1: Grades K-2
- consideration
- cooperation
- game rules
- games*
- gymnasium
- players
- playground
- sharing

LEVEL 2: Grades 3-6
- hearing disability
- wheelchair basketball

LEVEL 3: Grades 7-8
- exclusionary behaviors
- inclusive behaviors
- microcosm
- self-expression

LEVEL 4: Grades 9-12
- diversity*
- follower*
- international competitions
- leadership*
- Olympics
- Pan American Games
- professional sports*
- Special Olympics
- sportsmanship
- team championship
- World Cup Soccer

*Word or phrase appears more than once.

1. Hardware and Operating Systems

LEVEL 1: Grades K-2

- computer program
- CPU (central processing unit)
- delete/backspace
- diskette
- escape key
- function keys
- hard disk
- hardware
- home row
- keyboard
- monitor*
- mouse
- output*
- power-up
- printer
- reboot
- return/enter
- space bar

LEVEL 2: Grades 3-5

- fingering keys
- hazard
- input*
- internet
- intranet
- local network
- modem
- network
- storage

LEVEL 3: Grades 6-8

- bulletin board system
- CD-ROMs
- floppy disk
- memorization of keys
- on-line
- operating system

LEVEL 4: Grades 9-12

- current and emerging technology
- data scanners
- digital cameras
- hard drive crash
- input devices
- laptops
- monitor burn-out
- notebook*
- optical character recognition

- peripherals
- scanner
- sound processing
- touch screen
- voice/sound recorders

2. Software

LEVEL 1: Grades K-2

- games
- menu
- software programs
- special purpose programs
- typing
- word processor*

LEVEL 2: Grades 3-5

- add (computer records)
- back-up copies
- copy
- databases
- edit*
- file
- format*
- hardware platforms
- help systems
- Macintosh
- move (word processing)
- print*
- record*
- save (word processing)
- search (computer file)
- software applications
- sort (computer records)
- stored data
- tabs
- Windows (operating system)

LEVEL 3: Grades 6-8

- boolean search
- cells
- clip art
- columns
- desktop publishing software
- formulas*
- grammar checker
- graphics
- import
- outliner
- rows
- scanned images
- spell-checker

*Word or phrase appears more than once.

- spread sheet
- thesaurus*
- utilities

LEVEL 4: Grades 9-12

- export*
- galleries
- listservs
- macros
- mail merge
- merge (data)
- templates
- usenet newsreaders

3. Technology and Society

LEVEL 1: Grades K-2

- paging systems
- personal property (computer works)
- technology*
- telephone*
- tools
- VCRs

LEVEL 2: Grades 3-5

- copyright laws
- invention*
- software piracy
- technological benefits
- technological costs
- technological improvements

LEVEL 3: Grades 6-8

- computer fraud
- computer hacking
- engineer*
- explanations*
- scientific inquiry*
- scientists*
- solutions
- technological design
- technological revolutions
- virus (computer)

LEVEL 4: Grades 9-12

- acceptable use policies
- patents
- personal digital assistants
- scientific journals
- technological risks
- telecomputing
- virtual environment
- voice recognition software

4. Technological Design

LEVEL 1: Grades K-2

- machine

LEVEL 2: Grades 3-5

- constraint*
- designed objects
- natural objects

LEVEL 3: Grades 6-8

- aesthetics
- measures of quality
- resources*
- trade-off*

LEVEL 4: Grades 9-12

- artifacts*
- models
- simulation*

5. Nature and Operation of Systems

LEVEL 1: Grades K-2

- linear system
- simple system

LEVEL 2: Grades 3-5

- logo programming

LEVEL 3: Grades 6-8

- feedback*
- output*
- processes (system)
- subsystem

LEVEL 4: Grades 9-12

- complex systems
- system boundaries
- system failure
- systems analysis

*Word or phrase appears more than once.

1. Human Development, Identity and Behavior

LEVEL 1: Grades K-2
- behaviors
- community*
- family
- friends
- group*
- patterns of behavior
- rules*
- team*

LEVEL 2: Grades 3-5
- attitudes*
- culture*
- experience*
- identity
- mass communications media
- personal beliefs

LEVEL 3: Grades 6-8
- behavior patterns*
- ideas*
- needs and wants*
- punishments
- society
- subgroups*
- unacceptable behavior
- values*

LEVEL 4: Grades 9-12
- cultural beliefs*
- ethnicity
- gender*
- gradations
- institutional affiliations
- nationality
- social classes
- social distinctions
- socioeconomic status

2. Social Groups

LEVEL 1: Grades K-2
- roles*

LEVEL 2: Grades 3-5
- blue-collar workers
- church
- expectations
- home*
- membership*
- military units
- school
- scouts

- Shriners
- social group
- sororities
- Southerners
- street gangs

LEVEL 3: Grades 6-8
- affiliation
- belief systems*
- blind respect
- cohesion*
- companionship
- ethnic origin
- region*
- social class*
- stereotyping
- subculture
- superiority

LEVEL 4: Grades 9-12
- cross-cultural
- social organization

3. Learning, Inheritance, & Physical Development

LEVEL 1: Grades K-2
- imitating
- listening
- perspective*
- practice*
- senses*
- showing
- surroundings
- telling
- watching

LEVEL 2: Grades 3-5
- attitudes*
- consequences*
- experience*
- goals*
- group situations
- interests
- judgement*
- learned behavior patterns
- memory
- motivation*
- skills*
- talents

LEVEL 3: Grades 6-8
- inheritance
- innate
- input*

- olfactory stimuli
- perception*
- repertoire
- signals
- visual stimuli

LEVEL 4: Grades 9-12
- abnormal
- associations
- context*
- instinctive behavior
- mood*

4. Conflict, Cooperation, and Independence

LEVEL 1: Grades K-2
- argument
- disagreements
- disputes

LEVEL 2: Grades 3-5
- beliefs
- compromise
- customs*
- freedom
- point of view
- political institution
- religious institution
- social institution
- vote

LEVEL 3: Grades 6-8
- hostile actions
- individuality
- social class
- social conformity
- social power
- status
- tensions

LEVEL 4: Grades 9-12
- competition*
- conquest
- demonstrations
- economic change
- intergroup conflict
- majority
- migrations
- minority
- oppression
- political change
- retaliation
- social change
- status quo

*Word or phrase appears more than once.

1. Presenting an Argument

LEVEL 1: Grades K-2
- answer
- believe
- coherent
- convincing
- ideas*
- reasons
- true
- valid

LEVEL 2: Grades 3-5
- appeal
- argument*
- assertion
- authority*
- comparison*
- facts*
- fair
- fallacies
- reasoning*
- references*
- statement
- support*

LEVEL 3: Grades 6-8
- accounts
- biased samples
- central sample
- claims
- conclusions
- credibility*
- distinctions
- expertise
- false
- quantitative data
- samples

LEVEL 4: Grades 9-12
- charts*
- connections*
- construct
- contradict
- critical assumption
- graph*
- judge
- logic*
- point*
- prove
- slant
- subtle

- tables
- techniques*
- validity*

2. Logic and Reasoning

LEVEL 1: Grades K-2
- no benchmarks

LEVEL 2: Grades 3-5
- no benchmarks

LEVEL 3: Grades 6-8
- connectors ["if...then," "and," "not," "or"]
- deductive
- example*
- formal
- general rule
- overgeneralize
- rules*
- values*

LEVEL 4: Grades 9-12
- confirmatory bias
- counter example*
- exception
- explicit*
- faulty
- implicit*
- logical quantifier ["some," "none," "all"]
- necessary
- probabilities*
- scientific studies
- sufficient

3. Comparing, Contrasting, and Classifying

LEVEL 1: Grades K-2
- behavior*
- classify*
- color*
- criteria*
- difference*
- event*
- motion*
- number
- object*
- pattern*

- person
- place*
- shape*
- similarities*
- size*
- sound*
- texture*
- thing
- weight*

LEVEL 2: Grades 3-5
- ethnic, religious, and cultural characteristics
- familiar
- population*
- products*
- sense

LEVEL 3: Grades 6-8
- analogy*
- category
- consumer*
- cost*
- durability
- features*
- frequency*
- important
- membership*
- occurrence
- performance
- relevant*
- sources*
- trade-off*

LEVEL 4: Grades 9-12
- comparison table
- qualitative traits
- quantitative traits

4. Scientific Inquiry

LEVEL 1: Grades K-2
- reasonable

LEVEL 2: Grades 3-5
- experiment*
- formulate
- hypothesis*
- notebook*
- observations*
- record*
- results*
- systematic*
- verify*

*Word or phrase appears more than once.

LEVEL 3: Grades 6-8
- conjectures*
- control group
- experimental group
- findings
- interpret*
- outcome*
- reformulate

LEVEL 4: Grades 9-12
- explanations*
- field data
- grid*
- grid cells
- procedures*
- spatial sampling
- statistic*
- transparent

5. Problem Solving

LEVEL 1: Grades K-2
- problem*
- solution*

LEVEL 2: Grades 3-5
- goals*
- issues
- obstacles
- solve*

LEVEL 3: Grades 6-8
- action*
- consequences*
- predict*
- resolve
- strategy*

LEVEL 4: Grades 9-12
- advice
- causes
- constraint*
- electrical system

- expert
- feasability
- frame
- isolate
- many-step branching logic
- mechanical system
- objectives
- reframe
- resources*
- schematic diagram
- summation
- troubleshooting

6. Decision Making

LEVEL 1: Grades K-2
- activities
- decisions
- defend*

LEVEL 2: Grades 3-5
- alternatives

LEVEL 3: Grades 6-8
- decision-making grid
- external features
- factual
- implement
- matrix
- selection
- service industries*

LEVEL 4: Grades 9-12
- advocate
- balance sheet
- benefits*
- current
- factors
- international policy
- national policy
- pending
- turning point

*Word or phrase appears more than once.

1. Group Contribution

LEVEL 5: Grades K-8

- active listening
- challenge
- climate*
- conflict*
- group*
- initiative
- interact
- practices
- progress
- strengths of others
- supportive

2. Conflict Resolution

LEVEL 5: Grades K-8

- acknowledgment
- aggressive
- beliefs*
- blame
- clarification*
- communication
- conversation*
- critic
- criticism
- effective
- emotional state
- guidelines
- habitual
- impact*
- individual*
- ineffective
- interest*
- mini-max position
- mutually agreeable
- negotiating
- opponent*
- organizational
- passive
- psychological state
- response*
- seriousness
- token agreement

3. Diversity

LEVEL 5: Grades K-8

- customer needs
- opposite gender
- religious orientation
- satisfy

4. Interpersonal Communication

LEVEL 5: Grades K-8

- accommodate
- adjust
- body position*
- confrontations
- constructive
- content*
- deliverance
- dialogues
- emotions
- empathy
- eye contact*
- feedback*
- friendliness
- inflammatory
- nondefensive
- nonverbal
- objectivity
- politeness
- react
- speaker
- tone*
- voice tone

5. Leadership Skills

LEVEL 5: Grades K-8

- accomplishments
- contribution*
- enlist
- follower*
- leader*
- shared
- vision
- win

*Word or phrase appears more than once.

1. Goal Setting

LEVEL 5: Grades K-8

- accomplishing
- contingency
- cumulative
- direction*
- evaluation
- long term
- milestones
- options
- proximity
- purpose*
- rank
- routine
- schedule
- wants*

2. Self-Appraisal

LEVEL 5: Grades K-8

- analysis
- compensating
- distribute
- document
- educational background
- employability
- experience*
- improvement
- inventory
- lifestyle*
- log*
- motivational pattern
- peak
- style*
- successes
- summarize*
- strengths and weaknesses
- work
- work experience
- working environment

3. Risk Taking

LEVEL 5: Grades K-8

- common knowledge*
- course of action
- emergency*

- emergency procedure
- hazard
- hazardous procedure
- injury
- preventative measures
- risks
- safety problem
- safety procedure
- security problem
- stress*

4. Perseverence

LEVEL 5: Grades K-8

- difficulty
- energy*
- mental energy
- perseverance
- persist
- physical energy
- prolonged
- purpose*

5. Self-Concept

LEVEL 5: Grades K-8

- affirmations
- body language
- dispassionate
- lessons
- limited resources
- living
- mistakes
- negative effect
- overreacting
- positive effect
- self-esteem*
- self-statements
- "shoulds"
- succeed

6. Impulsivity

LEVEL 5: Grades K-8

- assess
- judgement*
- situation*
- suspend

*Word or phrase appears more than once.

1. Using Basic Tools

LEVEL 1: Grades K-2

- assemble
- audio equipment
- cardboard
- clamp
- constructions
- erector sets
- hammer
- hard lenses
- interlocking blocks
- metal*
- operate
- paper*
- parts
- plastic
- reassemble
- ruler*
- scissors
- screwdriver
- task
- wood*

LEVEL 2: Grades 3-5

- measure*
- mechanical
- mix*
- prescribed amount
- safety

LEVEL 3: Grades 6-8

- device*
- disassemble
- fasten
- hand tools*
- inspect
- power tools
- soft metal
- unfasten

LEVEL 4: Grades 9-12

- instructions
- instruments
- join
- manual
- smooth
- work space

2. Information Sources

LEVEL 1: Grades K-2
- no benchmarks

LEVEL 2: Grades 3-5
- no benchmarks

LEVEL 3: Grades 6-8
- no benchmarks

LEVEL 4: Grades 9-12

- component*
- cross sections
- data matrix
- diagrammatic decision points
- factor specification
- flowchart
- inconsistency*
- intersection
- linear path
- malfunction
- mechanism
- organizational chart
- schematic diagram
- symbols*
- test points
- textual
- two-column chart
- visual*

3. Money Management

LEVEL 1: Grades K-2
- no benchmarks

LEVEL 2: Grades 3-5
- no benchmarks

LEVEL 3: Grades 6-8
- no benchmarks

LEVEL 4: Grades 9-12

- budget
- credit
- expenses
- forecasts
- goods and services*
- income*
- sound buying principles
- purchasing

4. Pursuing Specific Jobs

LEVEL 1: Grades K-2
- no benchmarks

LEVEL 2: Grades 3-5
- no benchmarks

LEVEL 3: Grades 6-8
- no benchmarks

LEVEL 4: Grades 9-12

- contacts
- deductions
- employer
- job application*
- job interview
- letter of application
- letter of inquiry
- organization*
- personnel office
- salary*
- vacation benefits

5. Work Force Preparation

LEVEL 1: Grades K-2
- no benchmarks

LEVEL 2: Grades 3-5
- no benchmarks

LEVEL 3: Grades 6-8
- no benchmarks

LEVEL 4: Grades 9-12

- appraisal
- aptitudes
- career action plan
- career goals
- character*
- child care
- classifieds
- college*
- educational opportunities
- employment profile
- employment tests
- entry-level job
- fee basis
- insurance
- job references

*Word or phrase appears more than once.

- junior college
- license
- life decisions
- market trend
- occupational apprenticeship
- preparation
- private employment agency
- resumé*
- Social Security card
- training
- unemployment insurance
- word of mouth
- work permit
- worker's compensation

6. Life Skills

LEVEL 1: Grades K-2
- no benchmarks

LEVEL 2: Grades 3-5
- no benchmarks

LEVEL 3: Grades 6-8
- no benchmarks

LEVEL 4: Grades 9-12
- apartment rental
- banking services
- car maintenance
- checking account
- contracts
- health care
- Internal Revenue Service
- public transportation
- regulations
- savings account
- telephone skills

7. Work Ethic

LEVEL 1: Grades K-2
- no benchmarks

LEVEL 2: Grades 3-5
- no benchmarks

LEVEL 3: Grades 6-8
- no benchmarks

LEVEL 4: Grades 9-12
- assigned
- attendance record
- congeniality
- constructive criticism
- appropriate dress
- ethical
- guidance
- hygiene*
- job responsibilities
- loyalty
- organize
- plan*
- preferences
- prepare
- priorities
- request
- respect
- supervisors
- work station

8. Operating within Organizations

LEVEL 1: Grades K-2
- no benchmarks

LEVEL 2: Grades 3-5
- no benchmarks

LEVEL 3: Grades 6-8
- no benchmarks

LEVEL 4: Grades 9-12
- compatible
- skills*
- visible

*Word or phrase appears more than once.

References

American Association for the Advancement of Science. (1993). *Benchmarks for Science Literacy*. New York: Oxford University Press.

American Federation of Teachers. (1985, September). "Critical Thinking: It's a Basic." *American Teacher*, p. 21.

American Federation of Teachers. (1998). *Making Standards Matter 1998.* Washington, DC: Author.

Anderson, C. W., & Smith, E. L. (1984). "Children's Preconceptions and Content-area Textbooks." In G. Duffy, L. Roehler, & J. Mason (Eds.), *Comprehension Instruction: Perspectives and Suggestions.* New York: Longman.

Anderson, J. C., & Freebody, P. (1981). "Vocabulary Knowledge." In J. T. Guthrie (Ed.), *Comprehension and Teaching* (pp. 77–117). Newark, DE: International Reading Association.

Anderson, J. R. (1990). *Cognitive Psychology and its Implications* (3rd ed.). New York: W. H. Freeman.

Anderson, J. R. (1995). *Learning and Memory: An Integrated Approach.* New York: John Wiley & Sons.

Anderson, M. (1992). *Impostors in the Temple: American Intellectuals Are Destroying Our Universities and Cheating Our Students of Their Future.* New York: Simon and Schuster.

Beck, I. L., McKeown, M. G., & Omanson, R. C. (1984, April). *The Fertility of Some Types of Vocabulary Instruction.* Paper Presented at the Annual Meeting of the American Educational Research Association, New Orleans, LA.

Becker, W. C. (1977). "Teaching Reading and Language to the Disadvantaged: What We Have Learned from Field Research." *Harvard Educational Review, 47,* 518–543.

Bennett, W. J. (1992). *The De-Valuing of America: The Fight for Our Culture and Our Children.* New York: Summit Books.

Berliner, D. C. (1979). "Tempus Educare." In P. L. Peterson & H. J. Walberg (Eds.), *Research on Teaching.* Berkeley, CA: McCutchan.

Berliner, D. C. (1984). "The Half Full Glass: A Review of Research in Teaching." In P. L. Hosford (Ed.), *Using What We Know about Teaching.* Alexandria, VA: Association for Supervision and Curriculum Development.

Berliner, D. C. (1992, February). *Educational Reform in an Era of Disinformation.* Paper Presented at the American Association for Teacher Education, San Antonio, TX.

Berliner, D. C., & Biddle, B. J. (1995). *The Manufactured Crisis: Myths, Fraud, and the Attack on American Public Schools.* Reading, MA: Addison-Wesley.

Berliner, D. C., & Biddle, B. J. (1998). "The Lamentable Alliance Between the Media and Social Critics." *The School Administrator, 8*(55), 12–18.

Bernstein, R. (1994). *Dictatorship of Virtue: Multiculturalism and the Battle for America's Future.* New York: Knopf.

Beyer, B. K. (1988). *Developing a Thinking Skills Program.* Boston: Allyn & Bacon.

Bloom, A. (1987). *The Closing of the American Mind: How Higher Education Has Failed Democracy and Impoverished the Souls of Today's Students.* New York: Simon and Schuster.

Borg, W. R. (1980). "Time and School Learning." In C. Demham & A. Lieberman (Eds.), *Time to Learn* (pp. 33–72). Washington, DC: National Institute of Education.

Bracey, G. W. (1997). *Setting the Record Straight: Responses to Misconceptions about Public Education in the United States.* Alexandria, VA: Association for Supervision and Curriculum Development.

Brandt, R. (1995). "Overview: What to Do with Those New Standards." *Educational Leadership, 52*(6), 5.

Bruner, J. S. (1960). *The Process of Education.* Cambridge, MA: Harvard University Press.

Burling, R. (1970). *Man's Many Voices: Language in its Cultural Context.* New York: Holt, Rinehart and Winston.

Carnevale, A. P., Gainer, L. J., & Meltzer, A. S. (1990). *Workplace Basics: The Essential Skills Employers Want*. San Francisco: Jossey-Bass.

Carson, C. C., Huelskamp, R. M., & Woodall, T. D. (1993, May/June). "Perspectives on Education in America: An Annotated Briefing, April 1992." *The Journal of Educational Research, 86*(5), 259–310.

Center for Civic Education. (1994). *National Standards for Civics and Government*. Calabasas, CA: Author.

Clark, H. H., & Clark, E. V. (1977). *Psychology and Language*. San Diego, CA: Harcourt Brace Jovanovich.

Coleman, J. S. (1972). "The Evaluation of Equality of Educational Opportunity." In F. Mosteller & D. P. Moynihan (Eds.), O*n Equality of Educational Opportunity* (pp. 140–161). New York: Vintage Books.

Coleman, J. S., Campbell, E. Q., Hobson, C. J., McPartland, J., Mood, A. M., Weinfield, F. D., & York, R. L. (1966). *Equality of Educational Opportunity*. Washington, DC: U.S. Government Printing Office.

College Board, The. (1983). *Academic Preparation for College: What Students Need to Know and Be Able to Do*. New York: College Entrance Examination Board.

Collins, A. M., & Quillian, M. R. (1969). "Retrieval Time for Semantic Memory." *Journal of Verbal Learning and Verbal Behavior, 8,* 240–247.

Conant, E. H. (1973). *Teacher and Paraprofessional Work Productivity*. Lexington, MA: D.C. Heath.

Condon, J. C. (1968). *Semantics and Communication*. New York: Macmillan.

Consortium of National Arts Education Associations. (1994). *National Standards for Arts Education: What Every Young American Should Know and Be Able to Do in the Arts*. Reston, VA: Music Educators National Conference.

Core Knowledge Foundation. (1998). *Core Knowledge Sequence: Content Guidelines for Grades K–8*. Charlottesville, VA: Author.

Core Knowledge Foundation. (1999). "About Core Knowledge" [On-line]. Core Knowledge Web Site. http://www.coreknowledge.org/CKproto2/about/index.htm (address current as of 1/5/99).

Costa, A. (Ed.). (1985). *Developing Minds: A Resource Book for the Teaching of Thinking.* Alexandria, VA: Association for Supervision and Curriculum Development.

Crafton, L. K. (1996). *Standards in Practice: Grades K–2.* Urbana, IL: National Council of Teachers of English.

D'Souza, D. (1991). *Illiberal Education: The Politics of Race and Sex on Campus.* New York: Free Press.

de Bono, E. (1985). "The CoRT Thinking Program." In J. W. Segal, S. F. Chipman, & R. Glaser (Eds.), *Thinking and Learning Skills: Vol. 1. Relating Instruction to Research* (pp. 363–388). Hillsdale, NJ: Erlbaum.

Dewey, J. (1916). *Democracy and Education.* New York: Macmillan.

Diegmueller, K. (1995, April 12). "Running out of Steam." *Struggling for Standards: An Education Week Special Report.* Washington DC: Education Week.

Dow, P. (1991). *Schoolhouse Politics: Lessons from the Sputnik Era.* Cambridge, MA: Harvard University Press.

Doyle, W. (1992). "Curriculum and Pedagogy." In P. W. Jackson (Ed.), *Handbook of Research in Curriculum* (pp. 465–485). New York: Macmillan.

Educational Policies Commission. (1961). *The Central Purpose of American Education.* Washington, DC: National Education Association.

Education Week on the Web. (1998). "Executive Summary: The Urban Challenge," in *Quality Counts '98* [On-line]. Available: http://www.edweek.com/sreports/qc98/intros/in-n.htm (address current as of 1/5/99).

Farkas, F., Friedman, W., Boese, J., & Shaw, G. (1994). *First Things First: What Americans Expect from Public Schools.* New York: Public Agenda.

Finn, C. E., Jr. (1990). "The Biggest Reform of All." *Phi Delta Kappan, 71*(8), 584–592.

Finn, C. E., Jr. (1991). *We Must Take Charge: Our Schools and Our Future.* New York: The Free Press.

Finn, C. E., Jr .(1998, March 25). "Why America Has the World's Dimmest Bright Kids." *Wall Street Journal*, Sec. A, p. 22.

Finn, Jr., C. E., Petrilli, M. J., & Vanourek, G. (1998, November 11). "The State of State Standards: Four Reasons Why Most 'Don't Cut the Mustard'," *Education Week, 18,* pp. 56, 39.

Fisher, C. W., Berliner, D. C., Filby, N., Marliave, R. S., Cahen, L. S., & Dishaw, M. M. (1980). "Teaching Behaviors, Academic Learning Time and Student Achievement: An Overview." In C. Denham & A. Lieberman (Eds.), *Time to Learn.* Washington DC: National Institute of Education.

Fisher, C. W., Filby, N., Marliave, R. S., Cahen, L. S., Dishaw, M. M., Moore, J. E., & Berliner, D. C. (Eds.). (1978). *Teaching Behaviours, Academic Learning Time and Student Achievement.* San Francisco: Far West Laboratory of Educational Research and Development.

Forgione, P. D., Jr. (1998). "Commissioner's Statement." In U.S. Department of Education, National Center for Education Statistics, *Pursuing Excellence: A Study of U.S. Twelfth-Grade Mathematics and Science Achievement in International Context* (pp. 5–6). Washington, DC: U.S. Government Printing Office.

Futrell, M. H. (1987, December 9). "A Message Long Overdue." *Education Week,* 7(14), 9.

Gaddy, B. B., Hall, W. T., & Marzano, R. J. (1996). *School Wars: Resolving Our Conflicts Over Religion and Values.* San Francisco: Jossey-Bass.

Gandal, M. (1995a). *Making Standards Matter: A Fifty-State Progress Report on Efforts to Raise Academic Standards.* Washington, DC: American Federation of Teachers.

Gandal, M. (1995b). "Not All Standards Are Created Equal." *Educational Leadership,* 52(6), 16–21.

Gandal, M. (1996). *Making Standards Matter, 1996: An Annual Fifty-State Report on Efforts to Raise Academic Standards.* Washington, DC: American Federation of Teachers.

Gandal, M. (1997). *Making Standards Matter, 1997: An Annual Fifty-State Report on Efforts to Raise Academic Standards.* Washington, DC: American Federation of Teachers.

Geography Education Standards Project. (1994). *Geography for Life: National Geography Standards.* Washington, DC: National Geographic Research and Exploration.

Glaser, R., & Linn, R. (1993). "Foreword." In L. Shepard, *Setting Performance Standards for Student Achievement* (pp. xiii–xiv). Stanford, CA: National Academy of Education, Stanford University.

Harnischfeger, A., & Wiley, D. (1978). *Conceptual and Policy Issues in Elementary School Teaching: Learning.* Paper Presented at the Annual Meeting of the American Educational Research Association, Toronto.

Hattie, J. A. (1992). "Measuring the Effects of Schooling." *Australian Journal of Education, 36*(1), 5–13.

Hirsch, E. D., Jr. (1987). *Cultural Literacy: What Every American Needs to Know.* Boston: Houghton Mifflin.

Hirsch, E. D., Jr. (1988). *Cultural Literacy: What Every American Needs to Know: With an Updated Appendix.* New York: Vintage Books.

Hirsch, E. D., Jr. (Ed.). (1991a). *What Your First Grader Needs to Know: Fundamentals of a Good First-Grade Education.* New York: Delta.

Hirsch, E. D., Jr. (Ed.). (1991b). *What Your Second Grader Needs to Know: Fundamentals of a Good Second-Grade Education.* New York: Delta.

Hirsch, E. D., Jr. (Ed.). (1992a). *What Your Fourth Grader Needs to Know: Fundamentals of a Good Fourth-Grade Education.* New York: Delta.

Hirsch, E. D., Jr. (Ed.). (1992b). *What Your Third Grader Needs to Know: Fundamentals of a Good Third-Grade Education.* New York: Delta.

Hirsch, E. D., Jr. (Ed.). (1993a). *What Your Fifth Grader Needs to Know: Fundamentals of a Good Fifth-Grade Education.* New York: Delta.

Hirsch, E. D., Jr. (Ed.). (1993b). *What Your Sixth Grader Needs to Know: Fundamentals of a Good Sixth-Grade Education.* New York: Delta.

Hirsch, E. D., Jr. (1996). *The Schools We Need and Why We Don't Have Them.* New York: Doubleday.

Hirsch, E. D., Jr. (Ed.). (1997). *What Your First Grader Needs to Know: Fundamentals of a Good First-Grade Education* (Rev. ed.). New York: Delta.

Hirsch, E. D., Jr. (Ed.). (1998). *What Your Second Grader Needs to Know: Fundamentals of a Good Second-Grade Education* (Rev. ed.). New York: Delta.

Hirsch, E. D., Jr., & Holdren, J. (Eds.) (1996). *What Your Kindergartner Needs to Know: Preparing Your Child for a Lifetime of Learning.* New York: Delta.

Hirsch, E. D., Jr., Kett, J., & Trefil, J. (1988). *The Dictionary of Cultural Literacy: What Every American Needs to Know.* Boston: Houghton Mifflin.

Hirsch, E. D., Jr., Kett, J., & Trefil, J. (1993). *The Dictionary of Cultural Literacy: What Every American Needs to Know* (2nd ed.). Boston: Houghton Mifflin.

House, E. R., Emmer, C., & Laurence, N. (1988, September). *Cultural Literacy and Testing.* (CSE Technical Report 291). Los Angeles, CA: UCLA Center for Research on Evaluation, Standards, and Student Testing. UCLA.

International Baccalaureate. (1993). *Group 5 Mathematics Guide* (Edition 1.2). Geneva, Switzerland: Author.

International Baccalaureate. (1995). *Middle Years Programme: Mathematics* (Edition 1.1). Geneva, Switzerland: Author.

Jacobs, H. H. (Ed.). (1989). *Interdisciplinary Curriculum: Design and Implementation.* Alexandria, VA: Association for Supervision and Curriculum Development.

Johnson, D. W., Maruyama, G., Johnson, R. T., Nelson, D., & Skon, L. (1981). "Effects of Cooperative, Competitive and Individualistic Goal Structures on Achievement: A Meta-Analysis." *Psychological Bulletin, 89*(1), 47–62.

Johnson, J., & Farkas, S. (with Berg, A., Friedman, W., & Duffett, A.). 1997. *Getting By: What American Teenagers Really Think about Their Schools.* New York: Public Agenda.

Joint Committee on National Health Education Standards. (1995). *National Health Education Standards: Achieving Health Literacy.* Reston, VA: Association for the Advancement of Health Education.

Karweit, N. L. (1983). *Time on Task: A Research Review.* Baltimore: Johns Hopkins University Press.

Kendall, J. S., & Marzano, R. J. (1996). *Content Knowledge: A Compendium of Standards and Benchmarks for K–12 Education.* Aurora, CO: Mid-continent Regional Educational Laboratory.

Kendall, J. S., & Marzano, R. J. (1997). *Content Knowledge: A Compendium of Standards and Benchmarks for K–12 Education* (2nd ed.). Aurora, CO: Mid-continent Regional Educational Laboratory.

Kimball, R. (1990). *Tenured Radicals: How Politics Has Corrupted Our Higher Education.* New York: Harper and Row.

Kingsley, C.D. (Ed.). (1918). *Cardinal Principles of Secondary Education: A Report of the Commission on the Reorganization of Secondary Education, Appointed by the National Education Association*, Bulletin, 1918, No. 35. Washington, DC: Department of the Interior, Bureau of Education, Government Printing Office.

Levine, L. W. (1996). *The Opening of the American Mind: Canons, Culture, and History.* Boston: Beacon Press.

Marzano, R. J. (1991). "Language, the Language Arts and Thinking." In J. Flood, J. M. Jensen, D. Lapp, & J. R. Squire (Eds.), *Handbook of Research on Teaching the English Language Arts* (pp. 559–586). New York: Macmillan.

Marzano, R. J. (1992). *A Different Kind of Classroom: Teaching with Dimensions of Learning.* Alexandria, VA: Association for Supervision and Curriculum Development.

Marzano, R. J. (1998a). *A Theory-Based Review of Research on Instruction* (Technical Report). Aurora, CO: Mid-continent Regional Educational Laboratory.

Marzano, R. J. (1998b). Unpublished Data on Time Necessary to Teach Standards. Aurora, CO: Mid-continent Regional Educational Laboratory.

Marzano, R. J., & Hutchins, C. L. (1983). *Measuring Academic Efficiency at the School Level* (Technical Report). Aurora, CO: Mid-continent Regional Educational Laboratory. (ERIC Document Reproduction Service No. ED 241–576)

Marzano, R. J., & Kendall, J. S. (1996). *A Comprehensive Guide to Designing Standards-Based Districts, Schools, and Classroom.* Alexandria, VA: Association for Supervision and Curriculum Development.

Marzano, R. J., Kendall, J. S., & Cicchinelli, L. F. (1998). "What Americans Believe Students Should Know: A Survey of U.S. Adults." Aurora, CO: Mid-continent Regional Educational Laboratory.

Marzano, R. J., & Marzano, J. S. (1988). *A Cluster Approach to Elementary Vocabulary Instruction.* Newark, DE: International Reading Association.

Marzano, R. J., & Pickering, D. J. (with Arredondo, D. E., Blackburn, G. J., Brandt, R. S., Moffett, C. A., Paynter, D. E., Pollock, J. E., & Whisler, J.). (1997). *Dimensions of Learning Teacher's Manual* (2nd ed.). Alexandria, VA: Association for Supervision and Curriculum Development.

Marzano, R. J., & Pickering, D. J. (with Arredondo, D. E., Blackburn, G. J., Brandt, R. S., Moffett, C. A., Paynter, D. E., Pollock, J. E., & Whisler, J.). (1997). *Dimensions of Learning Trainer's Manual* (2nd ed.). Alexandira, VA: Association for Supervision and Curriculum Development.

Marzano, R. J., & Riley, A. (1984). Unpublished Data. Aurora, CO: Mid-continent Regional Educational Laboratory.

McKeown, M. G., & Curtis, M. E. (Eds.). (1987). *The Nature of Vocabulary Acquisition*. Hillsdale, NJ: Erlbaum.

Mid-continent Regional Educational Laboratory. (1991). *A+: Achieving Excellence: An Educational Decision-Making and Management System for Leadership, Efficiency, Effectiveness, Excellence*. Aurora, CO: Author.

Mullis, I. V. S., Owen, E. H., & Phillips, G. W. (1990). *America's Challenge: Accelerating Academic Achievement (A Summary of Findings from 20 Years of NAEP)*. Princeton, NJ: Educational Testing Service.

Myers, M. (1997). Personal Communication.

Nagy, W. E. (1988). *Teaching Vocabulary to Improve Reading Comprehension*. Newark, DE: International Reading Association.

Nagy, W. E., & Anderson, R. C. (1984). "How Many Words Are There in Printed School English?" *Reading Research Quarterly, 19,* 303–330.

Nagy, W. E., & Herman, P. A. (1984). *Limitations of Vocabulary Instruction* (Tech. Rep. No. 326). Urbana, IL: University of Illinois, Center for the Study of Reading. (ERIC Document Reproduction Service No. ED 248 498)

Nagy, W. E., Herman, P. A., & Anderson, R. C. (1985, April). *The Inference of Word and Text Properties on Learning from Context*. Paper Presented at the Annual Meeting of the American Educational Research Association, Chicago.

National Assessment of Educational Progress. (1992). *Item Specifications: 1994 National Assessment of Educational Progress in Geography*. Washington, DC: National Assessment Governing Board.

National Assessment of Educational Progress. (n.d.). *Mathematics Framework for the 1996 National Assessment of Educational Progress*. Washington, DC: Author.

National Association for Sport and Physical Education. (1995). *Moving into the Future, National Standards for Physical Education: A Guide to Content and Assessment.* St. Louis: Mosby.

National Center for History in the Schools. (1994a). *National Standards for History for Grades K–4: Expanding Children's World in Time and Space.* Los Angeles: Author.

National Center for History in the Schools. (1994b). *National Standards for United States History: Exploring the American Experience.* Los Angeles: Author.

National Center for History in the Schools. (1994c). *National Standards for World History: Exploring Paths to the Present.* Los Angeles: Author.

National Center for History in the Schools. (1996). *National Standards for History: Basic Edition.* Los Angeles: UCLA, Author.

National Commission on Excellence in Education. (1983). *A Nation at Risk: The Imperative for Educational Reform.* Washington, DC: Government Printing Office.

National Council for the Social Studies. (1994). *Expectations of Excellence: Curriculum Standards for Social Studies.* Washington, DC: Author.

National Council of Teachers of English and the International Reading Association. (1996). *Standards for the English Language Arts.* Urbana, IL: National Council of Teachers of English.

National Council of Teachers of Mathematics. (1989). *Curriculum and Evaluation Standards for School Mathematics.* Reston, VA: Author.

National Council on Economic Education. (1997). *Voluntary National Content Standards in Economics.* NY: Author.

National Education Association. (1893). *Report of the Committee of Ten on Secondary School Studies.* Washington, DC: Government Printing Office.

National Education Commission on Time and Learning. (1994). *Prisoners of Time.* Washington, DC: U.S. Department of Education.

National Education Goals Panel. (1991). *The National Education Goals Report: Building a Nation of Learners.* Washington, DC: Author.

National Governors Association. (1996, March). *1996 National Education Summit Policy Statement.* Washington, DC: Author.

National Research Council. (1996). *National Science Education Standards*. Washington, DC: National Academy Press.

National Science Board Commission on Precollege Education in Mathematics, Science and Technology. (1983). *Educating Americans for the 21st Century*. Washington, DC: National Science Board Commission.

National Standards in Foreign Language Education Project. (1996). *Standards for Foreign Language Learning: Preparing for the 21st Century*. Lawrence, KS: Author.

New Standards Project. (1997a). *Performance Standards: English Language Arts, Mathematics, Science, Applied Learning: Volume 1: Elementary School*. Washington, DC: National Center on Education and the Economy, and the University of Pittsburgh.

New Standards Project. (1997b). *Performance Standards: English Language Arts, Mathematics, Science, Applied Learning: Volume 2: Middle School*. Washington, DC: National Center on Education and the Economy, and the University of Pittsburgh.

New Standards Project. (1997c). *Performance Standards: English Language Arts, Mathematics, Science, Applied Learning: Volume 3: High School*. Washington, DC: National Center on Education and the Economy, and the University of Pittsburgh.

Nickerson, R. S. (1988). "On Improving Thinking Through Instruction." In E. Z. Rothkopf (Ed.), *Review of Research in Education: Vol. 5* (pp. 3–58). Washington, DC: American Educational Research Association.

Nickerson, R. S., Perkins, D. N., & Smith, E. E. (1985). *The Teaching of Thinking*. Hillsdale, NJ: Erlbaum.

Park, C. (1976). "The Bay City Experiment. . . as Seen by the Director." *Journal of Teacher Education, 7,* 5–8.

Pearsall, M. K. (Ed). (1993). *Scope, Sequence, and Coordination of Secondary School Science: Vol. 1. The Content Core: A Guide for Curriculum Designers*. Washington, DC: National Science Teachers Association.

Pulliam, J. D. (1987). *History of Education in America* (4th ed.). Columbus, OH: Merill Publishing Company.

Quellmalz, E. S. (1987). "Developing Reasoning Skills." In J. B. Baron & R. J. Sternberg (Eds.), *Teaching Thinking Skills: Theory and Practice.* New York: W. H. Freeman.

Ravitch, D. (1983). *The Troubled Crusade: American Education 1945–1980.* New York: Basic Books.

Ravitch, D. (1995). *National Standards in American Education: A Citizen's Guide.* Washington, DC: Brookings Institute.

Ravitch, D., & Finn, C. E., Jr. (1987). *What Do Our 17-Year-Olds Know?* New York: Harper & Row.

Regional Educational Laboratories. (1998). "Taking Stock of States' Curriculum-Based Reform Efforts: An Interim Report of the Laboratory Network Program's Curriculum, Learning, and Instruction Project." Aurora, CO: Mid-continent Regional Educational Laboratory.

Reuter, G. S. (1963). *The Length of the School Day.* Chicago: American Federation of Teachers.

Ross, J. A. (1988). "Controlling Variables: A Metanalysis of Training Studies." *Review of Educational Research, 58*(4), 405–437.

Rossmiller, R. A. (1982). *Managing School Resources to Improve Student Achievement.* Paper Presented at the State Superintendent's Conference, Madison, WI.

Sadowski, M. (1998). "Time and Learning." *The Harvard Education Letter, 14*(2), 3–5.

Schmidt, W. H., McKnight, C. C., & Raizen, S. A. (1996). *Splintered Vision: An Investigation of U.S. Science and Mathematics Education: Executive Summary.* Lansing, MI: U.S. National Research Center for the Third International Mathematics and Science Study, Michigan State University.

Secretary's Commission on Achieving Necessary Skills, The. (1991). *What Work Requires of Schools: A SCANS Report for America 2000.* Washington, DC: U.S. Department of Labor.

Segal, J. W., Chipman, S. F., & Glaser, R. (Eds.) (1985). *Thinking and Learning Skills: Vol. 1. Relating Instruction to Research.* Hillsdale, NJ: Erlbaum.

Shaw, P. (1989). *The War Against the Intellect: Episodes in the Decline of Discourse.* Iowa City: University of Iowa Press.

Shepard, L. (1993). *Setting Performance Standards for Student Achievement: A Report of the National Academy of Education Panel on the Evaluation of the NAEP Trial State Assessment: An Evaluation of the 1992 Achievement Levels.* Stanford, CA: The National Academy of Education, Stanford University.

Sierra-Perry, M. (1996). *Standards in Practice: Grades 3–5.* Urbana, IL: National Council of Teachers of English.

Silver, E. (1986, July). *Research in Mathematical Problem Solving in the United States of America.* Paper Presented at the United States-Japan Seminar in Mathematics Problem Solving, Honolulu, Hawaii.

Smagorinsky, P. (1996). *Standards in Practice: Grades 9–12.* Urbana, IL: National Council of Teachers of English.

Smith, P. (1990). *Killing the Spirit: Higher Education in America.* New York: Viking.

Stahl, S. A., & Fairbanks, M. M. (1986). "The Effects of Vocabulary Instruction: A Model-Based Meta-Analysis." *Review of Educational Research, 56*(1), 72–110.

Stevenson, H. W., & Stigler, J. W. (1992). *The Learning Gap: Why Our Schools Are Failing and What We Can Learn from Japanese and Chinese Education.* New York: Touchstone.

Stiggins, R. J. (1994). *Student-Centered Classroom Assessment.* New York: Merrill.

Stodolsky, S. S. (1989). "Is Teaching Really by the Book?" In P. W. Jackson & S. Haroutunian-Gordon (Eds.), *Eighty-ninth Yearbook of the National Society for the Study of Education, Part I* (pp. 159–184). Chicago: University of Chicago Press.

Sykes, C. J. (1988). *Profscam: Professors and the Demise of Higher Education.* New York: Kampmann and Co.

Sykes, C. J. (1990). *The Hollow Men: Politics and Corruption in Higher Education.* Washington, DC: Regnery Gateway.

Tyack, T., & Tobin, W. (1994). "The 'Grammar' of Schooling: Why Has it Been So Hard to Change." *American Educational Research Journal, 31*(3), 453–479.

Uchida, D., Cetron, M., & McKenzie, F. (1996). *Preparing Students for the 21st Century.* Reston, VA: American Association of School Administrators.

U.S. Department of Education, National Center for Education Statistics. (1998). *Pursuing Excellence: A Study of U.S. Twelfth-Grade Mathematics and Science Achievement in International Context.* Washington, DC: U.S. Government Printing Office.

Viadero, D. (1993, June 16). "Standards Deviation: Benchmark-Setting Is Marked by Diversity." *Education Week*, pp. 1, 14–17.

Walberg, H. J. (1997). "Uncompetitive American Schools: Causes and Cures." In *Brookings Papers on Educational Policy.* Washington, DC: The Brookings Institute.

Wang, M. C., Haertel, G. D., & Walberg, H. J. (1993). "Toward a Knowledge Base for School Learning." *Review of Educational Research, 63*(3), 249–294.

Whittington, D. (1991). "What Have 17-Year-Olds Known in the Past." *American Educational Research Journal, 28*(4), 759–780.

Wiggins, G. (1994). "Toward Better Report Cards." *Educational Leadership, 52*(2), 28–37.

Wilhelm, J. D. (1996). *Standards in Practice: Grades 6–8.* Urbana, IL: National Council of Teachers of English.

Yoon, B., Burstein, L., & Gold, K. (n.d.). *Assessing the Content Validity of Teachers' Reports of Content Coverage and its Relationship to Student Achievement* (CSE Rep. No. 328). Los Angeles: Center for Research in Evaluating Standards and Student Testing, University of California, Los Angeles.

Zahler, K. A., & Zahler, D. (1989). *Test Your Countercultural Literacy.* New York: Arco.

Index